Communication

Experience Communication

Second Edition

EXPERIENCE COMMUNICATION, SECOND EDITION

Published by McGraw-Hill Education, 2 Penn Plaza, New York, NY 10121. Copyright © 2019 by McGraw-Hill Education. All rights reserved. Printed in the United States of America. Previous edition © 2015. No part of this publication may be reproduced or distributed in any form or by any means, or stored in a database or retrieval system, without the prior written consent of McGraw-Hill Education, including, but not limited to, in any network or other electronic storage or transmission, or broadcast for distance learning.

Some ancillaries, including electronic and print components, may not be available to customers outside the United States.

This book is printed on acid-free paper.

1 2 3 4 5 6 7 8 9 LCR 21 20 19 18

ISBN 978-1-260-14223-5 (Looseleaf)
MHID 1-260-14223-X
ISBN 978-1-260-39724-6 (Bound)
MHID 1-260-39724-6

Brand Manager: *Sarah Remington*
Product Developer: *Elizabeth Murphy*
Marketing Manager: *Laura Young*
Content Project Manager: *Lisa Bruflodt*
Buyer: *Laura Fuller*
Designer: *Jessica Cuevas*
Cover Image: *©GaudiLab/Shutterstock.com*
Content Licensing Specialist: *Brianna Kirschbaum*
Compositor: *Lumina Datamatics*
Printer: *LSC Communications*

All credits appearing on page or at the end of the book are considered to be an extension of the copyright page.

Library of Congress Cataloging-in-Publication Data

Names: Child, Jeff, author.
Title: Experience communication / Jeffrey T. Child.
Description: Second edition. | New York, NY : McGraw Hill Education, [2019]
Identifiers: LCCN 2017046584 (print) | LCCN 2017046653 (ebook) | ISBN
  9781260142181 (Online) | ISBN 9781260142235 (looseleaf : acid-free paper) |
  ISBN 9781260142198 (softcover : acid-free paper)
Subjects: LCSH: Communication--Study and teaching (Higher) | Communication in education.
Classification: LCC P91.3 (ebook) | LCC P91.3 .C45 2019 (print) | DDC
  302.2/0711--dc23
LC record available at https://lccn.loc.gov/2017046584

The Internet addresses listed in the text were accurate at the time of publication. The inclusion of a website does not indicate an endorsement by the authors or McGraw-Hill Education, and McGraw-Hill Education does not guarantee the accuracy of the information presented at these sites.

mheducation.com/highered

Experience Communication

Experience Communication is an integrated program built to address the communication challenges your students face—in the classroom, online, and in the workplace.

Our research has shown, and instructors across the country agree, that college students today face a wide range of communication challenges. Some of these challenges are perennial, while others accompany the host of new technologies that are changing the way students communicate. *Experience Communication* recognizes that for today's students, meeting these challenges is vital to gaining and maintaining employment, creating and sustaining diverse relationships, and cultivating those relationships through face-to-face and mediated communication channels.

Experience Communication meets these challenges by covering the basic core concepts of the introductory communication course while addressing the particular needs of today's students. Our approach is focused on providing ample opportunity for students to improve their communication skills and to practice transferring them to contexts outside the classroom. For example, throughout the chapters, Skill Builder boxes prompt students to practice such skills as neutralizing defensiveness in everyday communication or analyzing their own social media presence to better understand how that presence might appear to others, including prospective employers. These features offer a wealth of practical applications for real-life communication scenarios.

The second edition of *Experience Communication* expands the scope and coverage of public communication. Chapter 7 is uniquely focused on Mediated Communication and Social Media, coverage that is coupled with engaging, real-world applications. Students will think more critically about their use of social media and the different communication contexts in which they play an increasingly important role. In support of this coverage, a new feature, Connecting Globally, discusses the ways in which computer-mediated communication facilitates opportunities for intercultural awareness and exchange, as well as requires students to be more adaptable in their communication styles.

We are thrilled to be sharing this exciting second edition of *Experience Communication* with you. We welcome your thoughts on how we can continue to create an engaging program that is responsive to the needs of contemporary students and instructors.

—Jeffrey T. Child

Permission granted by Robert Christy, coordinator of photography, Kent State University

Author Jeffrey T. Child.

About the Author

Jeffrey T. Child is Associate Professor of Communication at Kent State University, where he teaches Family Communication, Advanced Interpersonal Communication, Communication Research Methods, High Impact Speaking, College Teaching and Communication, and Communication, Uncertainty, and Privacy Management. His primary area of research is in exploring privacy management practices across various communication contexts. He received his Ph.D. in Communication from North Dakota State University and a Bachelor of Science in Speech Communication from Wayne State College. In 2018, he will take over as editor of the *Journal of Family Communication*.

MCGRAW-HILL CONNECT: AN OVERVIEW

McGraw-Hill Connect offers full-semester access to comprehensive, reliable content and learning resources for the Communication course. Connect's deep integration with most learning management systems (LMS), including Blackboard and Desire2Learn (D2L), offers single sign-on and deep gradebook synchronization. Data from Assignment Results reports synchronize directly with many LMS, allowing scores to flow automatically from Connect into school-specific gradebooks, if required.

The following tools and services are available as part of Connect for the Communication course:

Tool	Instructional Context	Description
SmartBook	■ SmartBook is an engaging and interactive reading experience for mastering fundamental communication content. ■ The metacognitive component confirms students' understanding of the material. ■ Instructors can actively connect SmartBook assignments and results to higher-order classroom work and one-on-one student conferences. ■ Students can track their own understanding and mastery of course concepts and identify gaps in their knowledge.	■ SmartBook is an adaptive reading experience designed to change the way students read and learn. It creates a personalized reading experience by highlighting the most impactful concepts a student needs to learn at that moment in time. ■ SmartBook creates personalized learning plans based on student responses to content question probes and confidence scales, identifying the topics students are struggling with and providing learning resources to create personalized learning moments. ■ SmartBook includes a variety of learning resources tied directly to key content areas to provide students with additional instruction and context. This includes video and media clips, interactive slide content, mini lectures, and image analyses. ■ SmartBook Reports provide instructors with data to quantify success and identify problem areas that require addressing in and out of the classroom. ■ Students can access their own progress and concept mastery reports.
Connect Insight for *Instructors*	■ Connect Insight for Instructors is an analytics resource that produces quick feedback related to learner performance and learner engagement. ■ It is designed as a dashboard for both quick check-ins and detailed performance and engagement views.	■ Connect Insight for Instructors offers a series of visual data displays that provide analysis on five key insights: • How are my students doing? • How is this one student doing? • How is my section doing? • How is this assignment doing? • How are my assignments doing?
Connect Insight for *Students*	■ Connect Insight for Students is a powerful data analytics tool that provides at-a-glance visualizations to help students understand their performance on Connect assignments.	■ Connect Insight for Students offers details on each Connect assignment to students. When possible, it offers suggestions for the students on how they can improve scores. This data can help guide students to behaviors that will lead to better scores in the future.
Video Speech Assignment	■ Video Speech Assignment provides instructors with a comprehensive and efficient way of managing in-class and online speech assignments, including student self-reviews, peer reviews, and instructor grading.	■ The Video Speech Assignment tool allows instructors to easily and efficiently set up speech assignments for their course that can easily be shared and repurposed, as needed, throughout their use of Connect. ■ Customizable rubrics and settings can be saved and shared, saving time and streamlining the speech assignment process from creation to assessment. ■ Video Speech Assignment allows users, both students and instructors, to view videos during the assessment process. Feedback can be left within a customized rubric or as time-stamped comments within the video playback itself.

Speech Preparation Tools	■ Speech Preparation Tools provide students with additional support and include Topic Helper, Outline Tool, and access to third-party Internet sites like EasyBib (for formatting citations) and Survey Monkey (to create audience-analysis questionnaires and surveys).	■ Speech Preparation Tools provide students with additional resources to help with the preparation and outlining of speeches, as well as with audience-analysis surveys. ■ Instructors have the ability to make tools either available or unavailable to students.
Instructor Reports	■ Instructor Reports provide data that may be useful for assessing programs or courses as part of the accreditation process.	■ Connect generates a number of powerful reports and charts that allow instructors to quickly review the performance of a given learner or an entire section. ■ Instructors can run reports that span multiple sections and instructors, making it an ideal solution for individual professors, course coordinators, and department chairs.
Student Reports	■ Student Reports allow students to review their performance for specific assignments or for the course.	■ Students can keep track of their performance and identify areas with which they struggle.
Pre- & Post-Tests	■ Instructors can generate their own pre- and post-tests from the test bank. ■ Pre- and post-tests demonstrate what students already know before class begins and what they have learned by the end.	■ Instructors have access to two sets of pre- and post-tests (at two levels). Instructors can use these tests to create a diagnostic and post-diagnostic exam via Connect.
Tegrity	■ Tegrity allows instructors to capture course material or lectures on video. ■ Students can watch videos recorded by their instructor and learn course material at their own pace.	■ Instructors can keep track of which students have watched the videos they post. ■ Students can watch and review lectures by their instructor. ■ Students can search each lecture for specific bites of information.
Simple LMS Integration	■ Connect seamlessly integrates with every learning management system.	■ Students have automatic single sign-on. ■ Connect assignment results sync to the LMS's gradebook.

Instructor's Guide to Connect for *Experience Communication*

When you assign Connect you can be confident—and have data to demonstrate—that your students, however diverse, are acquiring the skills, principles, and critical processes that constitute effective communication. This leaves you to focus on your highest course expectations.

Tailored to you Connect offers on-demand, single sign-on access to students—wherever they are and whenever they have time. With a single, one-time registration, students receive access to McGraw-Hill's trusted content.

Easy to use Connect seamlessly supports all major learning management systems with content, assignments, performance data, and LearnSmart, the leading adaptive learning system. With these tools you can quickly make assignments, produce reports, focus discussions, intervene on problem topics, and help at-risk students—as you need to and when you need to.

Experience Communication SmartBook

A Personalized and Adaptive Learning Experience with Smartbook SmartBook with Learning Resources is the first and only adaptive reading and study experience designed to change the way students read and master key course concepts. As a student engages with SmartBook, the program creates a personalized learning path by highlighting the most impactful concepts the student needs to learn at that moment in time and delivering learning resources—videos, animations, and other interactivities. These rich, dynamic resources help students learn the material, retain more knowledge, and get better grades.

Enhanced for the New Edition! With a suite of new learning resources and question probes, as well as highlights of key chapter concepts, SmartBook's intuitive technology optimizes student study time by creating a personalized learning path for improved course performance and overall student success.

SmartBook highlights the key concepts of every chapter, offering the student a high-impact learning experience (left). Here, highlighted text and an illustration together explain the communication process. Highlights change color (right) when a student has demonstrated his or her understanding of the concept.

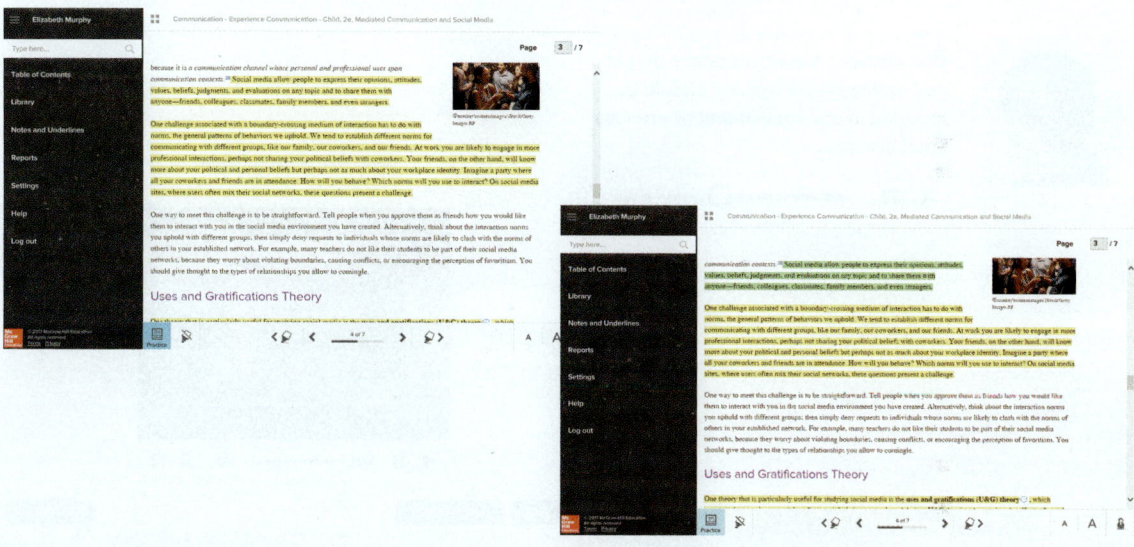

eBook Alongside SmartBook, there is also Connect eBook for simple and easy access to reading materials on smartphones and tablets. Students can study on the go without internet connection, highlight important sections, take notes, search for materials quickly, and read in class. Offline reading is available by downloading the eBook app on smartphones and tablets, and any notes and highlights created by students will be synced between devices when they reconnect. Unlike SmartBook, there is no pre-highlighting, practice of key concepts, or reports on usage and performance.

Preface   ix

Hundreds of interactive learning resources Presented in a range of interactive styles, *Experience Communication* Learning Resources support students who may be struggling to master, or simply wish to review, the most important communication concepts. Designed to reinforce the most important chapter concepts, every Learning Resource is presented at the precise moment of need. Whether video, audio clip, or interactive mini-lesson, each of the 200-plus Learning Resources was designed to give students a life-long foundation in strong communication skills.

More than 800 targeted question probes Class-tested at colleges and universities nationwide, a collection of engaging question probes—new and revised, more than 800 in all—give students the information on the introductory communication concepts they need to know, at every stage of the learning process, in order to thrive in the course. Designed to gauge students' comprehension of the most important *Experience Communication* chapter concepts, and presented in a variety of interactive styles to facilitate student engagement, targeted question probes give students immediate feedback on their understanding of the text. Each question probe identifies a student's familiarity with the instruction and points to areas where additional remediation is needed.

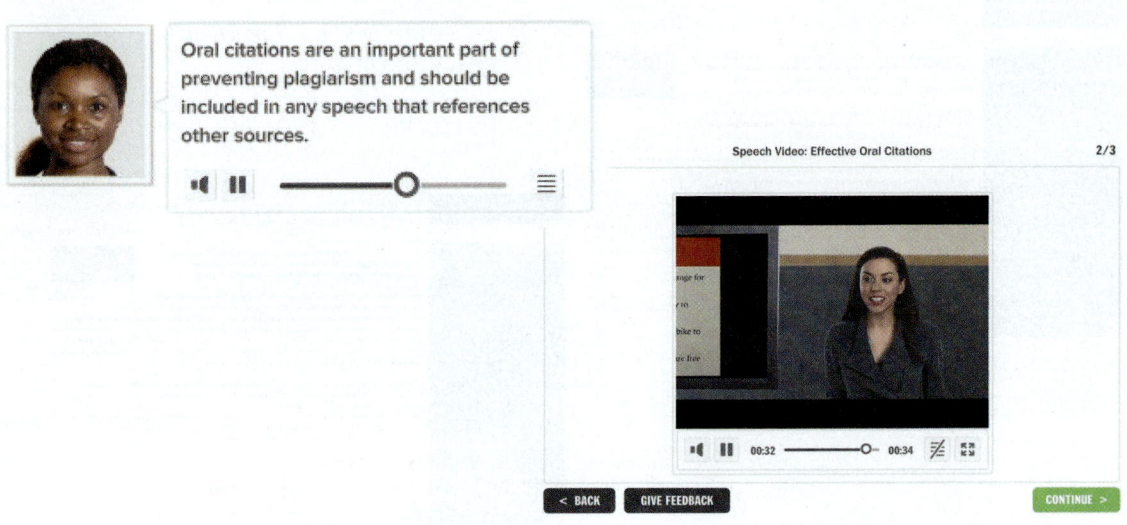

A strong focus on skill building *Experience Communication* focuses on building skills that are transferrable to contexts outside the classroom—skills that can be applied across an entire life.

Expanded scope and coverage of public communication An entire chapter is devoted to providing students with a strong conceptual basis for understanding the scope of public communication, which increasingly happens over mediated channels. A new box feature, Connecting Globally, introduces students to the ever-expanding relationships between mediated communication and intercultural communication, covering topics relevant to students' lives, including the role of mediated communication in interpersonal relationships, and how values related to privacy, surveillance, and disclosure vary from one culture to another.

Boxed Features Whether communicating with their peers, their loved ones, their colleagues, or their communities, students must continually adapt and build on their communication skills. This edition of *Experience Communication* includes a variety of boxed features to support students in developing these skills and applying them to their lives.

Connecting Globally boxes discuss the ways in which, in an increasingly global world, computer-mediated communication facilitates opportunities for intercultural awareness and exchange. Throughout the chapters, these boxes cover topics highlighting this intersection and teach students to be more adaptable in their communication styles.

Skill Builder boxes encourage students to practice key communication skills, such as neutralizing defensiveness in everyday communication or analyzing their social media presence. These features offer a wealth of practical applications for real-life communication scenarios.

Challenge Yourself boxes take the skill-building approach one step further, providing answers to students' most challenging communication questions on subjects ranging from gaining and maintaining employment, creating and sustaining diverse relationships, and cultivating those relationships through face-to-face and mediated channels.

Video Speech Assignment

Designed for use in face-to-face, real-time classrooms, as well as online courses, Video Speech Assignment allows you to evaluate your students' speeches using fully customizable rubrics. You can also create and manage peer review assignments and upload videos on behalf of students for optimal flexibility.

Students can access rubrics and leave comments when preparing self-reviews and peer reviews. They can easily upload a video of their speech from their hard drive or use Connect's built-in video recorder. Students can even attach and upload additional files or documents, such as a works-cited page or a PowerPoint presentation.

Peer Review Peer review assignments are easier than ever. Create and manage peer review assignments and customize privacy settings.

Speech Assessment Connect Video Speech Assignment lets you customize the assignments, including self-reviews and peer reviews.

Feedback Connect saves your frequently used comments, simplifying your efforts to provide feedback.

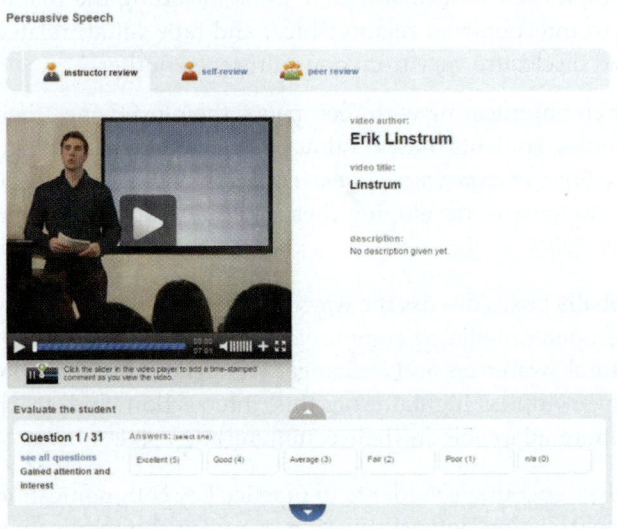

Data Analytics

Connect Insight provides at-a-glance analysis on five key insights, available at a moment's notice. The first and only analytics tool of its kind, Insight will tell you, in real time, how individual students or sections are doing (or how well your assignments have been received) so that you can take action early and keep struggling students from falling behind.

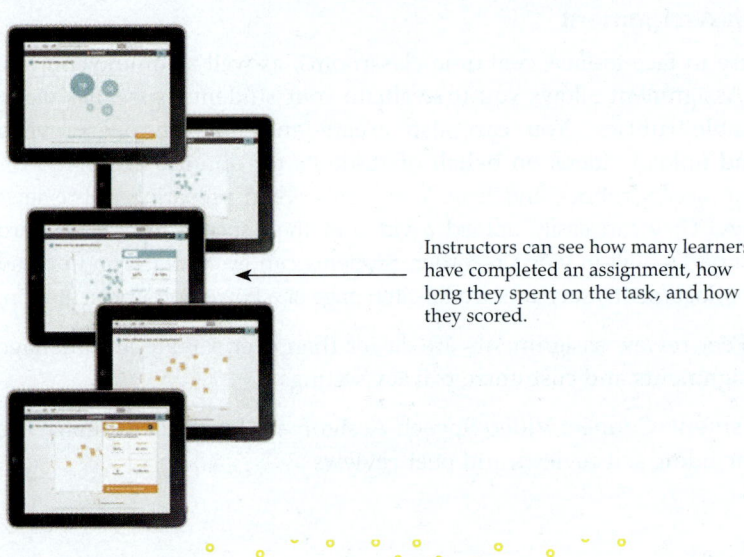

Instructors can see how many learners have completed an assignment, how long they spent on the task, and how they scored.

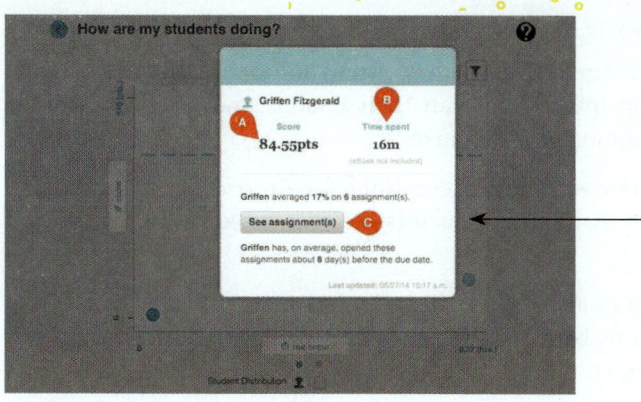

Instructors can see, at a glance, individual learner performance: analytics showing learner investment in assignments, and success at completing them, help instructors identify, and aid, those who are at risk.

LearnSmart Instructor Reports allow instructors to quickly monitor students' activity, making it easy to identify which students are struggling and to provide immediate help to ensure those students stay enrolled in the course and improve their performance. The Instructor Reports also highlight the concepts and learning objectives that the class as a whole is having difficulty grasping. This essential information lets you know exactly which areas to target for review during your limited class time.

Some key LearnSmart reports are listed below.

Progress Overview report—View student progress for all LearnSmart modules, including how long students have spent working in the module, which modules they have used outside of any that were assigned, and individual student progress through LearnSmart.

Missed Questions report—Identify specific LearnSmart probes, organized by chapter, that are problematic for students.

Most Challenging Learning Objectives report—Identify the specific topic areas that are challenging for your students; these reports are organized by chapter and include specific page references. Use this information to tailor your lecture time and assignments to cover areas that require additional remediation and practice.

Metacognitive Skills report—View statistics showing how knowledgeable your students are about their own comprehension and learning.

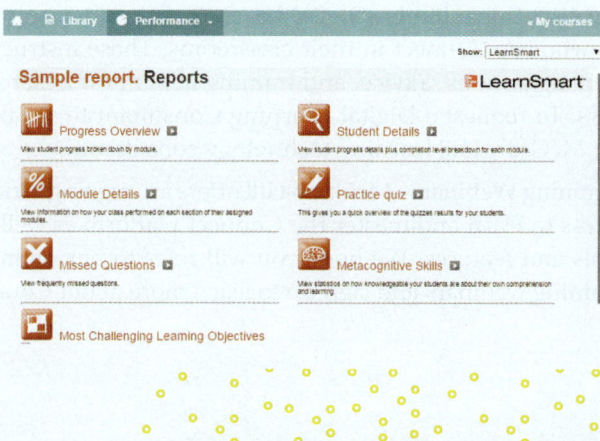

Classroom Preparation Tools

Whether before, during, or after class, there is a suite of *Experience Communication* products designed to help instructors plan their lessons and to keep students building upon the foundations of the course.

Powerpoint Slides The PowerPoint presentations for *Experience Communication* provide chapter highlights that help instructors create focused yet individualized lesson plans.

Test Bank The *Experience Communication* Test Bank is a collection of more than 1,000 examination questions based on the most important mass communication concepts explored in the text; more than 100 of the questions are new or revised for this edition.

Instructor's Manual Written by the author, this comprehensive guide to teaching from *Experience Communication* contains lecture suggestions and resources for each chapter.

Support to Ensure Success

- **Digital Success Academy**—The Digital Success Academy on Connect offers a wealth of training and course creation guidance for instructors and students alike. Instructor support is presented in easy-to-navigate, easy-to-complete sections. It includes the popular **Connect** video shorts, step-by-step *Click through Guides*, and *First Day of Class* materials that explain how to use both the Connect platform and its course-specific tools and features.

- **Implementation Team**—Our team of Implementation Consultants is dedicated to working online with instructors—one-on-one—to demonstrate how the Connect platform works and to help incorporate Connect into a customer's specific course design and syllabus. Contact your Digital Learning Consultant to learn more.

- **Learning Specialists**—Learning Specialists are local resources who work closely with your McGraw-Hill learning technology consultants. They can provide face-to-face faculty support and training.

- **Digital Learning Consultants**—Digital Learning Consultants are experienced instructors who use Connect in their classrooms. These instructors are available to offer suggestions, advice, and training about how best to use Connect in your class. To request a Digital Learning Consultant to speak with, please e-mail your McGraw-Hill learning technology consultant.

- **National Training Webinars**—McGraw-Hill offers an ongoing series of webinars for instructors to learn and master the Connect platform as well as its course-specific tools and features. We hope you will refer to our online schedule of national training webinars and sign up to learn more about Connect!

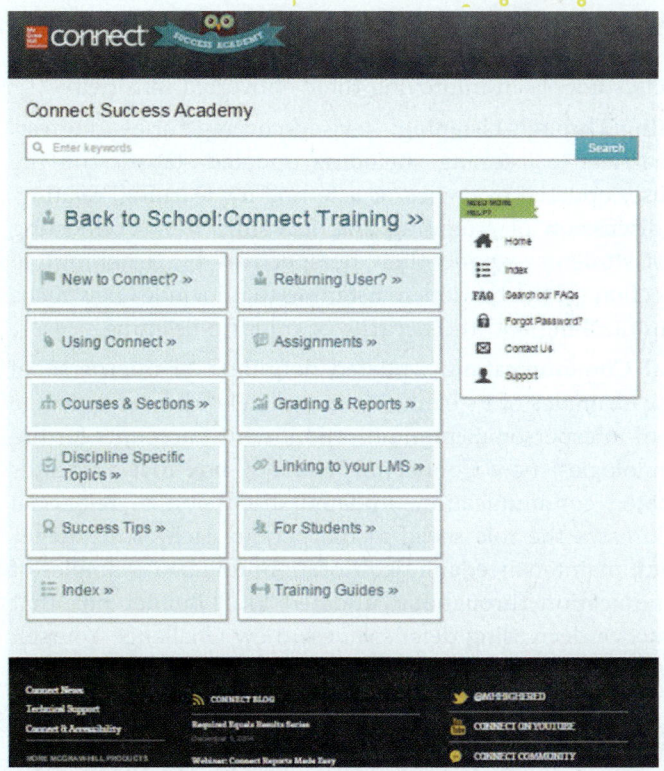

CONTACT OUR CUSTOMER SUPPORT TEAM

McGraw-Hill is dedicated to supporting instructors and students. To contact our customer support team, please call us at 800-331-5094 or visit us online at **http://mpss.mhhe.com/contact.php**

CHANGES TO THE SECOND EDITION: HIGHLIGHTS

Chapter 1 Communication, Perception and Your Life: Updated discussion of the relationship between self-image and communication includes examples from contemporary culture; new Connecting Globally box helps students take vacations from social media

Chapter 2 Communicating Verbally: Updated coverage of the social function of communication; new Skill Builder box that discusses practicing effective verbal communication and listening skills; new Connecting Globally box that examines the varying degree to which different cultures use social media to focus on the self; updated examples of American slang in Table 2.2; Challenge Yourself box that guides students in using correct grammar and avoiding profanity and slang

Chapter 3 Communicating Nonverbally: New Connecting Globally box that discusses issues of privacy and national security in the Global Village; revised Skill Builder box that instructs students in improving their nonverbal sensitivity

Chapter 4 Communicating Through Listening: Revised coverage of hearing versus listening and the barriers to listening, including updated statistics on the potential hazards of noise; updated examples of listening for learning, relating, and pleasure; revised discussion of attending and focusing; new Connecting Globally box that helps students expand their perspectives by "listening" to social media; updated section on the barriers to listening that includes new focus on the drawbacks of multitasking and the benefits of mindful listening

Chapter 5 Interpersonal Communication: Updated definition of interpersonal communication and new examples of its elements; completely updated coverage of the changing nature of interpersonal communication, which accounts for the impact of evolving technologies; new Connecting Globally box that addresses children's use of mediated communication; updated discussion of relational development, which addresses the role social media play in each of the stages of relational development, maintenance, and deterioration; updated examples of the dark side of communication throughout; updated Skill Builder box that prompts students to practice decreasing defensiveness; new Challenge Yourself box that helps students initiate conversations about sex with new or potential partners

Chapter 6 Intercultural Communication: Discussions of dominant cultures and nondominant or co-cultural groups, including updated definitions and examples of each; new Challenge Yourself box that provides guidance on speaking out against prejudice and hate speech; updated examples of ethnocentrism and stereotyping; new Skill Builder box that encourages students to reflect on their own cultural identity; new Connecting Globally box that compares cultural attitudes toward privacy and "the right to be forgotten"

Chapter 7 Mediated Communication and Social Media: Coverage of the different forms of mediated communication that includes an updated definition and examples of media convergence; revised discussion of the relationship between mass media and culture that includes new examples of gate-keeping and agenda-setting; updated definition of social media and statistics on its uses; new description and examples of CMC's applications in interpersonal communication, journalism and news reporting, and political communication; new Connecting Globally box that looks at social media use around the globe; Skill Builder box that shows students how to analyze and adjust their social media presence

Chapter 8 Organizational and Small-Group Communication: Revised Skill Builder box that shows students how to analyze organizational culture; updated discussion and examples of types of small groups, including assigned and emergent groups, task-oriented groups, and relationship-oriented groups; new Connecting Globally box that explores how issues of mediated communication and privacy affect global business

Chapter 9 Topic Selection and Audience Analysis: Updated coverage of narrowing a topic using Google Scholar and Google News; revised and updated coverage of conducting demographic analysis; new Connecting Globally box that demonstrates how user-generated content can be used to analyze an audience; updated examples in discussion of adapting language and topic to audience's needs

Chapter 10 Organizing Your Presentation: Revised coverage of gaining and maintaining audience attention, stating the purpose or thesis, and establishing qualifications; new sample outline that demonstrates the six principles of outlining; new Connecting Globally box that provides tips on storing and organizing website links; new Skill Builder box that shows students how to critique their introduction and conclusion

Chapter 11 Gathering Information and Supporting Materials: Updated discussion of the importance of information literacy in the digital age, including the process of gathering information and avoiding information overload and anxiety; coverage of primary versus secondary sources that takes a closer look at the role of bias; completely updated coverage of MLA documentation; updated topic example in Figure 11.5, a Google Scholar search; new examples that demonstrate how to learn more about a topic by experiencing it; new Skill Builder box that prompts students to practice proper oral citations; new Connecting Globally box on finding reliable and trustworthy statistics

Chapter 12 Communication Apprehension and Delivery: Revised discussion of systematic desensitization that walks students through each step of the technique with greater detail and specific tips; revised Skill Builder box that encourages students to conquer anxiety by developing their public speaking skills; additional examples for eliminating pauses and distracting bodily movement and improving fluency and pronunciation; new Connecting Globally box that instructs students in using eye contact over mediated channels

Chapter 13 Public Presentations to Inform: New discussion and examples of stating an immediate purpose and creating information hunger; new Connecting Globally box that shows students how to identify fake news; additional coverage of using visual aids in an informative presentation

Chapter 14 Public Presentations to Persuade: New Skill Builder box that teaches students the technique of persuading by listening and seeking common ground; new Connecting Globally box that explores the persuasive potential of social media profiles; updated discussion and new examples of inductive versus deductive arguments; updated coverage on the ethics of appeals to pathos, including fear appeals

Chapter 15 Using Communication Skills as You Enter the Workplace: Updated data in Figure 15.1, which shows what skills are most commonly sought by employers; an updated list of top ten attributes employers look for on a résumé in Figure 15.5; new Connecting Globally box that encourages students to use social media and face-to-face communication in their search for employment

Acknowledgments

We thank the many instructors across the country who offered insights and suggestions to improve the quality of the instructional material and student experience throughout the entire *Experience Communication* program:

Lawerence Albert *Morehead State University*
Ashley Alfaro *Tarrant County College Southeast*
Ennis Allen *Prince Georges Community College*
Emily Anzicek *Bowling Green State University*
Len Assante *Volunteer State Community College*
Rachelle Biderman *Hawkeye Community College*
Tonya Blivens *Tarrant County College Southeast*
Derek Bolen *Angelo State University*
Kathy Brady *University of Wisconsin Whitewater*
Ellen Bremen *Highline Community College*
Braze Brickwedel *Tallahassee Community College*
Guy Bruno *Edison Community College*
Amy Bryant *Nashville State Community College*
Christy Burns *Jacksonville State University*
Aaron Burtch *Lipscomb University*
Michael Caudill *Western Carolina University*
Jason Chapa *South Texas College*
Virginia Chapman *Anderson University*
John (Shiao-Yun) Chiang *State University College–Oneonta*
Kevin Clark *Austin Community College*
Sarah Clements *Pulaski Technical College*
Preston Coleman *University of North Georgia–Gainesville*
Julie Copp *Saint Louis Community College–Flors Valley*
Kelly Crue *Saint Cloud Technical and Community College*
Shirley Crum *Coastal Carolina Community College*
Phil Dalton *Hofstra University*
William Davis *Westchester Community College*
Jethro De Lisle *Tacoma Community College*
Allison DeStefano *Waubonsee Community College*
Nicolas Docan-Morgan *University of Wisconsin–La Crosse*
Allen Dutch *Georgia Highlands College*
Dawn Esser *Southwestern Iowa Community College*
Emilie Falc *Winona State University*
Robert Fussell *Guilford Technical Community College–Jamestown*
Angela Gibson *Shelton State Community College*
Jessica Gleason *Gateway Technical–Kenosha*
LaKresha Graham *Rockhurst University*
Luke Green *Saint Cloud Technical and Community College*
Douglas Hoehn *Bergen Community College*
Cheryl Hunter *NHTI Concord Community College*
Robert Kagan *Central Connecticut State University*
Linda Kalfayan *Westchester Community College*
Brian Kline *University of North Georgia–Gainesville*
Charles Korn *Nova Community College–Manassas*
Benjamin Krueger *Winona State University*
Amy Lenoce *Naugatuck Valley Community College*
Darren Linvill *Clemson University*
Martin Machover *Rockland Community College*
Lucas Messer *Scottsdale Community College*
Shellie Michael *Volunteer State Community College*
Barbara Midence *Miami Dade College*
Robert Mild *Fairmont State University*
Yolanda Mitchell *Pulaski Technical College*
Lauren Morgan *College of Dupage*
Jeffrey Nelson *Kent State Trumbull*
Lee Ann Nelson *Saint Charles County Community College*
Thomas Notton *University of Wisconsin–Superior*
Travice Baldwin Obas *Georgia Highlands College*
Christie Oberste *Pulaski Technical College*
Tami Olds *Nova Community College–Loudoun*
Darren Osburn *Saint Charles County Community College*
Lisa Packard *Gateway Technical–Kenosha*
Danielle Parsons *University of Rhode Island–Kingston*
Lisa Pavia-Higel *East Central College*

Andrea Pearman *Tidewater Community College–Virginia Beach*
Richard Pineda *University of Texas at El Paso*
Tom Preston *University of North Georgia–Gainesville*
Marlene Preston *Virginia Technical*
Deborah Prickett *Jacksonville State University*
Shannon Proctor *Highline Community College*
David Schrader *Oklahoma State University–Stillwater Campus*
David K. Scott *Northeastern State University*
Natalie Shubert *Ohio University–Athens*
Karen Solliday *Gateway Technical–Kenosha*
Don Spitler *Pulaski Technical College*
Steve Stuglin *Georgia Highlands College*
Charlotte Toguchi *Kapiolani Community College*
Carrie Tomko *Kent State University*
Dana Trunnell *Prairie State College*
Curt VanGeison *Saint Charles Community College*
James Wilson *Shelton State Community College*
Emily Workman *Guilford Technical Community College–Jamestown*

Brief Contents

PART 1 Communication Basics

1. Communication, Perception, and Your Life 2
2. Communicating Verbally 21
3. Communicating Nonverbally 43
4. Communicating Through Listening 60

PART 2 Communication Contexts

5. Interpersonal Communication 74
6. Intercultural Communication 100
7. Mediated Communication and Social Media 120
8. Organizational and Small-Group Communication 152

PART 3 Public Speaking Basics

9. Topic Selection and Audience Analysis 184
10. Organizing Your Presentation 202
11. Gathering Information and Supporting Materials 224
12. Communication Apprehension and Delivery 250

PART 4 Speaking to Inform and Persuade

13. Public Presentations to Inform 276
14. Public Presentations to Persuade 299
15. Using Communication Skills as You Enter the Workplace 324

Glossary 349
Name Index 359
Subject Index 361

Contents

PART 1 Communication Basics

1 Communication, Perception, and Your Life 2

Why Study Communication? 3
What Is Communication? 4
The Components of Communication 6
- People 6
- The Message 6
- The Channel 7
- Feedback 7
- Code 7
- Encoding and Decoding 8
- Noise 9

Three Models of Communication 9
Perception Affects Communication 11
- What Is Perception? 11
- What Occurs in Perception? 12

Differences in Perception 12
- Physiological Features 12
- Past Experiences 13
- Roles 13
- Present Feelings 13

Errors in Perception 14
Self-Image and Communication 15
- *Chapter Review* 18

2 Communicating Verbally 21

The Functions of Verbal Communication 22
- The Instrumental Function 22
- The Creative Function 22
- The Analytical Function 24
- The Social Function 24

How Words Communicate 25
- Two Processes for Interpreting Messages 25
- Two Kinds of Meaning 26

The Rules of Verbal Communication 27
- Rules Regarding Place 27
- Rules Regarding Conversational Partners 29
- Rules of Engagement 30

Words to Avoid 31
- Profanity 31
- Sexist Words 32
- Racist Words 32
- Ageist Words 33
- Grammatical Errors 33

Words to Use Carefully 34
- Slang 34
- Overused Expressions 35
- Jargon 35
- Words That Disguise 35

Strategies for Improving Your Verbal Communication 36
- Ask, "What Did You Mean?" 37
- Say It in Your Own Words 37
- Describe Without Judgment 37
- Define Your Terms 37
- Build Your Vocabulary 37
- Paint Pictures with Your Words 38
- Make Accurate Observations 38
- Make Inferences Carefully 38
- Be Specific and Concrete 38
- Use Figures of Speech 39
- Use the Language of the Locals 39
- *Chapter Review* 40

3 Communicating Nonverbally 43

What Is Nonverbal Communication? 44
How Are Verbal and Nonverbal Communication Related? 44
What Are Nonverbal Codes? 45
- Bodily Movement and Facial Expression 46
- Physical Attractiveness 47
- Space 48
- Time 50
- Touch 50
- Vocal Cues 51
- Clothing and Other Artifacts 52

Why Are Nonverbal Codes Difficult to Interpret?   54
   One Code Communicates a Variety of Meanings   54
   A Variety of Codes Communicate the Same Meaning   54
How Can You Improve Your Nonverbal Communication?   55
   Chapter Review   56

4 Communicating Through Listening   60

The Importance of Listening   61
   Why Listen?   61
   Hearing vs. Listening   62
Types of Listening   64
   Listening to Discern Content and Intent   64
   Listening for Learning   64
   Listening for Relating   65
   Listening for Pleasure   65
Attention and Listening   66
   Attending and Focusing   66
   Scanning and Choosing   66
   Listening and Remembering   67
Barriers to Listening   68
   Chapter Review   70

PART 2 Communication Contexts

5 Interpersonal Communication   74

Defining Interpersonal Communication   75
The Changing Nature of Interpersonal Relationships   77
The Stages of Interpersonal Relationships   79
   Relational Development   80
   Relational Maintenance   82
   Relational Deterioration   83
The Dark Side of Interpersonal Relationships   86
Improving Your Interpersonal Communication Behaviors   88
   Using Affectionate and Supportive Communication   88
   Influencing Others   89
   Bargaining   90
   Maintaining Behavioral Flexibility   90
The Healthy Interpersonal Relationship   92
   Chapter Review   94

6 Intercultural Communication   100

Defining Intercultural Communication   101
Studying Intercultural Communication   105
Biases That Affect Intercultural Communication   107
   Ethnocentrism   107
   Stereotyping   109
   Prejudice   109
Characteristics That Distinguish One Culture from Another   110
   Individualistic vs. Collectivist Cultures   110
   Uncertainty-Accepting vs. Uncertainty-Rejecting Cultures   111
   Implicit-Rule vs. Explicit-Rule Cultures   112
   M-Time vs. P-Time Cultures   113
Improving Intercultural and Co-Cultural Communication   116
   Chapter Review   117

7 Mediated Communication and Social Media   120

Understanding Mediated Communication   121
   Why Study Mediated Communication?   121
   The Forms of Mediated Communication   123
Mass Communication and Mass Media   123
   The Influence of Mass Media on Behavior   124
   The Relationship Between Mass Media and Culture   126
   Thinking Critically About Mass Media Messages   128
Computer-Mediated Communication and Social Media   129
   The Features and Uses of Social Media   130
   Uses and Gratifications Theory   133
   Evaluating Your CMC Interactions   135
   Thinking Critically About CMC Messages   136
Social Media Use Across Contexts   137
   Interpersonal Communication   137
   Organizational Communication   139
   Public Relations and Crisis Communication   140

Journalism and News Reporting   140
Political Communication   141
Health Communication   141
Global Communication   142

Protecting and Presenting Yourself on Social Media   143
Managing Your Privacy Online   143
Presenting Yourself Online   146
Chapter Review   147

8 Organizational and Small-Group Communication   152

What Is Organizational Culture?   153
Investigating Organizational Culture   153
Understanding Organizational Structure   156
Analyzing Organizational Communication Practices   157

Communicating in Small Groups and Teams   160
Types of Small Groups   161
Norms and Roles in Small Groups   162
Group Climate and Cohesion   164
Decision Making and Problem Solving   167

Organizational Leadership   169
Communication Skills for Leaders   169
Types of Power and Leadership   170

Cultivating Positive Relationships in Small Groups   173
Interacting Effectively in Small Groups   173
Achieving Communication Competence   174
Managing Conflict   176
Preparing for Ethical Dilemmas   177
Chapter Review   179

PART 3   Public Speaking Basics

9 Topic Selection and Audience Analysis   184

How to Select an Appropriate Topic   185
Survey Your Interests   185
Use Brainstorming   185
Assess Your Knowledge of and Commitment to the Topic   186
Determine Your Topic's Age   187

Narrow Your Topic   187
Audience Analysis   188
Three Levels of Audience Analysis   189
Four Methods of Audience Analysis   191
Tips for Analyzing Your Audience   196

Adapt to the Audience   196
Adapting Yourself   196
Adapting Your Language   197
Adapting Your Topic   197
Adapting Your Purpose and Thesis Statement   198
Chapter Review   200

10 Organizing Your Presentation   202

The Introduction   203
Gaining and Maintaining Audience Attention   204
Arousing Audience Interest   205
Stating the Purpose or Thesis   205
Establishing Your Qualifications   206
Forecasting Development and Organization   206

The Body   207
The Principles of Outlining   208
The Rough Draft   209
The Sentence Outline   211
The Key-Word Outline   212
Organizational Patterns   213
Transitions and Signposts   216
Tips for Using Note Cards   216

The Conclusion   217
The References   221
Chapter Review   222

11 Gathering Information and Supporting Materials   224

Gathering Information in a Digital World   225
Data, Information, and Knowledge   225
Information Literacy   226
Information Overload and Information Anxiety   227
The Information-Gathering Process   227

Gathering Information from Library Resources   230
Use Books, Articles, and Periodicals   230
Use Electronic Databases   233
Use Surveys and Statistics as Evidence   233

Contents   **XXV**

Gathering Information from the Internet   236
- Use Search Engines and Virtual Libraries   236
- Use Google Scholar   237
- Use Internet Search Tools and Resources   239

Gathering Information Through Personal Experience and Independent Research   239
- Experience Your Topic   240
- Conduct Independent Research   241

Evaluating, Citing, and Documenting Your Sources   242
- Evaluate Sources of Information   242
- Avoid Plagiarism   243
- *Chapter Review*   247

12 Communication Apprehension and Delivery   250

Why Care About Delivery Skills?   251
- What Is Delivery?   251
- What Is Communication Apprehension?   252
- Experiencing Communication Apprehension   252

Reduce Your Fear of Public Speaking   254
- Systematic Desensitization   254
- Cognitive Restructuring   255
- Skills Training   257
- Choosing the Right Anxiety-Reducing Technique for You   259

The Four Modes of Delivery   259
- The Extemporaneous Mode   259
- The Impromptu Mode   260
- The Manuscript Mode   260
- The Memorized Mode   261
- Choosing the Right Mode of Delivery for Your Presentation   261

The Vocal Aspects of Presentation   261
- Projection and Volume   262
- Rate   262
- Pauses   262
- Fluency   263
- Pitch   263
- Pronunciation   264
- Articulation   265
- Enunciation (Pronunciation Plus Articulation)   265
- Vocal Variety   266

The Bodily Aspects of Presentation   266
- Gestures   266
- Facial Expressions   267
- Eye Contact   268
- Movement   269

Delivery Tips for Non-Native Speakers   271
- *Chapter Review*   272

PART 4 Speaking to Inform and Persuade

13 Public Presentations to Inform   276

Prepare an Informative Presentation   277
- What Is Your Goal?   277
- What Is Your Purpose?   278

Effectively Present Information to an Audience   278
- Create Information Hunger   279
- Demonstrate Information Relevance   280
- Reveal Extrinsic Motivation   280
- Design Informative Content   282
- Avoid Information Overload   282
- Organize Content   283

Skills for an Informative Presentation   284
- Defining   285
- Describing   285
- Explaining   286
- Illustrating   287
- Using Analogies   287
- Narrating   287
- Demonstrating   288

Use Visual Resources to Inform   288

A Sample Informative Speech Outline and Note Cards   290
- *Chapter Review*   297

14 Public Presentations to Persuade   299

Prepare a Persuasive Presentation   300
- What Is Your Immediate Purpose?   300
- What Is Your Long-Range Goal?   301

Introduce Your Persuasive Presentation   301
- Revealing the Purpose of the Presentation   301

What Purposes Are Persuasive? 302
Why Should You Try to Persuade? 302
Understand Persuasion 305
Using Argument to Persuade: Fact, Policy, and Value 305
What Is the Difference Between Evidence and Proof? 306
How Can You Test Evidence? 307
Three Forms of Proof 308
Logos, or Logical Proof 308
Ethos, or Source Credibility 310
Pathos, or Emotional Proof 310
Organize Your Persuasive Message 311
The Monroe Motivated Sequence 311
Ethical Considerations 313
Skills for Persuasive Speaking 313
Providing Examples 313
Using Comparison and Contrast 314
Using Testimonials 315
A Sample Persuasive Speech Outline and Note Cards 315
Chapter Review 322

15 Using Communication Skills as You Enter the Workplace 324

Contemporary Jobs in Communication 325
Producing a Winning Résumé 325
Style 325
Content 327
Format 331
Writing a Convincing Cover Letter 334
Mastering the Job Interview 337
Create a Good First Impression 338
Speak with Clarity 339
Demonstrate Interest 339
More Tips for the Interview 339
Understand the Job 339
Understand the Company 339
Prepare for Behavioral-Based Interview Questions 340
Building Connections 342
Use Social Media to Expand Your Professional Network 342
Use Internships as a Networking Opportunity 343
Use the Informational Interview to Learn 344
Chapter Review 346

Glossary 349
Name Index 359
Subject Index 361

 **Communication**

Experience

part 1

Communication Basics

Why study communication? Throughout these chapters, we will examine some compelling reasons. We'll begin with the basics of communication and the factors that affect the ways we communicate. We will also see that listening is an important, and often overlooked, communication skill.

©Wavebreak Media Ltd/123RF

CHAPTER 1

Communication, Perception, and Your Life

Why Study Communication?
What Is Communication?
The Components of Communication
Three Models of Communication
Perception Affects Communication
Differences in Perception
Errors in Perception
Self-Image and Communication
Chapter Review

©Radius Images/Getty Images RF

CHAPTER 2

Communicating Verbally

The Functions of Verbal Communication
How Words Communicate
The Rules of Verbal Communication
Words to Avoid
Words to Use Carefully
Strategies for Improving Your Verbal Communication
Chapter Review

©Goodshoot/Fotosearch RF

CHAPTER 3

Communicating Nonverbally

What Is Nonverbal Communication?
How Are Verbal and Nonverbal Communication Related?
What Are Nonverbal Codes?
Why Are Nonverbal Codes Difficult to Interpret?
How Can You Improve Your Nonverbal Communication?
Chapter Review

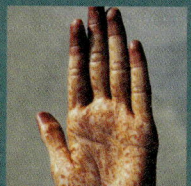
©Jacqueline Veissid/Getty Images RF

CHAPTER 4

Communicating Through Listening

The Importance of Listening
Types of Listening
Attention and Listening
Barriers to Listening
Chapter Review

chapter 1

Communication, Perception, and Your Life

©Wavebreak Media Ltd/123RF

In this chapter we will take a look at why studying communication is so important. We will also describe the process of perception and explore the concepts of self-image and identity management, all powerful influences on communication.

LEARNING OBJECTIVES

After reading this chapter, you should be able to:

- List the benefits of studying communication.
- Define communication and explain the roles that meaning and context play in it.
- Name and describe the components of communication.
- Name and describe the three models of communication.
- Describe the process of perception and its impact on communication.
- Explain the factors that affect and shape people's perceptions.
- Explain how and why errors in perception occur.
- Describe the ways in which self-image and identity management affect communication.

WHY STUDY COMMUNICATION?

Communication is your link to others at home, at work, and on the street. Although communication isn't always easy, you can improve your communication skills with study and practice. That improvement typically begins with understanding why the study of communication is important.

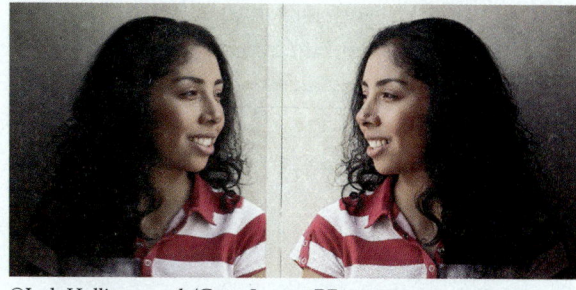
©Jack Hollingsworth/Getty Images RF

1. *Studying communication can improve the way others see you.* Compare a person who stumbles over words, falls silent, interrupts, and uses inappropriate language with someone who has a good vocabulary, listens when you speak, and smoothly exchanges ideas with you. The second type of person is what we call a competent communicator, and most of us prefer to relate to him or her. As you become increasingly competent, you will find that others will seek you out for conversations, assistance, and advice.

2. *Studying communication can make you more sensitive in your relationships.* By studying communication, you can learn specific ways to improve your relationships. A good example relates to listening. Men in our culture are rarely praised for being empathic or even considerate listeners. Women are widely perceived as talkers but also as better listeners. The actual style of listening often differs between men and women. Women engage in more relational listening, where people are more of the focus, whereas men engage in more action-oriented listening, where figuring out what to do about what is said is a greater focus.[1] Poor listening or engaging in the wrong style of listening can cause one partner in a relationship to think the other doesn't really care; that relationship may be doomed. Both men and women can learn to be effective listeners by following the practical advice on listening in **Chapter 4**.

3. *Studying communication can teach you important thinking skills.* Whether you are learning how to gather and evaluate information or to present an argument using evidence, you are working to hone your skills as a critical thinker,[2] problem solver, and decision maker. By studying communication and becoming more aware of the ways in which you communicate with others, you'll also become better at defining your own position on important issues, discerning which arguments and evidence are strong or weak, and analyzing which arguments and evidence your audience is likely to accept as proof.

4. *Studying communication can help you learn how to resolve conflicts at home, at work, and on the street.* Conflict is often resolved through effective communication, whether in person, on the telephone, or by e-mail.[3] You have also likely experienced conflicts that have gone unresolved and friendships that have been lost or relationships put on hold. In such cases, a meaningful exchange is often the key to finding a resolution. John Gottman, a social psychologist, and his fellow researchers even predicted which marriages would end in divorce by observing couples' inability to resolve conflict.[4,5]

©Tetra Images/Getty Images RF

Good communication principles and practices can resolve disputes between individuals, as well as between organizations, political parties, and nations.

5. *Studying communication can boost your confidence by helping you learn how to communicate in pairs, groups, and large audience contexts.* In a study based on the responses from 344 students at a large public university, those who had completed a communication course were more likely than those who hadn't to feel confident, comfortable with how others perceived them, satisfied with their ability to reason with others, and able to use language appropriately in a variety of communication situations.[6]

6. *Studying communication will encourage you to expand your comfort zone in communicating with others.* As you stroll through a mall, deposit money in a bank, go to a movie, or work at your job, about one in every five people you come in contact with will speak English as a second language. According to the 2013 American Community Survey, conducted by the U.S. Census Bureau, over 61.8 million Americans speak a language other than English in their home, and 44 percent of the people who speak a language other than English at home are native-born.[7] Learning how to communicate in today's world, whether English is your first language or not, requires an understanding of communication and culture and how those two concepts are related.

7. *Studying communication can help you succeed professionally.* A look at job postings online will give you an immediate understanding of the importance of improving your knowledge and practice of communication. What communication skills are employers seeking? The ability to speak clearly, succinctly, and persuasively is crucial to many jobs,[8] including sales positions,[9] as are public speaking skills.[10] Employers also value strong interpersonal skills[11] and an ability to work in teams or groups.[12] Professionals in fields as diverse as accounting, auditing, banking, counseling, engineering, information science, public relations, and sales have all noted the importance of oral communication skills.[13] The variety of these careers suggests that communication skills are important across the board. In fact, a recent survey from the Pew Research Center finds that most Americans agree that by and large the most important skill children must learn to succeed in life is communication.[14]

WHAT IS COMMUNICATION?

Communication comes from the Latin word *communicare*, which means "to make common" or "to share." The root definition is consistent with our definition of **communication**—*the process of using messages to generate meaning.*

Communication is considered a process because it consists of a series of actions, activities, or behaviors we engage in to achieve a particular result. In communication, the result of this process is, ideally, the conveyance and interpretation of meaning through messages. In other words, communication is not an unchanging product, nor is it an object you can hold in your hand; it is an activity in which you participate.

When you smile at another person, you send a message—that you are friendly or that you are interested in that person. When a radio announcer chooses particular words—for example, *emergency*, *crisis*, or *disaster*—to describe an event, she creates a particular kind of message. Because of the importance of word choice, a public speaker might spend days choosing just the right words, as well as considering his bodily movements, gestures, and facial expression to get across the desired message. In each of these examples, the person hopes to generate common meanings through the messages he or she provides.

Meaning, also covered in **Chapter 2**, is an understanding of the message as the speaker intended. People are not always successful in generating meaning. For example, a college professor may be very knowledgeable about a subject but has a hard time putting this knowledge in terms that students can relate to or understand. Understanding the meaning of another person's message cannot occur unless the two communicators have common meanings for words, phrases, and even movements and gestures. When you use language, common meanings facilitate a response that indicates that the message has been understood. For example, suppose you ask a friend for a ride home. She says nothing but walks with you to her car. You and your friend share the same meaning of the message exchanged.

But a message can be interpreted in more than one way, especially if the people involved have little shared experience. Let's say you ask a new friend to "meet at a restaurant for lunch around noon." You may assume that means he'll arrive at noon, no more than 5 to 10 minutes late, but he thinks "around noon" means that the arrangement is loose. You arrive at the restaurant a few minutes before noon, but he does not appear until 12:30. You end up waiting, but you are not happy when he arrives so terribly late, by your understanding of the situation. In such a case, you could have determined more accurately what he was planning or thinking by *negotiating*. So, for example, if your new friend had said, "Would 12:30 or 12:45 be OK?" you might have responded, "No, that would be too late for me." Or you might have provided additional information to him—for example, by saying, "I have a class at 1:30, and I don't want our meal to be rushed, so it would be great if you could be there by noon." And if he said, "But you said 'around noon,'" you would explain, "Oh, I'm sorry. I really meant *at* noon."

Although we do not include this concept in our formal definition of communication, it is important to note that all communication happens in a **context**, meaning it occurs within *a set of circumstances or a situation*. Contexts for communication include both face-to-face and mediated situations. For example, two friends talking on the way to class or five business acquaintances in a small-group setting are examples of face-to-face contexts. Students using e-mail to interact with pen pals across the country or a parent on a business trip touching base with family via FaceTime are examples of interaction contexts that rely on mediated communication. At many colleges and universities, the material covered in communication courses is defined by interaction context: interpersonal, global and intercultural, mediated, and organizational or small-group. In other words, communication occurs in a variety of contexts. **Part 2** looks at a number of these contexts in depth.

THE COMPONENTS OF COMMUNICATION

In this section you will see how communication really works by learning about its components: people, messages, channels, feedback, code, encoding and decoding, and noise. In the next section, by looking at three models of communication, you will see how each component has a part to play in the process of generating, as well as potentially obstructing, the meaning of a message.

People

People are involved in the human communication process in two roles—as both the sources and the receivers of messages. A **source** *initiates a message*, and a **receiver** is *the intended target of the message*. Individuals do not perform these two roles independently. Instead, they are the sources and the receivers of messages simultaneously and continually.

People may vary in the way they respond to the same message; they may also vary in the way they convey the same message. An individual's characteristics, including race, sex, age, culture, values, and attitudes, affect the way he or she sends and receives messages. A teenager, for example, uses slang expressions that an older person is less likely to use or perhaps even to understand. An acquaintance might use Facebook to maintain contact with you, your parents perhaps use text messages, and your grandparents probably use the telephone. In addition to the channels being different, the words that each communicator chooses will likely differ.

The Message

The **message** is *the verbal and nonverbal expression of the idea, thought, or feeling that one person (the source) wishes to communicate to another person or group of people (the receivers)*. As noted, the message includes the verbal symbols (words and phrases) you use to communicate your ideas, as well as the nonverbal ones— that is, your facial expressions, bodily movements, gestures, use of physical contact, and tone of voice. The message may be relatively brief and easy to understand or long and complex.

Communication can take the form of either intentional or unintentional messages. For example, if you wave to your friend when she enters a shopping center where you agreed to meet, that is intentional communication; you want her to see you and walk over to you. But if you just happen to have your hand in the air when she comes in (perhaps you are scratching your head) and she thinks you are waving to her, that is unintentional. Nevertheless, you still have communicated, and she may come toward you and begin to carry on a conversation, whether you wanted her to or not. Messages conveyed through mediated communication channels can also be distorted. For example, an e-mail to your friend conveys limited nonverbal messages, which can be crucial to correctly interpreting a verbal (written) message.

©Rolf Bruderer/Blend Images/Getty Images RF

The Channel

The **channel** is *the means by which a message moves from the source to the receiver of the message*. Airwaves, sound waves, twisted copper wires, glass fibers, and cable are all communication channels. So are phone calls, e-mails, text messages, face-to-face conversations, and so on. The channel used to convey a message can have great significance. Does anyone think that breaking off a serious relationship with someone by text is the right way? When the spouse of an active-duty soldier sees an armed forces car in front of the house, with two uniformed officers on their way to the door, that spouse can be pretty sure that this personal attention is not good news. Yes, the channel, the means of delivering a message, makes a serious difference. A delivery of flowers, an electronic get-well card, a surprise birthday cake—all of these are channels used to deliver a message, sometimes with words and sometimes with acts or items.

Feedback

Feedback is *the receiver's verbal and nonverbal response to the source's message*. Ideally, you respond to another person's messages by providing feedback, so that the source knows you received the message as intended. Feedback is part of any communication situation. Even no response, or silence, is feedback, as are confused looks and packing away of laptops by students in a lecture hall. Suppose you're looking for a restroom in a building you've never been in before. "Excuse me," you say to a passerby, "can you tell me . . . ," but the person keeps on going without acknowledging you. In this case, the intended receiver did not respond, yet even the lack of a response provides you with some feedback. You may think that the receiver didn't hear you, was in too much of a hurry to stop, or is unfriendly.

Code

A computer carries messages via binary code on cable, wire, or fiber; similarly, you converse with others by using a code called "language." A **code** is *a systematic arrangement of symbols used to create meanings in the mind of another person or persons*. As you will learn in **Chapter 2**, words, phrases, and sentences are "symbols" we all use to evoke images, thoughts, and ideas in the minds of others. If someone yells "Stop!" as you approach the street, the word *stop* is a symbol you are likely to interpret as a warning of danger.

©Image Source, all rights reserved RF

CHALLENGE YOURSELF

Why do I need to take a communication course when I have been communicating all my life?

Students taking an introductory communication course often ask themselves this question. Although it may be true that you have been communicating all your life, it's likely that you have not always communicated with success. The aim of this course is to give you the opportunity to learn how to communicate more effectively, competently, and efficiently. With practice you will find that not only will your communication improve, so will your relationships.

One challenge we all face is choosing the appropriate channel for the communication goals at hand. For example, it is likely that most of your interactions happen over mediated channels, such as text messaging and social media. Mediated communication can make it difficult to send and receive nonverbal messages, which are often crucial to our interpretations of verbal messages. For this reason, relationships can experience friction when conducted primarily via a mediated channel, such as text messaging.

To reduce friction, think about your own behaviors and the unintended messages you send when, say, you answer your cell phone, respond to a text message, or snap a photo to post to social media during a face-to-face interaction. Before you pick up your phone or device, consider the following questions:

- Will the person I am with feel less important if I text others while we are together?
- Will my date think I am not enjoying our time together if I interrupt to post a status update?
- Is it worth interrupting my face-to-face conversation to attend to a mediated message?

The proliferation of devices makes it difficult to turn away from our cell phone, television, and computer screens. When we make time for others by disconnecting from technology, we strengthen our connections.

Verbal and nonverbal codes are the two types of code used in communication. Verbal codes are the spoken language we use. "Stop!" in the previous example is a verbal code. Some examples of nonverbal codes, defined and discussed in **Chapter 3**, are facial expressions (like a smile or a furrowed brow), touch (a handshake), and the clothing and other artifacts you wear (your interview suit, a pair of earrings, a tattoo).

Encoding and Decoding

Because communication involves the use of codes, the process of communicating can be viewed as one of encoding and decoding. **Encoding** is *the process of translating an idea or a thought into words.* **Decoding** is *the process of assigning meaning to an encoded message.*

For instance, suppose you want to purchase a new car. You are trying to describe a compact model to your friend, who wants to help you with your purchase. You might be visualizing your uncle's car with the black interior, sporty design, and silver exterior. Translating this vision into words, or encoding it, you tell your friend only that you are interested in a car that is "small and well designed." Your friend, on hearing this, decodes your words and develops his own mental image. But his love of larger cars and your lack of precision affect this process; as a result, he envisions a sedan rather than the subcompact hatchback you were thinking of.

As you can see, misunderstanding often occurs because of the limitations of language, the inadequacy of descriptions, and a person's own biases. Nonetheless, encoding and decoding are essential to communication, and meanings can be further refined and clarified through negotiation—that is, through asking questions or paraphrasing: "Were you thinking of a sedan?" "No, actually, I prefer the look of a hatchback."

Noise

In the communication process, **noise** is *any interference in the encoding and decoding processes that reduces the clarity of a message.* Noise can include a variety of distractions—auditory ones, such as loud sounds; visual ones, such as a piece of food between someone's front teeth; and behavioral ones, such as someone standing too close for comfort. Noise can also be psychological, such as struggling to take seriously someone whose personality annoys you; physical, such as pain from a tooth; or semantic, such as uncertainty about what the other person's words mean. Noise is anything that interferes with receiving, interpreting, or providing feedback about a message. You can find out more about noise and other barriers to listening in **Chapter 4**.

©JGI/James Grill/Blend Images/Getty Images RF

THREE MODELS OF COMMUNICATION

Over the years, scholars have developed three basic models of the communication process: the action model, the interaction model, and the transaction model. Each model represents a particular way of understanding the communication process. We'll begin with the model that came first, the action model (**Figure 1.1**).

Figure 1.1 The Action Model of Communication

Figure 1.2 The Interaction Model of Communication

The action model is the most basic model, which depicts a one-way process in which a source encodes a message (puts it into language), then sends it through a channel (e.g., a text message or a face-to-face interaction) for the receiver to decode, or interpret. For example, you text a friend to tell her you will be late for your dinner plans. Your friend receives the message and interprets it to mean that she will need to change your reservation at the restaurant, so that you can meet a little later.

The second model is the interaction model, illustrated in **Figure 1.2**. Although the interaction model includes all the same components as the action model, it differs in two important ways. First, it sees communication as a two-way process; second, it recognizes the role of context and feedback. For instance, you text the same friend about dinner, but this time you take into account that this is her birthday dinner (the context) and that she is likely to be irritated by your change of plans (her feedback). Perhaps you write a text message to explain the reasons for your lag, in hopes that she will understand and not feel that her birthday plans have been ruined.

Finally, the transaction model differs from the other two in that it doesn't distinguish between the source and the receiver and does not see communication as a series of messages that get sent back and forth. Instead, the transaction model, laid out in **Figure 1.3**, sees communication as an ongoing conversation in which messages are sent in both directions simultaneously. As you begin to send your friend a second text to explain that you are having car trouble, she has already written back to say that she will change the reservation and meet you later that evening. In response to this message, you stop texting and call her to thank her for her understanding and to wish her a happy birthday. In other words, according to the transaction model, even as you are acting as the source of a message, you are also responding to feedback and acting as a receiver, all at the same time.

Figure 1.3 The Transaction Model of Communication

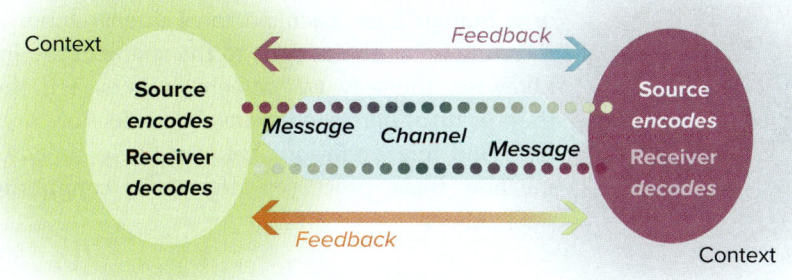

PERCEPTION AFFECTS COMMUNICATION

The definition of communication we have provided and the three models we have laid out still do not provide a complete picture of this complex topic. Another very important factor that affects communication is perception.

What Is Perception?

Perception is *the process of using the senses to acquire information about the surrounding environment or situation*.[15] The process of perception involves three stages: selection, organization, and interpretation. **Selection** refers to *the decisions we make to focus on some stimuli—sights, sounds, smells, and other sensations—and neglect others*. We all do this all the time—selecting the messages to which we attend. Perhaps you tend to tune out your nagging roommate but pay close attention to every word of praise from your boss. Selection also occurs when you size up people. Based on your experience with different people, you may treat them with respect, talk to them, or avoid them. Each of these treatments is a response to your perceptions of others.

Organization means *grouping stimuli into meaningful units*. In some cases we organize by distinguishing between the figure—or focal point of our attention—and the background against which that figure is set. An employer chooses your name from a list of applicants. For the employer, your name is the figure and all other names have fallen into the background. We also organize using *closure* (the tendency to fill in missing information), *proximity* (perceiving distinct objects as related because of their physical closeness), and *similarity* (grouping objects because they share attributes). You perceive your new boss to be unkind because you overheard him raising his voice (closure); an acquaintance believes you and your best friend to be dating because you are always seen together (proximity); you anticipate getting along with your brother's girlfriend because in a photo she resembles a good friend of yours (similarity).

Finally, perception involves **interpretation**, *the assignment of meaning to stimuli*. Have you ever seen an inkblot test? This well-known test of human

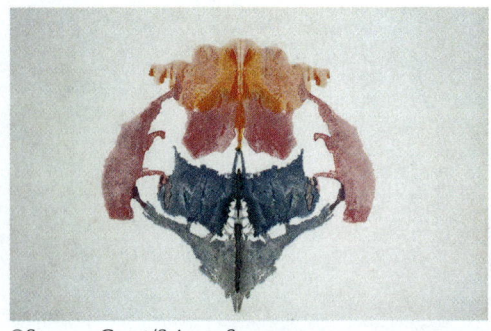
©Spencer Grant/Science Source

psychology relies on the principle of interpretation. Where one person sees a butterfly, another interprets the shapes to be a man's dress coat, a pair of angels, or a human face. Each person's interpretation is the meaning he or she assigns to the shape of the inkblot. Likewise, the way we perceive others—and the way they, in turn, perceive us—involves selection, organization, and interpretation. You can likely already imagine how these processes affect your communication with others.

What Occurs in Perception?

You meet with your supervisor, thinking she is going to praise you for all the extra work you have done lately, so you approach your meeting perceiving her in a warm and friendly way. When she instead tells you she's reducing your hours because profits are down, your perception of her changes, and the nature of your communication with her (the tone of your voice, the words you choose) are likely to change as well. When this kind of mismatch occurs—between what one expects and what occurs—surprise can turn to anger and disappointment (and no more extra work for that ungrateful supervisor).

Since each person's perceptions are unique, communication is a complicated matter. You will have a better understanding of how complex perception is and how your individual perceptions influence your communication with others once you consider the following two kinds of perception:

- *Active perception.* This is the process by which the mind selects, organizes, and interprets what one senses. You could think of each person you communicate with as having a video camera with a unique lens; as those people aim their camera at different things, they see different colors, degrees of light, and perspectives.

- *Subjective perception.* This is the process by which one attributes meaning to sensed stimuli. To understand this process, consider how much your inner state affects your perceptions. If you have a bad headache, the pain probably will affect the way you feel about your children, the way you respond to the workers at the shop, and even the way you see yourself in a mirror. These perceptions will likely change when your headache subsides in a few hours.

DIFFERENCES IN PERCEPTION

The uniqueness of human experience is based largely on differences in perception. These differences result from physiological features, past experiences, roles, and present feelings.

Physiological Features

People differ from each other in a multiplicity of physiological ways: for example, sex, height, weight, body type, and acuity of the senses. Each of these features affects the way you see yourself and the way you interact with others. Just imagine if you were a different race and sex or if you had hearing or vision loss, how those features would influence your perceptions and, in turn, how you would communicate with others. If you are particularly attractive, you may be accustomed to people looking at you and giving you favored attention. If you are short, the whole world looks very tall. If you have trouble hearing, you might avoid the telephone, especially cell phones, and prefer to text.

Past Experiences

Your *past experiences lead you to see the world in a way that is difficult to change*. This concept is known as **perceptual constancy**. For example, a bad experience in a given situation may cause you to avoid that situation in the future, just as a good one might encourage you to seek out that situation. In addition, your past experiences affect how you perceive certain categories of people—men, women, professors, police, politicians—whether in a positive or negative way. These perceptions also influence your current and future communication with those categories of people. You may choose never to remarry if you have gone through a difficult divorce. You might seek help from a police officer because your father spent his career in policing; or, you might avoid the police if your brother was treated poorly during an arrest. You might perceive education to be valuable if everyone you know who completed college has a successful job; or, you might view school as unnecessary to success if your mother holds a prestigious job with little higher education. In short, a variety of personal experience colors our beliefs and perceptions.

©Jonathan Newton/*The Washington Post*/Getty Images

Roles

A **role** is *a part a person plays in a social context*.[16] The roles we attribute to others affect the way we perceive them, and vice versa. If you play the role of a leader or a loner or a nerd, this will affect the way others perceive you and how receptive they are to your messages. If you label others as athletes, single moms, or beauty queens, that perception will affect your communication with them—the topics you choose to discuss, the vocabulary you use, and the credibility you give to their opinions.

Present Feelings

How you feel at the moment affects your perceptions—what you see and hear and how it looks and sounds to you—and these perceptions alter your communication. Great news about your mother's health, a brief fight this evening before class, or a disagreeable e-mail from your boss—all these life experiences influence your perceptions and how or whether you communicate with the people around you.

How can you apply this information about perception to your own life? Imagine you are talking to a classmate about an assignment but he looks away and does not respond to you. Your first thought might be that he is distant and uninterested or that he doesn't like you. The truth might be that he is catching a cold and doesn't want to talk because his throat hurts. Or he may be reluctant to get involved because he has helped classmates with their work in the past and gotten no gratitude for his effort. Or it might be something far more basic—that he is hungry and is just trying to get away from you so he can go eat! Clearly, his present circumstances and internal states are influencing his communication with you.

Students of communication who know about the role of perception in communication have a better idea of how to manage such situations. When faced with someone acting unpredictably, they would start by checking their own perceptions and inquiring about the other person's perceptions. They would give the other person a chance to say what is troubling him: "You are not answering me. Am I being unreasonable in asking for your help?" In any case, a person who is knowledgeable about how perception influences communication has an advantage in the exchange.

ERRORS IN PERCEPTION

Once we understand the active nature of perception and recognize that people hold unique perceptions as a consequence, we can see that we might make errors when we perceive other people. Many types of perceptual errors exist. In **Chapter 6**, we take a closer look at one of the most common errors, stereotyping. Stereotypes occur when we make a hasty generalization about a group based on a judgment about an individual from that group. Stereotypes often lead to prejudices, a topic also discussed in **Chapter 6**.

Therefore, an important skill is perceptual checking—a process of describing, interpreting, and verifying that helps you understand another person and his or her message more accurately. The three steps of perceptual checking are

1. Describe to the other person the observed behavior—including the verbal and nonverbal cues.
2. Suggest plausible interpretations of that behavior or feature.
3. Seek verification or rebuttal of your interpretations by asking for clarification, explanation, or amplification.

For example, imagine that you are assigned a group research project in one of your classes. Another member of the group asks you to produce all your primary sources for the project. You presented this source material weeks ago. You respond by saying, "I understand that you want me to give you my primary sources" (describe the behavior or the message). "I might just be acting paranoid, but this makes me feel that you don't trust me" (first interpretation). "Why do you want my primary sources?" (request for clarification).

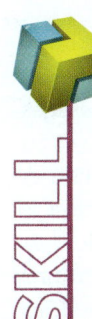

SKILL BUILDER

LEARN TO CHECK YOUR PERCEPTIONS

With a partner in class, identify a physical feature that you believe affects your communication with others, such as your height, weight, skin color, age, hairstyle, clothing, jewelry, scars, or tattoos.

- First say how you think this feature affects your communication with others.
- Next let the other person say how he or she perceives this feature.
- Then switch roles and repeat.

Discuss with your partner how your perceptions about the features you identified were similar or dissimilar to each other. How do you think your life experiences have contributed to the perceptions you hold about your own physical features? What about the physical features of others around you? By practicing these steps, you and your partner are checking your perceptions about features that affect your communication.

Perceptual checking can be even more important in personal and romantic relationships—especially if the person you are dating grew up in a different family situation or social group than you did. Whatever the relationship, though, you will want to avoid suggesting interpretations that cause the other person to feel defensive. **Chapter 5**, on interpersonal relationships, offers some very important advice as to how to avoid defensive interactions with the people in your life.

SELF-IMAGE AND COMMUNICATION

How you see yourself can make a big difference in how you communicate.[17] The great philosopher, sociologist, and psychologist George Herbert Mead said that the self originates in communication.[18] Through verbal and nonverbal symbols, which are the basis of communication, a child comes to accept the expectations of others and, in turn, takes on certain roles. When people are treated as though they are inferior, or intelligent, or gifted, or unattractive, they often act accordingly.

Many communication scholars and social scientists believe that people are products of how others treat them and of the messages others send them. Venus and Serena Williams have won over forty combined Grand Slam titles and five Olympic gold medals in tennis. They also happen to be sisters, who were coached, from very young ages, by their father Richard Williams. He taught them to be sensible and balanced, but also incredibly competitive in their sport. Most likely the sisters had an inherent physical ability for playing tennis, but they may not have achieved success without the early messages received from their father and coach.[19] Like the Williams sisters, each of us establishes a self-image based on the messages we receive and the categories others apply to us. A

©Kyodo News/Getty Images

Self-Image and Communication 15

recent study suggests that a mother's messages to her daughter about body image affect the daughter's perceptions about her own body image, and the way she treats her body.[20] In other words, positive, negative, and neutral messages all play a role in how we think about ourselves.

Communication itself is probably best understood as a dialogic process. A **dialogue** is simply *a conversation, discussion, or negotiation*, so communication is a process that occurs in the context of our interactions with other people.[21] A competent communicator considers the other person's needs and expectations when selecting messages to share. Thus, communication begins with the self, as defined largely by others, and involves others, as defined largely by the self.

For example, you can have **intrapersonal communication**, which is *the kind of discussion and decision making that occurs within your own mind*. Consider a situation of importance, such as asking the boss for more responsibilities so that you can earn a larger salary. Before you ever enter the boss's office, you will likely consider what you plan to say, rehearse in your mind how you are going to say it, and even consider what your response is going to be, no matter how the discussion proceeds. Yes, you worry, try out lines, and guess what will be said without uttering a word out loud. You are experiencing intrapersonal communication.

Of course, few of our daily interactions are as rehearsed as the one just described, and as we move from one encounter to the next, we present ourselves to people in a variety of ways, both consciously and unconsciously. Self-presentation can be defined as the way we portray ourselves to others.

A key part of self-presentation is **identity management**— *the control (or lack of control) of what we communicate and what it conveys about us*. Through identity management, we try to present an idealized version of ourselves in order to reach desired ends. A good example is a social media profile you update frequently. The identity you project in that profile depends in part on whether you use that site for personal or professional reasons, or a combination of those. If you intend the profile to attract potential dating partners, you might manage your identity by posting more selfies, or photos of yourself, doing things you enjoy in order to enhance perceptions of you as a fun or caring person. On a professional site like LinkedIn, your aim is to find a job or advance your career, so you highlight your accomplishments and take care to promote a professional identity by posting information that is accurate and free of grammatical errors. We all practice identity management in face-to-face interactions as well, presenting the self we want others to see.

People manage their identity and the impressions they make using three elements of communication: manner, appearance, and setting.[22] Manner is the way an individual typically interacts with others through verbal and nonverbal symbols. A person's manner might be brusque or silly, businesslike or immature, friendly, warm, or gracious. Appearance may be tied to a role an individual

©John Lund/Marc Romane/agefotostock RF

CONNECTING GLOBALLY

TAKE A VACATION FROM SOCIAL MEDIA

Interaction through social media has become an important part of our daily routines. However, despite its many benefits, some people argue that social media consumes too much of our time, encourages self-centered behaviors, negatively affects our productivity, and keeps us from engaging with others face to face.

How much time do you think you spend checking or posting to a social media site? Have you ever wondered what life is like without social media? To experience the benefits of "unplugging," some people take planned breaks from social media. Here's how to do it:

- Post to your primary social media accounts a message explaining that you are temporarily taking a break from social media.
- Disable your notifications so that you can truly experience the benefits of stepping away.
- Keep a journal about your experience of life without social media.

The following questions might help you frame your journal entries exploring your relationship to social media:

- What are the major benefits and drawbacks of taking a break from social media?
- Do you feel like you are missing out on anything, or do you enjoy being able to unplug?
- If you are comfortable sharing your thoughts, ideas, and personality through social media, how does it feel to interact face to face? With which mode of interaction are you more comfortable and why?
- Do you tend to use social media to get your information about the issues and trends impacting society? If so, how do you go about gathering information without social media? Has your understanding of global and local issues changed during your social media hiatus? How so?
- Do you think other people you know would share your experience of unplugging from social media? Will you recommend the experience to your friends?

plays (such as an administrative assistant versus a barista or rock musician), a value one holds (wearing jewelry versus not), one's personality (easygoing versus formal), or one's view of the communication setting (unimportant as opposed to crucial). The setting includes the immediate environment (the space in which you are communicating, such as a church as opposed to a coffee shop), as well as other settings in which you display who you are (your home and the way you decorate it, the type of car you drive). Thus, if you are concerned that your work manner comes across as stuffy and uptight, you might try to cultivate different impressions by asking colleagues to meet up outside of work, in a more casual setting.

Although communication is complicated, it occurs almost every minute of your life. If you are not communicating with yourself (thinking, planning, reacting to the world around you), you are actively and subjectively perceiving others and responding to their behavior. Even if others did not intend messages for you, you gather observations and draw conclusions. A person yawns and you believe she is bored with your message. A second person looks away and you conclude that he is not listening to you. A third person smiles (perhaps because of a memory of a joke she heard recently) and you believe she is attracted to you. We are continually interpreting the meanings of others' verbal and nonverbal messages, as well as behaving in ways that have communicative value for them.

CHAPTER REVIEW

Communication is far more than the transmission of information. To communicate involves multiple variables—its verbal, nonverbal, and behavioral aspects; the channel used; the characteristics and perceptions of the sender and the receiver; the relationship of the sender to the receiver; and the context in which the communication occurs. Each of these variables—including the communicator's self-perception and identity-management processes—affects every aspect of communication.

KEY TERMS

communication, 4
context, 5
message, 6
receiver, 6
source, 6
channel, 7
code, 7
feedback, 7
decoding, 8
encoding, 8

noise, 9
interpretation, 11
organization, 11
perception, 11
selection, 11
perceptual constancy, 13
role, 13
dialogue, 16
identity management, 16
intrapersonal communication, 16

STUDY QUESTIONS

1. List at least 10 ways you use communication in a single day, from the moment you wake in the morning until you fall asleep at night. How can you become a more competent communicator with regard to each of the items on your list?
2. Why do we call communication a process? What parts of the process influence meaning, and how do people arrive at a shared meaning of a message?
3. Give three specific examples of feedback that college students receive. How does this feedback shape their thinking and behavior?

4. Give examples from your own experience of perceptions organized by closure, proximity, and similarity.
5. Of the four factors that produce differences in perception, which do you think is most powerful? Why? Do you think one can be ranked as more important than the others? Why or why not?
6. Think of a time when perceptual checking would have helped you better understand another person's message. Describe how you would, in that instance, follow the three steps of perceptual checking.
7. List various identities you present in your daily life. How do you manage each via manner, appearance, and setting?

ENDNOTES

1. Johnston, M. K., Weaver, J. B., Watson, K. W., & Barker, L. B. (2000). Listening styles, biological or psychological differences? *International Journal of Listening, 14*, 32–46.
2. Allen, M., Berkowitz, S., Hunt, S., & Louden, A. (1999). A meta-analysis of the impact of forensics and communication education on critical thinking. *Communication Education, 48*, 18–30.
3. Markman, H. J., Renick, M. J., Floyd, F. J., Stangel, S. M., & Clements, M. (1993). Preventing marital distress through communication and conflict management training: A 4- and 5-year follow up. *Journal of Consulting and Clinical Psychology, 61*, 70–77.
4. Gottman, J. M., & Levenson, R. W. (1999). Rebound from marital conflict and divorce prediction. *Family Process, 38*, 287–292.
5. Scott, E. (2011). *Conflict resolution skills for healthy relationships: The key to less relationship stress? Effective conflict resolution skills!* Retrieved from http://stress.about.com/od/relationships/a/conflict_res.htmAbout.com Guide
6. Ford, W. S. Z., & Wolvin, A. D. (1993). The differential impact of a basic communication course on perceived communication competencies in class, work, and social contexts. *Communication Education, 42*, 215–233.
7. Zeigler, K., & Camarota, S. A. (2014, October). One in five U.S. residents speaks foreign language at home. *Center for Immigration Studies.* Retrieved from http://cis.org/One-in-Five-US-Residents-Speaks-Foreign-Language-at-Home
8. Adams, S. (2014, November 12). The 10 skills employers most want in 2015 graduates. *Forbes.* Retrieved from http://www.forbes.com
9. Nichols, M. (2006, September 15). Listen up for better sales. *BusinessWeek Online*, 12.
10. Bates, J. (2004, December 15). Unaccustomed as I am . . . *Nursing Standard, 19*(14–16), 25.
11. Johnson, L. M., & Johnson, V. E. (1995, January/February). Help wanted—accountant: What the classifieds say about employer expectations. *Journal of Education for Business, 70*(3), 130–134.
12. Cano, C. P., & Cano, P. Q. (2006). Human resources management and its impact on innovation performance in companies. *International Journal of Technology Management, 35*, 11–27.
13. Hanzevack, E. L., & McKean, R. A. (1991). Teaching effective oral presentations as part of the senior design course. *Chemical Engineering Education, 25*, 28–32; Horton, G. E., & Brown, D. (1990). The importance of interpersonal skills in consultee-centered consultation: A review. *Journal of Counseling and Development, 68*, 423–426; LaBar, G. (1994). Putting together the complete hygienist. *Occupational Hazards, 56*, 63–66;

Messmer, M. (1997, August). Career strategies for accounting graduates. *Management Accounting, 4*–10; Nisberg, J. N. (1996). Communication: What we hear, what we say vs. what they hear, what they say. *The National Public Accountant, 41,* 34–38; Ridley, A. J. (1996). A profession for the twenty-first century. *Internal Auditor, 53,* 20–25; Simkin, M. G. (1996). The importance of good communication skills on "IS" career paths. *Journal of Technical Writing & Communication, 26,* 69–78.

14. Goo, S. A. (2015, February 19). The skills Americans say kids need to succeed in life. *Pew Research Center.* Retrieved from http://www.pewresearch.org
15. Perception. *Encarta Dictionary.* (2011).
16. Role. *Encarta Dictionary.* (2011).
17. Yahaya, A. (2009). The relationship of self-concept and communication skills towards academic achievement among secondary school students in Johor Bahru. *International Journal of Psychological Studies.* Retrieved from www.ccsenet.org/journal/index.php/ijps/article/view/3931
18. Mead, G. H. (1967). *Mind, self, and society from the standpoint of a social behaviorist* (Charles W. Morris, Ed.). Chicago: University of Chicago Press.
19. Araton, H. (2015, August 27). Williams sisters leave an impact that's unmatched. *The New York Times.* Retrieved from http://nytimes.com
20. Arroyo, A., & Andersen, K. (2016). Appearance-related communication and body image outcomes: Fat talk and old talk among mothers and daughters. *Journal of Family Communication, 16,* 95–110.
21. For further reading see Czubaroff, J. (2000). Dialogical rhetoric: An application of Martin Buber's philosophy of dialogue. *Quarterly Journal of Speech, 86,* 168–189.
22. Wiggins, J. A., Wiggins, B. B., & Zanden, J. (1993). *Social psychology* (4th ed.). New York: McGraw-Hill.

Blue and Yellow Cube Icon, Connecting Globally Icon, Mountain Icon, Chapter Review Arrows Circle Icon: ©McGraw Hill Education

chapter 2

Communicating Verbally

©Radius Images/Getty Images RF

This chapter will look at the functions and rules of verbal communication, with three goals in mind: to demonstrate the multiple ways you use verbal communication, to help you avoid errors and offenses, and to guide you in making the best possible impression with your words.

LEARNING OBJECTIVES
After reading this chapter, you should be able to:

- Name and explain the four primary functions of verbal communication.
- Explain the meanings and processes by which words communicate.
- Explain the rules that influence and guide verbal communication.
- Recognize the categories of words speakers should avoid to present themselves as thoughtful and balanced verbal communicators.
- Recognize the categories of words speakers should use in moderation to present themselves as thoughtful and balanced verbal communicators.
- List and give examples of strategies that will improve a speaker's verbal communication.

THE FUNCTIONS OF VERBAL COMMUNICATION

©J. Hardy/PhotoAlto RF

Imagine that today, in one of your classes, a teacher told you that your assignment is due in two weeks; another teacher told you to tell a story in which two characters have a conflict; a third teacher asked you to analyze the school's parking policy; and a fourth stopped you on your way out of class to ask whether you were feeling OK. All four teachers were trying to get messages across to you, mainly with words—with verbal communication.

However, if one of those teachers looked you directly in the eye while speaking, pointed a finger at you, or pounded her fist on a desk, these forms of nonverbal communication would also have meaning and affect your response to the message. We communicate with each other with words, or verbal communication, as well as with eye contact, movement, and gestures (nonverbal communication), and the two forms work together to create a message.

This chapter focuses on **verbal communication**, which is *the use of language to convey meaning*. **Language** is *the code we use to communicate with each other*, a code that follows rules to encourage understanding. **Meaning** is more of a challenge to define, because it refers to *whatever message someone is trying to convey to others, as well as how that message is interpreted*. Although you use verbal communication every day, you may not be aware of the many roles it plays in your relationships. To understand verbal communication, let's look at four of the functions it performs: the instrumental, creative, analytical, and social functions.

The Instrumental Function

The first teacher mentioned earlier—the one who told you when your assignment was due—was using the **instrumental function** of verbal communication. That is, she was *using language as a directive—a means of getting others to think or do something*. When

©Photosindia/Getty Images RF

you use language in an instrumental way, you are using it as a tool or, as the term implies, as an instrument.[1] Instrumental language is unadorned, straightforward, and very descriptive[2]: "The assignment is due in two weeks," "You need to change the oil in your car every 5,000 miles," and "You should vote or quit griping about our leadership." Scientific and technical communication tends to be instrumental: a chemist's formula, an engineer's instructions for building a robot, and the fix for a computer problem are examples of language used instrumentally.

The Creative Function

The second teacher—the one who asked you to tell a brief story—was promoting the **creative function** of verbal communication, in which *imagination meets writing or speaking ability*. Called *elocutio* by the Roman rhetorician Quintilian in AD 95,[3] this function was one of the five canons (principles) of rhetoric. As an illustration of modern-day creativity with language, social media have spawned inventive acronyms and abbreviations (*lol, sup, idk, omg*) for quick texting and tweeting, in which the message needs to fit within a 140-character limit.[4] People are usually a pretty good judge of their own creative capabilities. Media- and journalism-related professions often look for people who can use language in more creative ways to write compelling stories and produce advertisements full of vivid imagery. In a recent study people who self-identified as creative were more inventive with their language and were more likely to come up with unique uses for everyday objects.[5] However, if it doesn't come naturally to you, creative use of language can be learned. When you are asked to use language in an imaginative way, a range of rhetorical devices are at your disposal—for example, metaphors, similes, hyperbole (exaggeration), and alliteration. These figures of speech allow writers and speakers to play with language and expand its potential.

A **metaphor** (MET-ah-four) *creatively compares two things that do not at first seem alike*: "The morning rainstorm was a crushing blow to his plans," "This economy is a sinking ship," "I'm queen of the house," "Our country is the world's police officer." Martin Luther King Jr. was an expert at using metaphors to help people understand difficult concepts, like justice. In his "I Have a Dream" speech he compared the injustices faced by people of color to a fraudulent check written by the United States to people of color. Why was this metaphor so powerful? Because people have a hard time understanding concepts like justice, but money is a very tangible and concrete concept that we deal with daily.[6]

A **simile** (SIM-ah-lee) *creatively compares two unlike things, using the word "like" or "as"*: "He sweats like a sailor in a sauna," "She worked like an engine, never tiring and rarely resting," "Their team pulls together like huskies in the Iditarod." The writer, orator, and abolitionist Fredrick Douglass, who was himself a former slave, makes powerful use of simile when writing about his condition after receiving a beating: "I suppose I looked like a man who had escaped a den of wild beasts, and barely escaped them."[7] This image vividly conveys to readers the terror Douglass experienced as a slave. During his lifetime, Douglass used figurative and creative language to help his audience understand the evils of slavery, and his words maintain their impact today.

Hyperbole (high-PURR-baa-lee) is *the use of exaggeration to make a point*: "He looked as if he had been run over by a tank," "My girlfriend is the most beautiful woman in the world," "That cop is meaner than a pit bull." Hyperbole makes use of the extremes to get people to pay attention to the issue at hand. They are often used more effectively in advertising campaigns.

Alliteration is *the repetition of the initial sound of a word*: "The problem is the price of property," "His tiny, timid eyes looked tired," "She proudly pranced on stage," Alliteration is used primarily in poetry and advertising, where it can contribute to rhythm and memorization.

Words targeting the ear (as in speaking) rather than the eye (as in writing) require repetition. Listeners daydream and let their thoughts wander during presentations, so they may need to hear important points several times. To get a message across, then, speakers need to use creative techniques to enhance understanding. One well-known method is to preview by saying what you plan to cover, review by restating in other words what you just said, and summarize to wrap up the message.

Also, effective speakers offer multiple kinds of support for their arguments and ideas. In addition to basic explanations, speakers can incorporate relevant YouTube videos, demonstrations, comparisons, contrasts, and even stories and case studies. The creative use of language can contribute significantly to audience understanding.

The Analytical Function

When the third teacher asked you to analyze the school's parking policy, he was prompting you to use the **analytical function** of verbal communication, which involves *the use of critical thinking skills to evaluate and critique an issue or idea*. A first step in critical thinking is research. For this assignment, you need to find, read, and understand your school's parking policy and explain it in your own words. Next you need to evaluate it by asking questions such as these: "What is the reasoning behind this policy?" "Is this policy fair to students?" "Is this policy fair to nonstudent residents in the area?" "Should any parts of the policy be changed to reflect conditions that have changed since it was first enacted?" Finally, you can suggest improvements to the current policy. Together, all this work and the paper or presentation that resulted would fulfill the analytical function of verbal communication. Just taking this communication class and learning how to analyze research and prepare speeches will improve your critical thinking skills and your ability to engage in effective use of the analytical function of language.[8]

The Social Function

When your teacher stopped you on the way out of class to ask whether you were OK, she was demonstrating the **social function** of verbal communication, which refers to *the use of language to build and maintain relationships*. In your case the teacher was letting you know that she had noticed something about you (maybe that you looked down or tired) and that she cared. We also use verbal communication in a social way when we greet friends between classes, chat online, and text each other. The social function of language can have a positive impact on our emotional health, as in when we turn to social media for support and community with members of our online networks.[9]

One social function of language is achieved through **phatic communication**, *the most casual and often briefest exchanges that are intended to recognize the existence of another person and to demonstrate sociability rather than provide information*, as when you say "hi" in passing. Another social function is achieved through **trouble talk**, *exchanges in which people complain about something without expecting a solution*: "Things are awful at work under that new boss," "My clothes hardly fit anymore," and "I work too hard for too little." A third way in which language functions socially is in **conflict management**, *the use of language to resolve issues between individuals or groups*. Spouses, partners, and friends, as well as union members and management, both create and solve conflicts with verbal communication.

Verbal communication used for social functions can have great benefits. In fact, research shows that students who are more socially active feel a greater sense of belonging, a benefit which correlates with higher levels of engagement, motivation, and achievement in college.[10]

HOW WORDS COMMUNICATE

Verbal language, of course, is made up of words. But what is a word, and how does it communicate? Let's begin with two definitions.

©Fancy Photography/Veer RF

As **Figure 2.1** shows, a **word** is *a symbol that has been assigned meaning*. A **symbol** *represents an idea, a process, or a physical entity*. For instance, the word *car* is a symbol that we have collectively come to agree stands for a vehicle of a certain type. However, over time words and symbols change and new ones are introduced.[11] For example, as some cars became more trucklike and vanlike, we came up with new words to describe them—*SUV, wagon,* and *crossover*. The next section explains how we go about interpreting the words and symbols we encounter.

Two Processes for Interpreting Messages

For words to have meaning, we have to produce and interpret them. To do this, we use the processes of encoding and decoding, as defined in **Chapter 1**:

- You encode when you translate your thoughts into words. You are wondering if you are doing your job well, so you translate that thought into words to your supervisor: "Did I do that correctly?" You have interpreted the word *correctly* as the one that best communicates your concern. You are saying that you are concerned about whether you are meeting the employer's guidelines for a particular task. If you were concerned specifically with your speed, you could have asked, "Did I do that quickly enough?"

- When you decode, you assign meaning to someone else's verbal communication, translating his words into thoughts of your own. Your supervisor says to you, "Doesn't the cooking area need mopping?" You interpret his words to mean that he wants you to mop the cooking area, but you have to determine from the urgency in his voice whether he means "right now" or "anytime during this shift." The "urgency in his voice" is a nonverbal feature that coordinates with the verbal to make the message. In either case, you assign meaning to the other person's words. If, however, you decode the message to mean that it's OK to wait a few hours before mopping the floor and your

Figure 2.1 What Are Words?

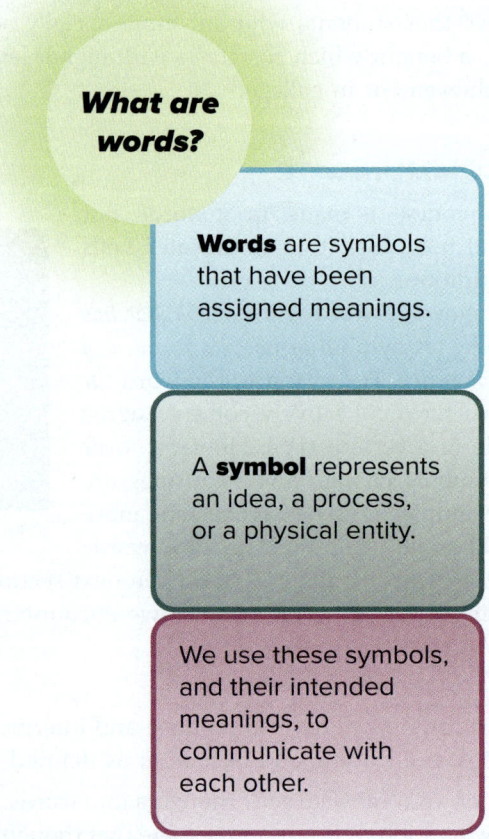

supervisor meant "right now," you may make a bad impression. He, of course, could have encoded his message with more precision—for example, "Please mop the kitchen area now."

Because language is an imperfect means of transmission, the thoughts that one person encodes never exactly match what the other decodes, so language often requires further interpretation or clarification, which you achieve when you ask, "Do you mean right now?" or "Can I do the mopping at the end of my shift?"

Two Kinds of Meaning

Words can carry two kinds of meaning: denotative and connotative. **Denotative meaning** is *the agreed-upon meaning, or the meaning you find in a dictionary*. The *Webster's New Collegiate Dictionary* says a *cat* is "a carnivorous mammal long domesticated and kept by man as a pet or for catching rats or mice." However, a dictionary meaning fails to capture your feelings for the felines you encounter in your life, which you may either adore or detest. Denotative meanings of words can be fluid, changing over time. For example, a primary meaning for the word *gay* was once *happy*, but now it also means homosexual; the word *troll* once referred to a mythological being, but its meaning has now expanded to include *to search* (as a verb) and *someone who deliberately provokes others on the Internet* (as a noun). The word *bandwidth* went from being a measure related to data transmission to one's ability to handle intellectual or emotional issues.[12]

New words, and new denotative meanings, sometimes enter the language. Such terms are called **neologisms**, *new words or new meanings for old words that are in the process of entering common use.* New technologies create many neologisms, such as *app, tweet cred, hash tag,* and *404.* The last term, meaning clueless, came from the Web's notation for "document not found." Hence, when someone calls a person 404, the message is that the person is clueless.[13]

Connotative meanings are *meanings people come to assign because of personal or individual experience.* For example, the word *cat* holds vastly different meanings for people because of their unique experiences with that variety of animal: some fill their homes with cats and pamper them as they would their children, whereas others suffer from serious allergies and swell up and itch at the sight of a cat. Another way to understand the difference between denotative and connotative meanings is to think, for example, of the word *mother.* Everyone knows what a mother is according to the denotative meaning. But each person has his own connotations for that word—laden with emotions that drown the denotative meaning in a flood of remembered experiences. Denotative meanings are general and shared, whereas connotative meanings tend to be individual and personal.

THE RULES OF VERBAL COMMUNICATION

The way you use words is often determined by the situation you are in. That is, you adapt your speech depending on where you are, whom you are with, and what the context is. Multiple rules and practices guide communication—some that you follow without even being aware of them, others that can benefit you as you gain awareness of them. These are the topics we turn to in this section.

Rules Regarding Place

You may already know that where you are affects the way you speak and the words you choose. When you are at home, where people know you well, you can be very informal and make certain assumptions—for example, that people will know what you mean by "the back room" or "that story Dad always tells." When you are out with friends, the formal rules of verbal communication may become extremely relaxed, because friends tend not to be very critical about your language. Among friends you can talk about topics you never would talk

SKILL BUILDER

PRACTICE EFFECTIVE VERBAL COMMUNICATION AND LISTENING SKILLS

One way to practice effective verbal communication is to interact with people who don't share your opinions. Identify someone who holds a differing opinion on a controversial issue and engage that person in a conversation in which you each exchange your thoughts and ideas. While you're talking and listening, practice the following recommendations from this chapter:

- **When you're unsure of your partner's meaning, stop and ask "What do you mean?"**
  - Listen for generalizations that lack fuller explanations.
  - Ask the other person to explain by saying, "I'm not sure I followed your argument, what did you mean when you said . . . ?" Doing so can help you learn more about the differing perspective without jumping to conclusions.
- **Take the opportunity to summarize the other person's major points in your own words.**
  - It is easy to misunderstand what other people have to say. Our interpretation of what we hear is informed by our personal experiences and worldviews. Even language choices can trigger misunderstandings.
  - When your partner has made an important point and explained their feelings on that point, stop and summarize: "I want to make sure I understood you correctly. When you were talking about this issue of . . . you said you feel . . . because. . . ."
  - Often people will clarify and refine their arguments when given the opportunity. This type of perception checking demonstrates that you care enough to verify an accurate understanding of another's perspective.
- **Focus on understanding your partner's perspective rather than trying to get your own point across.**
  - By focusing on another person's point of view without interjecting your own feelings and opinions, you validate their right to an opinion and you gain a better understanding of their unique position.
  - When people feel like their opinions have been heard, they will be more open to listening to differing opinions.

Sometimes it isn't possible to resolve differences of opinion, especially when the issues at hand reflect beliefs that are deeply held. However, there are mutual benefits to talking through sensitive issues. By practicing effective verbal communication skills, we increase our understanding of others' perspectives and teach them more about our own.

about at work, such as your love life, and you may not be so careful about the language you use.

When you are in the more formal setting of a classroom, however, you tend to be more careful with your speech, because you want to make a good

CONNECTING GLOBALLY

FOCUS ON YOURSELF—OR NOT—THROUGH SOCIAL MEDIA

In the dominant culture in the United States, it is standard social practice to make oneself the focus of conversation. In keeping with this norm, Americans tend to use social media to highlight their own personal and professional accomplishments.

But using social media to focus on the self is not common to all cultures. For example, in collectivistic cultures, people are more likely to use social media to highlight group or team accomplishments. In South Korea, for example, where modesty is highly valued, a person using social media might even downplay their own credentials. Differences in individual freedoms likewise influence social media use. Some Eastern cultures are denied certain freedoms of expression. This factor can limit, and in some cases prohibit, the use of social media.

Consider for a moment your own uses for social media. How often do your posts include details about your daily life? Have you ever taken a photograph of yourself to post to social media, a practice referred to, appropriately, as "taking a selfie"? Do you see these behaviors as a reflection of your culture?

---

impression on your professor. You also adapt your speech when you enter a place of worship—a church, synagogue, or mosque—and you speak differently at a funeral than you do in a bar. Certain places—courtrooms, for example—have strict and extensive rules and practices related to verbal communication and appropriate speech, especially related to tone and volume. In other places, the rules may be less clear—if you begin a loud argument in a restaurant, you may be asked to leave, but if you shout in a sports bar during an exciting game, you'll fit right in. Finally, when giving a public speech or when being interviewed for a job, you are under the most pressure of all to follow the formal rules of language and choose your words with care.

Rules Regarding Conversational Partners

Knowing how and when to adapt your verbal communication based on your relationship with your conversational partner is part of being an effective communicator. Close relationships with family and friends allow the greatest latitude in terms of the formal rules of grammar and word choice, but even in these close circles, profanity, sex, and various other topics may be taboo. Verbal communication with authority figures—for example, professors, police, and upper-level management—introduces a number of language restrictions and adaptations. Because of the differences in status, you likely know that you want to sound intelligent and well informed with your professor, you don't want to rile a police officer by saying anything that sounds rude or threatening, and you want to be

©SW Productions/Brand X/Corbis RF

respectful and emphasize your competence and commitment when speaking to your boss.

These rules don't only apply to face-to-face exchanges. When you communicate with your professor via e-mail, for example, you should use a formal tone. Begin with an appropriate opening (Dear Professor Franklin), put a clear description in the subject line (question about Wednesday's assignment), let your professor know which class you're in, write in complete sentences, avoid the abbreviations you use for texting with your friends, make your message clear and direct, review it for typos, and end with an appropriate salutation (Sincerely, Alison Corsino). Your professor will appreciate the respect you show with your businesslike tone and the care you took to craft a clear message.

Rules of Engagement

As noted previously, verbal communication comes to us loaded with rules about what can be said to whom, under what circumstances, and how it should be said. In addition, verbal communication comes with **rules of engagement**—*rules about initiating, conducting, and ending a verbal exchange.*

By convention, a public speech begins with an introduction that reveals something about the speaker and the topic. In one-to-one conversation, certain conventions have been established as to who can initiate the exchange—sometimes based on status or gender. For example, at a party or a bar, men are often expected to initiate a conversation with women, although such conventions have loosened up somewhat; in some business contexts, managers initiate meetings with those they supervise, rather than vice versa. In a very formal setting, like a courtroom, the judge is usually the only person who can initiate or permit an exchange, as when she asks questions of lawyers or jurors.

In addition, both public speeches and conversations follow particular organizational patterns. In a public speech the body, or main points, follows the introduction, whereas in a conversation turn taking begins. **Turn taking** means that *one person speaks and the other responds with a certain amount of give and take.* Usually, the signal that one person has said his piece is that he stops talking, so that the other person can respond, but sometimes the first speaker is only pausing to collect his thoughts, in which case the two speakers may have some awkward moments of speaking over each other as they try to determine whose turn it is or one says, "No, you."

Another aspect of language rules is called **code switching**, which means *shifting from one treatment of language to another based on the audience and place.*[14] A common case of code switching occurs when a politician alters her word choice, or even her accent, to appeal to a particular voting base. Another case of code switching occurs when college students talk one way to each other but another way in the presence of their professor. All of us know how to do some code switching depending on the place or audience.

In the context of the rules of engagement, nonverbal indicators can also act as signals between conversational partners. For example, a listener may nod to indicate understanding or encouragement or may look away to indicate distraction or boredom. Conversations can vary considerably in length, but when one person wants to stop the conversation, he signals this message either verbally or nonverbally—for example, saying, "Well, I've got to go now," or getting up to leave and putting on his coat. As with all other phases of a conversation, ending one can have its awkward aspects—as in the case that one person wants to continue talking but the other doesn't. All in all, we have multiple signals—subtle and overt—that we use in starting, continuing, and ending conversations. Moreover, as discussed earlier, we adapt our verbal behavior based on where we are and to whom we're talking.

©Paul Burns/Photodisc/Getty Images RF

WORDS TO AVOID

Another set of rules to make you a more effective communicator focuses on choosing the right words and avoiding the wrong ones. Remember that your word choices affect your credibility. Whether you are at work, with friends, or in the classroom, an ill-chosen word can make a difference; for instance, in the spring of 2013, a young man on his first day of work as a broadcast anchor uttered some profanity into a live microphone, only to lose his job minutes after his first broadcast.[15] The following sections describe some categories of words that can get you in trouble with your classmates, work colleagues, and even friends and family.

Profanity

Profanity is *language that is vulgar, abusive, or disrespectful of things sacred*. Many so-called swear words have a religious origin: *hell* and *damn* are examples. Inappropriate use of the words *God* and *Jesus* to express irritation or incredulity can also be considered disrespectful and offensive. Other forms of profanity refer to forbidden statuses or acts: "son of a ___" or "Mother ____." Many people find profanity offensive, so using such words can get you in trouble, especially with people you don't know. Even the Internet has rules about the use of profanity. A note on eBay, for example, says, "We don't allow hateful, offensive, profane, or vulgar language in almost all public areas of the website."

Some people think that profanity is never appropriate, but usage varies by place, age, and sex. Although everyone seems to know that swearing is inappropriate in a place of worship, profanity is fairly common on many college campuses and at athletic events. Also, those in their eighties and nineties seem to have less tolerance for profanity than do middle-aged and

©O. Dimier/PhotoAlto RF

younger people. And men tend to cuss more than women. Profanity has become so common that once-forbidden words are so overused that they have lost their impact.

But since you can't be certain what those around you—at school, at work, in an audience, or in your social circle—really think about such words, and they may judge you harshly if you use them, think carefully before you use words that are potentially offensive.

Sexist Words

Sexist language is *language that excludes individuals on the basis of gender*. The statement "A professor needs to read incessantly to keep up with his field" suggests that all professors are men. A nonsexist way to express this thought is "Professors need to read incessantly to keep up with their fields." People reveal sexism when they assume that all members of any category are all male or all female—for example, that all criminals are male or that all nurses are female. Sexist language also appears in many gender-specific compound words, such as *chairman* and *salesman*; instead, use the term *chair* or *salesperson*.

The use of sexist language varies by sex, with more women than men being victimized by sexist talk. In particular, the vast majority of hostile workplace charges come from women charging men with an offense. Sexism also varies by region. In some parts of the United States a female server might call a man "honey" without meaning anything much, whereas in other parts of the country that word might be seen as flirtatious or at least too personal to use with a stranger. And sexism can vary by age. Younger people are often more attuned to the offenses that accompany sexist language. An older generation may use profanity less but exhibit more sexist language. In any case, speakers in conversation or on the stage need to be aware that sexist words can get a person in trouble, sometime career-killing trouble.

Career-killing trouble comes when words create a hostile workplace. The Federal Communications Commission explains the situation this way: "**Hostile work environment harassment** *occurs when unwelcome comments or conduct based on sex, race or other legally protected characteristics unreasonably interferes with an employee's work performance or creates an intimidating, hostile or offensive work environment.*"[16]

Racist Words

Racist language is *language that is insulting because it associates skin color or ethnicity with stereotypical and usually negative characteristics*. The concepts of race and ethnicity—as well as stereotypes and prejudice—are discussed in detail in **Chapter 6**, on global and intercultural communication. Needless to say, racial and ethnic insults and labels are common in society. Also common is the debate about who is entitled to use certain labels. The standard rule is that, even though people within a race or an ethnic group may use such words with or about each other, that does not give outsiders permission to use them, and when they do, it can be deeply offensive.

So what should you do when someone around you uses an offensive racial or ethnic term or makes a racist "joke" in your presence? If you find a comment offensive, an appropriate response is, first, to refrain from laughing at the joke and, second, to tell the speaker that you find the comment offensive and why. These are not easy things to do, however—especially if the person who made the joke has more power than you do, like your boss. Even among friends, it can be difficult to call someone out on bad behavior. The same applies to sexist language and sexist "jokes." Learning how to navigate such difficulties can take time and experience. The more tuned in you are to the damage that such language can do, the better you will become at responding when you hear it.

Ageist Words

Ageist language is *language that denigrates people based on their age, whether young or old.* Classifying every young person as a *child* or a *kid* may be both offensive and inaccurate; referring to someone as a *young person,* an *adolescent,* or a *young adult* is more descriptive and precise. Ageism is also evident in language that infantilizes older persons and diminishes their status as vigorous and vital individuals. Older people may not think of themselves as old and may not appreciate being referred to as senior citizens or the elderly.[17,18] The key is to be respectful and thoughtful about applying labels and consider whether you need to refer to people's age at all—or for that matter, their sex, race, or ethnicity—when addressing them or speaking or writing about them. For example, journalists are trained to describe a subject by race, age, or ethnicity *only* if it is clearly relevant to the story they are presenting.

Grammatical Errors

Grammatical errors are *violations of the formal rules of written and spoken language.* When you use poor grammar in a classroom, a job interview, or a new relationship, you risk making a bad impression. Others may not mention your errors, but they may hold them against you. In **Table 2.1**, you will find examples of common grammatical mistakes and how to correct them.

Table 2.1 Common Grammatical Errors[19]

Incorrect	Correct	Explanation
"He *don't* care about me anymore."	"He *doesn't* care about me anymore."	Check subject–verb agreement: "don't" is the plural form of the verb "to do," so it should be used only with plural subjects ("They don't care"). "Doesn't" is the singular form of the verb, so it's used with singular subjects (he, she, Joe, Alice, etc.).
"I never *would of* thought he would act like that."	"I never *would have* thought he would act like that."	Distinguish spoken from written language: the contraction "would've" sounds like "would of" when spoken but, in fact, stands for "would have." People make this mistake when they confuse the sound of language with its written form.
"I'm not speaking to *nobody* in this class."	"I'm not speaking to *anybody* in this class."	Avoid double negatives: instead of "not . . . nobody," say or write "not . . . anybody."
"I should *have went* to school yesterday."	"I should *have gone* to school yesterday."	Use verb tenses correctly: "went" is the simple past tense of "go" and is never used with "have." "Have gone" is the present perfect tense, which is formed from the present tense of "to have" + a past participle of another verb—in this case "gone."

WORDS TO USE CAREFULLY

Because the categories of words discussed in the previous section can offend or insult your listeners, they seriously undermine your ability to communicate. In contrast, the categories of words discussed in this section can have a less serious but still negative impact. In some cases, however, these words or phrases may help you illustrate a point or use language creatively. As always, though, remember the rules regarding place and conversational partners.

Slang

Slang is *informal, casual language used among equals*. It is suitable for use among friends but is not suitable for more formal contexts. Such language may be unacceptable, offensive, or simply incomprehensible to your teacher, your boss, and even your family. Moreover, you may be so used to using some slang terms (*Dude, Bro, veg-out*) that you don't even think of them as slang. This is why it's important to reflect on your language use.

As you advance through your school and work career, make an effort to eliminate language that may undermine your progress. **Table 2.2** offers some examples of new American slang terms. Depending on the communication context, you might be better off using the more formal language listed in the right-hand column.

Ask, "What Did You Mean?"

As defined in **Chapter 1**, **perception checking** *involves checking in with your conversational partner to ensure you have a common understanding of an event that has occurred or a common definition of a particular phenomenon.* Before an exam, you might ask, "Did you say that you wanted to study together?" Many disagreements occur because people do not stop to make these simple checks on their perception.

Say It in Your Own Words

©PhotoAlto/Alix Minde/Getty Images RF

Paraphrasing is *restating another person's message by rephrasing it in your own words.* Paraphrasing is not simply repeating what you heard. When you say it in your own words, you allow the original speaker to make corrections, in case you misinterpreted what he said. The original speaker must actively listen to your paraphrase to determine whether you understood both the content and the intent of what was said: "So you're saying that we should include others in our study group?"

Describe Without Judgment

Description involves *giving an account of observed behavior or phenomena.* You offer a reasonably neutral description when you say, "I saw two cars run into each other because one car did not stop at the sign." You are judgmental when you say, "I saw that fool run a stop sign and bash that other car." Being descriptive instead of evaluative is difficult, but being descriptive can keep you out of many conflicts. Say what you see; don't judge what you see.

Define Your Terms

Defining terms is necessary in school and at work as well as in your personal life. When you ask, "Can you explain what you mean by *benefits*?" you have a better chance of avoiding misunderstandings with a potential employer. What, precisely, does an employer mean when she says you may have to work overtime? Major disputes continue to arise over the way human beings define *work hours, gun control, birth control,* and *marriage.*

Build Your Vocabulary

Building your vocabulary means adding new words to your language. Having a large vocabulary is a sign of intelligence; it means you have many words to choose from and can express yourself with precision. The best way to improve your vocabulary is to read and to look up terms you do not know in a dictionary, as you go. Another fun way to increase the number of words you have at your disposal is to subscribe to a word-of-the-day e-mail, such as the one available on *Merriam-Webster Online* (**www.merriam-webster.com/word-of-the-day/**). Keep in mind that

NASA,ESA, and the Hubble Heritage Team (STScI/AURA)

demonstrating a good vocabulary can help you impress others, but using words incorrectly will likely work against you. Before using a new word, familiarize yourself with its denotative and connotative meanings.

Paint Pictures with Your Words

Visual imagery helps you communicate complex ideas. For example, a physicist on the national news illustrated the discovery of hundreds of galaxies with the image of a pizza. Earth, he said, is one small dot on a pizza that is our galaxy. Now, he said, imagine hundreds of pizzas surrounding that one, each representing a galaxy like our Milky Way. By referencing an object whose size and shape we all know well, the physicist was better able to communicate the immensity of the known collection of galaxies.

Make Accurate Observations

Observations are *descriptions of what you directly saw, touched, tasted, smelled, or heard*. Even though we put considerable trust in what we observe, research tells us that memory, including in the context of witness identification, is not always reliable.[24] Therefore, be precise in your descriptions, and offer concrete details. Instead of saying, "She drove a nice car," say, "She drove a dark blue 2013 Mazda 6—very sporty." The first observation tells little about what you judge to be a "nice car"; the second demonstrates what style, color, and make you prefer.

Make Inferences Carefully

Inferences, as defined in **Chapter 9**, are conclusions we make based on some evidence, such as observations. For example, you can observe that someone took something without paying, but to say that person is a thief is an inference. Inferences, like observations, can be incorrect. The person might have forgotten to pay or might be the nephew of the owner and so has permission to take a candy bar off the shelf. We make observations all the time, and we draw inferences from observations. But we have to be careful about accuracy and error with both observations and inferences.

Be Specific and Concrete

A person who uses **concrete language** uses *words and statements that are specific rather than abstract or vague*. The statement "You have interrupted me three times since I began to talk. I feel as though you do not consider my point of view as important as yours" is concrete. In contrast, "You never consider my viewpoint" is vague. The first explanation would likely help the person interrupting you to correct his behavior, whereas the second, less specific statement might just make him defensive.

CHALLENGE YOURSELF

Does it really matter if I use correct grammar and avoid profanity and slang?

You don't have to speak correctly, but not doing so can hold you back. Your use of words can mark you as educated, intelligent, and knowledgeable—or not. The worst part about demonstrating weak language skills is that your partner, your friends, and your boss are unlikely to comment on the way you use words. Instead, they might just make a negative judgment. And even if someone does correct you, you may not, in the moment, feel grateful for the correction.

To improve your language use, speak and listen to others as much as possible. Watching television, reading books, listening to the radio or your professor's lectures, and carrying on conversations are all great ways to study language and to improve your own language use.

Slang can be useful when you're interacting with peers and friends. Older generations sometimes use slang to try to connect with a younger generation. However, you should be careful about when and how you use it. If your reasons for using it aren't clear, you can create more distance than closeness with your audience.

Swearing and profanity can also evoke strong negative reactions and alienate others, and those are good reasons to avoid it. However, swearing can also communicate how strongly you feel about an issue or topic. Used sparingly, and in the appropriate moments, with the right audiences, swearing can be appreciated and can even build solidarity.

While it is generally better to use restraint, we recommend that when you do reach for profane words, do so strategically, knowing that your words are likely to have the right impact. Keep in mind that you don't want people to reject your ideas on the basis of your language choices. Know your audience and adapt your message appropriately.

Not everyone you speak and listen to will use the strategies and rules discussed in this chapter. However, the more you expose yourself to the different ways people communicate, the better you will be at deciding where, when, and how to speak and doing so with confidence.

Use Figures of Speech

Figures of speech *draw relationships that help listeners remember.* Discussed earlier, in the section "The Creative Function," these figures of speech include metaphors like "you broke my heart," similes like "ugly as sin," and hyperboles like "a dessert to die for." Figures of speech are descriptive and in some cases can clarify a point. For example, describing blockage in a heart valve by specifying its size as a number of millimeters might not be helpful for most patients. Describing the valve's opening as the size of a drinking straw when it should be the size of a water hose is far clearer and more graphic.

Use the Language of the Locals

Regionalisms are *words and phrases specific to a particular region or part of the country.* For example, submarine sandwiches are *hoagies* in Philadelphia, *po' boys* in New Orleans, *grinders* in Boston, *torpedoes* in Los Angeles, *wedgies* in Rhode Island, and *heros* in New York City. Pay attention to the terms used by those around you when you're in a new location. Your mission is to use the correct words for the region.

CHAPTER REVIEW

In this chapter you learned about verbal communication's four functions: the instrumental, the creative, the analytical, and the social. You learned how words communicate through denotative and connotative meanings and through two processes for interpreting messages: encoding and decoding. You were also introduced to several sets of rules for communicating verbally, including rules that vary where you are and with whom, rules of engagement, and rules concerned with words to avoid and those to use in moderation. A list of specific strategies at the end of the chapter will help you continually improve your verbal communication.

KEY TERMS

creative function, 22
instrumental function, 22
language, 22
meaning, 22
verbal communication, 22
alliteration, 23
hyperbole, 23
metaphor, 23
simile, 23
analytical function, 24
phatic communication, 24
social function, 24
trouble talk, 24
conflict management, 25
symbol, 25
word, 25
denotative meaning, 26
connotative meanings, 27
neologisms, 27
code switching, 30
rules of engagement, 30

turn taking, 30
profanity, 31
hostile work environment harassment, 32
racist language, 32
sexist language, 32
ageist language, 33
grammatical errors, 33
slang, 34
cliché, 35
euphemism, 35
jargon, 35
ambiguous words, 36
description, 37
paraphrasing, 37
perception checking, 37
observations, 38
concrete language, 38
figures of speech, 39
regionalisms, 39

STUDY QUESTIONS

1. Provide your own example (not from the book) of the analytical function of verbal communication.
2. What are three words that are loaded with connotative meaning for you?

3. Offer one example of an instance in which you misjudged the importance of place in verbal communication. Examples of places with specific rules regarding communication include the classroom, the office, a job interview, and an event like a wedding or funeral.
4. Tell of one instance where you mistakenly used a word to avoid—for example, profanity—with negative consequences.
5. In the list of strategies for improving language, select one and provide an example of how you could apply that strategy in your daily life.

ENDNOTES

1. Leaper, C., & Gleason, J. B. (1996). The relationship of play activity and gender to parent and child sex-typed communication. *International Journal of Behavioral Development, 19,* 689–703.
2. Lindset, E. W., & Mize, J. (2001). Contextual differences in parent-child play: Implications for children's gender role development. *Sex Roles, 44,* 155–176.
3. McKay, B., & McKay, K. (2011, January 28). *Classical rhetoric 101—Invention.* Retrieved from www.artofmanliness.com/2011/01/26/classical-rhetoric-101-the-five-canons-of-rhetoric-invention/
4. Walther, J. (2012). Interaction through technological lenses: Computer-mediated communication and language. *Journal of Language and Social Psychology, 31,* 397–414.
5. Mattern, J. L., Child, J. T., Vanhorn, S. B., & Gronewold, K. L. (2013). Matching creativity perceptions and capabilities: Exploring the impact of feedback messages. *Journal of Advertising Education, 17,* 13–25.
6. Val, M. (2006). The "integrative" rhetoric of Martin Luther Kind Jr.'s "I have a dream" speech. *Rhetoric & Public Affairs, 9,* 51–78.
7. Frederick Douglass's *Narrative of the Life of Frederick Douglass: An American Slave Written by Himself.*
8. Allen, M., Berkowitz, S., Hunt, S., & Louden, A. (1999). A meta-analysis of the impact of forensics and communication education on critical thinking. *Communication Education, 48,* 18–30.
9. Chung, J. (2013). Social networking in online support groups for health: How online social networking benefits patients. *Journal of Health Communication.* doi: 10.1080/10810730.2012.757396
10. Zumbrunn, S., McKim, C., Buhs, E., & Hawley, L.R. (2014). Support, belonging, motivation and engagement in the college classroom: A mixed method study. *Instructional Science, 42,* 661–684.
11. Whorf, B. L. (1956). Science and linguistics. In J. B. Carroll (Ed.), *Language, thought and reality* (pp. 207–219). Cambridge, MA: MIT Press.
12. *Ordinary words with new meanings.* Retrieved from https://www.americanexpress.com/us/small-business/openforum/articles/11-ordinary-words-that-have-new-meaning-in-social-media-1/?linknav=us-openforum-search-article-link1
13. Ibid.
14. Genesee, F., & Bourhis, R. Y. (1982). The social psychological significance of code switching in cross-cultural communication. *Journal of Language and Social Psychology, 1,* 1–27.

15. Daily Mail (2013, April 21). Is this the shortest TV career in history? 'Nervous' brand new anchor is FIRED after his first words on air are 'f***, s***' *Daily Mail.* Retrieved from http://www.dailymail.co.uk
16. Federal Communications Commission. Retrieved from www.fcc.gov/encyclopedia/understanding-workplace-harassment-fcc-staff
17. Chrisler, J. C., Barney, A. & Palatino, B. (2016). Agism can be hazardous to women's health: Agism, sexism, and stereotypes of older women in the healthcare system. *Journal of Social Issues, 72,* 86–104.
18. *Slang. Commonly used American slang.* Retrieved from www.manythings.org
19. Ageist language. (2012, February 12). Retrieved from virtuallinguist.typepad.com/the_virtual_linguist/.../ageist-language.html
20. Chassin, J. (2017, January 20). 11 new slang terms to memorize if you want to stay cool. *Popsugar.* Retrieved from http://www.popsugar.com
21. Technopedia. Where IT terms, buzzwords, and technology jargon are explained. Retrived from https://www.techopedia.com/dictionary/tags/buzzwords-and-jargon
22. Euphemism list. Retrieved from www.euphemismlist.com/
23. http://muse.dillfrog.com/ambiguous_words.php
24. Wells, G. L., & Olson, E. A. (2003). Eyewitness testimony. *Annual Review of Psychology, 54,* 277–295.

Blue and Yellow Cube Icon, Connecting Globally Icon, Mountain Icon, Chapter Review Arrows Circle Icon:
©McGraw Hill Education

chapter

Communicating Nonverbally

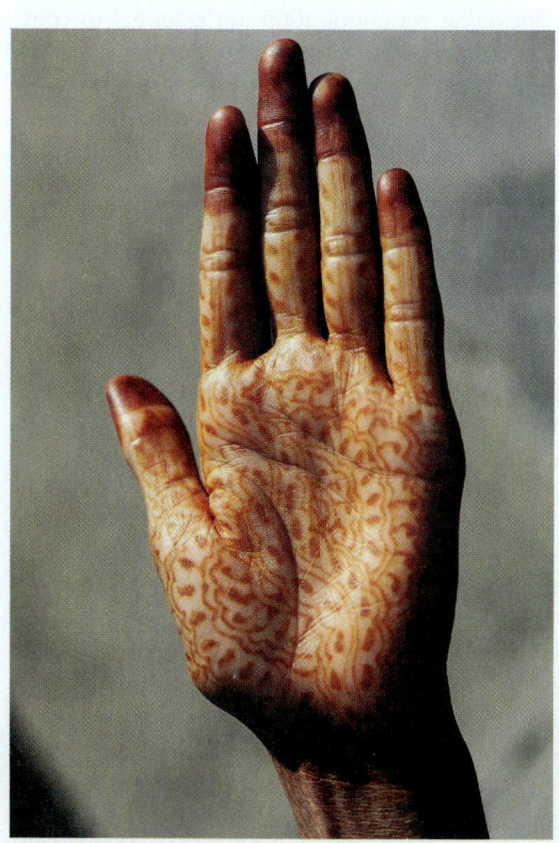
©Goodshoot/Fotosearch RF

Although everyone knows that the words we use are important, people often forget the importance of nonverbal communication. In this chapter we will define nonverbal communication, explain the relationship between verbal and nonverbal codes, and demonstrate the challenges of interpreting those codes. Finally, we will offer suggestions on how you can improve your nonverbal communication.

LEARNING OBJECTIVES

After reading this chapter, you should be able to:

- Define nonverbal communication.
- Explain the relationship between verbal and nonverbal communication.
- Define and describe the seven nonverbal codes: bodily movement and facial expression, physical attractiveness, space, time, touch, vocal cues, and clothing and other artifacts.
- Explain why nonverbal codes are difficult to interpret.
- Explain how you can improve your nonverbal communication.

WHAT IS NONVERBAL COMMUNICATION?

Nonverbal communication is *the process of using wordless messages to generate meaning.* Nonverbal communication includes nonword vocalizations, such as inflection, and nonword sounds, such as "ah" and "hmm." When you raise your hand in class or furrow your brow when concentrating on what your professor is saying, you are likewise communicating nonverbally.

Some people believe that nonverbal communication may be more important than the words we use. It is difficult to determine how much meaning comes from words and how much comes from the nonverbal cues we offer. However, we know that nonverbal messages often provide much more meaning than people realize.[1] Indeed, when we are not certain about another person's feelings, or about our feelings for him or her, we may rely far more on nonverbal cues—a smile, a touch on the arm, the clothes worn on a date—and less on the words they use.[2]

HOW ARE VERBAL AND NONVERBAL COMMUNICATION RELATED?

©L. Mouton/PhotoAlto RF

Both verbal and nonverbal communication are essential to communicating effectively. But how are the two related? A recent study examined the role of verbal and nonverbal elements of communication to determine which is most important in a persuasive message. The results showed that the content (the verbal portion of the speech) was most important in determining the effect of the speech. Emphasis and gestures, however, can make a speech seem lively and powerful.[3] In other words, both the verbal and the nonverbal elements of a speech play an important role in the outcome of communication.

Nonverbal communication works in conjunction with the words we use in six ways: to repeat, to emphasize, to complement, to contradict, to substitute, and to regulate.

Repetition *occurs when the same message is sent verbally and nonverbally.* The man who rubs his temples while telling his colleagues he has a splitting headache is engaging in repetition of his verbal message through nonverbal cues.

When we use **emphasis**, we are *using nonverbal cues to strengthen a message.* A speaker who shakes her finger while conveying important verbal information during a speech is emphasizing. Her use of emphasis helps audience members recall the information she is presenting.[4]

Complementing *goes beyond duplicating the message in two channels; the verbal and nonverbal codes add meaning to each other and expand the meaning of either message alone.* When we flirt we often complement our verbal messages with corresponding nonverbal messages, such as smiling and touching.[5] In contrast, **contradiction** is *when verbal and nonverbal messages conflict.* Two friends who say they want to resolve a

Table 3.1 Relationships Between Nonverbal and Verbal Cues

	Description	Example
Repetition	When the same message is sent verbally and nonverbally	You frown at a speaker while asking what she means.
Emphasis	The use of nonverbal cues to strengthen your message	You hug a friend while telling him how much you care about him.
Complementing	Goes beyond duplication of the message in two channels; the verbal and nonverbal codes add meaning to each other and expand the meaning of either message alone	You point to your favorite dessert in the bakery case as you describe to your friend how delicious it is.
Contradiction	Occurs when your verbal and nonverbal messages conflict	You sarcastically state that you are fine about something that has happened when you are not.
Substitution	Occurs when nonverbal codes are used instead of verbal codes	You roll your eyes, shrug your shoulders, or stick out your tongue instead of saying out loud how you feel.
Regulation	Occurs when nonverbal codes are used to monitor and control interactions with others	You walk away from someone who isn't finished talking to you.

difference but do not make eye contact and hold closed postures are exhibiting contradiction.

Substitution *occurs when nonverbal codes are used in place of verbal codes.* For example, starting in infancy, we are able to accurately decode facial expressions that convey common emotions like happiness, sadness, anger, or pain.[6] This is true even when strong verbal indicators are absent.

Finally, **regulation** is *the use of nonverbal codes to monitor and control interactions with others.* The daughter who looks away from her mom so she can control her emotions while being disciplined is using nonverbal communication to regulate verbal interaction. **Table 3.1** demonstrates each of these relationships between nonverbal and verbal communication and offers more examples of each.

WHAT ARE NONVERBAL CODES?

Nonverbal codes are *nonword symbols, gestures, or vocalizations that communicate meaning.* In contrast to verbal codes, which are most often to used to convey thoughts and ideas, nonverbal codes help us convey and infer emotions.[7] Have

©Steve Debenport/Getty Images RF

you ever shrugged your shoulders in answer to a question, moved away from someone who was becoming too friendly, or worn a particularly professional outfit when interviewing for a job? All of these represent nonverbal codes, and they fall into several categories, discussed in the following paragraphs.

Bodily Movement and Facial Expression

Kinesics is *the way we interpret nonverbal behavior related to movement, such as body language and facial expression.* Psychology professor Albert Mehrabian studied nonverbal communication by examining the concepts of liking, status, and responsiveness among the participants in communication situations.[8] Mehrabian explained these concepts in the following way:

- *Liking* is expressed by forward leaning, a direct body orientation (such as standing face to face), proximity, increased touching, a relaxed posture, open arms and body, a positive facial expression, and direct eye contact.
- *Status,* especially high status, is communicated nonverbally by bigger gestures, a relaxed posture, and less eye contact.
- *Responsiveness* is exhibited by movement toward the other person, spontaneous gestures, shifts in posture and position, and facial expressiveness.

Other researchers have categorized movement on the basis of its functions, origins, and meanings.[9] The categories they have identified—emblems, illustrators, affect displays, regulators, and adaptors—are described in **Table 3.2**.

Table 3.2 Categories of Movement Based on Functions, Origins, and Meanings

	Description	Example
Emblems	Nonverbal movements that substitute for words and phrases	▪ A curved index finger meaning "come here" ▪ An open hand held up meaning "stop"
Illustrators	Nonverbal movements that accompany or reinforce verbal messages	▪ Nodding or shaking your head when you say yes or no
Affect displays	Nonverbal movements to express emotion	▪ Showing joy for the winning team ▪ Slamming a door in anger
Regulators	Nonverbal movements that control the flow or pace of communication	▪ Moving away when you want the conversation to stop ▪ Looking away when you are not interested
Adaptors	Nonverbal movements that you might perform fully in private but only partially in public	▪ Gently scratching an insect bite in public but rubbing it vigorously or applying an ointment in private

Facial expressions, in particular, play an important role in our interactions.

- One study noted similarities in the facial expressions displayed by twins who were separated at birth, suggesting that genetics plays a role in the ways we express ourselves.[10]
- Another study found that children who are blind are as able as sighted children to effectively convey emotions through facial expressions.[11]
- Not all cultures display emotions using the same facial expressions. But with greater exposure to diverse cultures, anyone can improve their ability to infer the meanings of facial expressions of different cultural groups.[12]

This research demonstrates that facial expressions play a significant role in communicating. And learning how to effectively decode facial expressions for their emotional meaning will enhance your relationships with others.

Physical Attractiveness

Some characteristics—bright eyes, symmetrical features, and thin or medium build—are generally associated with physical attractiveness.[13] Physical attractiveness is equally important to men and women when considering who to date.[14]

Physical attractiveness affects many aspects of our lives. Generally, people who are physically attractive are privileged over those who are not.[15] This bias is stronger for women than for men.[16] Further, people are more likely to accurately describe the traits of those who are attractive over those whom they perceive to be unattractive. Women tend to raise their pitch when speaking to a man they find attractive.[17] Men and women deemed more attractive take home larger salaries than average-looking or plain people.[18] Attractive people are more likely to get offered a job when interviewed in comparison to average-looking people unless the attractive person is interviewed by a same-sex individual, who is more likely to find their attractiveness threatening.[19]

©JGI/Jamie Grill/Getty Images RF

The influence of physical appearance begins as early as age four. Children are treated differently by their day-care teachers based on their physical appearance.[20] Moreover, children's misbehaviors are viewed as isolated events if they are attractive, but as a chronic tendency to be bad if they are not. These patterns continue throughout one's life.[21]

Physical attractiveness affects both credibility and the ability to persuade others. Attractive people receive higher initial credibility ratings than do those who are viewed as unattractive.[22] Attractive women have more success in persuading the opposite sex than do attractive men, but less so as they grow older.[23]

CONNECTING GLOBALLY

PRIVACY AND SECURITY IN THE GLOBAL VILLAGE

Since the events of 9/11 Americans have been expected to sacrifice aspects of their individual privacy in exchange for greater national security. How much does your privacy mean to you? Consider the following questions addressing the ways in which privacy rights have changed over the last decade:

- When you go through the full body scanner in an airport security line, do you believe you are experiencing an invasion of privacy?
- Do you believe that governmental surveillance of cellphone networks and the Internet is justified?
- Do you think governments are honest about the extent to which they monitor individual citizens?

The answers to these questions highlight an ongoing debate about the exchange of individual privacy for governmental protection and national security. People around the world approach these questions differently. For example, trust in national political leadership impacts the degree to which people are willing to allow governmental surveillance, as demonstrated in the debates that took place during the 2016 campaign season. If you have the opportunity, discuss the issue of government surveillance with someone from another culture. What factors impact their desire for more privacy, or more security?

Space

Anthropologist Edward T. Hall introduced the concept of **proxemics**—*the study of the human use of space and distance*—in his book *The Hidden Dimension*.[24] Two concepts considered essential to the study of the use of space are territoriality and personal space.

©Marnie Burkhart/Corbis/Getty Images RF

- **Territoriality** refers to *your need to establish and maintain certain spaces as your own*. In a shared dormitory room, the items on the common desk area mark the territory. For example, you might place your notebook, pens and pencils, and tablet on the right side of the desk, and your roommate might place books, a cell phone, and a laptop on the left side. Although the desk is shared, you are each claiming part of the area.
- **Personal space** is the personal "bubble" that moves around with you. It is *the distance you maintain between yourself and others; the amount of space you claim as your own*. Large people usually claim more space because of their size, and men often take more space than women.

Figure 3.1 shows how people regularly use four distances when they communicate.[25] Beginning with the closest contact and the least personal space and moving to the greatest distance, they are intimate distance, personal distance, social distance, and public distance.

- **Intimate distance** *extends from your body outward to 18 inches; it is used by people who are relationally close.* This distance is employed to show affection, to give comfort, and to protect, and it usually elicits a positive response. This is because individuals tend to stand and sit close to people they are attracted to.[26] However, occasionally people overestimate how close another person feels to them and they sit or stand too close for the comfort of the second person. Communication researcher Judee K. Burgoon labeled this behavior as a personal space violation.
- **Personal distance** *ranges from 18 inches to 4 feet, and it is the distance most Americans use for conversation and other nonintimate exchanges.*
- **Social distance** *ranges from 4 to 12 feet, and it is used most often to carry out business in the workplace.* The higher the status of one person, the greater the distance.
- **Public distance** *exceeds 12 feet and is used most often in public speaking in such settings as lecture halls, churches, mosques, and synagogues.*

Figure 3.1 The Four Distances

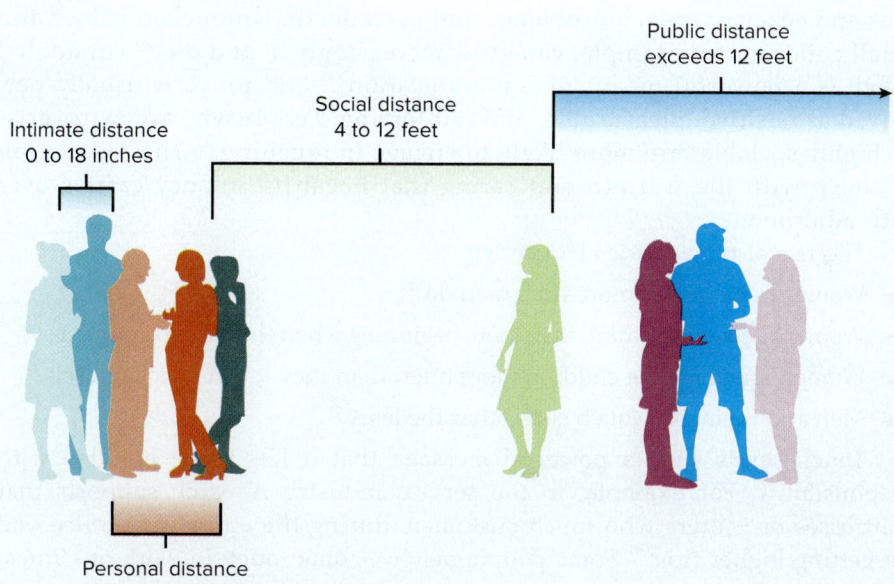

What Are Nonverbal Codes?   **49**

Time

Temporal communication, or **chronemics**, *refers to the way people organize, relate to, and use time and the messages that result.* Some people particularly value the past and collect photographs and souvenirs to remind themselves of times gone by. Others focus more intensely on the future and are always chasing dreams or planning future events. Still others live in the present and savor the current time. They try to live each day to its fullest and neither lament the past nor show concern for the future. Research about past, present, or future time orientations reflects that as people age they become more future oriented in their views of time, trying to prepare for what may come down the road.[27]

What kinds of messages relate to the way we use time? People who are perennially late might send the message that their time is more important than that of those around them, whereas those who tend to be early might be understood as being responsible and conscientious. People in different cultures view time differently, a topic we will cover in greater depth in **Chapter 6**, on global and intercultural communication.[28]

Touch

Tactile communication, also known as haptics, is *the use of touch in communication.* Because touch always involves invasion of another's personal space, it commands attention. It can be welcome, as when a parent holds a crying child, or unwelcome, as in an instance of sexual harassment.

Our need for, and appreciation of, tactile communication starts early in life.[29] Insufficient touching can lead to health disorders, such as allergies and eczema, speech problems, and even death. Untouched babies and small children, for example, can grow increasingly ill and die.[30] For adults, touch is a powerful means of communication,[31] and touch is usually perceived as positive, pleasurable, and reinforcing. People who are extroverts, or highly sociable, are more likely to engage in touching.[32] The association of touch with the warmth and caring that began in infancy carries over into adulthood.

The use of touch varies by gender:[33]

- Women value touch more than men do.[34]
- Women are touched more than men, beginning when they are six months old.[35]
- Women touch female children more often than they touch male children.[36]
- Men and their sons touch each other the least.[37]

Touch sends such a powerful message that it has to be handled with responsibility. For example, in the service industry research supports that waitresses or waiters who touch customers during the course of service end up getting higher tips.[38] Some people may welcome touch in work or clinical settings, but it is equally likely to be undesirable or annoying. Certainly, touch can be misunderstood in such settings.[39] When the right to touch is abused, it can result in a breach of trust, anxiety, and hostility. When touch is used to communicate concern, caring, and affection, it is often welcomed, desired, and appreciated.

Vocal Cues

Nonverbal communication includes some sounds, as long as they are not words. We call them **paralinguistic features**—*the nonword sounds and nonword characteristics of language, such as pitch, volume, rate, and quality.* The prefix *para* means "alongside" or "parallel to," so *paralinguistic* means "alongside the words or language."

The paralinguistic feature examined in this section is **vocal cues**—*all of the oral aspects of sound except words themselves.* Vocal cues include those outlined in **Table 3.3**.

These vocal cues are important because they are linked in our minds with a speaker's physical characteristics, emotional state, personality characteristics, gender characteristics, and even credibility. Vocal cues may convey information about the speaker's age, height, appearance, and body type.[40] When you talk to customer service agents, for example, on your cell phone, you form an impression of how they look and how their personalities might be described.

Table 3.3 Vocal Cues

Pitch	■ The highness or lowness of your voice
Rate	■ How rapidly or slowly you speak
Inflection	■ The variety or changes in pitch
Volume	■ The loudness or softness of your voice
Quality	■ The unique resonance of your voice, such as huskiness, nasality, raspiness, or whininess
Nonword sounds	■ Using "mmh," "huh," "ahh," and the like, as well as pauses or the absence of sound for effect in speaking
Pronunciation	■ Saying a word correctly
Articulation	■ Coordinating your mouth, tongue, and teeth to make a word understandable to others
Enunciation	■ Combining pronunciation and articulation to produce a word with clarity and distinction, so that it can be understood. A person who mumbles has an enunciation problem.
Silence	■ The lack of sound

Vocal cues are not only important in interpersonal settings but also essential to successful public speakers. Vocal cues can help a public speaker establish credibility with an audience and can clarify the message:

- Pitch and inflection can be used to make the speech sound aesthetically pleasing, accomplish subtle changes in meaning, and tell an audience whether you are asking a question or making a statement, being sincere or sarcastic, or being doubtful or assertive.
- A rapid speaking rate may indicate you are confident about speaking in public or that you are nervously attempting to conclude your speech.
- Variations in volume can be used to add emphasis or create suspense.
- Enunciation is especially important in public speaking because of the increased size of the audience and the fewer opportunities for direct feedback.
- Pauses can be used to create dramatic effect and arouse audience interest. Vocalized pauses—"ah," "uh-huh," "um," and so on—are not desirable in public speaking and may distract the audience.

Clothing and Other Artifacts

Objectics, or object language, refers to *the study of the human use of clothing and other artifacts as nonverbal codes.* **Artifacts** are *ornaments or adornments you display that hold communicative potential,* including jewelry, hairstyles, cosmetics, automobiles, canes, watches, shoes, portfolios, hats, glasses, tattoos, body piercings, and even the fillings in teeth. Your clothing and other adornments might communicate your age, gender, status, role, socioeconomic class, group memberships, and personality.

Conformity occurs when one tries to go along with the norms of a group in attitudes, clothing, language, or other behaviors. Conforming to current styles is correlated with an individual's desire to be accepted and liked.[41] People can also choose to deviate from the norms of a group, in which case clothing and other adornments may be used as a form of creative self-expression.[42]

©Clark Brennan/Alamy RF

Cultural and religious differences can often be apparent in the clothing people wear. For example, the dress of Muslim women, which tends to be modest and consist of loose and fairly heavy materials, is distinctive. Some Muslim women cover their entire body, including their face and/or hands, whereas others wear a simple hijab, or head covering, with long sleeves and long skirts. Like Muslim women, Orthodox Jewish women tend to dress modestly. Generally, they wear dark-colored, loose clothing and cover their elbows and knees. Married Orthodox Jewish women usually cover their hair as well. Some women from India who are Hindu may wear dhotis and saris, at least for formal occasions.

CHALLENGE YOURSELF

What should I know about body language, clothing, and accessories, so I don't make a fool of myself when it comes to socializing or looking for a job?

As you've learned throughout this chapter, nonverbal communication involves many cues, including bodily movement and facial expression, physical attractiveness, use of space, time orientation, use of touch, vocal cues, and clothing and other artifacts. Let's focus, for a moment, on this last set of cues—clothing and other accessories:

- Think about how much attention you pay, in a typical interaction, to this set of cues. Are you aware of the nonverbal messages your clothing and accessories might be sending? Are they representative of the types of messages you want to send?
- How would you dress for an interview? You would probably wear fairly conservative clothes, like a suit or a matching outfit in dark colors. You would not forget a belt or socks. Your jewelry—whether male or female—would be minimal. And good hygiene is essential.
- A different set of standards applies to going for coffee with friends. You can be more expressive on a social occasion than when you interview for a job.
- Can you add other suggestions about appropriate clothing and adornments? Have you ever erred in how you dressed? Have you observed others who have? What advice would you offer a younger sibling, or a student new to your school, about how to fit in, or, for that matter, stand out?

After considering clothing, think about the other kinds of nonverbal codes. If you feel confident about your own sensitivity to them, ask a trusted friend to provide feedback about your clothing, your use of space and touch, and your use of time in social or casual situations. If you are seeking a job, ask someone whose opinion you trust about how you might manage the same sets of cues in a formal setting. Find ways to improve by paying attention to the nonverbal behavior of others. All of us make mistakes from time to time with complex nonverbal cues. But by being both more thoughtful and more reflective, you can increase your chances of successful nonverbal communication.

©McGraw-Hill Education/John Flournoy

Body modifications, such as tattoos and piercings, are a type of artifact. Although they can be removed, the procedures may be both costly and time intensive. What do tattoos signal to others? Most people who adorn themselves with tattoos and piercings probably do so because they believe it adds to their overall attractiveness. A recent study, however, presented findings on how others perceive people with tattoos. Men with tattoos were viewed as more dominant than nontattooed men, and women with tattoos were seen as less healthy than women without tattoos.[43]

WHY ARE NONVERBAL CODES DIFFICULT TO INTERPRET?

Perhaps you have been in a situation where you misinterpreted someone's nonverbal cues. You thought that a touch on your arm communicated liking, that a frown meant someone disapproved of what you said, or someone looking elsewhere while you were talking suggested a lack of interest, but you later found out you were wrong. If you have had these experiences, you know that nonverbal codes are difficult to interpret. In this section, we talk about two reasons this is so.

One Code Communicates a Variety of Meanings

The ambiguity of nonverbal codes occurs in part because one code may communicate several meanings. For example, the nonverbal code of raising your right hand may mean that you are taking an oath, you are demonstrating for a cause, you are indicating to an instructor that you would like to answer a question, a physician is examining your right side, or you want a taxi to stop for you.

Although people in laboratory experiments have demonstrated some success in decoding nonverbal behavior accurately,[44] in actual situations receivers of nonverbal cues can only guess about the meaning.[45] Several lay authors have been successful in selling books suggesting that observers can learn to easily and accurately interpret specific nonverbal cues. Unfortunately, these authors have not been able to demonstrate any significant improvement among their readers.

A Variety of Codes Communicate the Same Meaning

Nonverbal communication is not a science: any number of codes may be used to communicate the same meaning. Consider the many nonverbal ways that adults communicate love or affection. You may sit or stand close to someone you love. You might speak softly, use a certain vocal intonation, or alter how quickly you speak.

Cultural differences are especially relevant in this context. How do you show respect to a speaker? In some cultures, listeners show respect by averting their eyes; in other cultures, listeners show respect and attention by looking directly at the speaker. Depending on her own culture, a speaker who is not familiar with the cultural practices of others might feel that people who look away are inattentive or people who look directly are overstepping the boundaries of privacy.

SKILL BUILDER

LEARN TO IMPROVE YOUR NONVERBAL SENSITIVITY

You can improve your nonverbal sensitivity by paying attention to the context, adapting to your audience, and providing feedback to others.

- **Consider the context.** Ask yourself if the physical setting, the occasion, and the situation require changes in your behavior. For example, let's say you are upset with your partner and want to talk about what's upsetting you right then and there. But what if you and your partner happen to be in a public place?

- **Adapt to your audience.** What if your partner gives nonverbal cues that he or she is distracted and uncomfortable? What does it mean if he or she is not looking at you but at the people around you who are witnessing your disagreement? What information is expressed in your partner's raised eyebrow, crossed arms, open posture, or facial expression? These nonverbal signals will impact how you adapt your approach to dealing with the disagreement.

- **Give and receive feedback.** Observe your audience, which is to say, your partner. What nonverbal signals might your partner use to convey that he or she would like to continue the conversation? Are you providing nonverbal feedback that lets your partner know that his or her needs and interests matter to you?

Arguments often happen on two levels, on a content level and a relational level. The content-level messages are the information that is exchanged. The relational-level messages are often expressed in nonverbal messages and tone. Look for examples of relational-level messages in the nonverbal behaviors a friend or partner conveys when receiving content messages from you. Effective communicators who are attuned to nonverbal cues pay attention to both content- and relational-level messages.

HOW CAN YOU IMPROVE YOUR NONVERBAL COMMUNICATION?

You can improve your nonverbal communication by being sensitive to context, audience, and feedback. The **context** includes *the physical setting, the occasion, and the situation.*

In conversation your vocal cues are rarely a problem unless you stutter, stammer, lisp, or suffer from some speech pathology. Vocal cues are perhaps most important in public speaking, because you have to be highly attuned to your volume and rate, you have to enunciate very clearly, and you have to introduce more vocal variety to keep the audience's attention. The strategic use of pauses and silence is also more important in public speaking than in conversations or small-group discussions.

©Realistic Reflections RF

The occasion and physical setting also affect the potential meaning of a nonverbal cue. For example, you may stand farther away from people in formal situations when space allows but closer to family members or strangers in an elevator.

You also have to adapt to the audience. When speaking to children, you must use careful enunciation, articulation, and pronunciation. With an older audience—or with younger audiences whose hearing has been impaired by too much loud music—you must adapt your volume. Generally, children and older people in both interpersonal and public speaking situations appreciate slower speech. Adaptation to an audience may also determine your choice of clothing, hairstyle, and jewelry.

Your attention to audience feedback can be very important in helping others interpret your nonverbal cues. If your listeners give quizzical looks, stare, or nod, you can interpret these as signals to talk louder, introduce variety into your pace or pitch, restate your points, or clarify your message. If your conversational partner or audience does not provide you with feedback, ask questions and check on their perceptions.

CHAPTER REVIEW

In this chapter you explored nonverbal communication first by learning what it means to communicate without words. You also learned about the relationship between verbal and nonverbal communication—that it can function to repeat, emphasize, complement, contradict, substitute, or regulate your verbal communication. Understanding this relationship can mean the difference between communicating effectively and obscuring your meaning with cues that are too easily misunderstood. The last section of this chapter therefore focused on how you can improve your nonverbal communication, no matter the context—whether you are on a date, speaking in front of your peers, or interviewing for a job.

KEY TERMS

contradiction, 44
complementing, 44
emphasis, 44
nonverbal communication, 44
repetition, 44
nonverbal codes, 45

regulation, 45
substitution, 45
kinesics, 46
personal space, 48
proxemics, 48
territoriality, 48

intimate distance, 49
personal distance, 49
public distance, 49
social distance, 49
chronemics, 50
tactile communication, 50

paralinguistic features, 51
vocal cues, 51
artifacts, 52
objectics, 52
context, 55

STUDY QUESTIONS

1. How much does nonverbal communication contribute to a message? Under what circumstances is it especially important?
2. Name two ways in which verbal and nonverbal communication work together, and give examples of each.
3. List two kinds of nonverbal codes, and explain how each contributes to a message. Describe scenarios from your own experience that illustrate each of the two codes.
4. Name two reasons people sometimes misinterpret nonverbal messages. Describe an experience you had or witnessed (including in a book or movie) when a message was misinterpreted for one of these reasons.
5. What are the three areas to focus on when working to improve your nonverbal communication? Give an example from your own experience to illustrate each.

ENDNOTES

1. Lapakko, D. (1997). Three cheers for language: A closer examination of a widely cited study of nonverbal communication. *Communication Education, 46*, 63–67.
2. Grahe, J. E., & Bernieri, F. J. (1999). The importance of nonverbal cues in judging rapport. *Journal of Nonverbal Behavior, 23*, 253–269; Vedantam, S. (2006, October 2–8). A mirror on reality: Research shows that neurons in the brain help us understand social cues. *The Washington Post National Weekly Edition, 23*(50), 35.
3. Nikolaus, J., Roessing, T., & Petersen, T. (2011). The effects of verbal and nonverbal elements in persuasive communication: Findings from two multi-method experiments. *Communications: The European Journal of Communication Research, 36*, 245–271.
4. Cook, S. W., Yip, T. K., & Goldin-Meadow, S. (2010). Gesturing makes memories that last. *Journal of Memory and Language, 63*, 465–475.
5. Hall, J. A., & Xing, C. (2015). The verbal and nonverbal correlates of the five flirting styles. *Journal of Nonverbal Behavior, 39*, 41–68.
6. Matsumoto, D., & Willingham, B. (2006). The thrill of victory and the agony of defeat: Spontaneous expressions of medial winners of the 2004 Athens Olympic games. *Journal of Personality and Social Psychology, 91*, 358–581; Pascalis, O., & Kelly, D. J. (2009). The orgins of face process in humans: Phylogeny and ontogeny. *Perspective on Psychological Science, 4*, 200–209; Schiavenato, M., Byers, J. F., Scovanner, P., McMahon, J. M., Xia, Y., Lu, N., & He, H. (2008). Neonatal pain facial expression: Evaluating the primary face of pain. *Pain, 138*, 460–471.
7. Hall, J. A., & Mast, M. S. (2007). Sources of accuracy in the empathic paradigm. *Emotion, 7*, 438–446.
8. Mehrabian, A. (1971). *Silent messages*. Belmont, CA: Wadsworth.

9. Ekman, P. (1997). Should we call it expression or communication? *Innovations in Social Science Research, 10,* 333–344; Ekman, P. (1999). Basic emotions. In T. Dalgleish & T. Power (Eds.), *The handbook of cognition and emotion* (pp. 45–60). Sussex, UK: John Wiley; Ekman, P. (1999). Facial expressions. In T. Dalgleish & T. Power (Eds.), *The handbook of cognition and emotion* (pp. 301–320). Sussex, UK: John Wiley; Ekman, P., & Friesen, W. V. (1967). Head and body cues in the judgment of emotion: A reformulation. *Perceptual and Motor Skills, 24,* 711–724.

10. Kendler, K. S., Halberstadt, L. J., Burera, F., Myers, J., Bouchard, T., & Ekman, P. (2008). The similarity of facial expressions in response to emotion-inducing films in reared apart twins. *Psychological Medicine, 38,* 1475–1483.

11. Galati, D., Miceli, R., & Sini, B. (2001). Judging and coding facial expressions of emotions in congenitally blind children. *International Journal of Behavioral Development, 25,* 268–278.

12. Elfenbein, H. A., & Ambady, N. (2003). When familiarity breeds accuracy: Cultural exposure and facial emotion recognition. *Journal of Personality and Social Psychology, 85,* 276–290.

13. Cash, T. F. (1980, July 7). If you think beautiful people hold all the cards, you're right, says a researcher. *People Weekly, 14,* 74–79; Kowner, R. (1996, June). Facial asymmetry and attractiveness judgment in developmental perspective. *Journal of Experimental Psychology, 22,* 662–675.

14. Kurzban, R., & Weeden, J. (2005). HurryDate: Mate preferences in action. *Evolution and Human Behavior, 26,* 227–244.

15. Williams, R. B. (2011, August 6). *Wired for Success* provides the findings of a study conducted by Biesanz, J., Human, L., & Lorenzo, G. which was published in *Psychological Science.*

16. Rhode, D. L. (2010). *The beauty bias: The injustice of appearance in life and law.* Oxford, UK: Oxford University Press.

17. Fraccaro, P. J., Jones, B. C., Vukovic, J., Smith, F. G., Watkins, C. D., Feinberg, D. R., Little, A. C., & DeBruine, L. M. (2011). Experimental evidence that women speak in a higher voice pitch to men they find attractive. *Journal of Evolutionary Psychology, 33,* 57–67.

18. Robbins, P. K., Homer, J. F., & French, M. T. (2011). Beauty and the labor market: Accounting for the additional effects of personality and grooming. *Labour, 25,* 228–251.

19. Agthe, M., Sporrle, M., & Maner, J. K. (2011). Does being attractive always help? Positive and negative effects of attractivenss on social decision making. *Personality and Social Psychology Bulletin, 37,* 1042–1054.

20. Cash, 164–182.

21. Knapp, M. L., Hall, J. A., & Horgan, T. G. (2014). *Nonverbal communication in human interaction* (8th ed.). Boston: Wadsworth, Cengage Learning.

22. Widgery, R. N. (1974). Sex of receiver and physical attractiveness of source as determinants of initial credibility perception. *Western Speech, 38,* 13–17.

23. Davies, A. P. C., Goetz, A. T., & Shackelford, T. K. (2008). Exploiting the beauty in the eye of the beholder: The use of physical attractiveness as a persuasive tactic. *Personality and Individual Differences, 45,* 302–306.

24. Hall, E. T. (1966). *The hidden dimension.* New York: Doubleday.

25. Ibid.

26. Burgoon, J. K. (1978). A communication model of personal space violations: Explication and an initial test. *Human Communication Research, 4,* 129–142.

27. Gonzalez, A., & Zimbardo, P. G. (2008). Time in perspective. In L.K. Guerrero & M.L. Hecht (Eds.), *The nonverbal communication reader: Classic and contemporary readings* (3rd ed., pp. 245–253). Long Grove, IL: Waveland Press.

28. Bruneau, T. J. (2007). Time, change, and sociocultural communication: A chronemic perspective. *Sign Systems Studies, 35*, 89–117.
29. Cecchini, M., Baroni, E., Di Vito, C., & Lai, C. (2011). Smiling in newborns during communicative wake and active sleep. *Infant Behavior & Development, 34*, 417–423.
30. Hertenstein, M. J. (2002). Touch: Its communicative functions in infancy. *Human Development, 45*, 70–94; Loots, G., & Devise, I. (2003). The use of visual-tactile communication strategies by deaf and hearing fathers and mothers of deaf infants. *Journal of Deaf Studies and Deaf Education, 8*, 31–43.
31. Aguinis, H., Simonsen, M. M., & Pierce, C. A. (1998). Effects of nonverbal behavior on perceptions of power bases. *Journal of Social Psychology, 138*(4), 455–475.
32. McCroskey, J. C., Heisel, A., & Richmond, V. (2001). Eysenck's Big Three and communication traits: Three correlational studies. *Communication Monographs, 68*, 360–366.
33. Lee, J. W., & Guerrero, L. K. (2001). Types of touch in cross-sex relationships between coworkers: Perceptions of relational and emotional messages, inappropriateness, and sexual harassment. *Journal of Applied Communication Research, 29*, 197–220.
34. Fisher, J. D., Rytting, M., & Heslin, R. (1976). Hands touching hands: Affective and evaluative effects of interpersonal touch. *Sociometry, 3*, 416–421.
35. Goldberg, S., & Lewis, M. (1969). Play behavior in the year-old infant: Early sex differences. *Child Development, 40*, 21–31.
36. Ibid., 241–248.
37. Jourard, S., & Rubin, J. E. (1968). Self-disclosure and touching: A study of two modes of interpersonal encounter and their inter-relation. *Journal of Humanistic Psychology, 8*, 39–48.
38. Crusco, A. H., & Wetzel, C. G. (2008). The midas touch: The effects of interpersonal touch on restaurant tipping. In L.K. Guerrero & M.L. Hecht (Eds.), *The nonverbal communication reader: Classic and contemporary readings* (3rd ed., pp. 226–231). Long Grove, IL: Waveland Press.
39. Kane, M. N. (2006). Research note: Sexual misconduct, non-sexual touch, and dual relationships: Risks for priests in light of the code of pastoral conduct. *Review of Religious Research, 48*, 105–110; Lee & Guerrero; Strozier, A. L., Krizek, C., & Sale, K. (2003). Touch: Its use in psychotherapy. *Journal of Social Work Practice, 17*, 49–62.
40. Kramer, E. (1963). The judgment of personal characteristics and emotions from nonverbal properties of speech. *Psychological Bulletin, 60*, 408–420.
41. Taylor, L. C., & Compton, N. H. (1968). Personality correlates of dress conformity. *Journal of Home Economics, 60*, 653–656.
42. Laurie, A. (2000). *The language of clothes.* New York: Holt.
43. Wohlrab, S., Fink, B., Kappeler, P. M., & Brewer, G. (2009, January). *Personality and Individual Differences, 46*(2), 202–206.
44. Horgan, T., & Smith, J. (2006). Interpersonal reasons for interpersonal perceptions: Gender-incongruent purpose goals and nonverbal judgment accuracy. *Journal of Nonverbal Behavior, 30*, 127–140.
45. Motley, M. T., & Camden, C. T. (1988). Facial expression of emotion: A comparison of posed expressions versus spontaneous expressions in an interpersonal communication setting. *Western Journal of Speech Communication, 52*, 1–22.

Blue and Yellow Cube Icon, Connecting Globally Icon, Mountain Icon, Chapter Review Arrows Circle Icon: ©McGraw Hill Education

chapter **4**

Communicating Through Listening

©Jacqueline Veissid/Getty Images RF

Listening is your most used communication skill. In fact, research shows that, as a college student, you spend roughly 51 percent of your time listening to others, including those in the mass media—on talk shows, news programs, podcasts, and the radio.[1] In this chapter you will learn why listening is such an important communication skill, which kinds of listening require the most effort, what factors affect your attention and focus, and the many barriers to effective listening, which you can overcome.

LEARNING OBJECTIVES
After reading this chapter, you should be able to:

- Explain the difference between hearing and listening.
- Describe the different types of listening.
- Understand the factors that affect attention.
- Know how to overcome barriers to listening.

THE IMPORTANCE OF LISTENING

Although listening is your most used communication skill, it is also very likely your least studied. You learned reading and writing from grade school through high school, and even into college, but did you ever study listening? As you transition into a career, listening will remain an important skill and one worth practicing.

Why Listen?

The data presented in **Figure 4.1** shows the average amount of time that working professionals spend listening, speaking, writing, and reading. According to this chart, as well as other sources referenced in this chapter, listening will play a vital role in your work life, whatever career you choose. In fact, it's possible that you will even spend more time listening than speaking on the job!

©Purestock/Getty Images RF

- According to an article in *Training & Development*, 80 percent of the corporate executives who were surveyed rated listening as the most important skill in the workforce.[2]
- Nearly 30 percent of those executives said that listening was the communication skill most lacking among their employees.[3]
- Underscoring the significance of these self-reports are the assessments of those in upper management, like the CEO of Best Buy, who asserts that, because customer interests rapidly evolve, not listening guarantees failure.[4]

Figure 4.1 Listening in the Workforce: Average Time Spent Listening, Speaking, Writing, and Reading

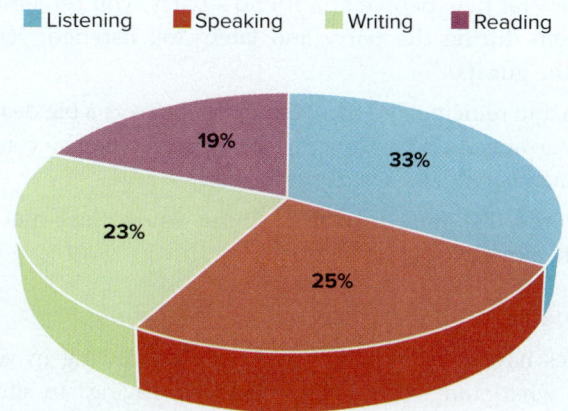

The Importance of Listening   **61**

©Ingram Publishing RF

Try to think of a job you've had where your communication skills made no difference. If you work in entry-level retail—from fast food to clothing—customers will care how you treat them. The following points taken from customer-service questionnaires at retail chains across the country demonstrate the impact your listening skills can have on the customers with whom you interact, and very likely on the outcome of your job. In almost any customer-service position, your performance will be measured in large part by your ability to:

- Get to know the customer base by listening when they ask questions or make requests.
- Ask questions about customers' lifestyles—and listen to their answers—to better understand their needs.
- Interact with customers, which includes receiving orders and preparing products according to those orders.
- Listen and respond appropriately to customer issues.

The importance of listening extends to all levels and all fields. In health-related fields, from personal care specialists to dental hygienists and licensed practical nurses, communication is vital to the experiences of the patients being treated. Receptionists, secretaries, administrative assistants, service managers, cashiers, telemarketers, and truckers are expected to communicate well with visitors, customers, and clients. A friendly FedEx or UPS driver can spread goodwill to 50 people each day simply by having good communication skills. In the world of business, people at every level need to know how to listen and speak in ways that maintain positive relationships.

Your ability to listen affects your personal life, too. Consider the following situations that invite good listening skills:

- Your partner asks you to pick up three items on the way home from work. You not only listen but remember to bring home all three items. Your partner thinks you are wonderful.
- You meet several new people at a friend's party; you remember their names and use them during the party and later. You listened, remembered, and impressed the guests.
- You listened and remembered that your mother makes a big deal out of Mother's Day, so you arrange to be with her on her special day. She communicated; you listened, remembered, and acted appropriately.

In other words, listening to people—those you've just met and those you love—pays off in more positive relationships.

Hearing vs. Listening

How many times have you sat in class with words flowing in your ears only to forget, later on, what your teacher and peers were saying? In situations like this, the reason for your difficulty recalling information lies in the difference between

Figure 4.2 The Difference Between Hearing and Listening

Hearing
- **Hearing** is sound entering your ears, something you cannot prevent.
- Unless you have earbuds or earplugs in your ears, you cannot keep the sounds from entering.

Listening
- **Listening** is the act of interpreting those sounds in your brain.
- This occurs when you are paying attention but does not occur if you are busy texting when you are supposed to be listening.

hearing and listening, as illustrated in **Figure 4.2**. **Hearing** is *the act of receiving sound*; you cannot stop sound from entering your ears. **Listening** is *the act of interpreting the sounds you hear, to determine their meaning.*

In other words, it is possible to be present in class and absent at the same time. You may be physically present, and you may even appear to be listening, but your mind can easily become engaged in other matters, like texting a friend, updating your Facebook page, or admiring the person two rows ahead.

Noise, as defined in **Chapter 1**, is any physical or psychological interference that reduces the clarity of a message. The following list includes everyday examples of noise that interfere with listening, and their potential effects:

- Each year in the United States texting while driving results in over 400,000 accidents and 3,000 deaths.[5]
- In 2017, Apple was sued for not implementing safety features that would lock iPhones while cars are in use, a measure believed to reduce distracted driving.[6] Drivers who are distracted have a harder time listening for dangers, such as sirens or screeching brakes.
- Listening to loud, fast music significantly diminishes your ability to comprehend things you read or hear.[7]
- Checking devices may also reduce your ability to listen. An article in *Advertising Age* reported that smartphones and other personal communication devices might be diminishing face-to-face communication skills, such as listening.[8]
- A study examining the relationship between multitasking and academic performance found that using Facebook and texting while studying can lead to lower grades.[9]

Now you know why listening is so important. You are able to differentiate between hearing and listening and can identify the noise that often gets in the way. But knowing *about* listening and learning to become an effective listener are two different things. In the next section, you will see that there are several types of listening, and each requires a different kind of attention. As you will

The Importance of Listening

learn, practicing your listening skills, and adapting to the kind of listening required, can advance your opportunities both professionally and personally.

TYPES OF LISTENING

Your purpose in listening largely determines how actively you try to process information. If you are just listening to music to relax, you do not have to work very hard to listen; in fact, listening is more pleasure than work. But if you are listening in a class and your purpose is to learn, understand, and remember, that listening takes sustained effort. Anyone who sits through college lectures understands how hard one has to focus to sustain attention in a class.

Listening to Discern Content and Intent

"Isn't it warm in here?" says a woman, one of many at a crowded meeting. The content of her words indicates only that she is seeking agreement from others about the temperature. But very likely the intent of her message is to have someone open a window, turn on a fan, or start the air conditioning. "Where is the salt?" says a father, a man of few words. On the content level, his inquiry is simply about location, but the intent is to have someone pass the salt. **Content** is *the literal meaning of a message,* whereas **intent** is *what the speaker really wants.* Notice in both examples that an active listener has to be prepared to interpret another person's message, because the content often only suggests what the person wants. When your boss says, "Is it closing time already?" as you prepare to leave your job a little early, you understand that he isn't really just inquiring about the time. In other words, you know how to read the intent behind his content.

Listening for Learning

Learning to listen well will help you succeed in school. Listening skills will also be crucial in your efforts to gain and keep a job. When your professor is explaining what will be covered in the next class session, when your supervisor is describing what she wants in an oral report to be delivered to the CEO, when you are listening to your supervisor evaluate your job performance, and when you are listening to customers' complaints and compliments about service in the workplace, your listening requires focus.

Listening to learn is sometimes referred to as active listening, or critical listening. Active listening is a vital skill for those interested in working in the healthcare industry.[10] From diagnosing patient symptoms to dosing medication and providing adequate post-operation care, breakdowns in effective listening can have dangerous and even deadly consequences.

Source: Cade Martin/CDC

SKILL BUILDER

LEARN TO LISTEN IN CONVERSATION

Sometimes listening during a conversation can be a challenge all its own. Follow these practical tips to show others you are listening:

- Face the other person. Don't act as if you are trying to get away.
- Make eye contact. Keep your eyes on the other person instead of looking around for other opportunities.
- Occasionally agree, disagree, or make a noise to indicate that you are receiving the message.
- "Play back" a piece of the message in your own words (paraphrase) or repeat the other person's words back to her (repetition).
- Respond in some way consistent with what the other person is saying: add to what he is saying, provide an example, bring up another line of argument, or provide evidence.

In the educational setting, when listening to learn, you may have to write down what you hear, then return to that information later and review it. Research also finds that students who use their mobile phones to look up relevant information during class earn higher grades.[11] However, when used for unrelated activities, cell phones easily distract from listening to learn. Sending or receiving unrelated texts messages during class will hurt your chances of learning the course material.

Listening for Relating

Empathic listening is *the attempt to understand another person.* You engage in empathic listening by trying so hard to understand the other person that you put yourself in that person's shoes. For instance, Nicole tells her friend between classes that she could hardly focus because of a fatigue headache from a sleepless night. Her friend listens empathically and says, "I feel so sorry for you. Those headaches not only hurt your head but are so distracting. I'll share my notes from class with you in case you missed something." The ability to listen empathically is often the foundation on which close relationships are built. Empathic listening is a social skill connected to other concepts like being able to demonstrate emotional sensitivity effectively with others in conversation.[12]

Listening for Pleasure

Listening to relaxing, fun, or emotionally stimulating information—like music, podcasts, or

©momcilog/Getty Images RF

audio books—is known as **listening for pleasure**. Listening can be as involving and exciting as attending a live concert or as mellow as putting yourself to sleep listening to your favorite artist. The type of music that we listen to, whether actively or passively, can have emotional impacts. One way to manage our moods is though the type of music we select.[13] An athlete might select upbeat music for motivation during a workout, whereas a yoga instructor might select calming music to play during a guided meditation.

ATTENTION AND LISTENING

Our ability to listen can change depending on how much we hear and how long we attend to it. Some sounds prompt an immediate reaction, whereas others require more effort and attention. The key is that we engage in different kinds of attention, which affects how we choose what to listen to and what to remember.

Attending and Focusing

We respond to what we hear in one of two ways: automatically or selectively. With **automatic attention**, *we listen in spite of ourselves, without effort.* A siren, a loud noise, or your name shouted from across the room can capture your automatic attention. We respond immediately and automatically to sharp sounds, dangerous sounds, and warning sounds. If you are walking alone down a dark street late at night and a police car hits the siren just a few yards away, you can be sure it will get your automatic attention.

©Peathegee Inc./Getty Images RF

In contrast, **selective attention** is *the sustained focus we choose to give to things that are important to us.* Your favorite music, conversation with your spouse, statements made by your dinner companion, and your professor at the front of the class all can draw a person's selective attention. The trouble with selective attention is that it's difficult to sustain over time. The classroom, especially in a lecture, is a great example of a place where listening takes effort, even if you choose to listen.

Experts agree that, except for listening for pleasure, listening takes effort, focus, and purpose to sustain, but doing so can make all the difference. For example, many of us rely too much on selective attention as a listening strategy in our personal relationships. This can lead to listening behaviors that foster defensiveness, rather than engagement, such as when we use selective listening to identify errors in logic or to try to poke holes in someone else's argument.[14]

Scanning and Choosing

Listening involves **scanning and choosing**—*a process of taking in stimuli and choosing what to listen to and how.* A useful analogy can be seen in the use of social media sites. When on these sites, we quickly scan our surroundings and analyze them, assessing the importance of several items of interest and noting how they relate to one another.[15] Think about the timeline in a Twitter feed. You would not open Twitter and focus on only one tweet; rather, you would quickly scan hours' worth of tweets to see what is trending. You would quickly give selective attention to each tweet and then determine what trends are present, which you'd like to follow, and so on. Similarly, as you walk across campus, you hear traffic, people talking, and wind blowing, but you scan that environment for sounds that have meaning for you. When you hear someone call your name, all the other sounds fade into the background and you choose where to focus.

©Plattform/Getty Images RF

Listening and Remembering

We listen, but how much do we actually remember? Your psychological sticky note, **short-term memory**—*where you temporarily store information*—is limited in both the quantity of information it can store and the length of time it can retain

GLOBALLY CONNECTING

LISTEN TO SOCIAL MEDIA TO EXPAND YOUR PERSPECTIVES

Social media is a great tool for strengthening our existing relationships because it allows us to keep in contact with, and learn more about, the people in our social circles. However, social media also make it possible for us to interact with people all over the globe, and to learn more about the issues, topics, and perspectives that engage them. In fact, a 2016 report by the Pew Research Center[18] noted that most Americans turn to social media to learn about what's going on in the world, to share information, and to debate issues affecting global society.

Never before has it been easier to share user-generated content than in the age of digital communication. But not everything we read on social media—not even everything deemed "news"—is an accurate reflection of issues and events. **Chapter 11** on Gathering Information and Supporting Materials offers advice and resources for evaluating the credibility of sources you might share with your social media network.

The next time you come across a story about a group of people, a topic, or an issue you know little about, verify its credibility, then share it through social media. In your post, highlight something new you learned from reading the article and invite your social media audience to do the same. By verifying, sharing, and endorsing information through social media, you can enhance others' understanding of important issues.

Attention and Listening **67**

it.¹⁶ Specifically, short-term memory can retain only seven simple items, plus or minus two. Here's an easy way to remember this: telephone numbers have nine digits because that is about all most people can remember. You might notice that most speeches are limited to three main points—your average audience is lucky to remember that many!¹⁷

Your **long-term memory** is *reserved for facts, figures, and concepts that you know you have to remember*, at least until the next test. To move input gleaned from listening to long-term memory takes excitement, rehearsal, or extraordinary effort. Most of us are so thin-skinned that we remember many of the negative things that are said to us. However, to remember the name of a person we've just met, we have to repeat it in our minds over and over until it earns a place in our long-term memory.

BARRIERS TO LISTENING

The best way to become an effective listener is to know what stands in the way. The barriers to listening are common. But as our cultural listening habits change, these barriers evolve and new ones emerge. These days, with so much in front of us, and so much to do, many of us engage in a common barrier to listening known as multitasking. **Multitasking** is *trying to do two or more tasks at once,* sometimes with very negative results. Driving while texting can cause fatal accidents, for example. Research supports that one of the most important factors associated with effective listening involves being attentive, active, and fully present, the reverse traits of multitasking.¹⁹

Physical and mental distractions, too, can keep you from focusing on a message or can cause your mind to wander. As adults we constantly struggle to tune out these distractions. To better understand the various types of barriers to listening, consider the examples in **Table 4.1**.

As you can see, barriers to listening include not only the noises around you but also your perceptions of others and yourself. Your perceptions of others are influenced by factors such as status, stereotypes, and the sights and sounds that surround you.

When **status** affects your listening, you are *devoting attention to someone you think is particularly important.* When you **stereotype**, you *treat individuals as if they were the same as others in a given category.* The way someone looks, or the sound of that person's voice, can also affect the degree to which you listen.

Finally, you play an important role in the kinds of listening in which you engage. Much like stereotyping, when you are listening with a **personal bias**, you are *letting your own prejudices interfere with your ability to interpret information accurately.* Perhaps the most common barrier to listening, however, is **pseudolistening**, *pretending to listen but letting your mind or attention wander to something else.*

In today's noisy world, listeners of all skill levels can struggle to keep their minds—and their listening—focused. Research finds that mindfulness is an important part of being empathetic, engaging in active listening, and providing

Table 4.1 Barriers to Listening

Type of Barrier	Explanation and Example
Noise	
Physical distractions	All the distractions in the environment that keep you from focusing on the message Example: loud music at a party
Mental distractions	The wandering of the mind when you are supposed to be focusing on something Example: thinking about lunch while listening to a teacher
Multitasking	Trying to do two or more tasks simultaneously Example: talking on your cell phone while reading Facebook updates
Factual distractions	Focusing so intently on details that you miss the main point Example: focusing on the name of a character in a book your friend mentions but missing the name of the book and the reason your friend told you about it
Semantic distractions	Overresponding to an emotion-laden word or concept Example: not listening to a teacher when she mentions "Feminist Theory"
Perception of Others	
Status	Devoting attention to someone you think is particularly important Example: not listening to a first-year student in a group activity full of more senior students
Stereotypes	Treating individuals—especially negatively—as if they were the same as others in a given category Example: assuming all young people are unemployable and want to live at home with their parents
Sights and sounds	Letting appearances or voice qualities affect your listening Example: not listening to a person with a screechy voice
Yourself	
Egocentrism	Seeing yourself on stage and in the spotlight in every conversation Example: changing the topic of conversations to your own problems
Defensiveness	Acting threatened and feeling that you must defend what you have said or done Example: assuming others' comments are criticisms of you
Experiential superiority	Looking down on others as if their experience with life were not as good as yours Example: not listening to those with less experience
Personal bias	Letting your own prejudices interfere with your ability to interpret information accurately Example: assuming that people are generally truthful (or deceitful)
Pseudolistening	Pretending to listen but letting your mind or attention wander to something else Example: daydreaming while your professor is lecturing

CHALLENGE YOURSELF

What do I need to know about effective listening? I spend much of my time in college listening to others, but my grades show that I'm not getting much out of all that talk.

On average, we remember most of what we listen to for about twenty seconds, about 50 percent of a message immediately after listening to it, and only 25 percent after a short delay. Simply learning how to sharpen your memory can make you a more effective listener.

- **Listen closely, then paraphrase.** In conversation you can lengthen your listening capacity by paraphrasing what you think the person said.
- **Take notes.** Taking notes on your laptop or notebook is a method of helping you remember what you hear. The act of writing the words embeds them in your mind and allows you to review them later.
- **Make connections.** Linking what you hear to something else you know well can help you remember what you have learned. For example, you might remember the four modes of speech delivery discussed in **Chapter 12** by recalling the phrase "I'm me," whose acronym (IMME) stands for impromptu, memorized, manuscript, and extemporaneous. Linking new information to what you already know and believe aids your memory. If someone tells you something bad about a politician you already dislike, you can easily store that information along with all the negative things you already believe.

Listening, writing down, and linking to something you know better are three ways to enhance your listening by helping you retain information longer. And when you want people to remember what *you* have to say, try using comparisons, contrasts, and figurative language to communicate in a memorable way.

emotional support to others.[20] **Mindful listening** includes *focusing full attention on the speaker by paraphrasing, smiling, nodding, and providing other nonverbal indicators of conversational engagement.* When a good listener catches his mind wandering to other things, or feels the urge to multitask, he puts in the effort to refocus and listen.

CHAPTER REVIEW

In this chapter you learned why listening is so important in school, at home, and in the workplace. You also learned how attention and memory relate to listening and the many barriers to listening that an effective listener needs to overcome. Because listening is not taught the way that reading and writing are, we might assume that listening is not so important. But listening is a skill that is useful to everyone, from an entry-level employee to the CEO of a company.

KEY TERMS

hearing, 63
listening, 63
content, 64
intent, 64
empathic listening, 65
listening for pleasure, 66
automatic attention, 66
selective attention, 66
scanning and choosing, 66

short-term memory, 67
long-term memory, 68
multitasking, 68
status, 68
stereotype, 68
personal bias, 68
pseudolistening, 68
mindful listening, 70

STUDY QUESTIONS

1. Describe a situation in which you were at your best as a listener. What factors of the situation contributed to your good listening? Now describe a situation in which you did not listen as well as you could have. What factors interfered with your listening?

2. Provide examples from the past couple days of when you engaged in each of the four types of listening. How well did you do in each case? Where were you, and whom were you with? What, if anything, interfered with your ability to listen well?

3. Explain the difference between automatic attention and selective attention. Give examples of each from your recent experience.

4. Which barriers listed in the chapter tend to interfere most often with your ability to listen well? Give an example. Which barriers tend not to bother you much at all? Why don't they?

ENDNOTES

1. Janusic, L. A., & Wolvin, A. D. (2009). 24 hours in a day: A listening update to the time studies. *The International Journal of Listening, 23,* 104–120.

2. Salopek, J. (1999, September). Is anyone listening? Listening skills in the corporate setting. *Training & Development, 53,* 58–59.

3. Ibid.

4. Nett, W. (2011, September 23). Best Buy chairman says listening skills crucial to thriving business. *Lubbock Avalanche Journal.* Retrieved from http://lubbockonline.com

5. US Department of Transportation. (2016). Facts and statistics about distracted driving. Retrieved from https://www.distraction.gov

6. Matyszczyk, C. (2017, January 24). Apple sued over car accident linked to texting. *CNET.* Retrieved from http://www.cnet.com

7. Thompson, W. F., Schellenberg, E. G., & Letnic, A. K. (2011, May 20). Fast and loud background music disrupts reading comprehension. *Psychology of Music.* doi:10.1177/0305735611400173

8. Skenazy, L. (2009, February 9). Smartphone apps great for marketing, bad for social skills. *Advertising Age,* np.

9. Junco, R., & Cotton, S. (2012, September). No A 4 U: The relationship between multi-tasking and academic performance. *Computers & Education, 59*(2), 505–514.
10. Jahromi, V. K., Tabatabaee, S. S., Abdar, Z. E., & Rajabi, M. (2016). Active listening: The key of successful communication in hospital managers. *Electron Physician, 8*, 2123–2128.
11. Mobile phones in the classroom: Examining the effects of texting, Twitter, and message content on student learning. *Communication Education, 64*, 344–365.
12. Gearhart, C. C., & Bodie, G. D. (2011). Active-empathic listening as a general social skill: Evidence from bivariate and canonical correlations. *Communication Reports, 24*, 86–98.
13. Krause, A. E., North, A. C., & Hewitt, L. Y. (2015). Music-listening in everyday life: Devices and choice. *Psychology of Music, 43*, 155–170.
14. Zenger, J., & Folkman, J. (2016, July 14). What great listeners actually do. *Harvard Business Review*. Retrieved from https://hbr.org
15. Davidson, K. (2011). *Now you see it: How the brain science of attention will transform the way we live, work, and learn.* New York: Viking.
16. Miller, G. A. (1994). The magical number seven, plus or minus two: Some limits on our capacity for processing information. *Psychology Review, 101*, 343–352.
17. Gilbert, M. B. (1988). Listening in school: I know you can hear me—but are you listening? *Journal of the International Listening Association, 2*, 121–132.
18. Gottifried, J., & Shearer, E. (2016, May 26). News use across social media platforms 2016. *Pew Research Center*. Retrieved from http://www.pewresearch.org
19. Bodie, G. D., Cyr, S. S., Pence, M., Rold, M., & Honeycutt, J. (2012). Listening competence in initial interactions I: Distinguishing between what listening is and what listeners do. *The International journal of Listening, 26*, 1–28.
20. Jones, S. M., Bodie, G. D., & Hughes, S. D. (2016). The impact of mindfulness on empathy, active listening, and perceived provisions of emotional support. *Communication Research*, 1–28.

Blue and Yellow Cube Icon, Connecting Globally Icon, Mountain Icon, Chapter Review Arrows Circle Icon: ©McGraw Hill Education

part 2: Communication Contexts

As your friendships grow and mature, and as communication technologies continue to develop, the ways in which you interact with people will also evolve and adapt. Knowing how to interact successfully with people who have unique customs, beliefs, values, and attitudes, and to do so across a variety of channels, will make you a better communicator, manager, and member of a group or team.

©Lars Niki RF

CHAPTER 5

Interpersonal Communication

Defining Interpersonal Communication
The Changing Nature of Interpersonal Relationships
The Stages of Interpersonal Relationships
The Dark Side of Interpersonal Relationships
Improving Your Interpersonal Communication Behaviors
The Healthy Interpersonal Relationship
Chapter Review

©Darren Calabrese/The Canadian Press/AP Photo

CHAPTER 6

Intercultural Communication

Defining Intercultural Communication
Studying Intercultural Communication
Biases That Affect Intercultural Communication
Characteristics That Distinguish One Culture From Another
Improving Intercultural and Co-Cultural Communication
Chapter Review

©Aleksandar Nakic/Getty Images RF

CHAPTER 7

Mediated Communication and Social Media

Understanding Mediated Communication
Mass Communication and Mass Media
Computer-Mediated Communication and Social Media
Social Media Use Across Contexts
Protecting and Presenting Yourself on Social Media
Chapter Review

©DLILLC/Corbis Images RF

CHAPTER 8

Organizational and Small-Group Communication

What Is Organizational Culture?
Communicating in Small Groups and Teams
Organizational Leadership
Cultivating Positive Relationships in Small Groups
Chapter Review

chapter 5

Interpersonal Communication

©Lars Niki RF

You know that interpersonal relationships can be complicated, and they sometimes require a lot of work. You also know how important and satisfying those relationships can be—especially if you have strong communication skills. In this chapter, you will learn some of the basic elements of interpersonal relationships and interpersonal communication, and learn strategies for improving your skills and building healthy interpersonal relationships.

LEARNING OBJECTIVES

After reading this chapter, you should be able to:

- Define interpersonal relationships and interpersonal communication.
- Describe the changing nature of interpersonal relationships.
- Name and explain the three stages of interpersonal relationships.
- Explain the dark side of relationships.
- Name strategies for improving your interpersonal communication behaviors.
- Describe the components of a healthy interpersonal relationship.

DEFINING INTERPERSONAL COMMUNICATION

Although scholars have advanced different definitions for the study of **interpersonal communication**, the definition we focus on here uses a message-centered framework. According to this framework, three primary factors distinguish interpersonal relationships: (1) establishing a communicative relationship, (2) generating shared meanings, and (3) accomplishing social goals.[1]

- **Establishing communicative relationships.** In order for a communicative relationship to exist, one person must acknowledge another's desire and intentions to talk about something important to him or her.

- **Generating shared meanings.** When a communicative relationship is established, feelings, opinions, ideas, values, and beliefs are exchanged through verbal and nonverbal communication channels in the hopes of achieving some sort of shared meaning.

    - A range of misunderstandings (about what might have been intended, meant, said, or done) often prevent shared meaning from occurring.

    - As noted in **Chapter 2**, the words we use reflect symbols that may have unique situated meanings for different people. For example, the word "annoying" to one person might mean an overbearing person, whereas for someone else it might mean boring. However, the more we communicate with others, the closer we come to sharing the same meanings.

©I Love Images/agefotostock RF

- **Accomplishing social goals.** Finally, people pursue a range of social goals through dialogue, including managing impressions; influencing behaviors; clarifying emotions; and initiating, maintaining, or ending relationships. Some of these social goals and stages of interpersonal relationships are explored further on in this chapter.[2]

Interpersonal communication occurs in **interpersonal relationships**, which may be defined as *associations between at least two people who are interdependent, who use consistent patterns of interaction, and who have interacted for an extended period of time*. Consider the elements of this definition in more detail.

- *Interpersonal relationships include two or more people.* Often, interpersonal relationships consist of just two people—a dating couple, a single parent and a child, a married couple, two close friends, or two coworkers. But interpersonal relationships can also involve more than two people—a family unit, a group of friends, or a social group.

- *Interpersonal relationships involve people who are interdependent.* **Interdependence** refers to *a situation in which people are mutually dependent and have an* *impact on each other*. For example, a father and son, a husband and wife, and a coworker and boss are all examples of relationships that often include a lot of back and forth interactions, where one person's perspectives influences the other's.

- *Individuals in interpersonal relationships use some consistent patterns of interaction.* These patterns may include behaviors generally understood across a variety of situations, as well as behaviors unique to the relationship. For example, some couples make use of FaceTime to keep in touch throughout the day, whereas others may depend more on written notes and oral communication. Determining how important relationships will maintain consistent patterns of interaction is often an important relational goal.

- *Individuals in interpersonal relationships generally have interacted for some time.* Although interpersonal relationships might last for a lifetime, they vary in duration. However, one-time interactions do not count as interpersonal relationships.

Five additional characteristics of interpersonal communication help us narrow this broad definition further (**Table 5.1**). First, interpersonal communication begins with you, including who you are and what you have experienced. Your culture, language, attitudes, and experiences all come into play in your interpersonal exchanges.

©Jakob Helbig/Getty Images RF

Second, interpersonal communication is transactional. This means that it is far more than an interaction in which one person serves as the speaker and, when he or she is finished, the other person "catches the ball" and takes a turn. Generally, our conversations move quickly, and the participants serve simultaneously as listeners and speakers. We observe nonverbal cues from our partner while we are speaking and while we are listening, and these observations continuously shape our messages and interpretations.

Third, interpersonal communication has two dimensions—a content dimension and a relationship dimension, as

Table 5.1 Characteristics of Interpersonal Communication
1. It begins with the self.
2. It is transactional.
3. It has both content and relationship dimensions.
4. It generally requires that communicators share physical proximity.
5. It is irreversible and unrepeatable.

described in **Chapter 1**. If you are interacting in a fairly impersonal setting—say, purchasing a ticket from a bus driver, asking a stranger for directions, or buying a loaf of bread at a new convenience store—you generally limit yourself to the content of your brief interaction.

In contrast, if you are trying to convince your partner to go out to dinner, to change his or her job, or to quit working for the evening and watch television with you, you have both content and a relationship to consider. Perhaps your partner likes to please you and generally follows your lead and your suggestions. Or maybe in the past you changed jobs to follow him or her, and it is your turn to take the lead. All these factors are as important as the content of your message and will therefore influence how you present it.

Fourth, interpersonal communicators generally share physical proximity. That is, they are in a position that they can both hear and see their conversational partner. Developments in technology, of course, have altered this feature somewhat, enhancing our ability to communicate intimately and accurately even when we do not share physical proximity. Consider all the tools you have to create a physically proximate space, even when you are across the country or around the world.

Fifth, interpersonal communication is irreversible and unrepeatable. We have all been angry at one time or another and made hurtful statements to our family members or friends. Or we have been careless in our use of language or in our listening habits. You might say that you did not mean what you said, but you cannot really take it back. Both you and your partner will recall the event—sometimes for a good long time.

Consider the opposite situation, meaning a time when you have shared your feelings and truly touched your partner. Your touch, your posture, and your words were all coordinated to tell him or her how much you care about your relationship. You might attempt to repeat that situation, but no other time will be quite the same. As with a special evening out, you can go to the same restaurant a second time, order the same menu items, and enact similar behaviors, but you cannot perfectly duplicate the original experience.

THE CHANGING NATURE OF INTERPERSONAL RELATIONSHIPS

Who are your friends? In the past, this question was not so difficult to answer. Friends were the people with whom you shared the details of your life, typically through face-to-face interactions. Today, with social networking sites such as Facebook, Twitter, Instagram, and LinkedIn, the answer is more complicated. People may count dozens, or even hundreds, of people as their "friends." But what level of intimacy do we really maintain with our social media contacts? How many are truly friends, and how many merely acquaintances? Social media makes it easier than ever before to maintain contact with close friends and family members.[3] But the quality of our interpersonal relationships is dependent on many factors, as we discuss in this chapter. One thing is for sure, the nature of our relationships has been transformed by social media.

CONNECTING GLOBALLY

HOW COMFORTABLE ARE YOU WITH WIFI-CONNECTED TOYS?

American multinational toy manufacturer Mattel recently introduced a new doll designed for kids of the digital communication era. *Hello Barbie* connects to WIFI networks to engage in the two-way transmission of dialogue. A child can ask the doll questions that then get sent to a server for processing. Personalized responses, devised by the company, are then spoken back to the child in Barbie's own voice. At any time, parents can access a recording of their child's *Hello Barbie* voice data.

A product that uses mediated communication to engage young children should undergo close scrutiny. Consider the following questions which focus on issues related to mediated communication, parental and peer interaction, and privacy.

- What if a child asks Barbie a sensitive question like, "Where did I come from?" Whose values will form the basis of the response the company provides?
- What is the role of peer interaction in a digital society? Should machines become more adaptive in order to replace playmates? Or, should kids be interacting with and learning from peers, including those of diverse backgrounds?
- What about the child's privacy? Would you be comfortable with a company having access to what your child says while playing with his or her toys? Should what your child says during playtime be recorded?

What other questions and concerns come to mind when you think about this development in mediated communication as it relates to children. Would you buy the new *Hello Barbie* for your child? Why or why not?

If friendships have changed in definition, romantic relationships have been transformed. In the past, romantic relationships that included a sexual element occurred between people who had a long-term, exclusive commitment to each other. Friends with benefits relationships (FWBRs) include two good friends who share sex but have no long-term emotional commitment. FWBRs have rules just as more traditional sexual romantic relationships do. Within FWBRs there is wide variation in terms of the focus on friendship qualities as well as focus on repeated sexual contact.[4] The partners need to agree on how attentive they will be, whether the sexual relationship is a secret, and how the individuals will communicate about the relationship.[5] FWBRs often also clarify that the relationship is temporary and includes negotiation of rules regarding emotion and attachment within the relationship.[6] These factors sometimes vary between men and women. Clearly, these relationships are as complicated as traditional romantic relationships.

College students may be the group most likely to experiment with new friendships and new romantic relationships. In addition to engaging in FWBRs, some students are also experimenting with online relationships. Two psychologists determined that 36 percent of college students have formed online friendships. Of those friendships, 22 percent were identified as romantic relationships. Respondents rated their online romantic relationships as superior to, or similar to, those they established off-line in satisfaction, strength, and ease of communication.[7]

Most likely, gay and lesbian romantic relationships have existed since people began to couple. However, they are more prevalent in the news today because of the evolving rights of gay and lesbian people to marry and parent children. The 2010 U.S. Census reported that 605,472 gay and lesbian families existed, and they lived in all states and virtually all counties in the United States.[8] The Human Rights Campaign estimates that the number of such families may be undercounted by as much as 62 percent.[9]

©Fuse/Getty Images RF

At the same time, heterosexual unions are decreasing. The rate of marriages in 2000 was 8.2 per 1,000 people in the United States, whereas the rate fell to 6.9 per 1,000 in 2014. At the same time, the divorce rate also decreased—from 4 per 1,000 in 2000 to 3.2 per 1,000 in 2014.[10] Although many people have the impression that the divorce rate has been increasing in recent times, that was true only in the first part of the twentieth century, and the rate peaked in the 1970s. Since that time, the overall rate has been continually decreasing.[11] However, this decline applies only to people in middle- or upper-income brackets; the divorce rate for the poor and those from racially and ethnically diverse populations has increased.[12]

The one family type that has increased over the past four decades is the single-parent family. Nearly all of these are single-mother families. Recent estimates suggest that 25 percent of children, or one in four, are raised in a single-parent household in the United States. This figure is higher than for all other developed countries. The single-mother family leads to a number of problems, including higher rates of poverty. In addition, more of the children drop out of school, become disconnected from the labor force, and become teen parents. Both the public and policymakers view these issues as significant, with lasting effects.[13]

As societal and technological changes alter the nature of relationships, you need to consider the options that are right for you. Whatever you choose—online relationships or face to face, FWBR or the more traditional approach to romance, cohabiting or marrying—good communication skills will play a crucial role. All successful relationships rely on clear, open communication.

THE STAGES OF INTERPERSONAL RELATIONSHIPS

Communication and relationship development are symbiotic; that is, communication affects the growth of relationships, and the growth of relationships affects communicative behavior.[14] When you become closer to another person, you are likely to communicate more often and more intimately, and the communication is likely to be more satisfying. Similarly, when you experience positive interactions with another person, you are more likely to feel close to him or her.

Relational Development

Communication theorist and researcher Mark Knapp created a model that has been useful in considering how people come together in relationships, as well as how they split apart.[15] Each has five stages. The coming together phase includes initiating, experimenting, intensifying, integrating, and bonding, as illustrated in **Figure 5.1**.

The **initiating stage** *begins with the first impressions you have of a potential partner*. Why do we begin relationships with some people, but not others? Five factors affect our relational development:

- **Proximity**— *the location, distance, or range between persons and things*—is the first factor. You are more likely to have a relationship with someone who is physically, emotionally, or attitudinally close to you.

- **Attractiveness** *includes physical attractiveness, how desirable a person is to work with, and how much "social value" the person has for others.*[16] Sharing similar standards for how to interact with others in a given group or community, also known as social values, can greatly increase the attraction between two people.

- **Responsiveness**, *the idea that we tend to develop relationships with people who demonstrate positive interest in us*, is another factor. For example, when you are interested in someone, you respond to his or her text messages quickly, or perhaps even immediately.

©Beau Lark/Corbis/VCG/Getty Images

- **Similarity**, *the idea that our relational partners usually like or dislike the same things we do*, is another feature of relational development. You might have friends in common or enjoy the same movies. Similarity can be a powerful factor in the initiating stage.

- Finally, **complementarity** is *the idea that we sometimes bond with people who provide something we do not have; in turn we may have qualities or characteristics they lack*. Whereas you may be slightly shy, your friend may be assertive. In situations that call for assertiveness, your friend may play that role for you.

Figure 5.1 Knapp's Relational Model for the Stages of Coming Together

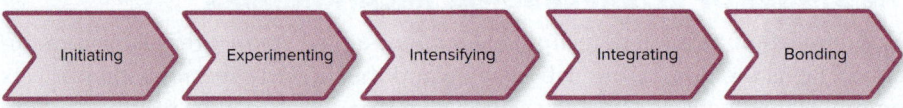

When deciding whether to pursue a new relationship, many people now turn to Facebook. After a first meeting, people often follow up by finding that person on social media in hopes of learning more about that person: interests, friendship network, and whether or not he or she mentions being "in a relationship." Next, people often look at the person's photos and check to see if they have friends in common. If the new acquaintance appears to reflect any of the five qualities listed earlier, then they often feel more comfortable pursuing that person by asking him or her out on a date or pursuing the experimentation phase.[17]

©JGI/Jamie Grill/Getty Images RF

The second stage is the **experimentation stage**. People in this stage *make an effort to find some common ground, including background, interests, attitudes, or values*. This stage is also referred to as the probing stage, because the individuals probe each other for information that would allow them to further the social connection between them. Some relationships end here, never developing into more than a mere acquaintance. One common goal in this phase is reducing the uncertainty about the other person, his or her attitudes, values, and stances on a range of issues and topics.[18] People often do this by becoming Facebook friends, texting, and hanging out with friends together to see if there is enough chemistry to intensify the relationship.

Relationships that do move forward go to the **intensifying stage**, *when the communication between two people changes and deepens*. At this point people begin to self-disclose. **Self-disclosure** is *the process of making intentional revelations about yourself that others would be unlikely to know and that generally constitute private, sensitive, or confidential information*. Although such self-disclosures are intentional, people can use disclosed information about themselves inappropriately. Here are three guidelines for appropriate self-disclosure:

- *Disclosure generally increases as relational intimacy increases.* Do not provide your life story to people you have just met.
- *Disclosure tends to be reciprocal.* When others offer you information about themselves, it is appropriate to reveal information to them.
- *Negative disclosure is directly related to the intimacy of the relationship.* As you become closer to another person, you can increasingly reveal negative information about yourself.

These guidelines become even more important as you establish relationships online. In online situations, you know far less about the other person. Too much disclosure early in a relationship could render you vulnerable to a predator, a poser, or someone with other malicious intent. Be careful in online situations. Negative information you share online may have a greater impact than it does in face-to-face communication, because you have far fewer clues about the receiver.

People stimulate relational development in many ways besides self-disclosure. They might offer gifts, ask for a romantic relationship commitment, or express affection verbally and nonverbally. Partners in some relationships may "test the waters" to see if particular advances are welcomed or frowned upon. These "secret" tests are intended to test the intensity of a relationship. They can include presenting the other person as a girlfriend or boyfriend (presentation) or seeing if the relationship lasts when a temporary physical separation occurs. Another important disclosure that often occurs in the intensifying stage is deciding to make a relationship Facebook official. Facebook official relationships are evaluated as more satisfying, committed, and stronger than relationships not tagged as "Facebook official."[19]

The fourth stage is the **integration stage**, and here the *two people begin to merge their lives*. Their status as a couple becomes obvious. The couple may engage in a sexual relationship at this stage, and they are more likely to disclose very personal information. Friends and family reinforce the relationship by including both of them, rather than just one of them, at social occasions. The people often merge networks, by adding more of one another's unique friends and family members as new Facebook friends.[20]

The final stage is referred to as the **bonding stage**, when *the couple communicate their relationship to others*. They might marry or celebrate their love through a commitment ceremony. This stage may last indefinitely, until death divides them.

Relational Maintenance

Once individuals have bonded, they enter a stage of **relational maintenance** in which they begin *establishing strategies for keeping the relationship together*. Although people in this stage reach stability and level off their relationship, the process is probably not best represented as a flat line. Instead, people become more intimate or closer at some periods and more distant at other times.

Communication theorists Barbara Montgomery and Leslie Baxter coined the **dialectic theory**, which suggests that *relationships include contrary tendencies or opposing values* like those described earlier.[21] These opposing values include **autonomy and connectedness**, meaning that we have *an interest in being close to others, but we also need to maintain a separate identity*. We also move between the need to be open and the need to be closed; we wish to *self-disclose and provide information about ourselves as well as to be private and keep secrets*. Most relational partners also experience **novelty and predictability**; that is, they wish to be able to *predict events in their relationship, and they yearn for the original and new*. In other words, our relationships in the maintenance stage are actually dynamic, moving forward and back; they are not stagnant or stable.

Another way of understanding the changes that occur in relationships is through the identification and discussion of "turning points."[22] A **turning point** is *a transformative event that alters the relationship in some way*.[23] Researchers have asked couples to reflect on changes in their relationships and to graph those changes. The turning points can propel the relationship toward more or less commitment. They might include outside events that occurred (the loss of a job or the offer of a new one in a different location), decisions the couple made (to buy a new house, have a child), a change in their social network (someone moving in or out), or circumstances beyond their control. Partners usually agree about half the time on the importance of the turning points they recall, but the extent of their agreement is not related to their satisfaction with the relationship.[24]

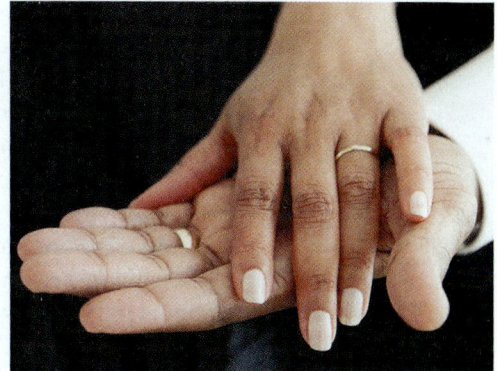
©JGI/Jamie Grill/Blend Images LLC RF

Although we initially develop relationships on the basis of factors like attractiveness and similarity, we maintain them for different reasons. After you have gotten to know someone, why do you choose to maintain the relationship? One reason is that maintained relationships invite certain levels of predictability, or certainty.[25] In this stage of the relationship, we are interested in our partner's ability to focus on us through empathic, caring, and concerned involvement.[26] Indeed, one of the key features of relationships during maintenance is that partners not only become more empathic but also begin to mirror each other's behavior.

Technology is an important part of how people maintain relationships today. One study finds that couples who watch the same television shows together are likely to have higher quality relationships than people who do not engage in joint TV viewing in maintaining their relationships.[27] Furthermore, dating partners who use text messages to maintain their relationships (by saying I love you and sending flirty texts throughout the day) had more satisfying and close relationships than people who did not use texting to maintain their relationships.[28]

Some couples achieve satisfying and long-term relationships. One study looked at couples who had been happily married for more than 40 years. Many of these marriages were characterized by stubbornness ("This marriage will succeed no matter what"), positive distortion ("She is the most beautiful woman in the world"), unconditional acceptance (regardless of faults), and the continuous push and pull of autonomy or independence versus unity or interdependence.[29]

©Deborah Jaffe/Corbis RF

Maintaining positive, satisfying relationships is not easy, but the people who are the most satisfied with their relationships are probably those who have worked hardest at maintaining them. Communicatively, people in long-term, satisfied relationships are distinctive from those in short-term or unhappy relationships. For example, people in long-term and satisfied relationships are more likely to use joint rather than individual identity pronouns ("we" and "us" rather than "I" or "me").[30]

Relational Deterioration

Not all relationships last. Some deteriorate and others end. About half of all marriages end in divorce; in second and third marriages, the failure rate is even higher. Why do interpersonal relationships end? Several factors encourage people to seek the conclusion, rather than the continuation, of a relationship. We consider a few of these factors here.

Hurtful messages *create emotional pain or upset, and they can encourage the end of a relationship.* Hurtful messages occur in most relationships; however, if they become a pattern or are so intense that one partner cannot forget them, they can be disruptive.

Deceptive communication—*the practice of deliberately making somebody believe things that are untrue*—can also lead to relational dissatisfaction and termination. All relational partners likely engage in some level of deception from time to time. Telling a "little white lie," avoiding telling the "whole truth," and omitting some details of an event are commonplace. In contrast, deliberate and regular deception can lead to the destruction of trust and the end of the relationship.

Aggressiveness *occurs when people stand up for their rights at the expense of others' and care about their own needs but no one else's.* Aggressiveness might help you get your way a few times, but ultimately others will avoid you and let their resentment show. People who engage in aggressive behavior may do so because they have formed negative self-concepts or because they learned this pattern of behavior growing up.

Aggressiveness is not the same as argumentativeness. **Argumentativeness** is defined as *a predisposition to recognize controversial issues, advocate positions, and refute opposing positions.*[31] Indeed, argumentative people may value argument as a normal social communicative activity. Argumentativeness may actually be a positive behavior for some cultures, whereas it may be negative for others.

Defensiveness *occurs when a person feels attacked*. Trust is essential to healthy relationships.[32] But trust must be established between individuals, and not be based on roles, positions, or status. In other words, people should come to relationships without all the trappings of the roles they play outside the relationship. Can you imagine how unsuccessful the relationship would be between Prince William and his wife, Kate, if William entered, or tried to maintain, their relationship while being proud and boastful of his role as royalty? Most likely their marriage would not survive. You might not ever be in a relationship with someone who is quite so well known, but people sometimes get stuck in their roles as professor, pastor, or residence hall advisor. These roles can lead to defensiveness on the part of the "lower-status" partner. Reducing defensiveness is essential to building trust.

As mentioned earlier, Knapp's relational model includes stages of coming together and stages of coming apart. Here we consider the five stages of coming apart, as illustrated in **Figure 5.2**. First is the **differentiating stage**. During this time, *differences are emphasized, as opposed to commonalities*. The momentum of togetherness shifts to independent and individualist directions. People may complain of being held back by the commitment to their partner. Temporary separations may occur. One action that sometimes happens during this stage is that partners post fewer photos on Facebook of their partner and some even remove

Figure 5.2 Knapp's Relational Model for the Stages of Coming Apart

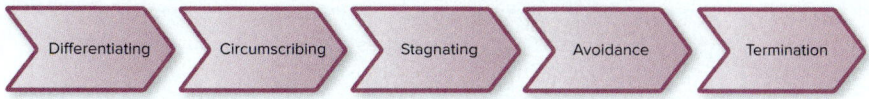

previous Facebook photos and memories as a way of beginning to move beyond the relationship and show more separation.[33]

Next is the **circumscribing stage**. The primary focus now is on *setting limits and boundaries on communication between the two people*. The couple no longer share intimate and private communication. Their interactions become shallow, and the range of topics significantly decline. The two may fear discussing deep topics because they lead to conflict.

If the decline of the relationship continues, it enters the third stage, stagnation, which builds on many of the problems of the circumscribing stage. Communication is even more limited and less frequent. In the **stagnation stage**, relationships are *sluggish and do not grow or progress*. The **avoidance stage** may follow. Now the *partners avoid each other, desiring separation*. Physical separation often occurs at this point. Finally, **termination** can occur as *the relationship stops completely*. Although it is possible to save a relationship from this stage of development, it is relatively rare. One thing that people frequently note experiencing as they go through these different stages of relational deterioration is that the declining relationship has less and less intimacy. This can help people feel better about making a change for a relationship that feels more personally rewarding.[34]

Communication theorist Jack Gibb distinguished between behaviors that encourage defensiveness and those that reduce it. He identified evaluation, control, neutrality, superiority, certainty, and strategy—outlined and defined in **Figure 5.3**—as promoting defensive behaviors in others.[35]

In contrast, behaviors for reducing defensiveness include description, problem orientation, empathy, equality, provisionalism, and spontaneity. People who use *description* report their observations, rather than making judgments or evaluations. People with a *problem orientation* do not act as though they have the solution but are eager to discuss multiple ideas. People who exhibit *empathy* demonstrate concern for others, as shown through careful listening for both content—what the other person states—and intent—what the other person actually means. *Equality* means that the communicator demonstrates that she is neither superior nor inferior to the other person. *Provisionalism* suggests that the communicator is open to other ideas. *Spontaneity* implies naturalness and a lack of premeditation. To decrease the likelihood of ending a relationship, replace behaviors that create defensiveness with those that reduce it, as demonstrated in **Table 5.2**.

Figure 5.3 Behaviors That Encourage Defensiveness

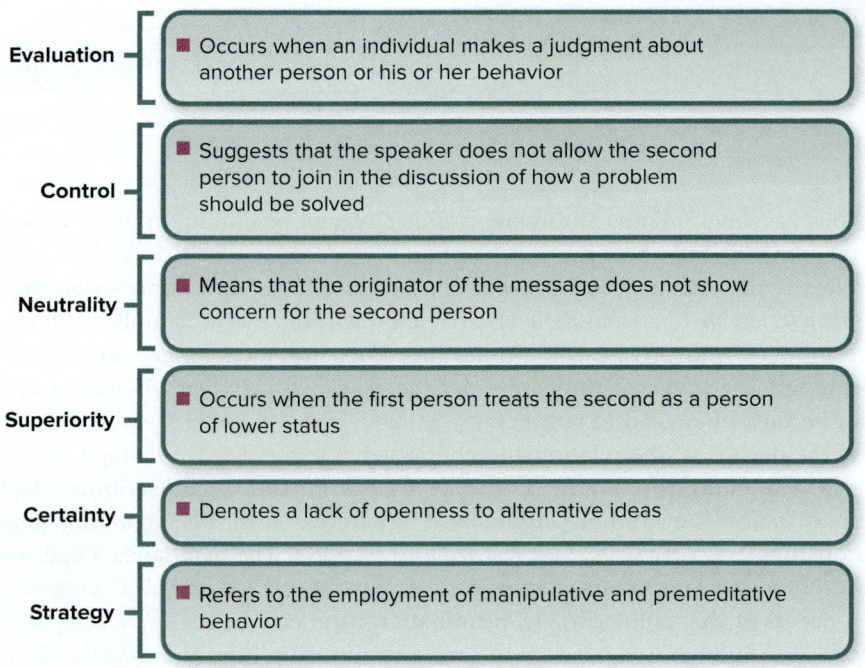

- **Evaluation**: Occurs when an individual makes a judgment about another person or his or her behavior
- **Control**: Suggests that the speaker does not allow the second person to join in the discussion of how a problem should be solved
- **Neutrality**: Means that the originator of the message does not show concern for the second person
- **Superiority**: Occurs when the first person treats the second as a person of lower status
- **Certainty**: Denotes a lack of openness to alternative ideas
- **Strategy**: Refers to the employment of manipulative and premeditative behavior

Table 5.2 Creating and Reducing Defensiveness

Create Defensiveness	Reduce Defensiveness
Evaluation	Description
Control	Problem orientation
Neutrality	Empathy
Superiority	Equality
Certainty	Provisionalism
Strategy	Spontaneity

THE DARK SIDE OF INTERPERSONAL RELATIONSHIPS

Although your interpersonal relationships may generally be pleasurable and positive, you might also have experienced painful and negative effects of relationships. What are some of the qualities of negative relationships? Obsession that includes jealousy certainly creates negative outcomes.[36] Similarly, misunderstanding, gossip, conflict, and **codependency**, or *the tendency to depend on the needs of,* *or the control by, another*, can lead to harmful results. Abuse, which can be sexual, physical, mental, and emotional, characterizes the most harmful and destructive of relationships.[37]

For many people, the thought of staying in a relationship that is abusive or violent seems absurd. Since relationships are ideally positive, generally focused on helping each other, and imbued with shared memories, why do some people maintain agonizing or distressing relationships?

These days examples of the dark side of relationships often take the form of cyberbullying. In 2012, fifteen-year-old Amanda Todd took her own life after 38-year-old Aydin Coban lured her in online, using false pretenses, and played on her vulnerabilities. Coban met Todd in a chat room and, lying about his age and his intentions, convinced her to share compromising photos of herself. He then used the images to blackmail her. Todd reacted by posting a YouTube video explaining how Coban had lured her in, a video that was viewed by millions of people around the world. After posting the video, she took her own life.[38]

BUILDER

LEARN HOW TO DECREASE DEFENSIVENESS

Have you ever heard yourself saying to a close friend or family member, "I hate how you always have to be right and never listen to me"? A less defensive statement would include more description, more of what is sometimes called a problem orientation. It would also include more empathy, equality, provisionalism, and spontaneity. Here is one example of a description statement that includes all these features:

"I don't always feel understood when I express my point of view on something that you feel strongly about. You probably didn't even know it bothers me. I'm sure there are ways that I can listen to you better as well. Do you have any ideas about how we can work on this?"

Rewrite the following statements in a way that would decrease their defensiveness. Use the categories generated by Jack Gibb. For example, replace *evaluation* statements with *description* statements.

- "What's wrong with you, anyway?"
- "Who's responsible for the mess in the library?"
- "I don't really care what you do."
- "We're not leaving here until I say we're leaving."
- "We don't need to meet. I know how to solve the problem."
- "I don't need your help."

Messages that create defensive relationships often take little thought. The more you practice responding with description, the more aware you will become of the work it can take to be mindful and craft messages that reduce defensiveness. That work will pay off in more productive problem-solving and in healthier relationships.

Even celebrity relationships can express a dark side. Singers Rihanna and Chris Brown have been in the news. Their on-again, off-again relationship was highlighted in 2009 when Brown assaulted Rihanna on the night before the Grammy Awards. Brown was arrested for domestic assault. Rather than going to jail, he pleaded guilty to the assault, plea bargained to do community service, and promised that he would undergo counseling. On several occasions before the assault, Rihanna had been seen with injuries and mysterious marks on her body that could have been the result of Brown's physical attacks. Nonetheless, the couple continued the relationship.

Most couples are optimistic when they initiate a relationship. Few people would enter a new relationship they believed was doomed to failure or that could cause them harm. Often the negative behaviors develop gradually. They may begin with harsh words, verbal aggression, or "playful" blows. The person who receives this treatment may rationalize that he or she deserves it. However, the violence generally escalates, and excuses can no longer be made.

©Stock-Asso/Shutterstock RF

Many options exist if you are in an abusive relationship. Consider counseling if you believe your partner is willing and motivated to change. If not, you may want to leave the relationship. Ending an abusive relationship is not a simple matter, however. You need to determine a plan that allows you to leave safely. You may need to enlist the help of family, friends, a social agency such as a crisis center, or the police. You can find help at the National Domestic Violence Hotline at (800) 799-SAFE.

IMPROVING YOUR INTERPERSONAL COMMUNICATION BEHAVIORS

Many of the communication behaviors discussed earlier in this text are important in interpersonal communication. For example, you need to (1) be aware of the role perception plays in relationships, (2) cultivate a good self-concept, (3) provide clear verbal and nonverbal cues to others, and (4) listen attentively and empathically as others provide messages to you.

Some additional behaviors are associated with effective interpersonal communication. For example, in interpersonal relationships you should show affection and support, learn how to influence others, understand how to bargain, and develop behavioral flexibility. Let's consider each of these.

Using Affectionate and Supportive Communication

Affection, the holding of fond or tender feelings toward another person, is essential in interpersonal relationships. You express your affectionate feelings for others nonverbally with touch, hugging, kissing, or caressing. You engage in verbal statements of affection, such as "I care about you," "I really like being with you," or "I love you."

A number of variables affect the appropriateness of statements of affection. Therefore, affectionate communication may be viewed as risk-laden. Among the factors you will consider when you choose to offer affectionate statements are your own and your partner's biological sex, the kind of relationship you have (platonic or romantic), the privacy and emotional intensity of the situation, and your predispositions.[39] Telling another person that you love him or her, for example, may hold significantly different meanings depending on your sex, your partner's sex, your past relationships, the degree of privacy of the situation in which you choose to share your feelings, and the other person's feelings about you.

©Andersen ross/Blend Images LLC RF

Although generally positive, the expression of affection may not always be so.[40] If the receiver of the affectionate message does not respond similarly, the sender may be embarrassed or feel a loss of face. Recall a time when you expressed affection toward another person but that person did not return the same warmth. How did you feel? In general, when people have particular expectations about communicative behavior and those expectations are not met, both trouble and change may follow.[41]

Supportive communication is also important in interpersonal relationships. Support may include giving advice, expressing concern, and offering assistance. Although people generally respond well to supportive communication, the type of support they prefer may vary with the receiver's age[42] and the support provider's goals.[43] In times of distress, comforting messages (suggesting a diversion, offering assistance, expressing empathy, and expressing optimism, for example) may encourage people to feel less upset. At the same time, the recipients of such messages may also feel humiliated or humbled. The distressed person is less likely to be upset about comforting messages when those messages are offered by a close friend rather than an acquaintance.[44] Comfort, then, is viewed as most positive in close interpersonal relationships, rather than in more distant ones.

Influencing Others

You might think that influencing others is generally a goal of public speaking or the mass media. However, influence is important in interpersonal communication as well. In general, **influence** is *the power a person has to affect other people's thinking or actions*. In interpersonal communication, influence has been studied widely. Two forms of influence are especially relevant: compliance-gaining and compliance-resisting.

Compliance-gaining may be defined as *attempts to persuade another person to do something he or she might not ordinarily do*.[45] Compliance-gaining occurs frequently in interpersonal communication. We ask a parent for financial assistance, or we encourage a relational partner to feel more committed. Children become more skillful at identifying situational and personal cues in possible compliance-gaining as they develop, with girls showing more sensitivity than boys.[46]

Compliance-resisting *occurs when targets of influence messages refuse to conform to requests.* When resisting requests, people often offer reasons for their refusal.[47] People who are more sensitive to others and more adaptive are more likely to engage in further attempts to influence, despite the resistance.[48] Indeed, they may address some anticipated obstacles when making their original request, later adapting their attempts to influence by offering counterarguments.

For example, if you are asking a friend to borrow his car, you can consider some of the reasons he might refuse. He might state that he needs his car at the same time you do, that the last time you borrowed his car you returned it with no gas, or that the only time he ever hears from you is when you want something from him. In your initial message, you might suggest to him that you believe you have been neglecting him, that you want to spend some time together, and that you have not been as considerate as you could have been with him. When he suggests that he needs his car at the same time you do, you might offer to use his car at a different time.

Bargaining

Often we engage in bargaining in our interpersonal relationships. **Bargaining** *occurs when two or more parties attempt to reach an agreement on what each should give and receive in the relationship.* Bargains may be explicit and formal, such as the kinds of agreements you reach with others to share tasks, to attend a particular event, or to behave in a specified way. Bargains may also be implicit and informal. For example, in exchange for receiving compliments from your relational partner, you help him or her with math homework. One member of the couple might make delicious evening meals in exchange for the partner's doing all the laundry. You may not even be aware of some of the unstated agreements you have with others.

A study on interpersonal bargaining identified three essential features of a bargaining situation:

1. All parties perceive the possibility of reaching an agreement in which each party would be better off, or no worse off, than if no agreement were reached.
2. All parties perceive more than one such agreement that could be reached.[49]
3. Each party perceives the others as having conflicting preferences or opposed interests.

What are some examples of bargaining situations? You may want to go out with friends when your partner would prefer a quiet evening at home. One member of the couple might prefer to go hiking, whereas the partner is more eager to take a cruise. In each of these instances, the disagreement can be resolved through bargaining.

Maintaining Behavioral Flexibility

Finally, interpersonal communication may be improved through behavioral flexibility. **Behavioral flexibility** is *the ability to adapt to new situations and* *relate in new ways when necessary.*⁵⁰ Behavioral flexibility allows you to relax when you are with friends or to be formal and professional while interviewing for a job. The key to behavioral flexibility may be self-monitoring, or awareness of the effect of your words on the audience in a particular context.

Flexibility is important in a variety of ways. Psychologists have suggested that women and men who are **androgynous**—who *possess both stereotypically male and stereotypically female traits*—are more successful in their interactions than are people who are unyieldingly masculine or absolutely feminine. Flexibility in gender roles is more useful than a static notion of what being a man or woman means in our culture. For instance, if you are a single parent, you may be called on to behave in a loving and nurturing way to your child, regardless of your sex. If your goal is to be a successful manager in a large corporation, you may have to exhibit competitiveness, assertiveness, and a task orientation, regardless of your sex. As you move from interactions with coworkers to interactions with family and friends, you may need to change from traditionally "masculine" behaviors to those that have been considered "feminine."

Behavioral flexibility is especially important in interpersonal communication, because relationships between people are in constant flux. For example, the family structure has gone through sharp changes in recent years. In addition, the United States has an increasingly older population. Changes in the labor force also require new skills and different ways of interacting with others. People travel more often and move more frequently. Finally, social media require enormous changes in how we communicate.

©Lane Oatey/blue Jean Images/Getty Images RF

What kinds of changes can you expect in your own life that will affect your relationships with others? You may change your job ten or more times. You may move your place of residence even more frequently than you change your job. You probably will be married at least once, possibly two or three times. You might have one child or more. You will experience loss of family members through death and dissolution of relationships. You may have a partner whose needs conflict with your own. You may find that social media both help and hinder your interactions with others. Last, other family members may view the world differently than you and challenge your perceptions. When your life appears to be most stable and calm, unexpected changes will occur.

How can behavioral flexibility assist you through life's changes? A flexible person draws on a large repertoire of behaviors. Such an individual is confident about sharing messages with others and about understanding the messages others provide. The flexible person self-discloses only when appropriate. The flexible person can demonstrate listening skills but is not always the one who is listening. The flexible person can show concern for a child who needs assistance, can be assertive on the job, can be yielding when another person needs to exercise control, and can be independent when called on to stand alone.

THE HEALTHY INTERPERSONAL RELATIONSHIP

Can we paint a portrait of a healthy interpersonal relationship? Actually, the material in this chapter gives us some broad brush strokes. First, by definition, and by practice, healthy relationships include people who are mutually dependent on each other. Psychological research demonstrates that healthy dependency includes perceptions of oneself as competent and of others as trustworthy. Healthy dependency results in security in intimacy and confidence in autonomy. Motivationally, a healthy person has a desire for closeness in a relationship, as well as autonomy and self-reliance. Behaviorally, the person functions autonomously but couples this with situation-appropriate help seeking.[51]

Second, individuals in healthy interpersonal relationships are consistent in their patterns of interaction. They do not behave randomly with no explanation. They do not switch from enthusiasm to despair. In general, their partners can predict how they will react to circumstances and to others.

Third, individuals in healthy relationships understand that their relationships will probably last for some time. A parent expects to have a relationship with a child long after the child has moved away from home. Romantic partners are not pursuing a "one night stand"; they want a relationship that can last for a long time, even a lifetime.

Fourth, individuals in healthy relationships understand that their interpersonal communication begins with themselves, and they take responsibility for their role in the relationship. They do not place blame on their partners; rather, they recognize that sometimes they are to blame. Similarly, they share in the positive outcomes of their relationship.

Thus, interpersonal relationships that work operate on the principle that they are transactional. Partners do not blame each other for "starting the battle." Instead, they know that both communicators are continually sending and receiving messages—from each other as well as from other people. A woman who blames her mother-in-law for interfering may not recognize that the mother-in-law seeks a closer relationship with her grandchild. The daughter-in-law and mother-in-law with a healthy relationship talk openly about their needs and how they can both be fulfilled.

In addition, healthy relationships include people who know that their communication includes both content and relationship dimensions. Perhaps your partner calls you by a nickname she's given you, when you are alone together or at home. "Sweetheart" and "dear" have a content dimension—that is, they both refer to you, as does your given name. On the other hand, the relationship dimension of these terms of endearment is also meaningful. Your partner understands this well if she knows that you do or do not appreciate being called "sweetheart" at dinner with friends or in line at the grocery store.

Although healthy relationships do not require that communicators share physical proximity all the time, some time together is likely part of the relationship. Couples today live apart for days, weeks, or even months at a time due to work or other obligations. Generally, though, they plan time to be together. Others begin their relationship online, but most eventually meet and spend time face to face. Most likely, although the jury is not in, healthy relationships include some sharing of physical proximity.

Healthy relational partners know they cannot "delete" or "erase" a careless remark, a hurtful statement, or the admission of caring more for another person. Thus, they are probably somewhat careful in their statements and disclosures. They recognize that communication is irreversible. They also know that, no matter how many times they attempt to "replay" a special day, evening, or even moment, it will not be the same.

Healthy relationships contain some levels of predictability—the knowledge that your friend or partner will help you out when you need it, will respond to your messages, will do what he or she has agreed to do. And partners in healthy relationships are empathic and caring; they demonstrate concerned involvement. They listen without judging. They attempt to put themselves in your shoes. They do not disregard your feelings or experiences. As these relationships develop, the partners are likely to use words like "we" and "us."

©Don Mason/Blend Images LLC RF

Healthy partners avoid hurtful messages. They do not try to create emotional pain or upset, and they do not signal that they want to end the relationship. They do not talk about past relationships, past sexual behavior, or past errors, including breaking the law, in order to provoke or upset their partners.[52] They also avoid deceptive communication. They are not aggressive—standing up for their own rights at the expense of their partner's.[53]

Violent behavior, abusive statements, and bullying are all off-limits. Do not hesitate to seek help if you encounter these behaviors.[54]

More education in building and maintaining healthy relationships—whether from a short course, from continuing education, or online—may be helpful. In addition, many online resources have been created to help couples learn to communicate better in their intimate relationships.[55] Finally, the suggestions listed earlier—using affectionate and supportive communication, learning to influence others in sensitive ways, learning to bargain successfully, and maintaining behavioral flexibility—are all keys to healthy relationships, whether among friends, family members, or lovers.

CHALLENGE YOURSELF

As I explore new relationships in college, how do I talk about sex with potential partners?

The topic of sex is sometimes shrouded in secrecy. But it doesn't have to be difficult to talk openly about sex. And doing so is important to you and your partner's health and safety. Just consider the benefits of an open and honest discussion: Talking about sex can help reduce the prevalence of unprotected sex, the transmission of sexually transmitted infections (STIs), and the occurrence of rape on college campuses.

To get a dialogue going, start by asking questions. Here are some examples of questions you might want to ask your partner, or that he or she may ask you:

- Do you believe sex should occur only after marriage?
- Is sex, for you, about procreation?
- Do you believe sex can be casual?
- Are you comfortable sharing any of your past sexual experiences with me?
- What kinds of sexual activities are you comfortable trying?
- What do you find most enjoyable sexually?
- What sexual activities are off limits and make you uncomfortable?
- How many sexual partners have you had?
- Have you had unprotected sex before?
- Have you ever contracted an STI?
- When was the last time you were tested for STIs?
- How many sexual partners have you had since you were last tested (or treated) for an STI?
- Are you willing to get tested again, together, before being sexually active?

Although it's important to talk honestly when you are beginning a sexual relationship, you should never feel pressured to talk about sex, or to have sex, before you feel ready. When you are ready, be open with your partner about what you need and want. During these conversations, use nonverbal behavior that communicates that you are listening without judgment.

CHAPTER REVIEW

Countless social scientific investigations provide insight into the components of a healthy relationship. In this chapter, you learned that the difference between a failed relationship and a healthy one frequently depends on the partners' communication skills. Relationships include three stages: development, maintenance, and deterioration. And some relationships have a dark side. The good news is that you can improve your interpersonal communication and the health of your relationships by reducing defensiveness and by knowing the difference between a healthy relationship and an unhealthy or abusive one.

KEY TERMS

interpersonal communication, 75
interpersonal relationships, 75
interdependence, 75
initiating stage, 80
proximity, 80
attractiveness, 80
responsiveness, 80
similarity, 80
complementarity, 80
experimentation stage, 81
intensifying stage, 81
self-disclosure, 81
integration stage, 82
bonding stage, 82
relational maintenance, 82
dialectic theory, 82
autonomy and connectedness, 82
novelty and predictability, 82
turning point, 82
hurtful messages, 84
deceptive communication, 84
aggressiveness, 84
argumentativeness, 84
defensiveness, 84
differentiating stage, 84
circumscribing stage, 85
stagnation stage, 85
avoidance stage, 85
termination, 85
codependency, 86
influence, 89
compliance-gaining, 89
compliance-resisting, 90
bargaining, 90
behavioral flexibility, 90
androgynous, 91

STUDY QUESTIONS

1. Define interpersonal communication and interpersonal relationships. What is the connection between the two?
2. How do your interpersonal relationships differ from those of your parents and grandparents? What are some factors that account for these differences?
3. Describe the stages of relational development, maintenance, and deterioration.
4. What are the characteristics of a dark relationship? Why do people sometimes become entangled in such relationships?
5. How can you improve your interpersonal behaviors?
6. Describe some of the components of a healthy relationship. Are any of these components reflected in your own relationships?

ENDNOTES

1. Burleson, B. R. (2010). The nature of interpersonal communication: A message-centered approach. In C. R. Berger, M. E. Roloff, and D. R. Ewoldsen (Eds.), *The handbook of communication science* (2nd ed., pp. 145–163). Thousand Oaks, CA: Sage.

2. Burleson, B. R. (2010). The nature of interpersonal communication: A message-centered approach. In C. R. Berger, M. E. Roloff, and D. R. Ewoldsen (Eds.), *The handbook of communication science* (2nd ed., pp. 145–163). Thousand Oaks, CA: Sage.
3. Sponcil, M. & Priscilla, G. (2013). Use of social media by college students: Relationship to communication and self-concept. *Journal of Technology Research, 4*, 1–13.
4. Mongeau, P. A., Knight, K., Williams, J., Eden, J., & Shawn, C. (2013). Identifying and explicating variation among friends with benefits relationships. *The Journal of Sex Research, 50*, 37–47.
5. Fahs, B., & Munger, A. (2015). Friends with benefits? Gendered performances in women's casual sexual relationships. *Personal Relationships, 22*, 188–203.
6. Hughes, M., Morrison, K., & Asada, K. J. K. (2005). What's love got to do with it? Exploring the impact of maintenance rules, love attitudes, and network support on friends with benefits relationships. *Western Journal of Communication, 69*, 49–66.
7. Nice, M. L., & Katzev, R. (2009). *Internet romances: The frequency and nature of romantic online relationships*. Retrieved from www.scribd.com/doc/10983206/Internet_Romances_The_Frequency_and_Nature_of_Romantic_Online_Relationships
8. U.S. Census Bureau (2011). Frequent asked questions about same-sex couples households. *US Census Bureau*. Retrieved from http://www.census.gov/hhes/samesex/files/SScplfactsheet_final.pdf
9. Retrieved from www.urban.org/publications/1000491.html
10. Centers for Disease Control and Prevention. *National marriage and divorce rate trends*. Retrieved from https://www.cdc.gov/nchs/nvss/marriage_divorce_tables.htm
11. Missouri Families.org. *Relationships: Quick answers*. Retrieved from http://missourifamilies.org/quick/divorceqa/
12. Wilcox, W. B. (2010). *The state of our unions: Marriage in America 2010*. Charlottesville, VA, & New York: National Marriage Project and Institute for American Values.
13. Armario, C. (2011, April 28). Single parents raise 25% of US children. *The Boston Globe*. Retrieved from www.boston.com/news/nation/articles/2011/04/28/single_parents_raise_25_of_us_children; Mather, M. (2010, May). *Population Reference Bureau: U.S. children in single-mother families*. Retrieved from www.prb.org/Publications/PolicyBriefs/singlemotherfamilies.aspx
14. Miller, G. R. (1976). *Explorations in interpersonal communication*. Beverly Hills, CA: Sage.
15. Knapp, M. L. (1978). *Social intercourse: From greeting to goodbye*. Needham Heights, MA: Allyn & Bacon.
16. McCroskey, J. C., & McCain, T. A. (1974). The measurement of interpersonal attraction. *Speech Monographs, 41*, 267–276.
17. Fox, J., Warber, K. M., & Makstaller, D. C. (2013). The role of Facebook in romantic relationship development: An exploration of Knapp's relational stage model. *Journal of Social and Personal Relationships, 30*, 771–794.
18. Solomon, D. H., Knobloch, L. K., Theiss, J. A., & McLaren, R. M. (2016). Relational turbulence theory: Exploring variation in subjective experience and communication within romantic relationships. *Human Communication Research, 42*, 507–532.
19. Lane, B. L., Piercy, C. W., & Carr, C. T. (2016). Making it Facebook official: The warranting value of online relationship status disclosures on relational characteristics. *Computers in Human Behavior, 56*, 1–8.
20. Fox, J. F., Warber, K. M., & Makstaller, D. C. (2013). The role of Facebook in romantic relationship development: An exploration of Knapp's relational stage model. *Journal of Social and Personal Relationships, 30*, 771–794.

21. Montgomery, B. M., & Baxter, L. A. (1998). *Dialectic approaches to studying personal relationships*. Mahwah, NJ: Erlbaum.

22. See, for example, Bullis, C., Clark, C., & Sline, R. (1993). From passion to commitment: Turning points in romantic relationships. In P. Kalbfleisch (Ed.), *Interpersonal communication: Evolving interpersonal relationships* (pp. 213–236). Hillsdale, NJ: Erlbaum; Surra, C. A. (1985). Courtship types. Variations in interdependence between partners and social networks. *Journal of Personality and Social Psychology, 49*, 357–375; Surra, C. A. (1987). Reasons for changes in commitment. Variations by courtship style. *Journal of Social and Personal Relationships, 4*, 17–33; Surra, C. A., Arizzi, P., & Asmussen, L. A. (1988). The association between reasons for commitment and the development and outcome of marital relationships. *Journal of Social and Personal Relationships, 5*, 47–63; Surra, C. A., & Hughes, D. K. (1997). Commitment processes in accounts of the development of premarital relationships. *Journal of Marriage and the Family, 59*, 5–21.

23. Baxter, L. A., & Pittman, G. (2001). Communicatively remembering turning points of relational development in heterosexual romantic relationships. *Communication Reports, 14*, 4.

24. Duck, S. (1994). Meaningful relationships: Talking, sense, and relating. Thousand Oaks, CA: Sage; Duck, S., & Sants, H. (1983). On the origin of the specious: Are personal relationships really interpersonal states? *Journal of Social and Clinical Psychology, 1*, 27–41.

25. Perse, E. M., & Rubin, R. B. (1989). Attribution in social and parasocial relationships. *Communication Research, 16*, 59–77.

26. Davis, M. H., & Oathout, H. A. (1987). Maintenance of satisfaction in romantic relationships: Empathy and relational competence. *Journal of Personality and Social Psychology, 53*, 397–498.

27. Ledbetter, A. (2017). Relational maintenance behavior and shared TV viewing as mediators of the association between romanticism and romantic relationship quality. *Communication Studies, 68*, 95–114.

28. McEwan, B. (2016). ILY & can u pick up some milk: Effects of relational maintenance via text messaging on relational satisfaction and closeness in dating partners. *Southern Communication Journal, 81*, 168–181.

29. Pearson, J. C. (1992). *Lasting love: What keeps couples together*. Dubuque, IA: William C. Brown.

30. Sillars, A., Shellen, W., McIntosh, A., & Pomegranate, M. (1997). Relational characteristics of language: Elaboration and differentiation in marital conversations. *Western Journal of Communication, 61*, 403–422.

31. Infante, D. A., & Rancer, A. S. (1982). A conceptualization and measure of argumentativeness. *Journal of Personality Assessment, 45*, 72–80.

32. Gibb, J. R. (1991). *Trust: A new vision of human relationships for business, education, family, and personal living* (2nd ed.). North Hollywood, CA: Newcastle.

33. Brody, N., LeFebvre, L. E., & Blackburn, K. G. (2016). Social network site behaviors across the relational lifespan: Measurement and association with relationship escalation and de-escalation. *Social Media and Society*, 1–16.

34. Frost, D. M., Rubin, J. D., & Darcangelo, N. (2016). Making meaning of significant events in past relationships. *Journal of Social and Personal Relationships, 33*, 938–960.

35. Gibb, J. R. (1991). *Trust: A new vision of human relationships for business, education, family, and personal living* (2nd ed.). North Hollywood, CA: Newcastle.

36. White, G. L. (2008). Romantic jealousy: Therapists' perceptions of causes, consequences, and treatments. *Journal of Couple and Relationship Therapy, 7,* 210–229.
37. Spitzberg, B. H., & Cupach, W. R. (2007). *The dark side of interpersonal communication* (2nd ed.). Mahwah, NJ: Erlbaum.
38. Omand, G. (2017, January 25). Amanda Todd case: Dutch trial starts for man suspected of cyberbullying. *Vancouver Sun.* Retrieved from http://www.vancouversun.com
39. Floyd, K. (1997). Affectionate communication in nonromantic relationships: Influences of communicator, relational, and contextual factors. *Western Journal of Communication, 61,* 279–298; Floyd, K. (1997). Communicating affection in dyadic relationships: An assessment of behavior and expectancies. *Communication Quarterly, 45,* 68–80; Floyd, K., & Morman, M. T. (1998). The measurement of affectionate communication. *Communication Quarterly, 46,* 144–162; Floyd, K., & Morman, M. T. (2000). Reacting to the verbal expression of affection in same-sex interaction. *Southern Communication Journal, 65,* 287–299.
40. Floyd, K., & Burgoon, J. K. (1999). Reacting to nonverbal expressions of liking: A test of interaction adaptation theory. *Communication Monographs, 66,* 219–239.
41. LePoire, B. A., & Yoshimura, S. M. (1999). The effects of expectancies and actual communication on nonverbal adaptation and communication outcomes: A test of interaction adaptation theory. *Communication Monographs, 66,* 1–30.
42. Caplan, S. E., & Samter, W. (1999). The role of facework in younger and older adults' evaluations of social support messages. *Communication Quarterly, 47,* 245–264.
43. MacGeorge, E. L. (2001). Support providers' interaction goals: The influence of attributions and emotions. *Communication Monographs, 68,* 72–97.
44. Clark, R. A., Pierce, K. F., Hsu, K., Toosley, A., & Williams, L. (1998). The impact of alternative approaches to comforting, closeness of relationship, and gender on multiple measures of effectiveness. *Communication Studies, 49,* 224–239.
45. Wilson, S. R. (1998). Introduction to the special issue on seeking and resisting compliance: The vitality of compliance-gaining research. *Communication Studies, 49,* 273–275.
46. Marshall, L. J., & Levy, V. M., Jr. (1998). The development of children's perceptions of obstacles in compliance-gaining interactions. *Communication Studies, 49,* 342–357.
47. Saeki, M., & O'Keefe, B. (1994). Refusals and rejections: Designing messages to serve multiple goals. *Human Communication Research, 21,* 67–102.
48. Ifert, D. E., & Roloff, M. E. (1997). Overcoming expressed obstacles to compliance: The role of sensitivity to the expressions of others and ability to modify self-presentation. *Communication Quarterly, 45,* 55–67.
49. Deusch, M., & Kraus, R. M. (1962). Studies of interpersonal bargaining. *Journal of Conflict Resolution, 6,* 52.
50. Pearson, J. C. (1983). *Interpersonal communication: Clarity, confidence, concern.* Glenview, IL: Scott, Foresman.
51. Haggerty, G., Blake, M., & Siefert, C. J. (2010). Convergent and divergent validity of the relationship profile test: Investigating the relationship with attachment, interpersonal distress, and psychological health. *Journal of Clinical Psychology, 66,* 339–354.
52. Anderson, M., Kunkel, A., & Dennis, M. R. (2011). "Let's (not) talk about that": Bridging the past sexual experiences taboo to build healthy relationships. *Journal of Sex Research, 48,* 381–391.

53. Schneider, I. K., Konijn, E. A., Righetti, F., & Rusbult, C. E. (2011). A healthy dose of trust: The relationship between interpersonal trust and health. *Personal Relationships, 18,* 668–676.
54. Cleary Bradley, R. P., & Gottman, J. M. (2012). Reducing situational violence in low-income couples by fostering healthy relationships. *Journal of Marital and Family Therapy, 38,* 187–198.
55. Hawkins, A. J., & Ooms, T. (2012). Can marriage and relationship education be an effective policy tool to help low-income couples form and sustain healthy marriages and relationships? A review of lessons learned. *Marriage and Family Review, 48,* 524–554.

Blue and Yellow Cube Icon, Connecting Globally Icon, Mountain Icon, Chapter Review Arrows Circle Icon: ©McGraw Hill Education

chapter 6

Intercultural Communication

©Darren Calabrese/The Canadian Press/AP Photo

Technology extends both our ability and our need to interact with people around the globe. On a daily basis, we are likely to connect with people from a variety of racial, ethnic, religious, and cultural backgrounds. The goal of this chapter is to increase your confidence and your ability to do so while making meaningful connections along the way.

LEARNING OBJECTIVES
After reading this chapter, you should be able to:

- Define and explain the differences among culture, race, ethnicity, and co-culture.
- Explain why the study of intercultural communication is important.
- Explain the three most common reasons for intercultural communication problems.
- Identify four broad characteristics that distinguish cultures from each other.
- Name strategies for improving communication with people from other cultures.

DEFINING INTERCULTURAL COMMUNICATION

Intercultural communication refers to *interactions between people from different cultural backgrounds.* This kind of communication occurs, for example, when a businessperson raised in the United States works with a Japanese businessperson on a mutually beneficial project. It also occurs when a U.S. student works on a school project with a student raised in Somalia, Pakistan, Mexico, or China. To accomplish mutual goals, they must adapt to their differences in language, attitudes about work, and culture-based customs.

A **culture** is *a unique combination of traditions and customs that is transmitted through learning and that shapes the beliefs and behavior of the people who live within it.* Cuba is a country, but we also regard the Cuban people as having a culture, because they speak Spanish, most are Roman Catholic, and they live under a Communist political system, eat particular foods, have close-knit families, and have a sense of a shared culture.

©Aruna Bhat/Alamy

Cultures develop in countries, or nation-states, over time such that the people who live there share similarities that come to characterize them. Language is a significant unifying feature of a culture. Japan has a single language, which dominates and therefore unifies the people who speak it. Religion, too, can be a significant unifying cultural feature, as Buddhism is in Thailand and Islam is in Saudi Arabia. Thus, a combination of features, such as language, religion, customs related to family, and dietary practices, creates a culture.

Two closely related terms that sometimes overlap and cause confusion are *race* and *ethnicity*. The concept of **race** generally refers to biological characteristics—in this sense, it refers to *a category of people distinguished by inherited features, such as skin color, facial features, or quality of hair.* But scientific evidence for racial distinctions is very weak. On close examination, the concept of race is vague, and it can be difficult to determine what the categories should be. For example, should "Hispanic" be considered a race? For one approach to this question, see **Figure 6.1**.

It can also be difficult to determine who belongs in which category and where the boundaries are between them. For example, we think of former President Barack Obama as African American; however, his father was African and his mother was Caucasian. He is only one among many Americans whose ancestors came from all corners of the world, bearing multiple variations of skin color, facial features, and hair qualities. As you can see in **Figure 6.1**, the Census

Figure 6.1 Reproduction of the Questions on Hispanic Origin and Race from the 2010 Census

→ **NOTE: Please answer BOTH Question 5 about Hispanic origin and Question 6 about race. For this census, Hispanic origins are not races.**

5. Is this person of Hispanic, Latino, or Spanish origin?
- ☐ **No**, not of Hispanic, Latino, or Spanish origin
- ☐ Yes, Mexican, Mexican Am., Chicano
- ☐ Yes, Puerto Rican
- ☐ Yes, Cuban
- ☐ Yes, another Hispanic, Latino, or Spanish origin — *Print origin, for example, Argentinean, Colombian, Dominican, Nicaraguan, Salvadoran, Spaniard, and so on.* ↗

6. What is this person's race? *Mark* ☒ *one or more boxes.*
- ☐ White
- ☐ Black, African Am., or Negro
- ☐ American Indian or Alaska Native — *Print name of enrolled or principal tribe.* ↗

- ☐ Asian Indian ☐ Japanese ☐ Native Hawaiian
- ☐ Chinese ☐ Korean ☐ Guamanian or Chamorro
- ☐ Filipino ☐ Vietnamese ☐ Samoan
- ☐ Other Asian — *Print race, for example, Hmong, Laotian, Thai, Pakistani, Cambodian, and so on.* ↗ ☐ Other Pacific Islander — *Print race, for example, Fijian, Tongan, and so on.* ↗

- ☐ Some other race— *Print race.* ↗

Source: U.S. Census Bureau, 2010 Census questionnaire.

©McGraw-Hill Education

Bureau acknowledges this fact by allowing people to check more than one box. Even more problematic than who fits where is the fact that, in the early nineteenth century, so-called racial differences came to be associated with differences in health, intelligence, and personality. Many societal ills, including stereotyping and prejudice (discussed later in the chapter), have flowed from such ideas, but there is no scientific evidence to support them.

In contrast to race, which is associated with physical features, the concept of ethnicity is related to cultural ones. An **ethnic group** *consists of people who share common cultural elements—for example, language or religion—as well as a common history.* Jewish, Irish, Polish, and Greek people are often referred to as belonging to ethnic groups. Within the category "Asian," which was once considered a single race, there are multiple, diverse cultures and ethnicities: Japanese, Chinese, Vietnamese, Thai, Korean, and so on (**Figure 6.1**). As you can see, the terms *race*, *ethnicity*, and *culture* can overlap, and there are no simple rules for sorting all this out. Some people identify their race or ethnicity by where their parents or grandparents came from, but many of us don't know all the threads of ancestry that produced us—for example, that somewhere three, four, or five generations back we had an ancestor who was Native American, Turkish, or Irish.

In all societies, we encounter the concept of a **dominant culture**, *the group that has the most power, influence, and rights*. In the United States, the dominant culture is composed of white, educated males who are employed, usually in managerial or professional occupations. The dominant group tends to make rules that work to its advantage, whether in the context of business, government, school, or the family. Religion can sometimes influence perceptions of dominant culture. For example, in the United States, most of the population (over 78 percent of people) identify with Christianity. Therefore, in the United States other religious groups are part of nondominant co-cultural groups.[1]

Nondominant, or **co-cultural**, **groups** are *made up of people in a region or area who have less power and influence,* for one reason or another. Examples of co-cultural groups in the United States include, but are not limited to women, ethnic minorities, gay and lesbian individuals, immigrants and refugees, persons who are physically or mentally challenged, and even neighborhood gangs and political groups that have formed to promote a cause. Those who are outside the dominant culture often are subjected to unequal treatment.

Individuals in a dominant cultural group in one area could be a part of a co-cultural group in another part of the world. For example, in Japan, Christians are a co-cultural minority group in a country where over 70 percent of people practice Buddhism.[2] Whereas dominant groups create rules, policies, and practices that perpetuate the continued existence of the dominant interests, the interests of co-cultural groups requires more care and attention to ensure their protection. Thus, understanding dominant and co-cultural groups requires sensitivity to the demographic makeup of an area, and to the lived experiences of people who do not hold positions of power or are unable to speak on behalf of their own interests.

Women are an unusual "co-culture" in the United States, because they outnumber men; yet women are classified as a co-culture because they have not been equal to men in terms of power, influence, and earning ability. Unlike many third-world countries, such as India, Pakistan, and Brazil, the United States has

Table 6.1	Women as a Co-Culture in the United States[4]
▪ The United States has more women than men (157 million vs. 152 million males).
▪ Women have more high school diplomas, bachelor's degrees, and master's degrees than men (31 million vs. 29 million for males), but males earn more doctorates and professional degrees.
▪ Women earn 79% of male salaries, a difference of more than 20%.
▪ Women's entry-level pay is about the same as men's, but college-educated women start to fall behind at 30 years of age.
▪ College-educated women hit a glass ceiling salary level of $60,000 per year at age 39, whereas men's salaries don't peak until 48 years of age, at an average of $95,000.

never had a female president. The Senate and House of Representatives have fewer women than do the parliaments of other countries, and large corporations and their boards of directors are very heavily male. Last but not least, women have never received equal pay (**Table 6.1**). Feminist scholar Cheris Kramarae, a communication professor, noted long ago that women are a "muted group," largely ignored in the workplace and often unheard even in group discussions.[3]

The Amish in America are also a co-culture and might be considered an ethnic group. The Amish people share religious beliefs, are relatively isolated from the dominant culture, have strict practices related to their dress and work, and have common German origins.

©Joe Raedle/Getty Images

Gay, lesbian, bisexual, and transgender individuals in the United States can also be considered a co-culture, as their sexuality unifies them, although contrasting with the heterosexuality of the dominant culture. Although this group is gaining rights, its members have faced extensive discrimination and have not yet achieved full and equal rights under the law in comparison to heterosexual individuals.

Why pay attention to co-cultures? First, democratic societies like ours are enriched by diversity and multiple unique contributions. Once banned by law, homosexuality has become increasingly accepted in American culture. Celebrities such Anderson Cooper on CNN, Jim Parsons on *The Big Bang Theory*, and Neil Patrick Harris[5] on *How I Met Your Mother* are among the many openly gay or lesbian celebrities who educate and entertain us. In 2016, Colton Haynes, a popular character on *Teen Wolf* and *The Arrow*, disclosed that he was gay.[6] If we do not learn to accept and appreciate those who differ from us, we limit our opportunities to advance, both personally and professionally.

CHALLENGE YOURSELF

How do I effectively confront and speak out against prejudice or hate speech?

Speech that expresses discriminatory or hateful views can make people feel disrespected and unsafe. While it's important to confront hate speech when you encounter it, doing so is not always easy or effective. How you choose to confront hateful speech will depend on the following factors:

- **Do you think the discriminatory language was used intentionally, or unintentionally?** Let's say someone makes a joke before considering how others might be hurt by it. In such a case a simple reminder can have the right impact. On the other hand, if someone says something purposefully hateful, a stronger message might be in order. If you overhear someone demeaning people with disabilities, you might respond by saying, "I don't appreciate your language. I find it disrespectful and inappropriate."

- **How important is the relationship?** If you care about the person who made the remark, you might try to influence that person's perspectives over time. If you have a relative who strongly dislikes anyone who is gay, and you are someone who wishes to create a culture of inclusiveness and respect, you might say: "We have different opinions about this issue. Can we agree to disagree on our perspectives and try not to offend one another when we spend time together?" If you do not have a close relationship with the person, you might be more direct and explain that intolerance and hate speech is simply unacceptable. Keep in mind that people often take incremental steps in changing their own deeply held opinions. If you want to maintain the relationship, be patient.

- **What keeps us from speaking up?** The *bystander effect* occurs when people are less likely to step in and help a victim, or speak up on that person's behalf, when they are in large groups. Remaining silent communicates an unchallenged assumption of agreement with hate speech. Are you comfortable with the assumptions that others might have if you choose not to speak up?

What might you do in a scenario in which all of these factors apply? For example, how might you respond to a close family member who says hurtful things about marginalized groups at family gatherings? Try a combination of the strategies recommended above. If these don't work, as a last resort you might decide to limit your contact with that person. In some circumstances, creating distance is the best solution for everyone involved.

No matter what strategies you choose, don't forget about the victims of hate speech. When you witness hate speech, tell the person who is the target that what was said is unacceptable. Ask if there is anything you can do to help support him or her. These messages go a long way.

Your voice has power. Speaking up can help create a more inclusive, accepting, and hospitable society, one where difference is seen as a source of strength rather than weakness.

STUDYING INTERCULTURAL COMMUNICATION

Not long ago, only select groups concerned themselves with intercultural communication—missionaries, jet-setting business executives, foreign correspondents, and political figures. Now, however, developments in technology have made intercultural and co-cultural communication more possible and more likely

©Fuse/Getty Images RF

than ever before. Around the world, people can cheaply communicate with each other on the Internet. Phone, video, and audio merge into a system that can allow for sight and sound. Cell phones, tablets, and laptop computers bring communication technology to our fingertips. Shifts in demographics, too, have created a world in which almost everyone engages in intercultural communication in their daily lives.

In short, we have increasingly been introduced to a variety of ethnic, national, and political groups. And this has occurred because of advancing technology, transnational jobs, international conflicts, military and humanitarian service, and the presence of immigrants, refugees, and new citizens in our communities. The national events on September 11, 2001, in particular, changed our perceptions of the world. Americans discovered that they knew little about the Islamic religion or the people of Afghanistan, Iraq, and Saudi Arabia and realized that they needed to educate themselves. Moreover, the composition of the U.S. population has shifted and continues to shift. As you can see in **Figure 6.2**, the percentage of Hispanics as compared with non-Hispanics has been increasing since 2000 and is projected to continue to increase.

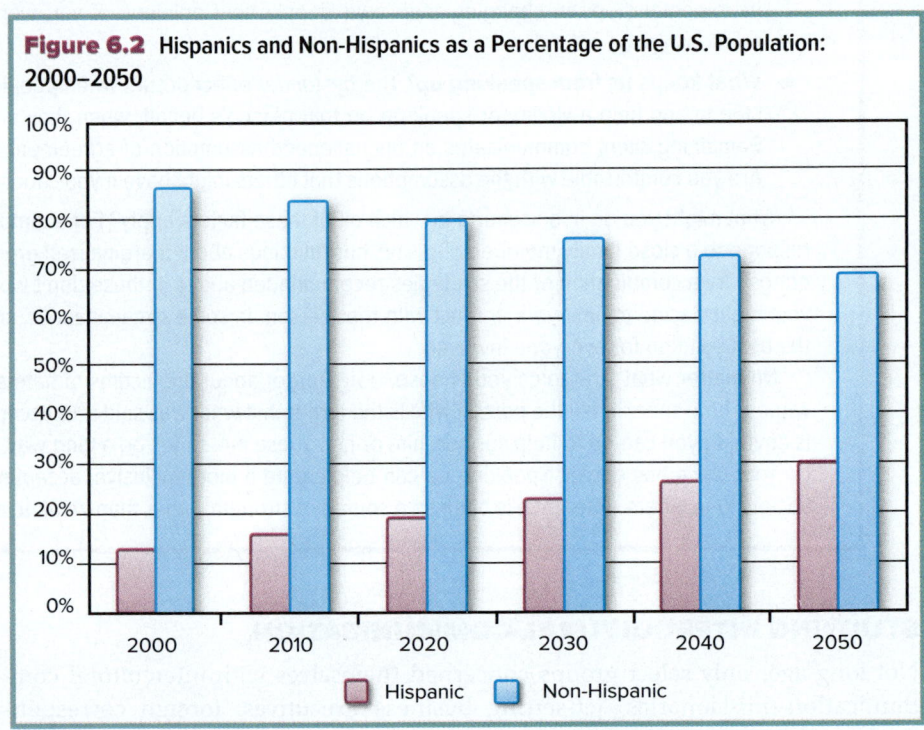

Figure 6.2 Hispanics and Non-Hispanics as a Percentage of the U.S. Population: 2000–2050

SOURCE: Congressional Research Service Report for Congress. (2011). Retrieved from **www.fas.org/sgp/crs/misc/RL32701.pdf**

Today chances are excellent that you will at least occasionally encounter individuals from unfamiliar groups—not just in the news but in your everyday life. Thus, you will need to know the basics of intercultural communication. In metropolitan Washington, DC, your server may be from Colombia, South America; your bus driver may be from Ethiopia; the student sitting next to you may be from the Sudan; and the cashier at the grocery store may have come from Vietnam. The story is similar in Miami, New York City, Detroit, and Chicago. America is now (and always was) an exotic salad with many cultures contributing to its overall flavor. The first reason, then, for studying intercultural communication is that communication with people from other cultures and co-cultures is becoming increasingly common.

A second reason to study intercultural communication relates to the economy. The United States sells corn, wheat, and cars in Asia and buys coffee from Colombia, bananas from Costa Rica, and oil from Africa, the Middle East, and South America. Much of our clothing comes from China and Panama, our shoes from Mexico, and our cars from Germany, Hungary, or Canada. Business is increasingly global, which means that you will almost certainly find yourself working with people from many cultures.

A third reason to study intercultural communication is, simply, curiosity about others. What does it mean to wear a turban or a headscarf? Why don't some people eat meat? Why do people from some cultures bow, whereas others shake hands or kiss? People from some cultures stand close when they converse; others maintain more physical distance. People from some cultures respect silence, whereas others avoid it. Learning about intercultural communication means that we can become better informed about our world.

BIASES THAT AFFECT INTERCULTURAL COMMUNICATION

Ethnocentrism

The most common problem that occurs during intercultural communication is **ethnocentrism**, *the belief that your own group or culture is superior to all other groups or cultures.* Common examples include the attitude that everyone in the world should speak English and the related idea that people in the United States should not have to learn languages other than English; that foods eaten in other cultures are disgusting rather than practical, nutritious, or even delicious; and that the Asian custom of bowing is odd, rather than something to try to understand.[7]

We cannot avoid operating to some extent from an ethnocentric perspective, but problems arise when we judge other cultures as inferior, rather than simply different. Generally, a lack of interaction with people from other cultures fosters high levels of ethnocentrism and encourages the notion of cultural superiority, which in turn creates defensiveness and barriers between communication partners.[8] One way to reduce ethnocentrism is to engage with and learn about other cultures. Take a semester studying abroad, or enroll in an intercultural communication course where a deeper appreciation for diversity and difference can be cultivated.[9]

In contrast to ethnocentrism, in which we use our own culture as the measure that others are expected to meet, **cultural relativism** involves *viewing other cultures as objectively as possible, without judgment.* It's a standard set by anthropologists and other social scientists as they work to describe a culture from the point of view of someone living within it. The foods of another culture; the style of dress; and the beliefs and practices regarding the family, the role of women, and punishment and criminal behavior are all cultural elements that social scientists attempt to view objectively, without judgment, in order to understand them in the context of that culture.

On the other hand, social scientists may strive to meet the standard of cultural relativism in their work, but they can still take moral stands or make moral judgments about another culture's beliefs or practices. For example, no social scientist needs to view violence against women or children as acceptable just because it occurs in someone else's culture. Ethnocentrism and cultural relativism are two ends of a spectrum. The ideal for intercultural communication

BUILDER

REFLECT ON YOUR OWN CULTURAL IDENTITY

Each of us is a product of our culture. Our cultural identities are shaped by characteristics that include race and ethnicity, religion, gender, skin color, and age, and these in turn influence how we see and respond to others. To better understand your cultural self and your own biases, complete the following exercise.

- Draw a circle in the middle of a piece of paper and write your name in it. Radiating out from this circle, draw other circles. In each of those, list aspects of yourself that define who you are. Examples include your gender identity, your country of origin or ancestry, your marital status, your religion or spiritual beliefs, your role in your family (mother, father, daughter, etc.), and your race or ethnicity.
- Reflect on why these aspects of yourself are important to you. How do they shape you?
- How do these aspects of your identity affect the way you view the world? For example, if you are a mother, does that affect your ideas about family? If you are biracial, how does that identity affect your view of race? How do you feel if someone ignores or disrespects one aspect of your identity?
- How does your identity influence your attitudes and beliefs about others? For example, if you are religious, are you able to appreciate the values of those who are not?
- Is there any aspect of cultural identity about which you are conscious of your own biases? What could you do to challenge these biases?

Asking yourself such questions can help you better understand your own complex cultural identity, as well as make you more aware of the cultural identities of others. Reflecting on these aspects of identity, and the biases they might inform, will deepen your cultural sensitivity.

lies somewhere between, in the acknowledgment that other people's values and norms may differ from your own but that, with respectful curiosity, people can work toward understanding.

©Joseph Turs/Getty Images RF

Stereotyping

Ethnocentrism is not the only bias people bring to intercultural communication. Equally dangerous is the tendency to stereotype, or generalize, all individuals in a group from the characteristics of a few. The result of stereotyping is that all members of the group are viewed in a limited way, especially if the stereotype is negative. Unfortunately, examples of negative stereotyping are all over the news. The Trump administration's recent ban of people from certain Muslim-majority countries reflects the negative stereotype that people from the Middle East, and Muslims specifically, are more likely to be violent extremists. As of 2010, 1.6 billion people belonged to the Muslim faith, making it the second largest religion in the world after Christianity.[10] And although, of these 1.6 billion, only a very few have committed terrorist acts on American soil, fear and a lack of familiarity has helped stereotyping to persist.

Even "positive" stereotypes can be insulting or limiting. For example, not all Jewish people are wealthy, not all Asians are gifted at math, and not all black Americans are great athletes. As you would expect, most people resent negative comments being made about them, whether as individuals or as members of a social group. In one study, however, participants also responded negatively to positive comments about their social group, if the comments reflected a stereotype.[11] People do not like being robbed of their individuality and being diminished to only one aspect of their identity.

If you feel that you are being stereotyped, what can you do? In one study, confrontation was a helpful strategy for both parties. Perhaps simply stating directly that the language being used or the assumptions being made make you uncomfortable or simply do not hold true in your experience. Confrontations of this kind should always be carried out with respect, never with aggressive words or actions. Although the person making a stereotyping comment may initially respond negatively to the person doing the confronting, he or she may be more hesitant to make such comments in the future.[12]

Prejudice

Whereas ethnocentrism involves thinking that your culture is better than others and stereotyping is viewing all members of a group as alike, the closely related concept of **prejudice** is *a negative attitude toward a group of people just because they belong to that group.* Often the people on the receiving end of prejudice belong to marginalized minority groups—people in poverty, people of color, people who speak a language other than English, gay men and lesbian women—but sometimes the group being discriminated against is larger than the group that exhibits the prejudice.

For example, as discussed earlier, in many countries, including the United States, women are subject to prejudicial treatment in the form of lower pay and fewer opportunities for corporate advancement, even though they are a majority. Much more so than men, women are also subject to demeaning and degrading comments related to their gender, as well as sexual objectification in the media, and women experience depression, anger, and lower self-esteem because of such prejudices.[13]

As with ethnocentrism and stereotyping, prejudice is often based in ignorance. That is, the person expressing the prejudice simply does not know much about the target of the prejudice, or the person simply dismisses the target group as deserving of its inferior status. Women and African Americans have made some headway against prejudice, but stereotypical attitudes and assumptions are hard to eliminate: you can see this when someone assumes that a man—not a woman—is the manager or owner of a business, that an African American man standing beside a luxury car is someone's driver, or that a Mexican man on a street corner must be a day laborer.

CHARACTERISTICS THAT DISTINGUISH ONE CULTURE FROM ANOTHER

Accepting that your own culture is not superior to, just different from, another person's culture is one way to improve your intercultural communication. Another way is to understand some of the values and norms of other cultures.

Suppose you are an American teaching in Japan. Your students' first assignment is to give a speech before the class. Even though you don't tell them to do so, they form groups and each group selects a spokesperson to give the speech. In contrast, in the United States, students would be unlikely to turn a public speaking assignment into a small-group activity unless specifically directed to do so. Neither behavior pattern is right or wrong; both are rooted in the culture of the country. If you didn't know anything about the norms and customs of the Japanese culture, you could be baffled by your students' behavior.

In this section, you will learn about four characteristics that distinguish cultures from each other: individualism versus collectivism, uncertainty-accepting versus uncertainty-rejecting, implicit rulemaking versus explicit rulemaking, and M-time versus P-time orientations. Keep in mind that these characteristics are general tendencies; they are not always true of a culture and are not true of everyone in a culture.

Individualistic vs. Collectivist Cultures

Much of what is known about individualistic and collectivist cultures comes from a study in 1980 of more than 100,000 managers from 40 countries.[14]

Although neither China nor Africa was included, the study is a classic in its comprehensiveness.

Individualistic cultures *value individual freedom, choice, uniqueness, and independence*. These cultures place "I" before "we" and value competition over cooperation, private property over public or state-owned property, individual achievement over group accomplishments, and individual opinion over what anyone else might think. In an individualistic society, people are likely to leave the family home or geographic area in which they were raised to pursue their dreams, they have only limited loyalty to organizations, they are unafraid of moving for advancement, and they may leave religious institutions that no longer meet their needs.

Loyalty to other people also has limits. Individualistic cultures have high rates of divorce and unmarried parents. Individualistic cultures have sayings like, "God helps those who help themselves," and "The squeaky wheel gets the grease," both of which favor individual action over group cooperation. According to this 1980 study, the top-ranking individualistic cultures are those of the United States, Australia, Great Britain, Canada, and the Netherlands.[15]

Collectivist cultures, in contrast, *value the group over the individual*. These cultures place "we" before "I" and value commitment to family, tribe, and clan; people in collectivist cultures tend to be loyal to their spouse, employer, community, and country. They value cooperation over competition, as well as group-defined social norms and duties over personal opinions.[16] It can be more difficult for someone in a collectivist culture to voice disagreement with a group, because doing so means calling out an individual difference rather than demonstrating harmony with the group as a whole.[17] Illustrating collectivist cultures are the Ethiopian proverb, "When spider webs unite, they can tie up a lion," and the Asian saying, "The nail that sticks up gets hit by the hammer." The Ethiopian proverb enforces the idea that collective action brings surprisingly powerful results, and the Asian saying discourages individual action over that of the group. The highest-ranking collectivist cultures in the 1980 study were those of Venezuela, Pakistan, Peru, Taiwan, and Thailand.[18]

Uncertainty-Accepting vs. Uncertainty-Rejecting Cultures

Uncertainty-accepting cultures *tend to be tolerant of ambiguity and diversity, and they are more often democracies than dictatorships or countries led by powerful royalties*. The

©Gareth Brown/Getty Images

populations of uncertainty-accepting cultures tend to be diverse in ethnicity, religion, and race. In addition, they are more likely to accept political refugees and immigrants.

The United States, Canada, and the United Kingdom are democratic countries that have attracted some of the most diverse populations in the world. They embrace general principles related to tolerance, as in England, which accepts immigrants from over 50 British Commonwealth countries that were once British colonies.[19] Other countries that ranked high in uncertainty-acceptance in the 1980 study were Denmark, Sweden, Singapore, Hong Kong, Ireland, and India.[20]

Uncertainty-rejecting cultures *have difficulty with ambiguity and diversity.* Most are not democracies. These cultures are more likely to have many rules regarding behavior, and they are more likely to reject outsiders, such as immigrants, refugees, and migrants, especially if they look different from and act differently than the majority population. South Korea and Japan, for example, do not welcome diversity, except for the uneasy presence of U.S. soldiers. Other countries that ranked high on the study's uncertainty-rejecting scale were France, Spain, Greece, Portugal, Belgium, Peru, Chile, Russia, China, and Argentina.[21]

©Dave Moyer RF

Cultures' tendency to be uncertainty-accepting or uncertainty-rejecting can have a powerful effect on intercultural communication. Those in uncertainty-accepting cultures tend to welcome outsiders, including offering citizenship. However, today, we are seeing that acceptance of outsiders can erode, even in uncertainty-accepting cultures, when the outsiders become numerous, refuse to integrate into the dominant culture, or come from cultures that are viewed with suspicion or prejudice. Countries like Germany and France have become less tolerant of outsiders because of an influx of Muslim immigrants, and the United States has a controversial relationship with Mexicans who have entered the country illegally. Nonetheless, some countries absolutely reject outsiders, whereas others grapple with these issues in considering paths to citizenship for immigrants.

Implicit-Rule vs. Explicit-Rule Cultures

An **implicit-rule culture** is one in which *cultural rules are embedded in tradition and followed faithfully.* For example, a traditional Arab woman knows that one rule of her culture is that she is to walk a few paces behind her husband. Individuals in such cultures are unlikely to question societal rules. People from implicit-rule cultures tend to be more polite, less aggressive, and more accommodating than those from explicit-rule cultures. Implicit-rule cultures are typically found in the Middle East, Africa, and Latin America.[22]

An **explicit-rule culture** is one in which *policies, procedures, and expectations are more likely to be discussed or negotiated.* For example, American parents negotiate with their children: "You can stay up late if you help with the dishes and clean your room." Compared with people from implicit-rule cultures, people from explicit-rule cultures tend to be more combative, less willing to please, and less concerned about offending others. Explicit-rule cultures are typically found in northern and western Europe and the United States.[23]

You might think about the differences in this way: in an implicit-rule culture, the social rules are part of who and what people are. The rules are ancient and unquestioned. Sex, status, and seniority dictate where each person sits around the decision-making table, and those at the table are unlikely to question their placement. In contrast, in an explicit-rule culture, rules are more likely to be developed, discussed, and negotiated. At dinner parties and even at decision-making meetings, people's placement around the table may largely be determined by who gets there first.

M-Time vs. P-Time Cultures

The fourth distinguishing characteristic relates to perceptions of time. Cultures associated with **M-time**, or *a monochronic time schedule, compartmentalize time to meet personal needs, and they separate tasks from social activities.*[24] M-time is dominant in Canada, the United States, and northern Europe.

People in M-time cultures see time as something that can be wasted or saved. Americans, for example, tend to schedule times for working out, going to the doctor, holding meetings, and taking the family out to dinner. Time is segmented, dedicated to work or social life (but usually not both), and thought

CONNECTING GLOBALLY

THE RIGHT TO BE FORGOTTEN VARIES BY CULTURE

Have you ever had something posted about you that you online didn't like? Maybe it was an off-the-cuff comment, or an unflattering photo, or even some embarrassing video footage that ended up online. When communicating over mass media channels, managing your identity and controlling your standards for privacy can be difficult.

Depending on where in the world you live, your ability to control the distribution of content shared through third-party sites will vary dramatically. For example, in 2012, the European Union passed legislation allowing its citizens to request the deletion of personally damaging information from websites or search engines. In the United States, "the right to be forgotten" has no legal basis. On the contrary, because the U.S. Constitution guarantees freedom of speech; to limit the availability of information is considered censorship.

What do you believe about the so-called "right to be forgotten"? Should the United States enforce limitations on those rights, on the grounds of censorship? How would you describe your cultural values on the questions of privacy, disclosure, and surveillance?

of in terms of future events and activities. Within this scheme, getting to any appointment on time is treated with considerable importance. People within M-time cultures rely more on a day planner and organized appointments, showing up on time throughout the day, than in P-time cultures.

Cultures associated with **P-time**, or *polychronic time schedules, view time as "contextually based and relationally oriented."*[25] What does this mean? For those in P-time cultures, time is not saved or wasted; it is only one factor in a much larger and more complicated social context. Someone in a P-time culture would wonder, why halt a conversation with an old friend to hurry off to an appointment on a relatively unimportant issue?

In other words, relationships trump time considerations in some contexts. Inhabitants of P-time cultures orchestrate their relational and task obligations with the fluid movements of jazz, whereas those in M-time cultures treat life as a march, in which people strive mainly to stay on schedule and be efficient, valuing tasks over relationships. Typical P-time cultures are found in Latin America, the Middle East, Asia, France, Africa, and Greece. North America is predominantly M-time because of the strong European influence, but some co-cultures in the United States exhibit P-time tendencies.

Businesspeople in P-time cultures do conduct business, but they do it very differently than those in M-time cultures. For example, a businessperson in a P-time culture might have a large waiting room outside her office, and the people in that waiting room may use the space and time to meet with each other and resolve issues. In other words, a great deal of business in P-time cultures is conducted in public rather than in a series of private meetings, as it would be in M-time cultures. In an M-time culture, the waiting room at a place of business is often silent, with everyone occupied with his paperwork or smartphone, each waiting for a turn to be heard.

If you live in an M-time culture and you travel to other parts of the world, including most countries in Latin America and the Middle East, you will probably experience a disconnect or disorientation. You may feel psychologically stressed, as others always seem to be late. On the other hand, you may note that, once your P-time associates arrive, they focus exclusively on you. They are not distracted by schedules or other commitments.

Notice in **Table 6.2** how these cultural characteristics tend to cluster. In the left-hand column, you will see that the same cultures cluster under individualistic, uncertainty-accepting, explicit-rule, and M-time usage. The cultures that share these characteristics are northern European or Commonwealth countries (e.g., Australia and Canada) that were strongly influenced by Great Britain. Much of the rest of the world tends to be collectivist, uncertainty-rejecting, implicit-rule, and P-time-oriented, including China, the South American continent, and much of Africa. However, the world is not so simple to explain. Western influence has pushed those who engage in global business toward the column on the left, such that, in a predominantly Chinese culture, as in Hong Kong and Singapore, people now conduct business in a very Western manner. Moreover, American businesspeople have learned the importance of

Table 6.2 Cultural Characteristics

Individualistic Cultures Tend To . . .	Collectivist Cultures Tend To . . .
■ Value individual freedom; place "I" before "we" ■ Value independence ■ Value directness and clarity ■ *Examples*: United States, Australia, Great Britain	■ Value the group over the individual; place "we" before "I" ■ Value commitment to family, tribe, and clan ■ Value cooperation over competition ■ *Examples*: Venezuela, Pakistan, Taiwan, Thailand
Uncertainty-Accepting Cultures Tend To . . .	**Uncertainty-Rejecting Cultures Tend To . . .**
■ Be willing to take risks ■ Avoid rules; seek flexibility; reject hierarchy ■ Value individual opinion, general principles, and common sense ■ *Examples*: United States, Great Britain, Denmark	■ Be threatened by ideas and people from outside ■ Establish formal rules for behavior; prefer stability, hierarchy, and structure ■ Embrace written rules, regulation, and rituals ■ *Examples*: Japan, France, Spain, Greece, Argentina
Explicit-Rule Cultures Tend To . . .	**Implicit-Rule Cultures Tend To . . .**
■ See cultural rules as explicit; explain and discuss procedures ■ Be straightforward, and people have to cope with embarrassment or insult ■ *Examples*: Northern and western Europe, United States	■ See cultural rules as set and not to be questioned ■ Prefer "saving face" to soothing an insulted person ■ *Examples*: Middle East, Africa, Latin America
M-Time Cultures Tend To . . .	**P-Time Cultures Tend To . . .**
■ Compartmentalize time, separating work from social time and task time from relational time ■ View time as something that can be wasted or saved ■ *Examples*: North America, northern Europe	■ Factor in time as one element of a larger context, which includes family, social responsibilities, and tasks ■ Value social relationships and time considerations together ■ *Examples*: Latin America, Middle East, Asia, France, Africa

SOURCE: Adapted from Dodd, C. H. (1998). *Dynamics of intercultural communication* (5th ed.). New York: McGraw-Hill.

establishing relationships with people in the Middle East, Africa, and South America before proposing business deals. The good news is that, driven by global economics, people in different cultures are strongly encouraged to learn more about each other.

IMPROVING INTERCULTURAL AND CO-CULTURAL COMMUNICATION

Effective intercultural communication can take considerable time, energy, and commitment. Although some people would like "10 easy steps," no foolproof plan is available. However, the following strategies should give you some ways to increase your comfort and competence in intercultural contexts and help you avoid potential problems.

1. *Conduct a self-assessment.* What are your attitudes toward other cultures and co-cultures? Be specific about your own discomforts and lack of information. Those attitudes likely influence your communication with others, so an honest assessment of your communication style, beliefs, and prejudices is a good first step toward more open and respectful communication.
2. *Practice supportive communication behaviors.* Supportive behaviors, such as empathizing with the situation of the other person, encourage success in intercultural and co-cultural exchanges.
3. *Develop sensitivity toward diversity.* Recognize that you can learn something from people from other countries and cultures. Don't be afraid to ask respectful questions; you may be surprised by what you learn.
4. *Avoid stereotypes.* Don't make assumptions about another's culture; get to know individuals for themselves.
5. *Avoid ethnocentrism.* You may know your own culture the best, but that familiarity does not make your culture superior to all others. You will learn more about the strengths and weaknesses of your own culture by becoming more familiar with other cultures.
6. *Develop code sensitivity.* **Code sensitivity** is *the ability to adapt to the verbal and nonverbal language of the individual with whom you are communicating, regardless of cultural or co-cultural differences.* The more you know about another's culture, the better you will be at adapting. Be open-minded about your differences. Can you patiently wait in silence when communicating with someone who is Native American or Japanese, who might be comfortable with quiet gaps in the conversation as she thoughtfully sizes you up?
7. *Use and encourage descriptive feedback.* Providing and receiving feedback are crucial in intercultural communication so that people make sure their messages are clear and understood. Feedback should be immediate, honest, specific, and clear. Say, "I don't understand. Could you repeat that?," or "What time do you mean when you say 'I'm coming over tomorrow'?," or "Are you saying that you'd prefer not to see the movie?".
8. *Make time to open communication channels.* Intercultural communication can be frustrating. Misunderstandings are likely because of all the differences among people, so everyone involved in intercultural communication may need to spend time negotiating the meanings of messages. Many cultures encourage tea or coffee time together as a way to connect and get to know one another in

a relaxed atmosphere. Sometimes conversational partners can clarify their meanings by writing down words that are difficult to communicate. Patience is key to mutual understanding.

9. *Manage conflicts that arise over beliefs and practices.* Think ahead about how you might handle minor and major differences. Minor differences include very different conceptions of time and different ideas about touching or appropriate ways of dressing. Major conflicts can arise over beliefs, such as the appropriate role of women or acceptable behavior for children. We all need to exercise caution about judging other cultures and cultural practices, as no culture is above criticism.

©Eric Audras/Getty Images RF

10. *Be reflexive.* **Reflexivity** means *being self-aware and learning from interactions with the intent of improving future interactions*. When being reflexive, you assess an interaction, identify what went well and what could have gone better, and then learn from those observations. Through reflexivity you not only will improve your intercultural communication skills but will also become a more effective communicator in nearly every situation.

11. *Practice intercultural communication competence.* Of course, the most effective strategy for improving your intercultural communication competence is practice. Fortunately, the increasing diversity of our own culture means that such practice can take place with the people at the corner market, those at your place of employment, and even others in class.

 **CHAPTER REVIEW**

In this chapter, we explored the importance of intercultural communications skills. You learned about the concepts of culture, race, ethnicity, and co-culture. Because people from various cultures differ in their communication styles and behaviors, problems can arise; some of the attitudes that can lead to these problems are ethnocentrism, stereotyping, and prejudice. There are four main ways in which cultures differ from each other, and by using such strategies as being reflexive and providing feedback, you can improve your skills in communicating with people from different cultures.

KEY TERMS

intercultural communication, 101
culture, 101
race, 101
ethnic group, 103
dominant culture, 103
co-cultural groups, 103
ethnocentrism, 107
cultural relativism, 108
prejudice, 109
individualistic cultures, 111
collectivist cultures, 111
uncertainty-accepting cultures, 111
uncertainty-rejecting cultures, 112
implicit-rule culture, 112
explicit-rule culture, 112
M-time, 113
P-time, 114
code sensitivity, 116
reflexivity, 117

STUDY QUESTIONS

1. What is the difference between a race and an ethnicity? What are some of the problems surrounding the concept of race?
2. What are some reasons that students in the United States should learn about other cultures and co-cultures?
3. Explain the relationships among ethnocentrism, stereotyping, and prejudice.
4. The United States is regarded as an individualistic nation, but this is a broad generalization. Think of experiences from your life that show collectivist characteristics in this individualistic culture.
5. Explain at least one strategy for relating to people from other cultures and co-cultures that would improve relationships in your school. Give an example from your own experience.

ENDNOTES

1. Newport, F. (2011, December 23). Christianity remains dominant religion in the United States. *Gallup*. Retrieved from http://www.gallup.com
2. Japan: Religious facts. *CIA Factbook Statistics*. Retrieved from http://www.religionfacts.com/japan
3. Kramarae, C. (1981). *Women and men speaking*. Rowley, MA: Newbury House.
4. Flores, A. (2016, September 13). The big difference between women and men's earnings after college. *Center for American Progress*. Retrieved from http://www.americanprogress.org; Sahadi, J. (2016, April 12). *6 things to know about the gender pay gap on equal pay day*. CNN. Retrieved from http://www.money.cnn.com; Institute for women's policy research (n.d.). Pay equity and discrimination. Retrieved from http://www.iwpr.org
5. Nasson, T. (2013). Gay celebrities, gay movie stars, gay actors. Retrieved from www.wildaboutmovies.com/features/GAY_CELEBRITIES.php
6. Avery, D. (2016, October 11). 16 celebrities who came out this year. *Logo*. Retrieved from http://www.newnownext.com
7. Dodd, C. H. (1998). *Dynamics of intercultural communication* (5th ed.). New York: McGraw-Hill.

8. Fatemi, A. H., Khajavy, G. H., & Choi, C. W. (2016). Testing a model of intercultural willingness to communicate based on ethnocentrism, ambiguity tolerance, and sensation seeking: The role of learning English in Iran. *Journal of Intercultural Communication Research, 45,* 304–318.
9. Dong, Q., Day, K. D., & Collaco, C. M. (2008). Overcoming ethnocentrism through developing intercultural communication sensitivity and multiculturalism. *Human Communication, 11,* 27–38.
10. Desilver, D. (2017, January 31). World's Muslim population more widespread than you might think. *Pew Research Center.* Retrieved from http://www.pewresearch.org
11. Garcia, A. L., Miller, D. A., Smith, E. R., & Mackie, D. M. (2006). Thanks for the compliment? Emotional reactions to group-level versus individual-level compliments and insults. *Group Processes and Intergroup Relations, 9,* 307–324.
12. Czopp, A. M., Monteith, M. J., & Mark, A. Y. (2006). Standing up for change: Reducing bias through interpersonal confrontation. *Journal of Personality and Social Psychology, 90,* 784–803.
13. Swim, J. K., Hykers, L. L., Cohen, L. L., & Ferguson, M. J. (2001). Everyday sexism: Evidence for its incidence, nature, and psychological impact from three daily diary studies. *Journal of Social Issues, 57,* 31–53.
14. Hofstede, G. (1980). *Culture's consequences: International differences in work-related values.* Beverly Hills, CA: Sage.
15. Ibid.
16. Coleman, D. (1998, December 22). The group and self: New focus on a cultural rift. *The New York Times,* 40.
17. Saad, G., Cleveland, M., & Ho, L. (2015). Individualism-collectivism and the quantity versus quality dimensions of individual and group creative performance. *Journal of Business Research, 68,* 578–586.
18. Hofstede.
19. Know Britain: Commonwealth countries from A–J. Retrieved from http://www.know-britain.com/general/commonwealth_countries1.html
20. Ibid.
21. Samovar, L. A., Porter, R. E., & Stefani, L. A. (1998). *Communication between cultures* (3rd ed.). Belmont, CA: Wadsworth.
22. Dodd.
23. Ibid.
24. Ting-Toomey, S. (1997). Managing intercultural conflicts effectively. In L. A. Samovar and R. E. Porter (Eds.), *Intercultural communication: A reader* (8th ed., pp. 392–404). Belmont, CA: Wadsworth.
25. Ting-Toomey, S. (1997). Managing intercultural conflicts effectively. In L. A. Samovar and R. E. Porter (Eds.), *Intercultural communication: A reader* (8th ed., pp. 395). Belmont, CA: Wadsworth.

Blue and Yellow Cube Icon, Connecting Globally Icon, Mountain Icon, Chapter Review Arrows Circle Icon: ©McGraw Hill Education

chapter **7**

Mediated Communication and Social Media

©Aleksandar Nakic/Getty Images RF

Although you use it every day, and it saturates the world in countless ways, the term *mediated communication* might be new to you. In this chapter we will explore in depth the most popular form of mediated communication: social media. We will examine its various features and uses, as well as cover the skills most relevant to you as a user.

LEARNING OBJECTIVES

After reading this chapter, you should be able to:

- Identify the reasons for studying mediated communication.
- Describe how mass media influence behavior and shape culture.
- Demonstrate an understanding of various types of computer-mediated communication and how they affect interactions and relationships.
- Understand how to become a responsible and critical consumer of mass media.
- Know how to protect and present yourself on social media.

UNDERSTANDING MEDIATED COMMUNICATION

Mediated communication refers to *messages that are transmitted not directly from person to person but through some other communication tool, such as print, electronic, or digital communication devices.* Some mediated messages are generated for masses of people to consume (such as television programs); others are targeted to individuals or smaller groups (such as e-mail and text messages).

Mediated communication includes messages conveyed through television, radio, and print (like newspapers and magazines), as well as through computer- and Internet-based means (such as e-mail messages, text messages, websites, discussion boards, and social media sites). Given the prevalence of social media in our lives, this chapter will focus on these forms of mediated communication.

©Uppercut RF/Getty Images RF

Why Study Mediated Communication?

Imagine trying to get through an entire day without consuming, or making reference to, mediated forms of communication. You might have trouble distinguishing the sugar from the salt, because you would have to cover all product labels at home, and you might have trouble preparing a presentation at work, because you wouldn't have access to your research materials. You could not turn on a television, computer, or cell phone; check your Facebook account or e-mail; or look at newspapers, billboards, and magazines. Possibly the only way you could avoid all forms of mediated communication would be to go to a national park, leaving all your electronic devices at home, and take a walk in the wilderness.

One reason for studying mediated communication is to better understand how the messages that surround us influence behavior and shape culture. To understand the media's influence on your own behavior, do some self-reflection. Answer the following questions based on your behavior today:

- How frequently did you check your Facebook, Twitter, or Instagram account?
- Did you listen to music or stream a television show while doing other things?
- How much time did you spend reading a newspaper or a news site?
- Finally, did anything you read, saw, or heard in any of those media change what you thought or talked about with others?

©Csondy/Getty Images RF

Your answers to these questions will help you understand the impact of mediated communication in your life and in the culture at large.

CONNECTING GLOBALLY

SOCIAL MEDIA USE AROUND THE GLOBE

Although Facebook, YouTube, and Twitter are enormously popular in the United States and Europe, in China, where free speech is not encouraged, these sites are not accessible. In order to control the kinds of messages that are made public, the Chinese government has banned the use of certain social media sites and closely monitors those that are allowed.

Much like users in the United States and Europe, Chinese citizens use social media to interact with family and friends, to meet new people, to engage in citizen journalism, and to organize social movements. For example, in 2015, popular news TV host Chai Jing produced *Under the Dome*, a documentary about China's pollution problem. The video went viral through Chinese social media. When viewership exceeded 200 million, the government removed the video from streaming sites and censored discussions of it online.

Although the Chinese government makes great efforts to regulate social media use, it has been more successful at censoring traditional media, including newspapers, television, and radio. Meanwhile, Chinese social media sites like Weibo, Renren, and YouKu have grown in popularity. Weibo, China's version of Twitter, now boasts 261 million active daily users.[1]

People around the globe have different concerns about government surveillance and social media. Consider how your own social media use may be influenced by concerns about governmental surveillance:

- Does government surveillance affect your decisions about what you share through social media?
- How would you adapt your use of social media if freedom of speech were not a right guaranteed to you?
- Have you ever worried about being punished for something you've posted to social media?

If you have the opportunity, discuss your answers to these questions with someone from a different culture.

The second reason is to help you become a more critical consumer of the mediated messages you encounter. For example, have you ever thought about how the actors and models in advertisements influence your own body image? The magazines you read and the movies and television shows you watch are filled with advertisements intended to impact your self-image and to encourage you to buy products and services that promise to improve that self-image. Research indicates that media influence on self-image,[2] and body image in particular, is powerful.[3] We will discuss this power in greater detail later in this chapter, as well as strategies for turning a more critical eye on the media you encounter.

The third reason to study mediated communication is that doing so will improve your own mediated interactions. As you consider the many means through which you communicate electronically, you will learn to effectively convey the messages you intend in ways that are appropriate for the context. For example, you do not e-mail your instructor or employer with the same casual style and abbreviations you use with your friends and peers. Understanding these differences, and shaping your messages accordingly, will greatly improve your mediated interactions and their outcomes.

The Forms of Mediated Communication

Mediated communication can be broken down into two broad categories: mass communication and computer-mediated communication. **Mass communication** *involves the use of print and electronic technology by professional communicators to share messages over great distances for large audiences.*[4] **Mass media,** then, include *the specific means by which we use print and electronic technology to communicate.* **Computer-mediated communication (CMC)** is *human-to-human interaction using networked computer environments.*[5]

Even if you are not familiar with the term *CMC*, you likely use it every day. Facebook, e-mail, chat, and instant messaging are all examples of modes of CMC. **Figure 7.1** demonstrates one way to understand mass communication and CMC by breaking them down into the components of the traditional communication model (sender-message-receiver-feedback), discussed in **Chapter 1**.

©Lars Niki RF

Today everyone is a consumer of mediated messages. And content circulated through older technologies can reach different audiences through new communication technologies. For example, mass media sources like *The New York Times* can be accessed in print or online and are increasingly interactive. Reporters now post stories in written and video format, and readers interact with each other and with reporters by posting comments. Most books are now published in multiple formats, including those compatible with mobile devices. Parents can buy their kids' favorite DVDs or download the content for on-the-go watching. All of these are examples of how media is converging. The technical term for this, **media convergence** refers to *the ways in which different technologies have evolved to perform similar outcomes or tasks.*

MASS COMMUNICATION AND MASS MEDIA

Researchers have long studied our motivations for consuming media and find a variety of reasons for our behaviors.[6] We use media for information ("I need to know how to keep myself healthy"), entertainment ("This show always makes me laugh"), relaxation ("This show always helps me unwind at the end of the day"), escape[7] ("I sometimes use YouTube when I need a break from my paper"), habit/addiction fulfillment ("I can't end my day without checking my apps for notifications"), companionship ("When I watch *Ellen* I don't feel so alone"), excitement ("I wonder what will go down on the *Bachelor* this week"), social interaction ("I browse *The New York Times* every morning so I can hold conversation with friends and coworkers"), and co-viewing experiences ("Watching football is what I do with the guys").[8]

What motivates you to turn on the television or browse the Internet? How do your motivations differ from those of important people in your life? Maybe

Figure 7.1 Mass Communication, CMC, and the Communication Model

Mass Communication and the Communication Model

- **Sources/Senders:** Mass communication sources include the television, a newspaper reporter, an author, an announcer, and a studio production team.
- **Messages/Channels:** Common channels for transmitting mass communication messages include cable and satellite systems, printing presses, computers, and the Internet.
- **Receivers:** In mass communication, large groups are the intended recipients of the messages disseminated.
- **Feedback:** With modern technology, mass communication provides a channel for feedback from intended receivers. Take, for example, much of reality television, where viewers are asked to call in and vote for their favorite contestants. On blogs and websites, readers can leave comments.

CMC and the Communication Model

- **Sources/Senders:** CMC sources include e-mails, social media, instant messages, and texts.
- **Messages/Channels:** Common channels for transmitting mass communication messages include cell phones, computers, and the Internet.
- **Receivers:** In CMC, receivers can be individuals (as in an instant message exchange) or large groups (as when you post a message to a Facebook group).
- **Feedback:** Possible feedback to a social media post includes silence from an online community (no response), "likes" for your posts, and online commentary that either reinforces or changes how you think about what you posted.

you watch a particular program to be entertained, whereas your partner joins you for the experience of co-viewing. Reflecting on the different motivations for consuming mass media can help you evaluate the role it plays in your life.

The Influence of Mass Media on Behavior

A Nielsen report tracked media consumption patterns during 2016 and found that the average American spends just over 10 and a half hours a day consuming media, including watching TV, reading news, checking cell phone apps, surfing the web, and checking in on social media. Fifty percent of Americans now subscribe to in-home streaming services like Netflix, Amazon Prime, and Hulu, a statistic that is up from 2015.[9] Put another way, Americans devote more time to consuming media than to performing their full-time jobs.

How does media consumption affect our beliefs, perceptions, and behaviors? Media-effects researchers explore this question by focusing primarily on violence and body image, as illustrated in **Figure 7.2**.

Media Violence Research by media-effects scholars consistently demonstrates a relationship between the consumption of media violence and aggressive[10] or

Figure 7.2 Effects of Mass Media on Behavior and Culture

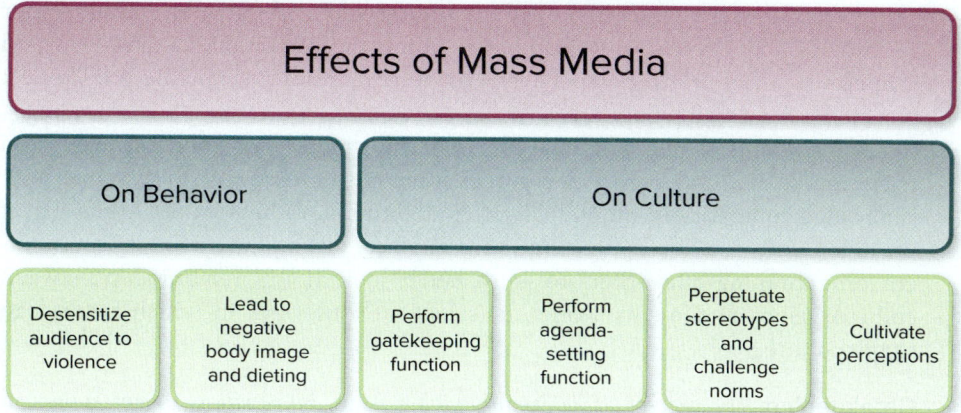

violent behavior.[11] One hypothesis researchers use to explain this relationship is that such programming desensitizes us to violence, making us more tolerant of it and more likely to respond to aggression and hostility with violent acts.[12]

Many factors contribute to violent behavior. For example, mental illness is believed to have played a role in the tragic mass killings in Tucson, Arizona, and Newtown, Connecticut. Nevertheless, the prevalence of media violence and its potential effects on viewers continues to be a focus in discussions of gun violence in the United States.

©Thanasis Zovoilis/Getty Images RF

Media and Body Image A second area of research focuses on how media consumption affects body image. Using extensive air-brushing and photo editing, the media project the impression that there is one ideal body for women (thin and young) and another for men (thin with developed muscles). Researchers found that the more media that men and women consumed, the more likely they were to be dissatisfied with their bodies and to demonstrate symptoms associated with eating disorders.[13]

Based on the findings on violence and body image in the media, you might conclude that the media's influence on our behaviors is entirely negative. But the media can be a positive force for both adults and children. Adults who watch a variety of programs can gain a greater appreciation and understanding of other cultures. Children's media consumption can help them acquire language and interpersonal skills, like empathy and conflict resolution.[14] However, to fully understand mass media's potential to positively impact our lives, we must also understand its relationship to the culture we live in.

The Relationship Between Mass Media and Culture

Whereas some scholars focus on the ways in which mass media influence our behaviors and cultural values, others examine the ways that media affect and shape our culture. Both perspectives are worth considering; media both reflect our culture and help shape it.

For example, some might argue that the ubiquity of sporting events on television, radio, and even video games intensifies the degree to which Americans value competition, individualism, and winning. Others would argue that if we didn't embrace these values in the first place, our media might reflect different programming altogether. To get a better look at this relationship between cultural values and media works, let's look at four ways in which media can shape culture.

Gatekeeping *The process of determining what news, information, or entertainment will reach a mass audience* is known as **gatekeeping**.[15] For example, when a new shopping complex opens in a community, gatekeeping occurs when newspaper editors determine whether the store's opening is important enough to justify sending reporters to the scene. If a story is written, it goes to a copy editor, who acts as a gatekeeper by deciding how the story will be framed, what tone the piece will take, and so on. Next the story goes to the city editor, who participates in gatekeeping by judging the importance of the story and thus determining its placement—on the front page or way in the back, above the fold or below. Front-page stories attract the attention of more readers and are therefore more likely to be the subject of broader discussion than are those buried in the middle of a paper.

Social media are also subject to gatekeeping practices. Facebook recently came under fire for manipulating the news feeds of half a million users.[16] Why does this manipulation of news feeds matter? Because the news that is shared is not always accurate, or even real. In 2016, 44 percent of Americans reported getting their news from social media posts by individuals in their networks.[17] This suggests that individual social media users have considerable gatekeeping power, perhaps more than traditional news organizations. While user-generated content is popular and prevalent, people who share news online do not necessarily know enough about the issues reflected in the news stories to be deemed trustworthy as sources.[18] It is increasingly important to evaluate news for credibility before clicking the share button on a social media site, a topic we highlight in the **Connecting Globally** box in **Chapter 13**. For starters, ask yourself whether coverage shared by a blogger, tweeter, or Facebook friend is more credible than information circulated by a news agency.

What we see and hear when we consume mass media is influenced by a range of gatekeeping activities. A news director at a television station, an acquisitions editor at a book publishing company, and even you, a user of social media, all participate in gatekeeping, and in doing so, help shape the cultural dialogue in meaningful ways.

Agenda-Setting *The process of influencing what topics are considered critical for discussion by society* is called **agenda-setting**.[19] Media officials and journalists may not explicitly tell us what to think, but they do set an agenda that influences the topics we think and talk about. Whereas gatekeeping determines what issues are critical to pass on to the public, agenda-setting involves more active promotion and discussion of particular issues. For example, CNN's multipart investigative TV series *Diversity in America* elevated the issue of diversity to a matter of universal public concern. In the most recent election cycle, Donald Trump frequently criticized media agencies, claiming that he was given unfair coverage because of a liberal bias in the media.[20] But it is not only the media that shape the agenda. In the age of the Internet, political bloggers, citizen journalists, and anyone with a Twitter account, can contribute to agenda-setting.

Perpetuating Stereotypes and Challenging Norms The media shape culture by perpetuating stereotypes while challenging societal norms. For instance, when the television show *Will and Grace* first aired in 1998, it was considered groundbreaking to place gay characters in prominent roles. The show exposed viewers to perspectives they were not used to encountering on prime-time television. These days television programming presents a diversity of characters and lifestyles in shows like *Glee*, *Transparent*, and *Modern Family*. The once-radical depictions of gay life on *Will and Grace* have more recently been criticized for relying on stereotypes of gay culture, while newer programs, like *Archer*, represent a less rigid structure of sexuality.

The media are full of stereotypes. Many television programs cast minority race characters in secondary roles, with white, middle-class men and women taking center stage. These depictions do little to challenge the norms about whose voices our society values most, thus helping perpetuate stereotypes. Although the characters we see on television are developed based on extensive marketing research and therefore reflect, to a large extent, what viewers want to see, the characters and situations presented also have the potential to alter our expectations and open (or close) our minds. In other words, television is shaped by our culture as much as it in turn shapes us.

Cultivating Perceptions Mass media also affect culture because of its **cultivation effect**. This means that *heavy television and media use leads people to perceive reality as consistent with media portrayals.*[21] Cultivation theory is often applied to the issue of media violence, with research indicating that those who view too much violence on television and other media come to perceive the world as a dangerous place.[22] Cultivation theory provides a potentially powerful analysis of how media affect us and has been applied to topics ranging from violence to mediated discussions about sex.

The Secret Life of the American Teenager is a popular TV program, as well as a focus for cultivation theory research. The show depicts teenage dialogues about

©Mike Theiss/National Geographic/Getty Images

sex and sexuality, revealing that few teenagers go to parents or medical professionals for trusted advice about sex. Instead, they turn to their peers to discuss the possible consequences of sex, such as unwanted pregnancy or STIs. Cultivation scholars who have done research on this topic argue that these depictions are likely to cultivate fear and avoidance among teenage viewers about openly discussing sex with adults.[23]

As you can see, the relationship between mass media and culture is complex. Media gatekeepers, like editors, producers, traditional journalists, bloggers, and citizen journalists, decide what information is passed on to us and in what forms. Our attitudes and perspectives are affected by which media we choose to consume and in what quantities. Mass media—from prime-time news to Netflix miniseries—likewise reflect our society's ideals and trends. As such, the media both shape, and are shaped by, culture.

Thinking Critically About Mass Media Messages

Mass media sometimes blur the distinction between news and entertainment, making it particularly important to critically evaluate and cautiously interpret mediated messages. To help you engage in more critical evaluation of the media, this section provides recommendations for increasing your overall media literacy skills and offers ways to counter some of the negative media effects.

Media literacy refers to *the ability to think critically about mediated messages and how they influence us.*[24] Sometimes when we turn on the television, the last thing we want to do is critically evaluate what we're watching. Nevertheless, media literacy experts prescribe a healthy dose of skepticism.[25]

Many media literacy efforts focus on increasing our understanding of how mass media messages are framed and created. Because the

©Lars Niki RF

technology used to produce such messages has become less expensive, almost anyone can produce mass media content. The large volume of messages disseminated on YouTube, Facebook, Twitter, and other message boards makes the task of finding accurate, unbiased information all the more challenging.[26]

Citizen journalists produce some of the most popular Internet videos, accessed by thousands of people each day on YouTube and Vimeo. As with other forms of media, this content must be carefully evaluated. In **Chapter 11** we discuss the process of gathering information and offer a list of questions to ask yourself with regard to every new source you evaluate.

COMPUTER-MEDIATED COMMUNICATION AND SOCIAL MEDIA

CMC can be categorized according to two prominent characteristics: the degree to which an interaction is synchronous or asynchronous. **Synchronous communication** *occurs when the people involved interact with one another at the same time as both senders and receivers of information.* **Asynchronous communication** *occurs when the people involved experience a delay in interacting with one another and take turns being senders and receivers of information.* **Figure 7.3** identifies the types of CMC associated with each type of interaction.

Social media are *platforms that include websites and applications that allow users to connect and interact with acquaintances, friends, family members, organizations, colleagues, and customers all over the world through the exchange of user-generated content.* You may have noticed that the word *media* is used with a plural verb, such as "media are." That's because there are so many types, especially in the case of social media. Let's begin by looking at who is using social media websites, also referred to as platforms, and why.

Figure 7.3 Synchronous vs. Asynchronous Communication

Synchronous Communication	Asynchronous Communication
■ The people involved interact with one another at the same time as both senders and receivers of information. Examples: • Face-to-face communication • Skype or Facetime video chat sessions • Cell phone conversations • Instant messaging • Online chat sessions	■ The people involved experience a delay in interacting with one another and take turns being senders and receivers of information. Examples: • E-mail • Discussion boards • Online support groups • Social media websites

Once known as the interaction domain of the millennial generation (those born roughly between 1980 and 2000), today social media attract users of all ages, as shown in **Figure 7.4**. In the early 2000s, the first type of social media to attract users was diary-based blogs, like MySpace, Blogger, and LiveJournal. In 2004, Facebook launched and rapidly grew in popularity, first among college students, and then more broadly when the site opened its registration to anyone in 2006. Today, more than 1 billion people log into their Facebook accounts daily.[27] In the later 2000s, sites like Twitter and YouTube established and expanded their user base as well.

Since 2009, Facebook has been the most popular social media website worldwide, but a growing number of platforms accommodate a variety of users. Having expanded beyond their use as a social networking tool, social media now play a much broader role in how we communicate. Later in this chapter, we will examine the effects of social media use across various contexts.

The Features and Uses of Social Media

Social media include a range of platforms, the four most common of which are blogs (including video blogs, or vlogs), microblogs, and social networking websites (**Figure 7.5**). The question of whether the widespread use of social

Figure 7.4 Who Is Using Social Media?

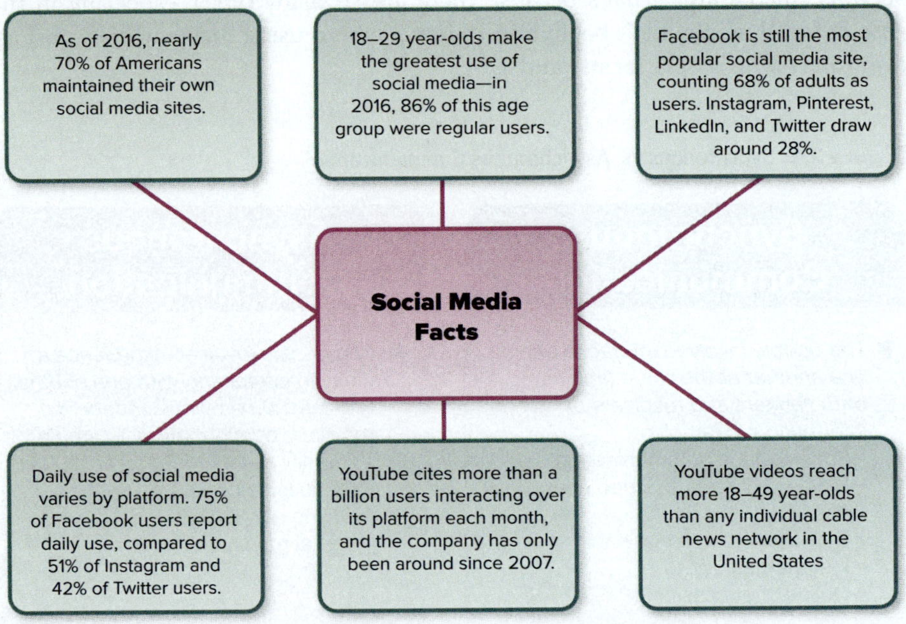

- As of 2016, nearly 70% of Americans maintained their own social media sites.
- 18–29 year-olds make the greatest use of social media—in 2016, 86% of this age group were regular users.
- Facebook is still the most popular social media site, counting 68% of adults as users. Instagram, Pinterest, LinkedIn, and Twitter draw around 28%.
- Daily use of social media varies by platform. 75% of Facebook users report daily use, compared to 51% of Instagram and 42% of Twitter users.
- YouTube cites more than a billion users interacting over its platform each month, and the company has only been around since 2007.
- YouTube videos reach more 18–49 year-olds than any individual cable news network in the United States.

Center: **Social Media Facts**

SOURCES: YouTube. (2017). YouTube statistics. Retrieved from **http://youtube.com/t/press_statistics**; Pew Research Center (2017, January 12). Social media fact sheet. Retrieved from **http://www.pewinternet.org**

Figure 7.5 Types of Social Media Platforms

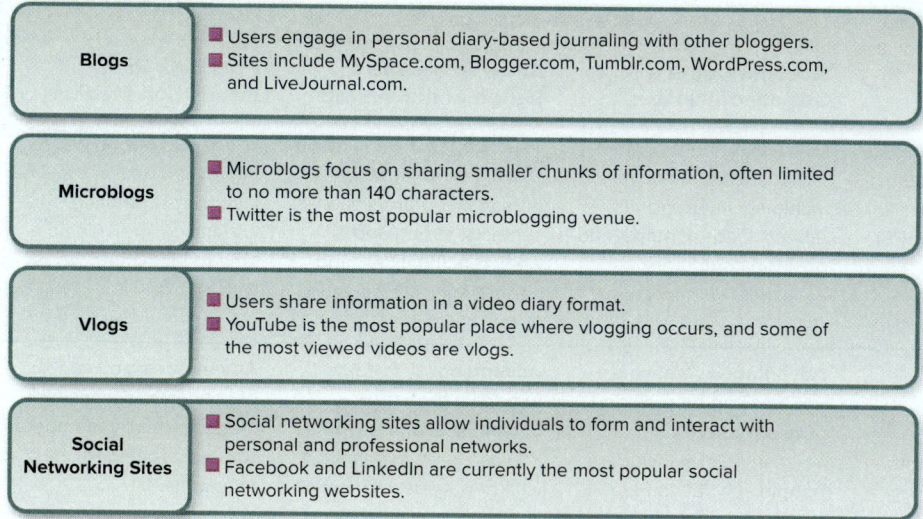

- **Blogs**
  - Users engage in personal diary-based journaling with other bloggers.
  - Sites include MySpace.com, Blogger.com, Tumblr.com, WordPress.com, and LiveJournal.com.

- **Microblogs**
  - Microblogs focus on sharing smaller chunks of information, often limited to no more than 140 characters.
  - Twitter is the most popular microblogging venue.

- **Vlogs**
  - Users share information in a video diary format.
  - YouTube is the most popular place where vlogging occurs, and some of the most viewed videos are vlogs.

- **Social Networking Sites**
  - Social networking sites allow individuals to form and interact with personal and professional networks.
  - Facebook and LinkedIn are currently the most popular social networking websites.

media is "good" or "bad" is a matter of much discussion and debate. Have you ever asked yourself any of the following questions?

Social media are neither entirely good nor entirely bad; the uses and applications of social media have both benefits and drawbacks. **Table 7.1** highlights some of the advantages and disadvantages of the most prominent features of social media.

Communication scholars describe social media as a **boundary-crossing medium** because it is *a communication channel whose personal and professional uses span communication contexts.*[28] Social media allow people to express their opinions, attitudes, values, beliefs, judgments, and evaluations on any topic and to share them with anyone—friends, colleagues, classmates, family members, and even strangers.

One challenge associated with a boundary-crossing medium of interaction has to do with norms, the general patterns of behaviors we uphold. We tend to establish different norms for communicating with different groups, like our family, our coworkers, and our friends. At work you are likely to engage in more professional interactions, perhaps not sharing your political beliefs with coworkers. Your friends, on the other hand, will know more about your political and personal beliefs but perhaps not as much about your workplace identity. Imagine a party where all your coworkers and friends are in

©monkeybusinessimages/iStock/Getty Images RF

Computer-Mediated Communication and Social Media **131**

Table 7.1 Important Characteristics of Social Media

Social Media...			
Enable Ease of Communication	**Accommodate a Variety of Devices**	**Allow Access to a Range of Individuals**	**Provide a Rich Interaction Medium**
Users exchange and share photos, status updates, videos, and Global Positioning System (GPS) location information.	Users contribute content from a host of devices, including smartphones, tablets, iPads, laptops, and desktop computers.	Users connect with known and unknown audiences, personal and professional contacts, strong and weak relational ties, and geographically close and distant relations.	Users achieve several interaction goals, including expediting, enhancing, or avoiding face-to-face interactions with others.
Advantages: A lot of information can be communicated easily. You can upload a photo that reflects a fond memory with someone, provide a brief caption, tag the friend, and rekindle a connection without saying much at all. Social media allow you to share details of your daily life in ways that you might not otherwise do—like posting a silly picture of your dog.	**Advantages:** Real-time updates can be provided from anywhere. You can quickly include people in what you are doing by posting a status update or sharing a thought about your day. You can share your digital photos, accompanying images with text and reflection. You can share news quickly, such as you might during an emergency or a natural disaster.	**Advantages:** It is easy to build a diverse communication network. You can keep in contact with people despite major life transitions, like taking new jobs or moving to new places. You might interact with others who share different political, racial, or religious identities that are not characteristic of your face-to-face network.	**Advantages:** You can observe interactions with friends or family members without needing to use a telephone. You can contribute your thoughts and ideas to the public sphere and see how others respond. When something happens in your life that you do not wish to relate multiple times, you can post it to everyone at once.
Disadvantages: You may inadvertently share information about others that upsets them. You might share more information than you intend to (information such as where we live, what we drive, when we are home, or when we are away from home).	**Disadvantages:** Social media can take up more time than you anticipate, or you may overdisclose because devices are so readily available. You might also put something in writing on a post that is hard to take back and that you regret.	**Disadvantages:** You may accidentally share a message to a broader audience than you intended. You may trust someone who lies to you and pretends to be something he or she is not (like an adult posing as a high school student).	**Disadvantages:** Some people might be offended if the primary way you interact with them is through social media, and some people might not even get your messages. People may misinterpret a message because of the lack of nonverbal cues.

attendance. How will you behave? Which norms will you use to interact? On social media sites, where users often mix their social networks, these questions present a challenge.

One way to meet this challenge is to be straightforward. Tell people when you approve them as friends how you would like them to interact with you in the social media environment you have created. Alternatively, think about the interaction norms you uphold with different groups; then simply deny requests to individuals whose norms are likely to clash with the norms of others in your established network. For example, many teachers do not like their students to be part of their social media networks, because they worry about violating boundaries, causing conflicts, or encouraging the perception of favoritism. You should give thought to the types of relationships you allow to comingle.

Uses and Gratifications Theory

One theory that is particularly useful for studying social media is the **uses and gratifications (U&G) theory**, which *suggests that people use social media to satisfy their own needs and desires*. U&G theorists do not view the effects of social media use as either positive or negative.[29] Instead, they argue that the impacts of social media use (such as isolation, engagement, or boredom), whether negative, positive, or neutral, are tied to the personality traits of the individual users, not the platform itself.

U&G theorists would explain the social media use of an extrovert, a person who thrives on social interaction with others, as satisfying his need to socialize. In contrast, according to U&G theorists, the lack of social media use by an introvert, a person who thrives in a quieter environment, satisfies her need for individual reflection. In other words, social media satisfy a range of needs. Moreover, a U&G theorist would be cautious in making statements such as "Social media isolate people," "Social media engage people," or "Social media create boredom," because they recognize the platform's flexibility, the variety of needs that people have, and the multiple ways such needs can be gratified via communication.

©Sam Edwards/Getty Images RF

Researchers exploring the characteristics of those who use the various types of social media have come to the following conclusions:

- *Some personality traits correlate with social media use.*
  - Extroverts use social media more frequently than do introverts.[30] Introverts gain strength from having more reflective moments, so they do not turn to social media as frequently as do extroverts. Extroverts, on the other hand, gain strength from interacting with people, a trait that can be easily expressed through social media.
  - Users who experience more social anxiety tend to use social media more frequently than do people who are less socially anxious.[31] For example, if you are concerned about saying the right thing in a given situation, you are more likely to want to test your message with a social media audience first. Less socially anxious people do not require as much feedback about the impressions they convey to others.

- Communication-based personality characteristics affect how people manage their privacy on social media. For example, people who are wary of lurkers on social media tend to take greater measures to protect their privacy and are more likely to use vague-booking, or posting intentionally vague social media updates, such as "I'm having the hardest week ever," or "I didn't see that coming."[32]

■ *People choose particular social media experiences based on their unique personality characteristics.*
- *Facebook users*: People with a greater need for entertainment and outlets for self-expression tend to interact frequently on Facebook.[33]
- *YouTube users*: Individuals who are motivated to interact socially, to be entertained, or to share viewing experiences gravitate to this platform.[34]
- *Social media users in general*: People who interact through social media can be divided into six general categories, as laid out in **Figure 7.6**.[35]

The unique profiles in **Figure 7.6** demonstrate how people use social media in different ways and for different reasons. What are the characteristics of your

Figure 7.6 Social Media User Profiles

Utilitarian users try to anticipate and think about all possible consequences before posting anything, to minimize problems.

Planners have a purpose for everything they post. They might discuss something controversial that has potentially adverse consequences if they feel there is a clear purpose for relaying the information.

Self-centered users present themselves clearly and do not necessarily care about the reactions of others when they post. Such a user is most driven by personal gain.

Unworried users don't give much extended thought to what they do when they interact through social media. They tend to engage in more mindless use of social media.

Sharing users freely share information through social media as a means of connecting with others. These users are likely to want to share everything they know through social media without much discrimination.

Protective users use caution not to reveal too much about themselves. These protective users of social media are often not concerned about violating other users' privacy expectations.

social media use? Do you tend to withhold pictures taken at a party, because you are concerned that a future employer might evaluate you negatively? If so, your behavior fits the utilitarian profile. Do you avoid posting phone numbers or specific meet-up location details? If you do, your behavior fits the protective orientation. And if you often know exactly what you are going to say through social media and have clear reasons for posting what you do, your behavior reflects a planning orientation.

You will identify with several of these user profiles at different stages of your life. When you are young, you might identify with the sharing profile, because you care about expanding your friendship network and finding potential dating partners. When you finish college and enter the job market, you might reflect the utilitarian, or consequence-driven, profile, because you realize that your social media interactions can affect your employment opportunities. Once you have a steady career, you might be an unworried user, especially if social media use is not as important to you as networking face-to-face within your company. Whatever your current perspective on social media use, you are likely to experience more rewarding interactions if you consider your goals as a user.

Evaluating Your CMC Interactions

A big difference between mass media and CMC is that the latter is interactive, meaning that it offers the potential for many to communicate. Using the Internet, romantic partners in long-distance relationships can maintain contact; members of the U.S. armed forces stationed overseas can communicate with family and friends; business can be conducted from almost any distance; videogame enthusiasts can compete with each other in virtually simulated worlds, forming friendships in the process. Some relationships exist entirely online.

Despite the evolving potential of CMC interactions, an important question remains: can strictly CMC-based interactions achieve deeper intimacy and enjoyment than face-to-face relationships? One group of theorists, describing what they call the **hyperpersonal perspective**, contend that, *in certain circumstances, CMC can be evaluated as more rewarding than face-to-face interaction.*[36]

©Design Pics/Kristy-Anne Glubish RF

Developed in the 1990s by communication scholar Joseph Walther, the hyperpersonal perspective debunked much of the research suggesting that CMC was an impersonal and unrewarding way to carry out relationships. Because CMC lacked the dimension of nonverbal communication, many people considered it an extremely limited medium for interaction. Not only did

Walther's work debunk the notion that CMC is merely impersonal communication but his propositions went on to suggest the circumstances under which CMC might be characterized as superior to face-to-face communication—or, as he calls it, a type of hyperpersonal interaction.

A hyperpersonal interaction can occur when a CMC user takes into account the following three factors when interacting online: (1) the ability to control one's self-presentation (i.e., the desire to edit and review messages before sending them), (2) the ability to control what cues one sends out (i.e., denying access to one's real name, identity, or images), and (3) the expectation that interaction partners may never actually meet face to face (i.e., the CMC relationship can exist in an entirely online context).[37]

If you prefer online dating, you might be familiar with one or more of the features of hyperpersonal interaction. Some online daters hide what they believe to be negative aspects of their identity (such as being a smoker or being overweight) to test how limiting this information, and in some instances engaging in positive distortions of the facts, changes the way people interact with them.[38]

CMC relationships sometimes evolve more quickly than face-to-face relationships. This happens in part because individuals tend to ask more direct questions through CMC, often as a way to make up for the lack of nonverbal cues.[39] This rapid disclosure can be highly rewarding, especially if, after you meet in person, you feel satisfied with the match. On the other hand, participants who construct a misleading online identity may appear to be more promising candidates than they actually are.

Many people continue to characterize CMC interaction as impersonal rather than hyperpersonal because they find interacting synchronously, or face to face, to be more rewarding. After all, face-to-face interaction allows for a far fuller range of both verbal and nonverbal messages. Nevertheless, Walther's research has changed the way communication theorists think about CMC and therefore remains crucial to any discussion of its value and applications.

Thinking Critically About CMC Messages

One of the most critical differences between face-to-face communication and CMC rests on content-level messages. As discussed earlier, this is because some forms of CMC (e-mail and text messages) lack nonverbal cues, such as tone. People using CMC have found some ways to try to convey tone and intent by using emoticons, capitalization, and boldface.

Although CMC expedites communication between people (think of the difference between sending a letter and sending an e-mail), the absence of nonverbal cues can result in misunderstandings. Consider the use of capitalization in CMC. A sender can use capitalization to emphasize part of a content-level message, such as "I DO NOT AGREE WITH THIS DECISION," or "PLEASE RESPOND BY THE END OF THE DAY." However, capitalization can also convey a range of relational-level meanings. If you use capitalization to highlight a sentence or two in a message, as in the previous examples, a receiver might think you are asserting that he is not intelligent enough to figure out what is critical. Moreover, many people don't like all caps because they feel they are being shouted at.

When deciding whether to use a CMC or face-to-face communication channel, always consider the verbal and nonverbal indicators that will be available to you. Research shows that people tend to interpret e-mail messages more negatively than senders intend,[40] because e-mails do not provide full access to nonverbal cues. If you think someone might misinterpret your e-mail, ask them to call you or try to arrange a face-to-face meeting instead of interacting through CMC.

With all of this in mind, if you are upset about a grade and wish to convey your frustrations to your professor, you might best manage this conversation in a medium that allows for the full range of both verbal and nonverbal expression. In face-to-face communication, nonverbal communication could help you convey the proper tone of respect with your content-level messages. Finally, there are circumstances in which sending an e-mail is more appropriate than engaging in face-to-face communication; you might introduce yourself to a new professional contact through an e-mail, as opposed to cold-calling or simply showing up at the place of business and risk interrupting.

SOCIAL MEDIA USE ACROSS CONTEXTS

Why do you use social media? Do you use them mostly to stay in touch with friends and family? Do you keep your personal network distinct from your work or school network? Perhaps you use one platform for socializing and another, like LinkedIn, for networking with others in your field. Of course, there are no right answers to these questions. Your use of social media most likely corresponds to your personal and professional goals. To illustrate, **Figure 7.7** lists common personal and professional uses of social media across communication contexts.

Each context presents unique challenges and opportunities for social media users. As the following examples illustrate, social media provide unique opportunities to share information, but they also require careful management.

Interpersonal Communication

Although many people use CMC to seek out new relationships, most people tend to use it to maintain existing ties.[41] Facebook is typically thought of as a way for individuals to connect with their peer networks.[42] But recent evidence suggests that many young adults also connect with their siblings, parents,[43] and extended family members through social media.[44] And the trend does not stop there:

- Compared with individuals from families with open communication, individuals from families that tend toward secretiveness are more likely to reject parental requests for Facebook site access.[45]

©KidStock/Getty Images RF

Figure 7.7 Examples of Social Media Uses Across Communication Contexts

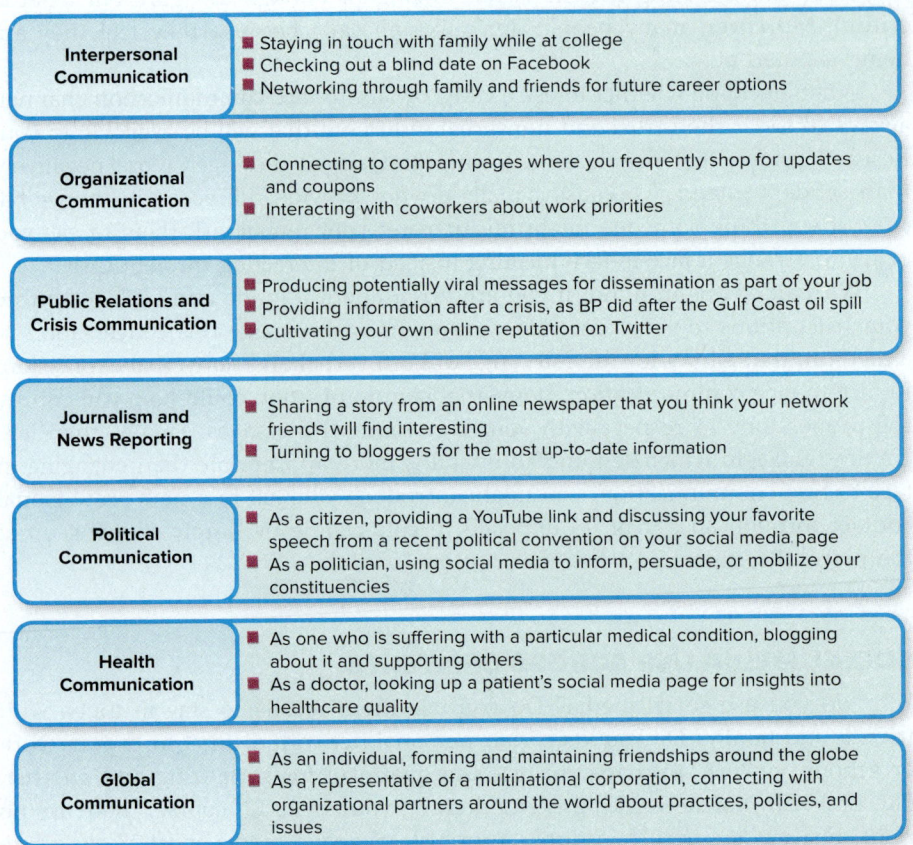

- In terms of family communication, young adults tend to interact most with siblings on Facebook and least with grandparents. Parents are somewhere in the middle. The younger generation also ends up providing more training for older generation family members about how to interact and manage privacy effectively through social media.[46]
- In a recent Pew Research Center study, the majority of parents (83 percent) reported being Facebook friends with their teenage children. Parents noted that the platform provides a convenient way to monitor their children's digital lives and to keep in touch.[47]

Just as familial networks benefit from the use of social media, so do friendship networks. For example, social media help us maintain existing friendships as we age and encounter new experiences. Social media help maintain both strong ties and weak ties. **Strong ties** are *relationships that we are highly committed to and that we devote substantial energy to maintaining,* *regardless of changes in our life circumstances.* With strong ties, such as those with your best friends, you are likely to interact face to face and over the phone, as well as through social media. In other words, social media provide yet another platform for strengthening your most vital relationships.

Social media are unique in that they offer significant opportunities for maintaining weak ties as well. **Weak ties** are *personal relationships to which we are not as committed overall and in which we would not invest as much time and energy to maintain.* Social media provide a great platform for maintaining relationships with people whom we might otherwise lose contact with, such as friends from high school or people who live far away. Instead of losing these friends, we may choose to maintain limited contact with these relationships by uploading images and videos, posting status updates, and reading about one another's lives through blog posts.

Organizational Communication

The use of social media is also changing organizational communication, a topic we will address in more detail in **Chapter 8**. Companies and organizations use sites like Facebook and LinkedIn to seek and confirm the information that prospective employees share during interviews and, ultimately, to make employment decisions.[48] As a result, employees have been fired for casual comments made to their social networks about their personal lives or their companies.[49] If an employer discovers information about you that conflicts with what is available through more formal organizational channels, you could lose your job, or you might not be hired in the first place.

Organizations also use social media to facilitate more effective internal and external organizational functioning. For example, some companies use social media so that members of the organization can work together on group projects or blog about pertinent workplace issues. Social media provide a venue for asking questions related to administrative matters or new work priorities and help facilitate external organizational communication practices, such as marketing, public relations, and crisis communication. Businesses use social media to connect with customers, respond to complaints, and interact with critical stakeholders.

©moorboard/Getty Images RF

If you are using social media to communicate on behalf of your organization, either internally or externally, use good judgment when choosing whom to welcome into your network. A recent study shows that most professionals who receive Facebook friend requests from coworkers accept the requests. However, some companies require employees to be more private about business matters; individuals at these companies tend to deny or ignore friend requests from coworkers.⁵⁰ Always be sure you understand your company's disclosure policies before you post messages that concern the company or are addressed to your fellow employees.

Public Relations and Crisis Communication

Over the past 10 years, public relations officers and crisis communication experts have increasingly used social media in their jobs. More and more companies are employing people whose primary responsibility is to craft messages that have the potential to "go viral." **Viral social media campaigns** are *video messages created with the intentions that people will forward and discuss them through social media and that the messages will be widely seen.*

Do you remember how you followed the results of the presidential election campaign? When it comes to natural disasters and breaking news, public relations representatives rely on all kinds of media outlets, including traditional media and social media, to keep people updated. Although social media allow companies to respond immediately to developing concerns—say, about a product recall—and to convey urgent messages, traditional media, such as news reports and press releases, also remain important sources of information.⁵¹ Individuals, too, can be sources of messages that go viral during crises, such as those who helped spark the uprisings in Egypt, Libya, and Syria.

Journalism and News Reporting

Many news agencies have developed a strong digital presence, allowing their audiences to read and respond to messages online or share commentary about events. Watching the nightly news, you have probably noticed the inclusion of social media messages or Twitter feeds, some created by professionals but also some by average television viewers who are social media users. *The New York Times* has adapted particularly well to media convergence by making subscriptions available in both print and digital formats. The electronic version of the daily *Times* includes written stories, video clips from its correspondents, links to YouTube videos, slide shows, citizen journalist or blog content, and a social media format that makes interacting, posting comments, and sharing content easy.

Today it is possible for anyone to create content to circulate online. With citizen journalists and nontraditional news sites circulating and distributing content about world events, the practice of gatekeeping now extends beyond large news agencies.⁵² For this reason it's absolutely critical to learn how to distinguish real reporting on actual events from fake news and mere opinion. When encountering a news story through social media, ask yourself: "Is the information presented objectively where assertions are backed up with evidence?," "Are expert opinions and researchers with credentials incorporated into the story?," and "Are the central facts conveyed in the article reinforced in other reputable sources?" If not, the hallmarks of objective informative reporting and source credibility are missing from that source.[53] Being critical of the news you read and share on social media can help prevent misinformation and confusion.

Political Communication

Social media, in all their forms, play a prominent role in political election cycles. When individuals and groups discuss their views on sites like Twitter, they inform our views on issues of policy, for instance. President Trump, who prefers to interact directly with his over 2 million Twitter followers rather than have his message circulated by traditional journalists, is a case in point. Interactive political discussions on social media can better our understanding of political activity on both a small and large scale.[54] For example, social media sites make it possible for a speechwriter to study trends in a political opponent's rhetoric and allow undecided voters to access information that will help decide their vote or party affiliation.

As with face to face communication, political discussions through social media can highlight deeply rooted differences. Unfortunately, social media users do not always share their political views in thoughtful ways, sometimes violating the rules of courteous dialogue. Anonymity and physical distance over social media embolden some people to be more direct and forceful in their political opinions than they would be face to face. Moreover, research shows that, unless someone is identified as an **opinion leader**, meaning that *a range of people consistently turn to that person for advice and informed perspectives on issues,* that person's views are unlikely to change the opinions of others.[55] Nonetheless, political messaging over social media signifies political involvement in the same way that placing a candidate sign in your front yard or a bumper sticker on your car has long served a similar purpose. Political engagement is important in a democratic society; to the extent that social media encourage engagement, they can be a positive force.

Health Communication

Increasingly, healthcare providers are struggling with the unique challenges social media present to their field. The Health Insurance Portability and Accountability Act (HIPAA), a series of regulations governing healthcare practices, requires healthcare providers to exercise extreme caution in protecting the privacy and security of patients' health information. In keeping with HIPAA regulations, most doctors do not allow patients to connect with them through social media in which patients reveal their identity.[56] However, when it comes to seeking support for healthcare issues, people frequently turn to social media networks, websites, or blogs to find people who also suffer from the same conditions.

Whereas most doctors deny Facebook friend requests from patients, some turn to social media to learn more about the patients they are treating. A social worker or therapist might want to observe what a patient is disclosing to an online social network, for example.[57] However, all it takes is one Facebook friend request to a primary physician to trigger a privacy breach that can affect the patient, the doctor, and the medical facility.

Global Communication

The term **global communication** refers to *exchanges between people whose communication practices, patterns, and understandings differ because they come from distinct cultures*. Global communication can occur in a person's own neighborhood, where people from many parts of the world live and work; on a college campus, where students of diverse backgrounds gather; on the Internet, which connects people all over the world; or in the more formal venues of international business, politics, and diplomacy.

Through advances in communication technology and social media, individuals around the globe can make contact with one another. Global communication therefore has become a prominent area of study. As never before, we can gain insights into cultural differences, share experiences, and connect as a global village. Just consider the number of important social movements that have been fueled and supported by social media, such as the Occupy movements, the People's Climate March, and more recently, the Women's March on Washington. Indeed, amid the chaos and violence of the Libyan revolution, social media became an important news source for people around the world, as well as a coordinating tool for those directly involved.

Organizations, too, are adjusting to this new global world by practicing outsourcing and establishing offices in countries with different legal and cultural

©Cynthia Edorh/Getty Images

practices. You may end up working for a global company where you will need to interact with people at times that don't correspond with the traditional workday. Social media, for example, can be a useful way to share information about different practices, policies, and issues with offices around the globe.

PROTECTING AND PRESENTING YOURSELF ON SOCIAL MEDIA

As we explored in **Chapter 1** on perception, impression management is the careful control of the information provided (in this case, through social media) when supporting desired viewpoints and impressions. One important way to do this is to give careful consideration to the ways you manage your privacy online.

Managing Your Privacy Online

Communication privacy management (CPM) theory *focuses on the processes people use to decide whether to reveal or conceal private information and how to manage the private information they share with others.*[58] CPM theory is particularly relevant when it comes to studying social media, privacy, and disclosure practices, because so many people around the globe use some type of social media. As a way of analyzing how people manage their privacy, CPM theory sets out three categories of rules that people adhere to: privacy co-ownership rules, privacy linkage rules, and privacy permeability rules.[59]

- **Co-ownership rules** *clarify your expectations for how much you expect people to check in with you before sharing information about you with others.* For example, you might ask the members of your social media network not to share information about your health with people outside the network, but that you are open to discussing it fully within the network. By establishing this rule, you clarify their responsibilities as co-owners of that private information. Or, you might establish a rule that you don't want any of your friends talking about your dating life before asking you first if it's okay to do so. Most people prefer to retain control over sensitive information that might be passed on about them.

- **Linkage rules** *clarify any specific people who should or should not have access to your private information.* Whereas co-ownership rules are more general parameters about sharing, linkage rules involve stipulations about sharing information with specific people. Thus, if you are seeking advice from your network about how to handle a disagreement with a relational partner, you could stipulate that they not share your concerns with your partner.

- **Permeability rules** *clarify how much private information, regarding specific topics, you are comfortable with others sharing.* Users of social media might navigate permeability rules by clearly establishing with their network which topics they can talk about online and which topics are off limits. Another example of a permeability rule might be asking a closer work friend to not talk about your personal life at work. Permeability rules specify specific topics that are okay or not to discuss with others.

Table 7.2 Top Motivators for Deleting Social Media Content

Social media users most frequently make decisions in order to:

1. **Manage conflict:** Deleting a post that creates tension or friction in an important relationship
2. **Ensure safety:** Removing an image that makes it too easy for people to know exactly where you live
3. **Prevent getting sued or ridiculed:** Removing rants that friends make about their jobs on your site
4. **Minimize job-related problems:** Removing posts that show you are away from home—for instance, when you took a sick day from work and your coworkers expected you to be at home
5. **Control impressions:** Removing a post that possibly portrays you to be interpreted as insensitive or immature
6. **Regulate emotions:** Removing posts that demonstrate an emotional reaction rather than a clear and rational thought, such as someone who verbally attacks another on your site
7. **Remove any indicators of sour relationships:** Deleting every picture and post of an ex-boyfriend or girlfriend and defriending that person

SOURCE: Child, J. T., Haridakis, P. M., & Petronio, S. (2012). Blogging privacy rule orientations, privacy management, and content deletion practices: The variability of online privacy management activity at different stages of social media use. *Computers in Human Behavior*, *28*, 1859–1872.

In addition to discussing, negotiating, and clarifying privacy rules, users of social media can also use privacy settings to ensure the protection of information. But even when you clearly lay out privacy-management parameters, **privacy turbulence** can occur, meaning that *those allowed to access your private information have not upheld the stipulated obligations.*

Research shows that most users of social media examine their posted information, photos, and content and make deletions.[60] This is a healthy sign. However, a smaller group of users never make deletions. This group views doing so as unnecessary, either because they practice caution before posting or because they simply do not care how others see them. The top seven reasons motivating deletions among social media users are described in **Table 7.2**.

Perhaps the most effective way to practice good privacy-management habits is to learn from the mistakes of others. The news is full of stories about people who did not believe they would be held accountable for what they communicated through social media. Consider these recent examples:

- Talking inappropriately about work on Facebook gets people fired all the time.

CHALLENGE YOURSELF

How should I manage social media to gain and maintain friendships without getting in trouble with others, including employers?

The default privacy settings on most sites are not designed to protect your privacy. On the contrary, companies profit from collecting your information and selling it to others. Changing your default settings can prevent your posts from potentially popping up in online search engines. It can also ensure that your information is available only to the people you have designated as friends.

- Explore the privacy options on each social media platform you use. For example, you may decide to establish different groups and then sort people according to the privacy norms you use in those groups. You can usually give a group unique access to part of your social media site. Each time you want to post something, consider which group or groups will have access to that content. You might choose to post similar content separately for each unique group, such as when you do not want members across groups to be able to discuss your posts with one another.

- Periodically return to the content you have posted and make deletions. Also, review your friend lists and unfriend individuals who shouldn't be on your site. If you haven't interacted with someone in a year, chances are, you won't miss having that person as a social media friend. Some people only want to be your friend so that they can passively observe your posts and access information about you.

- Be smart about what you post through all social media platforms, even seemingly ephemeral forms like Snapchat. Nothing that you capture and transmit through a mediated communication channel is completely private, untraceable, and uncapturable. Only share content that you don't consider confidential. If you follow this simple advice you will be less likely to experience privacy turbulence over social media.

- An individual was recently fired for going into extensive detail on Facebook about how he wanted to kill his boss. He had forgotten that one of his coworkers was a friend. The friend showed the boss the post, and the individual got fired.
- Another person revealed on Facebook that she wanted to use all of her sick time before quitting her job, only to be fired hours later.
- A newly hired employee was told that he would have to pass a drug test that would be administered the next day. Following the interview, he posted on Facebook "How do I pass a drug test in 24 hours?" This post got back to company.[61]

It is easy to misjudge the way a post will be taken by others. Just as face-to-face communication cannot be reversed, it can often be difficult to withdraw a written record, like a post. Because you can be held accountable for anything you say through social media, it is important to think before you post. It's also a good idea to stay away from social media when you are angry, upset, or emotional.

Presenting Yourself Online

A useful framework for understanding your interactions on social media is the concept of self-presentation.[62] Sociologist Erving Goffman used the metaphor of actors in a play to explain the ways we present ourselves in different social contexts. According to Goffman, the various situations in which you find yourself require that you act certain parts. For example, when you are in the classroom, you take on the role of student. At home, you are a son or daughter, a parent or spouse, a sibling or roommate. Some of these roles, like those you adopt at work or school, are more public—they take place "onstage." Others, like those you adopt at home or in private, are considered "backstage" roles.

In the context of social media, the internal dialogues, values, attitudes, and perspectives you do not share happen backstage. The images, messages, links, videos, and even friendships you post or make public take place onstage. Just

BUILDER

LEARN TO ANALYZE YOUR SOCIAL MEDIA PRESENCE

In this exercise you will choose one of your social media sites to analyze. If you want to analyze your Facebook page, an application like Wolfram Alpha can help you gather data about your user trends. Visit **www.wolframalpha.com** and type the phrase "Facebook report" into the search box. Now consider the following questions about your social media presence:

- What topics do you post about most often? What do think these topics say about who you are and what you value?
- In photos or videos posted of you, what locations appear most frequently? What activities are you engaging in?
- Who comments on your posts, and what is the nature and tone of their commentary? What impressions might these interactions give to those who don't know you?
- What organizations, causes, and groups are you affiliated with through social media?
- Who do you most wish to connect with through social media? Your family and friends, or maybe a potential employer?

After you've answered these questions, consider how you might adjust your social media presence to make the best impression to your friends, family, and potential employers.

as the clothes you wear to an interview communicate a certain message about you and your attitude toward the job, the content you share over social media acts as a sort of costume, conveying your social media identity to the personal and professional contacts in your network. Be certain that you present yourself in a manner that will best serve your goals.

CHAPTER REVIEW

This chapter identified the most common sources of mediated communication and discussed some of its most relevant features. We also examined the many aspects of interacting over social media, the ways you use social media across a variety of contexts, and how you can best present and protect yourself online. Mediated communication facilitates flexibility, efficiency, and variety in how we access and convey information. As technology continues to advance and to change the way we interact, mediated communication is all the more worthy of your attention and study.

KEY TERMS

mediated communication, 121
mass communication, 123
mass media, 123
computer-mediated communication (CMC), 123
media convergence, 123
gatekeeping, 126
agenda-setting, 127
cultivation effect, 127
media literacy, 128
synchronous communication, 129
asynchronous communication, 129
social media, 129
boundary-crossing medium, 131

uses and gratifications (U&G) theory, 133
hyperpersonal perspective, 135
strong ties, 138
weak ties, 139
viral social media campaigns, 140
opinion leader, 141
global communication, 142
communication privacy management (CPM) theory, 143
co-ownership rules, 143
linkage rules, 143
permeability rules, 143
privacy turbulence, 144

STUDY QUESTIONS

1. How do the components of the traditional communication model (sender-message-receiver-feedback) apply to mass communication sources of information?
2. Analyze a television program by describing how it challenges a societal norm or perpetuates a stereotype.
3. Explain the difference between synchronous and asynchronous communication channels. Then make two lists: in one, list all the circumstances in which you would prefer to communicate synchronously; in the other, list those in which you would choose an asynchronous communication channel. Explain your reasons for your choices.
4. Identify the seven contexts of social media use discussed in the text. Think of one example, not described in this text, of social media use in each context.
5. State one example of a co-ownership rule, a linkage rule, and a permeability rule that you have practiced.

ENDNOTES

1. China, I. (2016, May 12). 85% Weibo month active users from mobile in Q1 2016. *China Internet Watch.* Retrieved from https://www.chinainternetwatch.com/17509/weibo-q1-2016/
2. Chakroff, J. L., & Nathanson, A. I. (2008). Parent and school interventions: Mediation and media literacy. In S. L. Calvert & B. J. Wilson (Eds.), *The handbook of children, media, and development* (pp. 552–576). Oxford, UK: Blackwell.
3. Harrison, J., & Cantor, J. (1997). The relationship between media consumption and eating disorders. *Journal of Communication, 47,* 40–67.
4. Dominick, J. R. (2005). *Dynamics of mass communication: Media in the digital age.* New York: McGraw-Hill.
5. Thurlow, C., Lengel, L., & Tomic, A. (2004). *Computer mediated communication: Social interaction and the Internet.* Thousand Oaks, CA: Sage.
6. Rubin, A. M. (1984). Ritualized and instrumental television viewing. *Journal of Communication, 34,* 67–77.
7. Kim, J., & Haridakis, P. (2009). The role of Internet user characteristics and motives in explaining three dimensions of Internet addiction. *Journal of Computer-Mediated Communication, 14,* 988–1015.
8. Haridakis, P., & Hanson, G. (2009). Social interaction and co-viewing with YouTube: Blending mass communication reception and social connection. *Journal of Broadcasting and Electronic Media, 53,* 317–335.
9. Koblin, J. (2016, June 30). How much do we love TV? Let us count the ways. *The New York Times.* Available at http://www.nytimes.com
10. Husemann, L. R., Dubow, E. F., & Yang, G. (2013). Why it is hard to believe that media violence causes aggression. In K. E. Dill (Ed.), *The Oxford handbook of media psychology* (pp. 159–171). New York: Oxford University Press.
11. *Youth violence: A report of the surgeon general.* (2001). Retrieved from www.surgeongeneral.gov
12. Brockmyer, J. F. (2015). Playing violent video games and desensitization to violence. *Child and Adolescent Psychiatric Clinics of North America, 24,* 65–77.

13. Harrison & Cantor.
14. Chakroff & Nathanson.
15. Wilson, J., & Wilson, S. L. (1998). *Mass media/mass culture* (4th ed.). New York: McGraw-Hill.
16. Goel, V. (2014, June 29). Facebook tinkers with users' emotions in news feed experiment, stirring outcry. *The New York Times.* Retrieved from: http://www.nytimes.com
17. Gottfried, J., & Shearer, E. (2016, May 26). News use across social media platforms 2016. *Pew Research Center.* Retrieved from http://www.pewresearch.org
18. Beam, M. A., Hutchens, M. J., & Hmielowski, J.D. (2016). Clicking vs. sharing: The relationship between online news behavior and political knowledge. *Computers in Human Behavior, 59,* 215–220.
19. Lim, J. (2006). A cross-lagged analysis of agenda setting among online news media. *Journalism and Mass Communication Quarterly, 83,* 298–312.
20. Harper, J. (2016, October 17). Liberal bias in the media traced back to 1964. *The Washington Times.* Retrieved from http://www.washingtontimes.com
21. Bilandzic, H. (2006). The perception of distance in the cultivation process: A theoretical consideration of the relationship between television content, processing experience, and perceived distance. *Communication Theory, 16,* 333–355.
22. Gerbner, G. (1998). Cultivation analysis: An overview. *Mass Communication and Society, 1,* 75–77.
23. Reamer, N. D. (2012). *Mediated sexuality and teen pregnancy: Exploring the secret life of the American teenager.* Unpublished master's thesis, Kent State University.
24. Gennaro, C. D., & Dutton, W. H. (2007). Reconfiguring friendships: Social relationship and the Internet. *Information, Communication and Society, 10,* 591–618.
25. Jeong, S., Cho, H., & Hwang, Y. (2012). Media literacy interventions: A meta-analytic review. *Journal of Communication, 62,* 454–472.
26. Christ, W. G., & Potter, J. (1998). Media, literacy, media education, and the academy. *Journal of Communication, 48,* 5–15.
27. Facebook (2016, September 30). Facebook newsroom statistics. Retrieved from http://newsroom.fb.com/company-info/
28. Child, J. T., & Petronio, S. (2011). Unpacking the paradoxes of privacy in CMC relationships: The challenges of blogging and relational communication on the Internet. In K. B. Wright & L. M. Webb (Eds.), *Computer-mediated communication in personal relationships* (pp. 21–40). New York: Peter Lang.
29. Rubin, A. M., & Haridakis, P. M. (2001). Mass communication research at the dawn of the 21st century. *Communication Yearbook, 24,* 73–97.
30. Correa, T., Hinsley, A. W., & Zuniga, H. G. (2010). Who interacts on the Web? The intersection of users' personality and social media use. *Computers in Human Behavior, 26,* 247–253.
31. Ibid.
32. Child, J. T., & Starcher, S. (2016). Fuzzy Facebook privacy boundaries: Exploring mediated lurking, vague-booking, and Facebook privacy management. *Computers in Human Behavior, 54,* 483–490.
33. Hunt, D., Atkin, D., & Krishnan, A. (2012). The influence of computer-mediated communication apprehension on motives for Facebook use. *Journal of Broadcasting and Electronic Media, 56,* 187–202.

34. Haridakis & Hanson.
35. Child, J. T., Haridakis, P. M., & Petronio, S. (2012). Blogging privacy rule orientations, privacy management, and content deletion practices: The variability of online privacy management activity at different stages of social media use. *Computers in Human Behavior, 28*, 1859–1872.
36. Walther, J. B. (1996). Computer-mediated communication: Impersonal, interpersonal, and hyperpersonal interaction. *Communication Research, 23*, 3–43.
37. Ibid.
38. Ellison, N. B., Hancock, J. T., & Toma, C. L. (2012). Profile as promise: A framework for conceptualizing veracity in online dating self-presentations. *New Media and Society, 14*, 45–62.
39. Walther.
40. Byron, K. (2008). Carrying too heavy a load? The communication and miscommunication of emotion by email. *Academy of Management Review, 33*, 309–327.
41. Gennaro, C. D., & Dutton, W. H. (2007). Reconfiguring friendships: Social relationship and the Internet. *Information, Communication and Society, 10*, 591–618.
42. Pempek, T. A., Yermolayeva, Y. A., & Calvert, S. L. (2009). College students' social networking experiences on Facebook. *Journal of Applied Developmental Psychology, 30*, 227–238.
43. Child, J. T., & Westermann, D. A. (2013). Let's be Facebook friends: Exploring parental Facebook friend requests from a communication privacy management (CPM) perspective. *Journal of Family Communication, 13*, 46–59.
44. Child, J. T., Duck, A. R., Andrews, L. A., Butauski, M. & Petronio, S. (2015). Family members' management of privacy on Facebook. *Journal of Family Communication, 15*, 349–367.
45. Child, J. T., & Westermann, D. A. (2013). Let's be Facebook friends: Exploring parental Facebook friend requests from a communication privacy management (CPM) perspective. *Journal of Family Communication, 13*, 46–59.
46. Child, J. T., Duck, A. R., Andrews, L. A., Butauski, M. & Petronio, S. (2015). Family members' management of privacy on Facebook. *Journal of Family Communication, 15*, 349–367.
47. Gao, G. (2015, April 10). On social media, mom and dad are watching. *Pew Research Center*. Retrieved from http://www.pewresearch.org
48. Child & Westermann.
49. Frankel, A. (2011, September 12). NLRB judge: Employees can bitch about their jobs on Facebook. *Thomas Reuters*. Retrieved from http://blogs.reuters.com/alison-frankel/2011/09/12/nlrb-judge-employees-can-bitch-about-their-jobs-on-facebook/
50. Frampton, B. D., & Child, J. T. (2013). Friend or not to friend: Coworker Facebook friend requests as an application of communication privacy management theory. *Computers in Human Behavior, 29*, 2257–2264.
51. Shea, V. (1995). *Netiquette*. San Francisco: Albion.
52. Marchi, R. (2012). With Facebook, blogs, and fake news, teens reject journalistic "objectivity." *Journal of Communication Inquiry, 36*, 246–262.
53. Craft, S., Ashley, S., & Maksl, A. (2016). Elements of news literacy: A focus group study of how teenagers define news and why they consume it. *Electronic News, 10*, 143–160.
54. Himelboim, I., Lariscy, R. W., Tinkham, S. F., & Sweetser, K. D. (2012). Social media and online political communication: The role of interpersonal informational trust and openness. *Journal of Broadcasting and Electronic Media, 56*, 92–115.

55. Lazarsfeld, P., Berelson, B., & Gaudet, H. (1944). *The people's choice: How the voter makes up his mind in a presidential campaign.* New York: Columbia University Press.
56. Bosslet, G. T., Torke, A. M., Hickman, S. E., Terry, C. L., & Helfy, P. R. (2011). The patient–doctor relationship and online social networks: Results of a national survey. *Journal of General Internal Medicine, 26,* 1168–1174.
57. Ibid.
58. Petronio, S. (2002). *Boundaries of privacy: Dialectics of disclosure.* Albany: State University of New York Press.
59. Child, J. T., Pearson, J. C., & Petronio, S. (2009). Blogging communication, and privacy management: Development of the blogging privacy management measure. *Journal of the American Society for Information Science and Technology, 60,* 2079–2094.
60. Child, J. T., Petronio, S., Agyeman-Budu, E. A., & Westermann, D. A. (2011). Blog scrubbing: Exploring triggers that change privacy rules. *Computers in Human Behavior, 27,* 2017–2027.
61. Price, L. (2016, July 8). 20 tales of employees who were fired because of social media posts. *People.* Retrieved from http://www.people.com
62. Goffman, E. (1959). *The presentation of self in everyday life.* New York: Anchor Books.

Blue and Yellow Cube Icon, Connecting Globally Icon, Mountain Icon, Chapter Review Arrows Circle Icon: ©McGraw Hill Education

chapter 8

Organizational and Small-Group Communication

©DLILLC/Corbis Images RF

Many people consider their role in a group or organization to be an important part of who they are.[1] This chapter will examine the key concepts and practices of organizational culture and teach you how to function effectively in organizations and groups.

LEARNING OBJECTIVES

After reading this chapter, you should be able to:

- Define organizational culture, and discuss the proper methods for assessing the culture of an organization.
- Explain how small groups and teams function within organizations and the role communication plays.
- Describe leadership as a process of communication.
- Name and explain strategies for cultivating positive relationships in organizations.

WHAT IS ORGANIZATIONAL CULTURE?

Understanding an organization's culture means understanding the "right way to do things in the eyes of an organization or company."[2] In some organizations, employee interactions focus exclusively on work issues and employees are encouraged to leave their personal lives at home. In others, the culture is more open to what is known as work-life balance. **Organizational culture** refers to *the attitudes, values, and beliefs that are common among, and that characterize the interactions of, members of an organization.* Learning to quickly assess culture will help you adapt your behavior and communication practices.

©Ces'r Vera/Corbis RF

Often people are so immersed in their organization's culture that they are not even aware that it is a culture with a unique set of characteristics. In contrast, outsiders or newcomers, with their fresh eyes, are in a better position to become cultural detectives—that is, they can observe many behaviors and interactions that influence workplace culture and beliefs.[3]

Investigating Organizational Culture

Organizations communicate their cultural values in several ways: (1) the way employees use language and the stories they tell, (2) the rituals and routines they adhere to, and (3) the symbols and artifacts on display in the environment. **Table 8.1** provides a set of questions to consider for each of these three realms as you attempt to investigate an organization's overall culture. **Table 8.2** will help you determine what your findings may reveal.

Keep in mind that all three areas (language and storytelling, rituals and routines, and cultural markers) are critical to understanding organizational culture. Furthermore, employees will not always directly communicate aspects of their culture—sometimes because they are too used to them to perceive them. Nonetheless, it is important for you to understand and consider culture when evaluating whether you would be comfortable and effective working for a particular company.

However, you might have to depend on your own sleuthing abilities to extract information about organizational practices related to difference, diversity, and advancement. No human resources professional would say, "We do not promote women in this organization," but your observations may lead you to this conclusion. Still, be cautious in putting too much interpretation into any single marker of organizational culture. For example, an organization with written policies designed to promote work-life balance may experience complaints from employees who feel they have to pick up the slack for someone who is taking time off. Unfortunately, this attitude can actually deter people from taking advantage of such policies.[4] So, you should be

Table 8.1 Questions for Investigating an Organization's Culture

Language Use and Storytelling	Established Rituals and Routines	Prominent Cultural Markers (Symbols and Artifacts)

■ What terms or "lingo" does the group commonly use?
■ How do members refer to one another (e.g., coworker, colleague, associate, friend)?
■ Who is frequently discussed as a hero or role model?
■ Who, if anyone, is considered a villain? What stories are shared about this person?
■ How frequently does the group communicate formally (e.g., in meetings) versus informally (coffee breaks, lunch, or after work)?
■ What mode do they use to communicate with one another?
  • By e-mail?
  • Face to face?
■ Do members openly and respectfully engage in conflict?
■ Which topics do members avoid talking about at work?
■ Are there members that others avoid, or, alternatively, go out of their way to talk to?
	■ What procedures are followed for evaluating work?
	■ Who makes decisions? How many members are involved in decision making?
	■ How are members disciplined or rewarded?
	  • What procedures or activities are in place for rewarding people for exemplary work?
	  • When someone does not meet expectations, what procedures are followed?
	■ Which rules in the handbook or policy manual are most prominent?
	  • Does the company have antifraternization or dating policies?
	  • Is every aspect of work spelled out, or are policies flexible regarding the completion of tasks?
	■ What types of celebrations are in place to bring people together?
	  • How, if at all, does the organization formally acknowledge its heroes?
	  • How, if at all, does the organization bring people together socially?
		■ Does professional status determine the location of size of members' offices?
		■ Are executives or managers separated from general employees?
		■ Can members bring their children or pets to work?
		■ Does a security officer and/or receptionist monitor access to the organization?
		■ How do people dress—formally or casually? Do some members have earrings, tattoos, or unusual hair colors?
		■ What is the function of technology in the organization?
		  • Do members have access to computers, cell phones, or Internet-based technologies?
		  • Are they free to listen to music while they work?
		■ How diverse are the people in each level of the organization?
		  • What is the proportion of men to women at each level?
		  • Are the facilities accessible to members and clients with disabilities?

looking for themes supported across multiple indicators of organizational culture. You are not likely to find an organization that is completely congruent with your own preferences. Weigh the benefits and drawbacks of a company's organizational culture in relation to your own preferences. You might not take a job with an organization that stresses high productivity and

Table 8.2 Using Findings to Understand an Organization

Language Use and Storytelling	Established Rituals and Routines	Prominent Cultural Markers (Symbols and Artifacts)
■ When heroes are described as assertive, it may suggest that the organization values people who push for new opportunities. ■ When laughter is encouraged and members refer to one another using first names, the culture can be described as relaxed. ■ When groups meet frequently, this suggests a culture that values group participation and collaboration, versus independent decision making. ■ Understanding whom people turn to for answers, or whom they avoid, may suggest where power lies within the organization.	■ When rewards, such as monthly bonuses, are given to top performers, it suggests that productivity is valued. Rewards for other aspects of performance, such as mentoring newcomers or making charitable contributions, indicate other kinds of values. ■ When few events are planned to bring people together—picnics, or a monthly potluck meal—a more formal culture is in place, one that does not encourage the mingling of the personal and the professional. ■ When few people are consulted before important decisions are made, the culture is one where power is centralized. ■ When a yearly celebration is held for awarding employees, it suggests a supportive and appreciative culture.	■ When managers are segregated on their own floor or wing, with offices that are larger than those of general employees, management is valued more highly than employees. ■ When employees display personal pictures and artifacts, the organization demonstrates that members are valued beyond their formal roles in the workplace. ■ The presence of gatekeepers suggest a formal organization with strict hierarchy. ■ Upper management that lacks diversity in gender, race, or age may avoid advancing members who represent those groups. ■ Accessibility to all people demonstrates that diversity matters to an organization.

extensive time commitments if you know you need weekends to unplug completely from work.

As you evaluate the aspects of an organization's culture, keep in mind that who you are and where you come from will impact the conclusions you draw. For example, if you are a member of a dominant culture (as discussed in **Chapter 6**), your perspective on a particular organization's culture will differ in important ways from that of someone from a nondominant culture, or co-culture. A fully able-bodied individual may claim that her organizational culture is tolerant of diversity; however, if you speak to a member with a disability from the same organization, you might get a different answer. This is similarly true of gender inequalities. Asking a white, middle-class man whether women have equal opportunities within his company would gain you less insight than talking directly with women in the organization.

©Huntstock/age fotostock RF

SKILL BUILDER

ANALYZE ORGANIZATIONAL CULTURE

You can learn a lot from studying the organizational culture at your current workplace. Use the information below to identify the characteristics of organizational culture where you work. Do you see these characteristics as strengths or weaknesses?

- In **Table 8.1** identify at least two bullet points under each of the three main headings of organizational culture (language use and storytelling, established rituals and routines, and prominent cultural markers) that stand out to you in the context of your current workplace. Apply these characteristics to your observations.

- Using **Table 8.2** analyze and evaluate the characteristics you note. For example, if you notice that people are almost always promoted from within the organization, you might conclude that this organization values well-rounded employees who know the company well.

- Choose someone you trust from your current job, and discuss with them the characteristics of organizational culture that you noted, as well as your evaluations of them. Does your coworker agree about these characteristics and what they communicate about the organization? With your coworker's input, can you expand your list of observations?

- Finally, discuss with your coworker how you might reinforce the more positive aspects of organizational culture. How could you work together to change aspects of organizational culture that you find troubling? Start small. Organizations often have dominant cultural characteristics, meaning that small things can bring about significant change.

Your own values and observations about workplace culture are important to consider when you interview for a position. When you know the type of culture that appeals to you, you can seek out organizations that share your values and communication style. Perhaps you will even take on a leadership position where you are responsible for creating a culture that will attract others to the organization.

Understanding Organizational Structure

In addition to organizational culture, an organization's structure affects communication. Among the primary structural features that impact communication are hierarchy, differentiation and specialization, and formalization.

Hierarchy comprises *the levels of responsibility and relationships within an organization*. Some organizations stress hierarchy more than others. Those that are strongly hierarchical lay out clear procedures for whom employees report to up the entire chain of command. Moreover, individuals further up the chain of command rarely communicate directly with those in the lowest levels. Messages go through the hierarchy to reach appropriate audiences.[5] The military is a strongly hierarchical organization. Each person has a clearly defined rank, and a clear structure exists for who is in charge of decision making at each level of the organization. Although not as rigid as the military, colleges and universities also have hierarchies; students who have an issue with their instructor must take the matter to the instructor before other administrators. Organizations vary in the degree to which they depend on hierarchy. Organizations that place less stress on hierarchy empower multiple individuals to have a say in decision making.

Differentiation and specialization refers to *the division of labor in an organization and the degree to which each individual has a unique role and responsibility*.[6] Many fast-food and service industry jobs incorporate a high degree of differentiation and specialization of tasks to reduce uncertainty in the work environment. Each person knows precisely what he needs to do: one person takes the food orders, another fills the drink orders, and another fries the hamburgers.

In some settings this kind of specialization can make work mindlessly repetitious, but in other settings it can create a strong team of experts who can respond collectively to a wide range of concerns—more so than could one individual trying to manage multiple tasks. The emergency room of a hospital is an example of an organizational team that has members with a high degree of specialization and the ability to respond to a range of problems. General medical doctors and nurses work in shifts. If a patient arrives at the hospital needing more specialized expertise, on-call doctors are consulted and brought into the hospital.

Not every organization has highly specialized and differentiated roles. Some organizations incorporate **strategic ambiguity**, or *intentional uncertainty and vagueness*, so that they can adapt more easily to changing circumstances.[7] In either case, communication flows from the organization's approach to division of labor and specialization.

Formalization refers to *the rules, procedures, and norms that exist for carrying out work practices*. Highly formalized organizations have extensive rules and manuals in place to specify what people do and how they do it. Organizations with less formalization allow individuals a great deal of flexibility in how they carry out their work. For example, many student groups elect leaders (e.g., president and vice president) who fulfill their duties for their organizational groups with few formalized structures from the student body government. However, the same groups usually have handbooks that are shared within the group and that help provide formalization to carrying out leadership roles. An organization can incorporate both formalized and less formalized structures. A highly formalized organization can reduce creativity and innovation, whereas an organization with little formalization can be more chaotic.

Analyzing Organizational Communication Practices

The culture and structure of an organization affect its communication practices. In general, communication in organizations can be broken down into two types: formal and informal. **Formal communication** consists of *messages that follow prescribed channels of communication throughout the organization*. The most common way of depicting formal communication networks is with organizational charts, as in **Figure 8.1**.

Figure 8.1 Example of an Organizational Chart

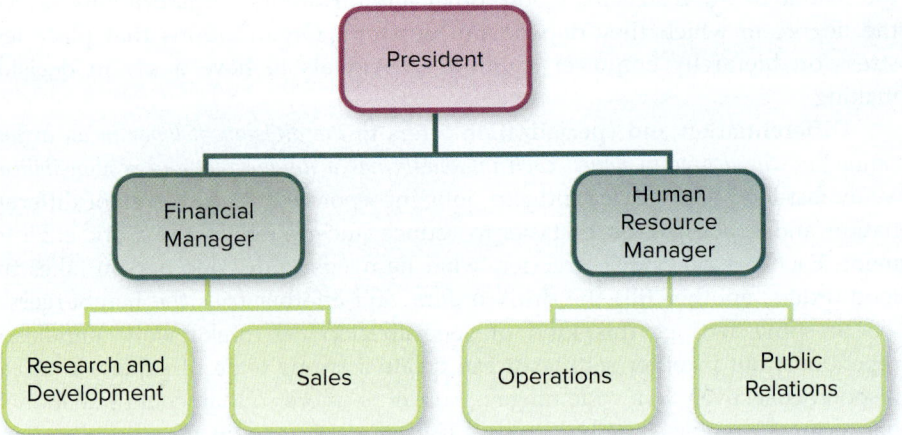

CHALLENGE YOURSELF

What can I learn about workplace communication, so that I can attract an employer's attention, interview well, and keep a good job?

Chapter 15 of this text offers plenty of tips to help you in your job searches, such as how to fine-tune your résumé and respond to interview questions. But perhaps the most important advice we can offer is to be proactive, positive, and persistent.

Proactive people who look for ways to do their jobs more effectively tend to stand out. Being proactive means making yourself indispensable to the functions of an organization. When you have become skilled with your assigned tasks, ask what else you can do to contribute. Once you've mastered one set of skills, be willing to learn and take on more.

When Hillary Clinton was first passed over for the democratic nomination for president, she didn't disengage from politics. She became Secretary of State and continued to learn about the international issues that would inform her future campaigns. She went on to become the first woman to gain an endorsement from a major political party.

Thomas Edison failed over 1,000 times in inventing the lightbulb. When asked about these failures, he is quoted to have said "I have not failed 1,000 times. Rather, I have discovered over 1,000 ways not to make a lightbulb."

These people exemplify what it means to be proactive, positive, and persistent. You too can be a person whom others seek out because of your positive attitude and your interest in new opportunities. For example, while pursuing your studies, you might approach an instructor who teaches something you find interesting. You could ask to be involved in her teaching or research practices. Many opportunities pass people by because they do not express an interest and create an opportunity to be more involved.

Finally, do not stop challenging yourself. Even if your ideas are at first dismissed, keep applying your creative energy to the goals of the organization. Doing so will open doors.

Organizational charts clearly indicate who is responsible for a given task and which employees are responsible for others' performance. Communication in formal networks typically flows in one of three ways:

- *Downward communication* occurs whenever superiors initiate messages to subordinates. Downward communication includes job instructions, job rationales, policies and procedures, performance feedback, and motivational appeals. When a boss sends a memo explaining that an upcoming training will introduce new procedures for handling complaints, this is an example of downward communication.

- *Upward communication* occurs when messages flow from subordinates to superiors. Upward communication includes monthly reports, scheduling issues, and feedback to supervisors about things like the effectiveness of policies and procedures. Telling your boss that you have a new idea for how the organization can relieve staffing needs is an example of upward communication.

- *Horizontal communication* flows between people who are at the same level of the organizational hierarchy. Horizontal communication includes task coordination, problem solving, information sharing, and conflict resolution. Asking a coworker what she thinks of the new hire is an example of horizontal communication.

Employees must learn the official and formal chain of command so they know where to take their issues and concerns. However, research demonstrates that bad news does not typically travel up to higher levels of management as frequently and clearly as it moves down the hierarchy.[8] A prominent example of this phenomenon occurred at Penn State University. In 2012, football coach Jerry Sandusky was convicted of sexually assaulting 10 male students over a twenty-year period. Although the first assault occurred in 1994, university leaders did not take action until 2011.[9] At the trial, other staff, including a school janitor, admitted to having known of the abuse but agreeing to look the other way. Why? People do not report bad news upward because they fear the negative repercussions of conveying bad news to a superior. They also worry about how bad news, if shared, could severely damage important relationships in the workplace.[10] Clearly, people in leadership positions need to respond appropriately to bad news, so that subordinates can feel safe conveying it to them.

Informal communication is *any interaction that emerges out of social interactions among organization members rather than following the rules of the formal chain of command.* Much information in organizations goes through informal channels, not through memos, meetings, or organization-wide announcements.[11] Examples of informal communication include hearing things from coworkers like, "Hey, did you hear that Sandra is going to quit?" or "Louis told me that he gets really defensive when people suggest new strategies that involve his department." Coworkers often find out about workplace romances through information communication channels.[12]

Informal communication is important because it allows the transmission of information that may be critical to know to be successful in an organization but that may never come through formal organizational channels.[13] For example, knowing who is dating who in the organization might matter before you decide who to trust in venting about work issues. Informal communication can also help you understand important aspects of organizational culture. Informal networks, sometimes referred to as "grapevine communication," are typically very accurate, with between 80 and 90 percent of the information being correct.[14] An understanding of formal and informal networks in organizations is critical as you join and make efforts to fit into a new organization.

Everything you have learned thus far in the chapter about evaluating organizational culture and understanding organizational structure will help you as you launch an effective job search. We explore this topic further in **Chapter 15**.

COMMUNICATING IN SMALL GROUPS AND TEAMS

Many workplace projects are put into the hands of small groups, and your ability to understand and work well in them will serve you throughout your career. Small groups drive and invigorate nearly all facets of our lives: our families, classrooms, clubs, sports teams, and community organizations. In this section we will examine small-group functioning from a communication perspective, exploring the types of small groups, norms and roles in groups, and group climate. Let's begin by defining the central concept.

Small-group communication is *the interaction among three to nine people who are working together to achieve an interdependent goal.*[15] This definition implies several things:

©Image Source RF

- Groups must be small enough for members to be aware of the collective nature of the group. For example, people who post comments on a particular blog are less likely to have a sense of group identity than are people who meet regularly, whether in an online forum or face-to-face, to address a particular issue, such as campus safety. Groups typically contain between three and nine people but may be larger if members perceive the group as an entity. Research shows that groups of three or four people are more productive than groups with five or more people.[16] If given a choice, working with a smaller group may produce better results.

- Interaction between members is the substance that creates and holds the group together. Communication practices and styles shape each group in unique ways and allow the group to function. As with all human communication, small-group communication involves sending verbal and nonverbal signals, which other people perceive, interpret, and respond to.

Chapter 8 Organizational and Small-Group Communication

- Group members are **interdependent**, which means they *cannot achieve their goals without the help of one another*. If you watch reality television shows like *Survivor*, you have seen examples of how groups of people must work as interdependent units to achieve success. Business consulting firms are now using a reality-show approach to teach the importance of interdependence for corporate work teams. Corporations pay $75,000 to have their team members locked in a house over some period of time to develop interdependent skills.[17]

Types of Small Groups

Think about the groups to which you belong. You may regularly study with other students from your accounting class, belong to a club on campus, and have a regular group of friends with whom you socialize. What are the key differences among these groups? In answering that question, first consider how you came to be a member. In this context, there are two types of groups:

- *Assigned groups* occur when individuals are appointed to be members. For example, if your boss brings together a task force to address inefficiencies in workplace practices, she might assign someone from HR, production, development, and marketing to form that committee. Wanting to be a member is not often sufficient to becoming a member of assigned groups.

©DLILLC/Corbis Images RF

- *Emergent groups* occur when individuals decide to form a cohesive group out of personal need or desire. A group of friends who meet at college and decide to work together to get a better grade in a class is an example of an emergent group. People who joined together to demonstrate at the recent Women's March likewise exemplify an emergent group.

We can also classify groups according to the function they serve:

- *Task-oriented groups* are formed for the purpose of completing tasks such as solving a problem or making a decision. A community task force convened to come up with novel solutions for combatting underage drinking is an example of a task-oriented group.

- *Relationship-oriented groups* are long-term groups that exist to meet individual needs. A family is a relationship-oriented group that provides emotional and other kinds of support for its members. Joining an online or face-to-face support group, like a cancer support group, can have tremendous benefits for individual adjustment and health.[18] This is another example of a relationship-oriented group.

©Huntstock/Getty Images RF

Classifying groups according to whether they are task-oriented, relationship-oriented, assigned, or emergent risks oversimplifying how groups actually work in your life. Because people form groups, and because groups can grow and change through communication, lines between types and functions can easily blur. For example, members of relationship-oriented groups, such as families, may start a business together, in which case they need to make strategic decisions and cooperate to complete work tasks.

Members of task-oriented groups may forge strong personal bonds and continue their relationships even after completing their assigned task. In fact, task-oriented groups can benefit from strong relational bonds that allow members to feel appreciated and valued. Also, if members of an assigned group establish positive relationships, the group can start to look and feel like an emergent group, in the sense that a relationship-oriented social group may emerge. Much as in our personal relationships, the quality of our group membership is constantly in flux.

Norms and Roles in Small Groups

Beginning with their very first interactions, group members establish the group's **norms**, which are *the beliefs about how individual members should interact and behave in a particular context*. Norms often develop naturally based on how members structure tasks and allow work to progress. However, norms can also be developed explicitly, as when group members openly discuss expectations for group members. Some groups even create a group contract.

Norms can make a group effective, as when the norm is for everybody to arrive on time, be well prepared, and get to work. Or they can make a group ineffective, as when the norms are for people to be casual about arrival time, to socialize instead of getting to work, or to take cell phone calls or return text messages while others are speaking. To ensure a productive set of norms, consider having a discussion about members' expectations for group functioning. The following questions may help in this discussion:

- What are the purpose and function of the group?
    - What does each member identify as the group goal?
    - What do members view as the mission statement?
- What will constitute ethical and unethical group interactions?
- What expectations do members hold for group functioning and behavior?
    - How will the group handle violations of group expectations?
    - What about arriving to a meeting late or failing to show up?
    - What if members fail to uphold individual obligations or complete work in a timely manner?
- How will the group make decisions when differences of opinion arise?
- How can members get in touch with one another for input or further assistance?

- How frequently should the group meet?
- What can the group do so that everyone gets the opportunity to contribute to ideas?
- How can the group ensure that everyone contributes to the output or final products?

The intent is to spend time making explicit what is implicit in group members' minds. If one member thinks that all decisions should run through the group but another member expects more flexibility, the group is likely to experience conflict. A discussion of decision-making procedures can lead to clarity. In addition, clarifying the roles that group members might fulfill will ease group functioning.

Every group member enacts a unique **role**, *a consistent pattern of interaction or behavior exhibited over time*. In movies, characters enact roles to drive the story; in small groups, members enact roles to drive the interaction of the group. Whereas actors learn their roles from scripts, group members create their roles spontaneously during interactions with others and while drawing on their unique skills and attitudes. Just as an actor plays different roles in different scripts, individuals enact diverse roles in the groups to which they belong.

Group roles are either formal or informal. A **formal role** (sometimes called a **positional role**) is *an assigned role based on an individual's position or title within a group*. For example, a person may be responsible for taking certain types of information to group meetings, for keeping track of finances, or for recording agenda items for future meetings. Once a person is assigned one of these formal roles, other group members have expectations for that person. If the person does not follow through—by supplying the information or keeping the records—others will be disappointed, and the group's efforts may be undermined.

©Andersen Ross/Brand X/Corbis RF

An **informal role** (sometimes called a **behavioral role**) is a *role that develops naturally or spontaneously within a group*. Informal roles emerge through interactions in the group, and they change to meet the group's emerging needs. Such roles reflect members' personality characteristics, habits, and typical ways of interacting in a group. If you are the type of person who likes to talk in front of others, you might take on the role of facilitator. On the other hand, if you are less talkative, you might take on behind-the-scene roles, such as conducting research or creating documents. Informal roles allow you to play to your strengths; of course, to develop informal roles, you may need to talk to other group members about your preferences and abilities.

Group member roles can be classified by their function as task, maintenance, or self-centered behaviors. **Task functions** are *behaviors that directly relate to the group's purpose, and they affect the group's productivity*; they are

Communicating in Small Groups and Teams **163**

implemented to focus group members productively on their assignment. **Maintenance functions** are *behaviors that focus on the interpersonal relationships among group members; they are aimed at supporting cooperation and harmony*. Both task and maintenance functions are considered essential to effective group communication. On the other hand, **self-centered functions** are *behaviors that serve the needs of the individual at the expense of the group*. The person performing self-centered functions manipulates other members for selfish goals that compete with group goals. Task, maintenance, and self-centered functions can in turn be broken down into several categories, as you can see in **Table 8.3**.

One thing that is important in the creation of norms for groups is to consider the needs of English-as-a-second-language (ESL) members of the group. Research shows that having various primary languages represented in a group does not impede cohesiveness and effectiveness of a group as long as members have frequent interactions.[19] Four strategies that you can think about when forming groups norms to help ESL students are (1) providing written information in advance, (2) asking someone in the group to take notes that can be copied and distributed to all, (3) viewing difference as a group strength, and (4) matching tasks to members' abilities. Take time to find out the strengths of all group members. ESL students make not speak as often, but this does not mean do not have highly develop skills in other areas.

Group Climate and Cohesion

You have probably attended group meetings where people were so comfortable with one another that they found it hard to get beyond socializing and down to business. That relaxed atmosphere describes the **group climate**, which is *the emotional tone or atmosphere members create within the group*. Three factors that contribute heavily to group climate are trust, supportiveness, and cohesiveness.

©John Giustina/Getty Images RF

- **Trust** refers to *a belief that members can rely on each other*. Two types of trust relevant to group work are task trust and interpersonal trust. Task trust develops when members have confidence that others will get their jobs done in support of the group's goals. Interpersonal trust emerges when members perceive that others are working in support of the group, rather than trying to achieve personal gain or accomplish hidden agendas.

- **Supportiveness** refers to an atmosphere of openness in which members care about each other. If you reveal to your study group that your mother has just passed away, supportive group members will focus on how to help you through your time of need; unsupportive group members will be more concerned that you maintain your role within the group and complete your work on time.

Table 8.3 Types of Task, Maintenance, and Self-Centered Functions

Type of Statement	Sample Statements
Task Functions	
Initiating and orienting	"Let's make a list of what we still need to do." "What has each member done since we last met?"
Information giving	"I was asked to find suitable venues for our event. Three possible locations exist."
Information seeking	"Who in the group has contacts in student government to check on that?"
Opinion giving	"I'm not sure that is the most effective way for us to raise funds."
Clarifying	"Paul, I'm not sure I understand the point you're trying to make. Can you clarify what you mean?"
Extending	"An additional benefit of pursing that idea is . . ."
Evaluating	"One problem I see with following this recommendation is . . ."
Summarizing	"So before we meet again next week, Mindy will talk to vendors and Mark will look at our expenses so far."
Coordinating	"If each member can get me their parts of the paper by Tuesday, I can compile them for further discussion at our next meeting."
Consensus testing	"Let's see if there is group agreement about this course of action."
Recording	"Let's make sure to get that in the minutes, so that we don't forget to follow up on that task."
Maintenance Functions	
Reinforcing norms	"Let's consider Mark's objections further. We decided to aim for consensus about all decisions."
Gatekeeping	"Pat, you look like you want to say something about the proposal."
Supporting	"I think Tara's point is well made, and we should look at it more closely."
Harmonizing	"Jared and Sally, I think there are areas where you agree, and I would like to suggest a compromise that might work for you both."
Tension relieving	"We're getting tired and cranky. Let's take a 10-minute break."
Dramatizing	"That reminds me of a story about what happened last year when . . ."
Showing solidarity	"We've really done good work here!" or "I'm so pleased with the decision we made tonight as a group."
Self-Centered Functions	
Withdrawing	"Do whatever you want; I don't care."
Blocking	"I don't care if we've already voted; I want to discuss it again!"
Status and recognition seeking	"I have a lot more expertise than the rest of you, and I think we should do it the way I know works."

Working against trust and supportiveness in groups is the quality of defensiveness. To help you consider the impact supportiveness and defensiveness can have on group climate, **Table 8.4** presents types of defensive and supportive behavior, illustrating each type with an example.

- **Cohesiveness** is the *attachment members feel toward each other and the group*. Highly cohesive groups are more open, handle disagreement more effectively,[20] and typically perform better[21] than groups with low levels of cohesiveness. More supportiveness and less defensiveness contribute to greater cohesion.

Although cohesiveness is generally desirable, dangers arise from too much cohesion. **Groupthink** is *a phenomenon that occurs when the desire for cohesion and agreement takes precedence over critical analysis and discussion*. According to sociologist

Table 8.4 Defensive and Supportive Behaviors and Statements

Behavior	Description	Sample Statement
Defensive Behaviors and Statements		
Evaluation	Insulting another person's idea	"That's a completely ridiculous idea."
Control	Dominating or insisting on your own way	"I've decided what we need to do."
Manipulating	Pushing compliance	"Don't you think you should try it my way?"
Neutrality	Claiming that you don't care how others feel	"It doesn't matter to me what you decide."
Superiority	Pulling rank, maximizing status differences	"As group leader, I think we should . . ."
Certainty	Being a "know-it-all"	"You guys are completely off base. I know exactly how to handle this."
Supportive Behaviors and Statements		
Description	Describing your own feelings without making those of others wrong	"I prefer the first option because . . ."
Problem orientation	Searching for the best solution without predetermining what that should be	"We want to produce the best results, and that may mean some extra time from all of us."
Spontaneity	Reacting honestly and openly	"Wow, that sounds like a great idea!"
Empathy	Showing you care about the other members	"Jan, originally you were skeptical. How comfortable will you be if the group favors that option?"
Equality	Minimizing status differences by treating members as equals	"I don't have all the answers. What do the rest of you think?"
Provisionalism	Expressing opinions tentatively and being open to others' suggestions	"Maybe we should try a different approach . . ."

Irving Janis, groupthink can destroy effective decision making. Several historical decision-making blunders have been attributed to groupthink, including the escalation of the Vietnam conflict, the space shuttle *Challenger* disaster, and possibly the *Columbia* shuttle disaster over Texas.[22]

Why are bad decisions usually associated with groupthink? Because when groups are too cohesive, faulty communication practices occur, where members do not challenge one another's ideas and make sure logical reasoning and soundness are upheld for all conclusions advanced by the group. Instead, desire to not offend someone or concern about holding up the process become more important and the focus of dialogue rather than ensuring the group makes the most thoughtful and critical decisions.[23] Although groupthink may be difficult for members to detect, researchers have identified the following observable signs:

- An illusion of invulnerability
- An unquestioned belief that nothing the group does could be wrong
- Collective efforts to rationalize faulty decisions
- Stereotypical views of enemy leaders as evil, weak, or ineffective
- Censorship of alternative viewpoints
- A shared illusion that all members think the same thing
- Direct pressure on members expressing divergent opinions to be quiet

Although Janis originally asserted that these were the characteristics that led to groupthink, and consequently resulted in a bad decision, recent studies suggest that these characteristics actually occur after the group has already made the poor decision.[24] Once groups make decisions, members try to create and reinforce a consensus in support of the decision, even in the face of evidence that the decision was poor, which leads to the groupthink characteristics.

Groupthink is possible in nearly every group. To prevent it, members should seek all pertinent information, carefully assess the credibility of information relevant to the decision at hand, assign members to present counterarguments, and maintain a commitment to finding the best possible outcome as supported by the available evidence.

Decision Making and Problem Solving

Generally, effective problem solving involves five steps: (1) discussing criteria for an acceptable solution, (2) brainstorming and identifying alternatives, (3) evaluating each alternative, (4) implementing the plan, and (5) evaluating the outcomes based on the original criteria. Each step is a potential antidote for groupthink.

Discussing Critical Criteria *The standards by which a group must judge potential solutions to a problem* is known as **criteria**. For example, a solution's potential effectiveness ("Will it work?"), acceptability ("Will people vote for our proposal?"), and cost

©Jim Arbogast/Getty Images RF

("Does this option keep us within the budget?") are common criteria. Discussing these criteria allows a team or group to reflect on its values and reasons for doing something in a new or different way. Group members will not always agree on what the critical criteria are, but agreeing is very important to the decision-making process. The more similar the group members are in age, gender, ethnicity, background, attitudes, values, and beliefs, the easier they can agree on criteria.

Two kinds of criteria are common. Absolute criteria are those that must be met; the group has no leeway. Important criteria are those that should be met, but the group has some flexibility. Group members should give the highest priority to absolute criteria. Ideas that do not meet the standard of absolute criteria should be ranked on how well they meet the standard for important criteria. Consider an organization that wants a new location for business. Its absolute criteria might be the maximum cost of the building and the accessibility of the parking and entrances. Important criteria might be having other industry close by and being near public transportation.

Identifying Alternatives One technique that can promote innovation and creative thought in groups is brainstorming.[25] While brainstorming, group members are free to identify multiple, succinct ideas and are asked to defer any judgment (positive or negative) until all ideas have been identified. Critical evaluation kills creativity, which is why the evaluation stage takes place *after* the group has run out of ideas.

A facilitator can guide brainstorming by first giving group members a few minutes to consider the question. This can help generate a range of possibilities. As ideas are presented, the facilitator records and displays them. Once ideas become repetitive, the facilitator wraps up the process, and the analysis and evaluation begin.

Evaluating Each Alternative At this stage, the group uses the criteria they identified earlier to judge the efficacy of the ideas generated through brainstorming. To do so, it is useful to analyze the listed ideas and determine whether some can be combined into meaningful categories—for example, ideas related to location, to cost, or to accessibility. Solutions failing to meet absolute or important criteria are quickly eliminated, with the primary focus on those that meet absolute criteria. Later in the chapter, you will read about managing conflict in groups, as conflict can easily arise during group problem solving and decision making.

Implementing the Plan After your group has spent a significant amount of time considering group goals, project criteria, and each possible idea or recommendation, it is time to test or fully implement ideas. If you have enough time, you might test some of your ideas with a smaller group of people who can provide feedback. Organizations do this all the time in what are called focus groups. Focus groups help companies refine product development, testing, and implementation. For example, if you are hoping to get other college students interested in attending a charity event you are planning, you might form a small group of students who meet your ideal target market and ask them to give you feedback. They can tell you if they would come to your event or what they think of your promotional materials. You might explore how you could adapt your plan to make it more appealing to them. Once the group feels comfortable with the plan that has been developed, members should consider the best way to implement it and decide who will take on the various responsibilities for carrying it out.

Evaluating the Outcomes Based on the Original Criteria After you have carried out your plan, you will need to reconvene as a group to evaluate it. The group should discuss and analyze how the outcome compared with its expectations. Did the group meet its goals? What can be learned from project implementation that can be carried into future projects? Engaging in this type of cyclical learning and evaluation at the end of a project helps ensure that groups continue to grow and learn in their work together.

ORGANIZATIONAL LEADERSHIP

As you work in groups, whether in the workplace or elsewhere, you will have opportunities to be a leader and even more opportunities to be led. What makes a good leader? Is leadership a skill people are born with? Can anyone learn to be a leader? As you will see, leadership by and large depends on effective communication skills.

Communication Skills for Leaders

People sometimes use the terms *leadership* and *management* interchangeably. Although some leaders perform management functions and vice versa, the roles and functions of leaders versus managers differ in significant ways. As **Figure 8.2** demonstrates,

Figure 8.2 Leadership vs. Management

Leaders and Leadership	Managers and Management
■ **Leadership** is *the process of using communication to influence the behaviors and attitudes of others.* ■ Leaders challenge the status quo and establish a strong vision for the future. Leaders motivate and inspire people toward the established change initiatives.	■ **Management** is *the process of using communication to maintain structure, order, harmony, and the efficacy of procedures and practices.* ■ Managers maintain the status quo. They monitor the organization and remove obstacles that prevent the execution of established priorities.

SOURCE: Hackman, M. Z., & Johnson, C. E. (2003). *Leadership: A communication perspective* (4th ed.). Prospect Heights, IL: Waveland Press.

leadership is *the process of using communication to influence the behaviors and attitudes of others*, whereas **management** is *the process of using communication to maintain structure, order, harmony, and the efficacy of procedures and practices.*

Think about the role of the president of the United States. This leader is expected to establish a vision and use language in a way that excites others to be a part of that vision. A manager, on the other hand, monitors the organization and removes obstacles that prevent the execution of a leader's vision. Managers ensure that employees come to work on time, follow proper protocol and procedures for getting things done, and execute the organizational priorities as outlined.

Research shows that some of the most important communication competencies associated with leadership include the ability to:

- Communicate ideas to the group clearly and appropriately without dominating the conversation
- Communicate a clear grasp of the task facing the group
- Facilitate discussion
- Encourage dialogue rather than forcing their own ideas on the group
- Place group needs over personal concerns
- Display respect for others during interaction
- Share in the successes and failures of the group[26]

Types of Power and Leadership

In general, people become leaders in one of two ways: they are designated as such or they emerge. A **designated leader** is *someone who has been appointed or elected to a leadership position* (such as a chair, team leader, coordinator, or facilitator). An **emergent leader** is *someone who exerts influence toward the achievement of a group's goal but who does not hold the formal position or role of leader.*

Having a designated leader can add stability to a group, but emergent leaders have their value as well. For example, a designated leader can focus resources and energy on central priorities, so that others in the group can focus on other functions. An emergent leader can be helpful for groups that confront a range of issues; moreover, it is nice for different people to step up to the front and lead the team from time to time, depending on the new challenge or issue. For example, a group of faculty members might be asked to develop a new recruiting strategy, and the person in the group with the most knowledge in this area might emerge as the leader. Then, when the group is asked to revise graduate student practices, someone more versed in that area can lead the group. As is the case with roles and types of groups, emergent leaders may also turn into designated leaders.

How do leaders, designated or emergent, gain their ability to influence others? They do this through the use of **power**, which is *the ability to influence others*.[27] In general, leaders use five kinds of power:

- *Reward power* is based on the ability to give followers what they want and need—for example, a leader who often uses pay bonuses or an advancement to show appreciation for a job well done.

©Andersen Ross/Getty Images RF

- *Punishment power* is based on the ability to withhold from followers what they want and need. An extreme form of punishment power is **coercion**, in which *compliance is forced through hostile acts*. A prime example is a parent who tries to get a child to comply by threatening to take away privileges, such as use of the Internet. Employers can threaten demotions or termination.

- *Referent power* is based on others' admiration and respect. Charisma is an extreme form of referent power that inspires strong loyalty and devotion from others. Your professors have referent power due to their ability to influence potential employers on your behalf through recommendations.

- *Expert power* is based on knowledge or expertise. A person who is sought out for a company because he or she has an established record for knowing how to implement new ideas has expert power. As students studying a specialized area or field, you are increasing your expert power.

- *Legitimate power* is given to a person because of a title, position, or role. Although legitimate power is important in influencing people, it is most effective when used in tandem with other bases of power. Consider a child who asks a parent why she has to go to bed at 8 PM. If the parent responds, "Because I say so," the child is more likely to rebel than if the parent also uses expert power to explain the reasons behind family rules.[28]

Depending on the kinds of power they use and the way they use it, leaders can be classified as one of three basic types: democratic, laissez-faire, or autocratic.

- *Democratic leaders* encourage members to participate in group decisions, even major ones. For example, a democratic leader asks, "What suggestions do you have for solving our problem?"

- *Laissez-faire leaders* take almost no initiative in structuring group discussions or actions. A laissez-faire leader is more like a nonleader, who is likely to say something along the lines of "I don't care; whatever you want to do is fine with me."

Organizational Leadership **171**

- *Autocratic leaders* maintain strict control over their group, including making assignments and giving orders. A typical autocratic leader says, "Here's how we'll solve the problem. First, you will. . . ." Autocratic leaders ask fewer questions than do democratic leaders but they answer more; compared with democratic leaders, they make more attempts to coerce and fewer attempts to get others to participate.[29]

Groups vary in the amount of structure and control their members want and need, but research findings about style have been consistent. Most people in the United States prefer democratic groups and are more satisfied in democratically rather than autocratically led groups.[30] However, most scholars believe that the style should match the needs of the situation. For example, if you are in a group working on a class project and the deadline is tomorrow, a democratic leadership style might not be effective, because it takes longer to generate decisions.

CONNECTING GLOBALLY

MEDIATED COMMUNICATION, PRIVACY, AND GLOBAL BUSINESS

Most businesses now provide employees with cell phones for professional and personal use. But what are the implications, with regard to privacy, for the employer who is paying for the phone, and the employee who is using it? Consider the following questions about mediated communication and privacy in the workplace.

- Would you accept a stipend from your company to pay for a cell phone that would be used, at least in part, for professional purposes? Would you prefer that your company provide you with a phone to be used strictly for professional purposes?
- If your company is paying the bill, do you think it has the right to seize that phone and view its contents?
- When is it appropriate to use social media to share some aspect of your job?
- How might the standards for professional social media use vary from one culture to the next? How should people working for the same company, but based in different parts of the world, handle organizational issues via social media?

These questions demonstrate the complexity of issues related to privacy, mediated communication, and global business practices. If you are ever in doubt about how to communicate through social media as part of your job, play it safe. Here are some tips:

- Find out if your organization has rules about social media use and follow them.
- Get to know the culture of your organization. More relaxed workplaces tend to embrace and even encourage social media use.
- Finally, you might opt to refrain from sharing information or opinions about your workplace through social media altogether.

CULTIVATING POSITIVE RELATIONSHIPS IN SMALL GROUPS

Many issues that arise in the work environment, and in all small groups, can bring about conflict. You can learn to interact in ways that will minimize the occurrence of conflict, and you can cultivate strategies for dealing with conflict when it does arise. There is much you can do to interact in small groups in ways that will help move effective group processes forward. We begin by reviewing strategies that may help minimize conflict among group members through more effective small-group interactions.

©Chris Schmidt/Getty Images RF

Interacting Effectively in Small Groups

Each member of a group must take responsibility to support the group's functions and to interact in ways that will advance group processes. How can you best do that? The ability to speak with polish is not essential, but the ability to speak clearly is. The following advice will help you interact effectively in small groups and teams, whether at work or elsewhere.

1. *Relate your statements to preceding remarks.* Clarify the relevance of your remarks to the topic by linking them to an idea raised by another group member:
   - Briefly mention the previous speaker's point—for example, "I want to piggyback on Bill's comment by noting that we can meet our goal by. . . ."
   - Then state your own point clearly and concisely.
   - Summarize how your point adds to the comments made by others—for example, "I agree with Bill. We need to fund-raise, but we can't get so caught up in raising money that we forget about our goal of volunteering."

2. *Communicate your ideas with clear and simple language.* You don't need to impress others with your vocabulary or long, complex sentences. For example, you don't need to say, "I unequivocally recognize the meaningful contribution made by my colleague." Saying "I agree" works just as well. Here are some guidelines for communicating simply and clearly in group discussions:
   - After connecting your idea to that of the previous speaker, state your point and then provide one piece of supporting information or additional explanation.
   - Give group members a context for your remarks. Not all comments are critical; some are just ideas. Letting others know how you intend your remark to be taken—that is, as a recommendation for going forward, a critical piece of evidence, or an idea for brainstorming—may influence how they react and respond.
   - When done, ask if anyone needs you to clarify your point.

3. *Get to the point quickly.* Don't be long-winded. The main advantage of small groups is their ability to approach a problem interactively and hear multiple points of view on a topic. If you monopolize the discussion, or leave little time for others to contribute to the group dialogue, that advantage may be diminished or lost completely. To learn to speak concisely, try the following:
   - Write down your idea before speaking. People tend to be wordier when they are trying to figure out what they want to say. If you've thought it out ahead of time, you'll be able to get right to the point.
   - Try to talk for no more than one minute at a time. Of course, this time limit is arbitrary; however, one minute should be enough time to get an idea out for consideration, and you can always answer questions to clarify as needed.
4. *State one point at a time.* A group member making a presentation may certainly state several points. However, during give-and-take discussion, stating only one idea promotes efficiency and allows others to respond:
   - As a group, appoint a process observer to keep the discussion moving and to prevent any member from bringing up more than one idea at a time. After the process observer intervenes a few times, these behaviors become second nature.
   - If you have several ideas, provide the less important points to group members in written form for later reflection. Save discussion time for the most important ideas.

By following these simple strategies, you establish norms that allow your small group to function effectively, and you take advantage of all members' expertise.

Achieving Communication Competence

Every workplace, as well as every small group, includes a variety of people, each with a unique personality. Maintaining positive relationships with all these individuals can be a challenge requiring effective verbal and nonverbal communication skills. Three key communication qualities can enhance workplace relationships: immediacy, supportiveness, and interaction management.

Immediacy When people engage in *communication behaviors intended to create perceptions of psychological closeness with others*, they are enacting **immediacy**. Immediacy can be created both verbally and nonverbally. Calling people by their first names, using "we" language, and telling stories are verbal behaviors that promote immediacy. Smiling, reducing the physical distance between those in the interaction, and using animated gestures and facial expressions are nonverbal behaviors that promote immediacy. For example, when you are excited about a course you are taking, you probably sit at the edge of your chair, lean forward, and smile more often, all positive immediacy behaviors. When you are bored in a lecture, you are more likely to pull out your cell phone, check your bag, slouch over and put your head on your hand, all negative or distancing immediacy behaviors.

Using immediacy has been shown to have positive effects in the workplace. For instance, it can improve the relationship between supervisors and subordinates[31] and encourage people to engage in higher levels of self-disclosure.[32] Immediacy reflects the popular notion that it is not necessarily what you say but how you say it that matters.

©John Lund/Drew Kelly/Blend Images LLC RF

Supportiveness People engage in **supportive communication** when they *listen with empathy, acknowledge the feelings of others, and engage in dialogue to help others maintain a sense of personal control.* Of course, supportive communication is an important skill in all contexts. To enhance your supportive communication skills, consider the following strategies.

1. *Listen without judging.* Being judgmental while listening to a coworker's explanation of a problem can cause you to lose your focus on what he is really saying.
2. *Validate feelings.* Even if you disagree with something your coworkers say, validating their perceptions and feelings—for example, "What you're saying makes a lot of sense, Maria"—is an important step in building a trusting relationship.
3. *Provide both informational and relational messages.* Supportive communication includes both helping and healing messages. Simply listening to someone vent is as important as providing advice.
4. *Be confidential.* When coworkers share feelings and personal reflections, maintaining their trust is essential. Telling others or gossiping will destroy your credibility as a trustworthy coworker.[33]

Interaction Management Workplace communication is somewhat different from other types of communication situations, because conversations tend to flow between the technical jargon associated with the workplace and other topics brought up to relieve stress and pass time. Thus, computer technicians might talk about megabytes and megapixels one minute and speculate about who will be voted off *Dancing with the Stars* the next. But this kind of topic switching can occur in any group setting—for example, when people switch topics from their personal lives to tasks that need attention.

Competent communicators engage in interaction management, which is an approach to communication that allows a clear flow between topics and ideas and in which people are aware of the communication styles and preferences of those around them and adapt appropriately. Pausing, changing pitch, listening carefully, and responding appropriately are skills related to interaction management. Being an effective communicator with coworkers and clients, or in any group, requires carefully observing the communication preferences of others. Recognizing that one person is consistently task-focused, whereas another always likes to chitchat about family is important; adapting your interactions will help you fit in and achieve individual and group objectives.

Managing Conflict

Communicating in organizations is not easy. In fact, a pervasive part of organizational life is conflict, both destructive and productive. Destructive conflict can harm relationships, whereas productive conflict can create a needed impetus for organizational change and development. People often view conflict negatively because they associate it with anger. However, **conflict** *occurs anytime two or more people have goals they perceive to be incompatible*. When one employee wants to work late to finish a joint project, but another wants to go home to be with his family, conflict can occur. In short, conflict is a fact of life, the rule rather than the exception. You can use a variety of techniques to manage conflict productively,[34] including any of those listed and described in **Table 8.5**.

In addition to the general techniques in **Table 8.5** for managing conflict, consider the tips in **Table 8.6** related to conflict and communication throughout your career in groups and teams where people will have differences of opinion.

Table 8.5	A Variety of Techniques for Managing Conflict
Avoidance	■ In using the avoidance style, you deny the existence of conflict or work around it. Although avoidance can provide time to think through a situation, continued avoidance allows conflict to simmer and flare up with more intensity.
Competition	■ In using the competition style, you view conflict as a battle and advance your own interests over those of others. Although competition may work for some situations, if your coworkers perceive that you view conflict as a win–lose situation every time, and that you must always win, they may come to question whether you really listen to and value their perspectives.
Compromise	■ In using the compromising style, you are willing to negotiate away some of your position as long as the other party is willing to do the same. Compromise can be an effective strategy, because both parties get at least some of what they want.
Accommodation	■ In using the accommodation style, you set aside your views and accept those of others. Accommodation can maintain harmony in relationships, but sometimes at the expense of airing your own perspectives and opinions.
Collaboration	■ In using the collaborative style, you rely on thoughtful negotiation and reasoned compromise whereby both parties agree that the negotiated outcome is the best possible alternative under the circumstances. Although collaboration takes more time and effort to enact, it typically results in the best possible outcome for all parties.

Table 8.6 Conflict Management and Communication Tips

Not all conflict is effectively managed through more communication. You will invariably encounter people with experiences and perspectives different from your own. Sometimes the best thing to do is agree to disagree without trying to change someone else's perspective.
When you do communicate about disagreements with others, listen just as much, if not more, than you speak. Communication is interactive, dynamic, and interdependent. This means that your responses to others should be based on what they say to you. When people spend too much time thinking about what their next point will be, rather than listening to what others are contributing to the dialogue, conflicts persist.
Paraphrase your understanding of other people's positions as you engage in managing conflict with them. Listen and try to understand new ideas. Sometimes simply by paraphrasing those ideas you can illuminate the source of a conflict. Also, by demonstrating that you are working to understand other people's positions, you may help them feel less guarded and defensive.
Not every conflict is resolvable. This is why the term *conflict* management is preferred over conflict *resolution*. Sometimes a resolution is not needed. People might simply need you to listen to what they have to say. By listening, you validate others' feelings.
Do not engage in conflict management when you are overly emotional. You never want to say something in a conflict that you will come to regret. Avoid saying such things by telling people when you need more time and space to think before you engage in more open discussion with them.
When you engage in conflict management with people, use "I" language instead of "you" language. It is easier to be open to someone else's opinions when they are phrased as individual perceptions. Refrain from speaking on behalf of large groups or making overly general claims like "everyone in this group thinks you're a slacker." Statements like this cause defensiveness and are unproductive. You might instead say something like "I feel you can make stronger contributions to this project."
Learn to separate conflict disagreements from the person airing the conflict. It is possible to dislike an idea and still highly value the person who contributed it. Be mindful of your nonverbal messages as you engage in conflict management, and remember that messages contain a content dimension as well as a relational one. When interacting with people who are unable to separate conflict disagreements from the person airing the conflict, be more cautious in what you say. You may even decide that more discussion is counterproductive.

Preparing for Ethical Dilemmas

You are likely to encounter several types of ethical dilemmas in organizations. Three common ones are aggressive communication, dishonesty, and sexual harassment.

When working in organizations, particularly those with a customer service focus, it is not uncommon to encounter situations in which anger turns to aggression. **Verbal aggressiveness** is *communication that attacks the self-concepts of other people in order to inflict psychological pain.*[35] This kind of aggression is common in organizational settings, although it is sometimes unrecognized by management. A recent summary of literature on workplace aggression identified the following types, some of which overlap:

- *Abusive supervision.* This occurs when a supervisor engages in sustained hostile behavior, both verbal and nonverbal. This does not, however, rise to the level of physical aggression.
- *Bullying.* Bullying occurs when *one or more individuals ridicule, make offensive statements to or about, tease, socially isolate, or otherwise abuse one or more other individuals over an extended period of time.*
- *Incivility.* This occurs when a person demonstrates frequent rude behavior that may or may not have the intent of being harmful. Uncivil people may or may not know they are being rude.
- *Social undermining.* Whereas incivility can occur unwittingly, **social undermining** is intentional and often planned. It is an *action meant to socially isolate another person from a larger group.*[36]

Verbal aggressiveness can cause embarrassment, feelings of inadequacy, humiliation, hopelessness, despair, and depression. If you feel you are the victim of workplace aggression, consult a human resources manager, a union representative, or a trusted manager for advice.

©Erica Simone Leeds RF

Several high-profile events resulting from the 2008 economic crisis underscored the impact of dishonesty in organizational communication. Specifically, financial institutions were blamed for not being honest when extending risky mortgages to individuals who went on to purchase homes they could not afford. The widespread lack of honesty and ethics played a large role in eroding consumer confidence during the crisis. All organizational members share the responsibility for behaving and communicating with honesty. When you suspect someone is being dishonest, it is important to say something to the individual and not allow people to practice unethical behavior. This type of assertive communication skill can be difficult, but it is critical in preventing a culture in which dishonest behaviors and interactions are commonplace. The fears that drive people to dishonest behaviors at work (e.g., the fear of offending a colleague or the fear of embarrassment for admitting when they're wrong) can often be countered by establishing open communication with coworkers.

Sexual harassment is a form of workplace aggression, defined by the Equal Employment Opportunity Commission (EEOC) as

> unwelcome sexual advances, requests for sexual favors, and other verbal or physical conduct of a sexual nature if (1) submission to the conduct is made a condition of employment, (2) submission to or rejection of the conduct is made the basis for an employment decision, or (3) the conduct seriously affects an employee's work performance or creates an intimidating, hostile, or offensive working environment.[37]

Simply put, *sexual harassment is unwelcome, unsolicited, repeated behavior of a sexual nature*. The EEOC definition outlines two, sometimes overlapping types of sexual harassment. The first type, quid pro quo, occurs when an employee is offered a reward or is threatened with punishment based on his or her participation in a sexual activity. For example, a supervisor might say, "I'll give you Friday off if you meet me at my place tonight." The second type of sexual harassment creates a hostile work environment, meaning that conditions in the workplace are sexually offensive, intimidating, or hostile and affect job performance. For example, if two males talk explicitly about the physical features of a female colleague in her presence, and she is offended by this exchange, sexual harassment has occurred.

A major obstacle to ending sexual harassment is the tendency of victims to avoid confronting the harasser. Most instances of sexual harassment are neither exposed nor reported. Instead, the victim usually avoids the situation by taking time off, transferring to another area, or changing jobs. The perpetrator is usually someone with authority and status—with power over the victim—and the victim feels that exposure or confrontation will backfire. Organizations take sexual harassment very seriously, and most have confidential channels for reporting problems. Although unpleasant to confront, sexual harassment must be reported through the appropriate organizational channels.

Although not all ethical issues can be eliminated with effective communication practices, some of the strategies recommended throughout this chapter can create a more positive and enjoyable work environment. Why do we end this chapter by discussing some of these negative aspects of organizational workplace culture? Such discussions may empower you to take a confident stance if you observe someone isolating another person in an organization or engaging in unproductive and aggressive communication practices.

CHAPTER REVIEW

This chapter provided you with a foundation for communicating in organizations and small groups of various types and sizes. You learned how to assess an organization's culture to determine the roles and norms that move its processes forward. You also learned how to approach and resolve conflict, a skill that is as important to the small group situation as it is to your one-on-one interpersonal relationships. Finally, you now have a better understanding of what is meant by leadership and how to enact the role of a leader effectively and ethically. With all these skills, you will be well prepared to work in groups in the classroom and workplace. As you move forward with your career, use all of these skills to determine your own role within your organization and to cultivate positive relationships with those around you.

KEY TERMS

organizational culture, 153
hierarchy, 156
differentiation and specialization, 157
strategic ambiguity, 157
formalization, 157
formal communication, 157
informal communication, 159
small-group communication, 160
interdependent, 161
norms, 162
role, 163
formal (positional) role, 163
informal (behavioral) role, 163
task functions, 163
maintenance functions, 164
self-centered functions, 164
group climate, 164

trust, 164
cohesiveness, 166
groupthink, 166
criteria, 167
leadership, 170
management, 170
designated leader, 170
emergent leader, 170
power, 171
coercion, 171
immediacy, 174
supportive communication, 175
conflict, 176
verbal aggressiveness, 177
social undermining, 178
sexual harassment, 178

STUDY QUESTIONS

1. Discuss the three main ways you can analyze an organization to learn about its culture. Use one of these methods to analyze the organization of your school.
2. Identify a few concrete strategies for interacting in small groups, and explain why these strategies would improve group functioning overall.
3. What is the difference between management and leadership? What role does communication play in enacting this difference?
4. What are three strategies for cultivating positive relationships in organizations?

ENDNOTES

1. Cheney, G. (1983). The rhetoric of identification and the study of organizational communication. *Quarterly Journal of Speech, 69*, 143–158.
2. Sun, S. (2008). Organizational culture and its themes. *International Journal of Business and Management, 12*, 137–141.
3. Pacanowsky, M. E., & O'Donnell-Trujillo, N. (1983). Organizational communication as cultural performance, *Communication Monographs, 50*, 126–147.
4. Kirby, E., & Krone, K. J. (2002). "The policy exists but you can't really use it": Communication and the structuration of work-family policies. *Journal of Applied Communication Research, 30*, 50–77.
5. Jones, E., Watson, B., Gardner, J., & Gallois, C. (2004). Organization communication: Challenges for the new century. *Journal of Communication, 54*, 722–750.
6. Cheney, G., Christensen, L. T., Zorn, T. E., & Ganesh, G. (2010). *Organizational communication in an age of globalization* (2nd ed.). Long Grove, IL: Waveland Press.
7. Eisenberg, E. (1984). Ambiguity as strategy in organizational communication. *Communication Monographs, 51*, 227–242.

8. Milliken, F. J., Morrison, E. W., & Hewlin, P. F. (2003). An exploratory study of employee silence: Issues that employees don't communicate upward and why. *Journal of Management Studies, 40,* 1453–1476.
9. Sablich, J., Fessenden, F., & McLean, A. (2012). Timeline: The Penn State scandal. *The New York Times.* Retrieved from www.nytimes.com/interactive/2011/11/11/sports/ncaafootball/sandusky.html
10. Milliken et al.
11. Susskind, A. M., Schwartz, D. F., Richards, W. D., & Johnson, J. D. (2005). Evolution and diffusion of the Michigan State University tradition of organizational communication network research. *Communication Studies, 56,* 397–418.
12. Cown, R. L., & Horan, S. M. (2014). Love at the office? Understanding workplace romance disclosures and reactions from the coworker perspective. *Western Journal of Communication, 78,* 238–253.
13. Fay, M. J., & Kline, S. L. (2011). Coworker relationships and informal communication in high-intensity telecommuting. *Journal of Applied Communication Research, 39,* 144–163.
14. Caudron, S. (1998). They hear it through the grapevine. *Workforce, 77,* 25–27.
15. Galanes, G. J., & Adams, K. H. (2009). *Effective group discussion.* New York: McGraw-Hill.
16. Wheelan, S. A. (2009). Group size, group development, and group productivity. *Small Group Research, 40,* 247–262.
17. Jana, R. (2009, March 23). Real life imitates real world. *BusinessWeek,* 42.
18. Chung, J. E. (2014). Social networking in online support groups for health: How online social networking benefits patients. *Journal of Health Communication, 19,* 639–659.
19. Lauring, J., & Selmer, J. (2010). Multicultural organizations: Common language and group cohesiveness. *International Journal of Cross Cultural Management, 10,* 267–284.
20. Kelly, L., & Duran, R. L. (1985). Interaction and performance in small groups: A descriptive report. *International Journal of Small Group Research, 1,* 182–192.
21. Barker, D. B. (1991, February). The behavioral analysis of interpersonal intimacy in group development. *Small Group Research, 22,* 76–91.
22. Ferraris, C. (2004, May). *Investigating NASA's intergroup decision-making: Groupthink and intergroup social dynamics.* Paper presented at the annual meeting of the International Communication Association Convention, New Orleans, LA.
23. Kramer, M. W., & Dougherty, D. S. (2013). Groupthink as communication process, not outcome. *Communication & Social Change, 1,* 44–62.
24. Henningsen, D. D., Henningsen, M. L., Eden, J., & Cruz, M. G. (2006). Examining the symptoms of groupthink and retrospective sense making. *Small Group Research, 37,* 36–64.
25. Blomstrom, S., Boster, F. J., Levine, K. J., Butler, E. M., & Levine, S. L. (2008).The effect of training on brainstorming. *Journal of the Communication, Speech, & Theatre Association of North Dakota, 21,* 41–50.
26. Barge, J. K., & Hirokawa, R. Y. (1989). Toward a communication competency model of group leadership. *Small Group Behavior, 20,* 167–189.
27. Wilmot, W. W., & Hocker, J. L. (2007). *Interpersonal conflict* (7th ed.). New York: McGraw-Hill.
28. French, J. R. P., & Raven, B. (1981). The bases of social power. In D. Cartwright & A. Zander (Eds.), *Group dynamics: Research and theory* (3rd ed.). New York: McGraw-Hill.
29. Foels, R., Driskell, J. E., Mullen, B., & Salas, E. (2000). The effects of democratic leadership on group member satisfaction. *Small Group Research, 31,* 676–702.

30. Brown, M. E., & Trevino, L. K. (2006). Socialized charismatic leadership, values congruence, and deviance in work groups. *Journal of Applied Psychology, 91,* 954–962.
31. Teven, J. J., McCroskey, J. C., & Richmond, V. P. (2006). Communication correlates of perceived Machiavellianism of supervisors: Communication orientations and outcomes. *Communication Quarterly, 54,* 127–142.
32. Lee, D., & LaRose, R. (2011). The impact of personalized social cues of immediacy on consumers' information disclosure: A social cognitive approach. *CyberPsychology, Behavior, and Social Networking, 14,* 337–343.
33. Albrecht, T. L., & Bach, B. W. (1997). *Communication in complex organizations: A relational approach.* New York: Harcourt Brace.
34. Wilmot & Hocker.
35. Infante, D., Riddle, B., Horvath, G., & Tumlin, S. (1992). Verbal aggressiveness: Messages and reasons. *Communication Quarterly, 40,* 116–126.
36. Herschovis, M. S. (2011). "Incivility, social undermining, bullying . . . oh my!": A call to reconcile constructs within workplace aggression research. *Journal of Organizational Behavior, 32,* 499–519.
37. U.S. Equal Employment Opportunity Commission. (n.d.). Retrieved from www.eeoc.gov/laws/types/sexual_harassment.cfm

Blue and Yellow Cube Icon, Connecting Globally Icon, Mountain Icon, Chapter Review Arrows Circle Icon: ©McGraw Hill Education

part 3

Public Speaking Basics

In this section you will learn skills that will help you become a competent public communicator. You will learn how to select a topic, analyze your audience, organize your presentation, and gather the most relevant and credible information and supporting materials. Finally, you will learn how you can apply delivery skills to overcome the very natural fear of speaking in public.

©Matej Kastelic/Alamy RF

CHAPTER 9 — **Topic Selection and Audience Analysis**
How to Select an Appropriate Topic
Narrow Your Topic
Audience Analysis
Adapt to the Audience
Chapter Review

©Hill Street Studios/Getty Images RF

CHAPTER 10 — **Organizing Your Presentation**
The Introduction
The Body
The Conclusion
The References
Chapter Review

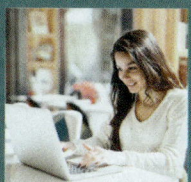
©nd3000/Shutterstock RF

CHAPTER 11 — **Gathering Information and Supporting Materials**
Gathering Information in a Digital World
Gathering Information from Library Resources
Gathering Information from the Internet
Gathering Information Through Personal Experience and Independent Research
Evaluating, Citing, and Documenting Your Sources
Chapter Review

©Steve Hix/Somos Images/Corbis RF

CHAPTER 12 — **Communication Apprehension and Delivery**
Why Care About Delivery Skills?
Reduce Your Fear of Public Speaking
The Four Modes of Delivery
The Vocal Aspects of Presentation
The Bodily Aspects of Presentation
Delivery Tips for Non-Native Speakers
Chapter Review

chapter 9

Topic Selection and Audience Analysis

©Matej Kastelic/Alamy RF

Imagine that you have been asked to provide a talk for a class at your local high school. You are given a great deal of freedom on the topic. How do you decide on the subject matter? How will you narrow the scope of the topic you choose? Deciding on an appropriate topic will often depend on the audience you are going to address. In this chapter, we will consider the best steps to take when choosing a topic that is right for you and your audience.

LEARNING OBJECTIVES

After reading this chapter, you should be able to:

- Know how to select an appropriate topic.
- Explain strategies for narrowing your topic.
- Use observation, inference, questionnaires, and the Internet to analyze your audience.
- Apply three levels of analysis to discover specifics about your audience.
- Demonstrate how to adapt yourself, your language, your topic, your purpose, and your thesis statement to your audience.

HOW TO SELECT AN APPROPRIATE TOPIC

Finding a topic that is right for you and your audience can be a challenge for a beginning speaker. Some speakers spend far too little time finding a suitable topic and end up speaking on something that audience members cannot connect with; others spend too long searching for topics, feel forced into making a last-minute decision, and sacrifice valuable preparation time. Although you should devote adequate attention to thoughtful topic selection, this step should require only a small amount of your speech preparation time. In this section you will learn some strategies for making an efficient, effective choice, beginning with two ways to quickly generate a list of ideas.

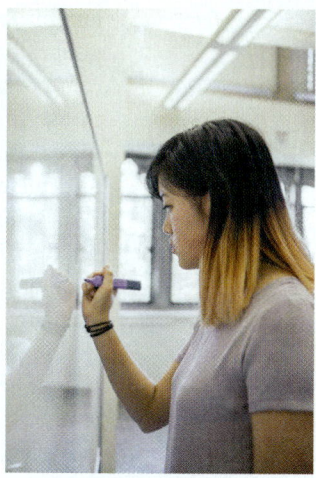
©Take A Pix Media/Blend Images/Newscom

Survey Your Interests

Public speaking starts with the self—with what you know, have experienced, or are willing to learn. To survey your interests, ask the following questions:

- What do you like best and least at work, about family life, about your community, and about our government, politics, and policies?
- How do you spend your leisure time—what do you like to read, what kinds of movies do you enjoy, and what television programs do you watch regularly?
- Do you enjoy sports and exercise? Do you regularly attend, or watch, certain sports but ignore others? Do you enjoy working out?
- What causes take up your time and energy? Do you work for environmental groups, do you care about the disparity between the rich and the poor, or do you buy only organic food?
- What types of news stories do you click on when scanning Facebook? What about your friends—are there any topics that they come to your Facebook page to learn more about?
- What particular issues bother you personally that you want to bring to the attention of others: discrimination, environmental concerns, or access to healthcare, for example?

If you choose a topic that is important to you, you will already know more about it than you do about a topic chosen at random. And you will be more motivated to do research on the topic and learn even more about it. Because of your passion and interest, you will probably speak with more gusto when you deliver your talk. You will, in turn, create more audience attention and enthusiasm.

Use Brainstorming

After you have surveyed your interests, you might consider brainstorming to generate multiple topics on which to speak. **Brainstorming** consists of *thinking of as many topics as you can in a limited time, so that you can select one that will be* *appropriate for you and your audience.* Selecting a topic from a list of many you've generated through brainstorming can be much easier than trying to think of just one perfect idea. In **Chapter 8** you learned about how brainstorming in a group is useful in problem solving and small-group decision making. Similarly, individual brainstorming can help you find topics for your public speeches, reports, and term papers.

Basic brainstorming is fairly straightforward, as demonstrated in the steps outlined in **Figure 9.1**. First, give yourself a limited amount of time, such as five minutes, and without trying to think of titles or even complete thoughts, write down as many potential topics as you can. Second, select the *three* items from your list that appeal to you the most as topics for your speech. Third, from those three topics, choose the *one* you think would most appeal to both you and your audience.

Assess Your Knowledge of and Commitment to the Topic

Once you have chosen a topic that interests you, you need to determine how the breadth and depth of your knowledge of your topic compares to that of your audience. Ideally, you should know more about the topic than does your audience. And you can add to what you know by talking to others, reading, and visiting relevant websites, resources for supporting material that are discussed in greater detail in **Chapter 11**.

But even a topic about which you're well informed is not a good choice for a presentation unless you feel some commitment to it. **Commitment** is *a measure of how much time and effort you put into a cause.* Do you volunteer in a childcare center, at a hospital, at the library, or at a food pantry? Have you had friends or relatives die of careless habits, diseases, or addictions? Do you work for a political party during elections?

Although important, commitment to a topic may not be enough to overcome poor preparation and speech performance. Research has found that it is not; the strongest predictor of speech performance is the work put into preparation.[1]

After all these considerations of your interest, knowledge, and commitment to the topic, you need to think about one other factor: the timeliness of the topic. Have you ever watched an old movie and observed how differently people used the telephone in the past? You no doubt observed how stylized the clothing was. You may have even noticed how much smoking occurred in the past compared

Figure 9.1 Brainstorming, a Simple but Useful Process

with today. Technology, clothing, and behavior change over time. Similarly, topics also change over time.

Determine Your Topic's Age

Topics, like people, live, change, and die. You will want to consider the age and development of your subject matter, as well as the age and development of your audience. Some topics have endured for decades, if not centuries:

- How much should government be allowed to intervene in our lives?
- Should the United States use military force to promote democracy?
- What can we do for the poor and marginalized in our society?
- What can we do about the privileged and overrewarded in our society?
- Should concern for the environment limit our exploration for oil?

Source: Rob Simpson/USCG

Although these questions can lead to appropriate speech topics, the speaker might need to be diligent in determining something fresh and new about the topic. Thus, older topics are not inappropriate to use as long as you dig deeper and frame the topic in a unique way to show your audience why it still matters to them in their daily lives.

On the other hand, some topics become dated rather quickly. You may know about the temperance movement only from a history course, and these days you don't hear many speeches on the evils of drinking alcohol. However, if you had been alive before and after the Civil War, this topic would have been relevant. Today people are more likely to speak on the ill effects of smoking and vaping, or of taking drugs, both legal and illegal.

Think about the speeches you hear in other classes, and more particularly in your communication class. Are you likely to hear some of the same topics over and over again? You might hear a number of speeches on abortion, euthanasia, capital punishment, drunk driving, drug legalization, eating disorders, and term limits for elected officials. Familiar topics may not be the best choice. Audience members may stop listening early when they hear yet another presentation on a common topic.

At the same time, you should not believe that a topic that has recurred is always prohibited. Current events can quickly recast an overly familiar topic into one that is relevant for the present. For example, the topic of gun control may have been considered outdated a few years ago, but more recent tragedies involving guns, including the mass shootings at the Aurora, Colorado, movie theater and at Sandy Hook Elementary School in Newtown, Connecticut, render this topic highly relevant again.

NARROW YOUR TOPIC

Many beginning speakers choose a topic that is too broad for their time limit. Animal cruelty, buying a car, and overcoming an addiction may meet the requirements of importance, knowledge, and commitment, but they are too broad. If

Table 9.1 Possible Presentation Topics

Privacy on social media sites	Keeping drugs out of sports
Protecting yourself from foodborne illnesses	Personality tests
Reducing the national debt	Computer viruses
Food preservatives	Violence in videogames
Humans' effects on the environment	Biosystems engineering
Benefits for vets	Who are the libertarians?
Genetic cloning	Changing nature of families
Conflict-resolution strategies	Healthy eating
Why tuition keeps rising	What are orphan trains?
Successful job hunting	Stop moving jobs overseas

you carefully narrow a topic *before* you begin your search for additional information, you can save much time and even more frustration. **Chapter 11** describes one way to narrow your topic—*concept mapping*, a technique for visually diagramming your primary topic and subtopics and the relationships among them.

Another way is to choose a broad and even abstract category, such as love, and list as many smaller topics as you can that are loosely related to it:

- The development of love over time
- Platonic love
- Obsessive love
- Crushes and "falling in love"
- How parents can demonstrate their love for a child
- Same-sex love
- Unconditional love
- Is it possible for a person to really love another person?

How will you know when your topic is narrow enough? Consider (1) the amount of information available about it, (2) the amount of time you have for your speech, and (3) whether you can discuss the topic in enough depth to keep audience members interested.

Chapter 11 shows how you can use Google Scholar to learn how research articles on a given topic are related. You might also visit news sites like *Google News* (**https://news.google.com/**) and scan the most popular topics and stories listed there. Newspaper articles tend to convey detailed information in a small amount of space, which is similar to your task as a public speaker. As you scan, try to identify the most relevant and insightful information on the topics that interest you. Then build your speech focus around this information.

Still another approach is to look at the examples of topics provided on the Internet. (You could look, for example, at the site "Speech Topics Help: 10,000+ Speech Topics" at **www.speech-topics-help.com/**.) **Table 9.1** also lists some possible topics.

AUDIENCE ANALYSIS

Next, you will need to determine your topic's importance to the audience. For example, you may be a committed environmentalist who knows a great deal about sustainable

©Helen H. Richardson/The Denver Post / Getty Images

agriculture, you may have lived on a small farm, and you may have good ideas about how to practice organic farming. But if most of your audience members have never set foot outside a large metropolitan area, you may have a challenge discussing sustainable agriculture with them. This topic probably has less relevance and importance for your audience than it does for you. **Audience analysis** is *the collection and interpretation of audience characteristics through observation, inference, questionnaires, and the Internet.* In this section we will discuss three levels of audience analysis and offer four methods for conducting it for your own speech.

Three Levels of Audience Analysis

Captive and Voluntary Audiences The simplest level of audience analysis is to make a distinction between captive and voluntary audiences. A **captive audience** *did not choose to hear you or your speech*; therefore, they will take more convincing than voluntary audiences. Your classmates are a largely captive audience. A **voluntary audience** *chooses to hear you speak about a particular topic.* A voluntary audience is easier to manage, because they actually seek information or ideas. A captive audience may recognize that they have no choice but to listen to your talk. They might be less critical and more agreeable than a voluntary audience. A voluntary audience, on the other hand, may have higher expectations for a speaker, since they took time or paid money to hear the speech. At the same time, they may already agree with the topic and the speaker's point of view, since they volunteered to be part of the audience.

Demographics The second level of audience analysis involves discovering the audience's demographics. The term *demographics* means "the characteristics of the people." **Demographic analysis** is *the collection and interpretation of data such as name, age, sex, place of birth, year in school, race, major subject, religion, and organizational affiliation.* Seasoned public speakers usually rely heavily on demographic information when considering which topics to present. As you look around your classroom, how many of your peers commute and how many live on campus? How many work full- or part-time versus focusing entirely on coursework? These questions pertain to the demographic makeup of your classroom. The answers you arrive at can help you infer your audience's needs and what they might find unique about your speech topic. You can collect demographic analysis through observation, inference, questionnaires, and the Internet.

A skilled speaker may guess that students majoring in engineering are highly logical and seek scientific explanations, whereas those in the humanities value narrative as proof and appreciate artistic strokes in language. Older people may be more likely to be widely traveled but also more set in their beliefs. Younger people may be less experienced but more adaptive to new technology. These judgments, of course, are not universal; we all need to be careful not to stereotype, a topic covered in **Chapter 6**. For a knowledgeable speaker, demographic information is just one aspect of audience analysis. Such a speaker will use additional methods to learn more about the audience's attitudes, beliefs, and values.

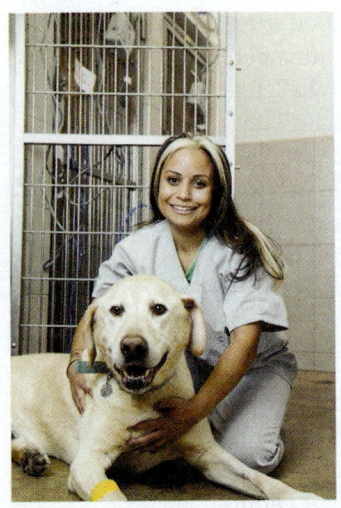
©Heidi Orcino/Getty Images

Attitudes, Beliefs, and Values The third level of audience analysis is to discern the audience's attitudes, beliefs, and values on an issue before giving the speech. How can you learn about these matters? Questionnaires and the Internet might be most useful as methods of discovery.

An **attitude** is *a predisposition to respond favorably or unfavorably to a person, an object, an idea, or an event*. Attitudes are quite stable and often difficult to change. You can assess the attitudes of audience members through questionnaires, as mentioned earlier; careful observation; or even informal conversations in which you ask the right questions. The following are some examples of attitudes:

Anti-government	Pro-business
Anti-gun control	Pro-choice
Anti-immigration	Pro-life
Anti-refugee	Pro-animal rights
Anti-tax	Pro-free trade

If you know that many of your classmates are pro-immigration and a few are originally from Mexico, you would be wise to steer clear of that discussion if your attitudes conflict with theirs.

CONNECTING GLOBALLY

USER-GENERATED CONTENT REFLECTS HUMAN VALUES

Some colleges are so diverse that the task of analyzing your audience can seem overwhelming. Although challenging to address, an audience with a mix of races, religions, and languages provides a speaker with an opportunity to address topics that matter to everyone, such as those relating to safety, security, food, shelter, and loving relationships.

Here are two ideas for using the unique functionalities of Facebook and Twitter to analyze your audience and develop your speech for a diverse classroom audience:

- ***Survey your Facebook network.*** Ask your friends what information they think your audience is likely to know and/or not know about your topic. Ask your Facebook network if they can think of more culturally diverse examples related to your topic that you might research. Their answers will help guide your library research.

- ***Check out Twitter.*** Twitter is especially helpful for learning about trends in people's thinking about a particular topic. Use the Twitter search function to see what people are currently saying about your topic and look for globally diverse examples that you might pursue further in library research.

As you learn more about the diverse perspectives of people around the world (and in your classroom!), be open-minded and generous in sharing this information with your audience. Showing you are aware of, and sensitive to, global perspectives will enhance your credibility as a speaker.

A **belief** is *a conviction.* Beliefs are usually more enduring than attitudes, but our attitudes often spring from our beliefs. Knowing your audience's beliefs about your topic can be a valuable aid in informing and persuading them. Some examples of beliefs follow:

Hard work always pays off.

Good people will go to heaven.

Taxes are too high.

Anyone can get rich.

Government should be small.

Education is important.

The strength of beliefs suggests that they are important to know about the people with whom you interact. Have you ever had a conversation with someone who bashed your beliefs? She may have ridiculed the president of the United States or a senator or representative for whom you campaigned. She may have stated that the current healthcare system will not work, it is too expensive, and most people do not understand how to receive quality care. She may have added that people should pay for their healthcare and that, if they cannot afford it, they do not deserve it. Unknowingly, she is disagreeing with your beliefs. This disagreement can seem even more pronounced in a public speech.

A **value** is *a deeply rooted belief that governs our attitude about something.* Both beliefs and attitudes can be traced to a value we hold. A questionnaire for ranking values is provided in the section on methods of analyzing the audience.

The values your audience members hold and the order in which they rank them can provide important clues about their attitudes and beliefs. The relationships among attitudes, beliefs, and values are illustrated in **Figure 9.2**. If you know that many of your classmates are majoring in business, you might infer that they hold the attitudes, beliefs, and values in **Figure 9.2**. On the other hand, what if most of the students in your class are philosophy majors who want to become more educated simply because they love ideas and new knowledge? If they are music majors and are not planning on teaching music, what might you infer? Simply knowing the majors of your classmates may provide you with helpful information and a start on understanding what they value. This knowledge, in turn, helps you avoid some topics and consider others.

Four Methods of Audience Analysis

Why should you analyze your audience? Suppose you are giving a speech arguing that a state should not take away an individual's right to belong to a union. To give an effective presentation, you should know not only state law (some states prohibit unions by denying workers the right to strike) but also how most of the individuals in your audience feel about unionization. If they agree with

Figure 9.2 The Relationship Among Attitudes, Beliefs, and Values

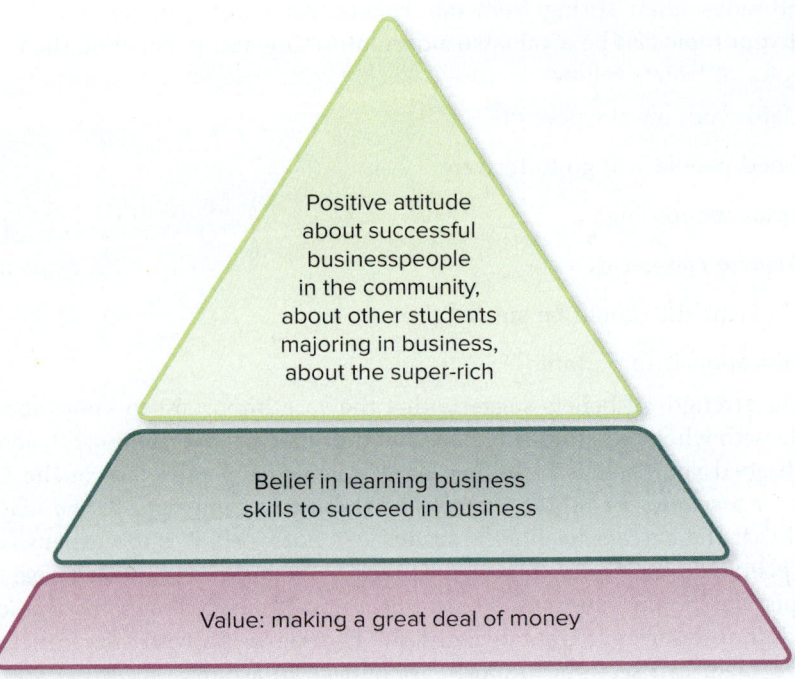

Positive attitude about successful businesspeople in the community, about other students majoring in business, about the super-rich

Belief in learning business skills to succeed in business

Value: making a great deal of money

SKILL BUILDER

"SIZE UP" YOUR AUDIENCE

Some of us are better than others at sizing up an audience. Whatever your skill level, you should practice analyzing audience characteristics. You might learn about the audience by looking at them, listening to their informal conversations, or observing their changes in behavior in response to other speakers. For example, ask yourself the following questions:

- What is the approximate age range of the audience?
- What cultures and ethnicities are represented?
- How many audience members commute to school? How many live on campus?
- How many have traveled to other parts of the world?
- How many are active in campus or community organizations?

Use the information that you gather from your audience analysis to refine your strategy for researching your speech topic. For example, one demographic characteristic of most college-aged students is that they have a broad knowledge base. So if you are speaking to a group of college students, you will want to dive deeper into your topic, going beyond the basic information. One thing is for sure, the time spent analyzing your audience and adapting your message will enhance the overall quality and effectiveness of your speech.

your view, you will probably take a different persuasive approach than if they disagree.

Audience analysis for public speaking is similar to target marketing in advertising and public relations. It can be as simple as "eyeballing" a group to estimate their age, sex, and race or as complicated as polling a group of people to discover their feelings on your topic. The insights you gain about them will help you make your speech more effective. Let's examine four methods of analyzing an audience: observation, inference, questionnaires, and the Internet.

Observation Effective public speakers must engage in active observation, using their five senses—particularly sight and hearing—to gather information about their audience. An effective lawyer observes jurors' verbal and nonverbal behavior and decides which arguments, evidence, and witnesses are influencing them. Activists and fundraisers usually spend years watching others and learning which approaches, arguments, and evidence an audience is most likely to accept.

©McGraw-Hill Education /Kefover/ Opatrany

As a student, your classroom presents an opportunity to acquire these observational skills. For every speech you give, you might listen to 20 or 25 given by others, each of which gives you a unique opportunity to discover your classmates' responses. Do they prefer speakers who come on strong or speakers who talk to them as equals? Do they like speeches about work, leisure, or ambition? Do they respond well to numbers and statistics, stories and examples, graphs and posters, or PowerPoint and Prezi? Observing and recording your classmates' responses to a variety of speakers, topics, and visual resources will give you a rich base of information about this audience.

Inference To draw an **inference** is to make *a tentative generalization based on some evidence*. The more evidence on which an inference is based, the more likely it is to be accurate. We infer from a man's wedding band that he is married and from a fellow student's military uniform that she has served in the military. We are basing these inferences on thin data, but they are probably correct.

An *indirect* inference is one we draw by observation. You might, for example, have noticed that most of the students at your college hold part-time jobs (an observation). You might infer that most students, like you, find the school expensive, the financial aid to be limited, and the cost of area housing high. If students need to work, you might avoid persuasive topics that encourage your classmates to engage in expensive hobbies and recreational activities. Instead, you might consider topics such as "good food on a budget," "ways to have fun without spending any money," and "how budgeting can work for you."

A *direct* inference is based on deliberately gathered data. You could ask either orally or in writing how many students in the class have part- or full-time jobs; how many are married, have families, and/or have grown children; how many hope to become wealthy; whether they were raised in an urban or a rural setting; and how many have strong religious ties. The answers to these questions provide valuable information about your audience.

Questionnaires A more formal way to collect data on which you can base inferences is to ask your audience to fill out a **questionnaire** in which you present *questions developed to obtain demographic and attitudinal information.*

You can gather and summarize demographic information from questions similar to the following:

_____ 1. I am a
    a. first-year student.
    b. sophomore.
    c. junior.
    d. senior.

_____ 2. I am
    a. 17–21 years old.
    b. 22–35 years old.
    c. 36–45 years old.
    d. over 45.

_____ 3. I am
    a. single.
    b. married.
    c. divorced or separated.
    d. widowed.

_____ 4. I have
    a. no children.
    b. one child.
    c. two children.
    d. more than two children.

The audience members do not have to identify themselves by name to provide this information. In fact, keeping the questionnaires anonymous encourages honest answers and does not reduce the value of the information. You do not need advanced math skills to find helpful information in such a questionnaire. Simply note the categories that are most common—for example, most students are married and have children. Note the categories into which no one falls. If most of the students are single and have no children, a speech on daycare, nutrition for babies and young children, or how to balance school, career, and your personal life is probably not appropriate.

You can collect attitudinal information in at least three ways. One way is to ask questions that place audience members in identifiable groups, as these questions do:

_____ 5. I am
    a. active in campus organizations.
    b. not active in campus organizations.

_____ 6. I see myself as politically
    a. conservative.
    b. liberal.
    c. independent.

_____ 7. I see myself as
    a. strongly religious.
    b. moderately religious.
    c. not religious.

The second way to gain attitudinal information is to ask people to rank their values, using a scale like that in **Table 9.2**. These rankings can provide additional information about the audience's attitudes and beliefs. If you can persuade some of your classmates, or the entire class, to do this, you will have information to help you prepare your speech. How does your ranking compare with those of your classmates? What other values might help you with your speech?²

The third way to collect data about people's attitudes is to list concepts and then ask the respondents their attitudes toward them, such as by using an attitudinal scale like the one in **Table 9.3**. The respondents' reactions to these and similar words or phrases can provide information that will help you adapt your speech to your audience.

Compile data that indicate the attitudes within your class on one of the topics listed in **Table 9.3**. What does this information tell you about how to approach your audience on this topic? Clearly, if the audience is sympathetic to your position, you will need to do less to inform them about the idea. You can also go further in persuading them to be even more proactive on the issue than they have been. If they are opposed to your ideas, you will need to offer both sides of the information, if informing, and/or a two-sided appeal, if persuading. Even though you might feel strongly about legalizing a lower drinking age, a majority of your classmates may disagree. You do not have to reject your topic, but you will need to tailor it for an audience with attitudes that are different from yours. The information you can gain through questionnaires is invaluable and may outweigh the effort you make to gather it.

Table 9.2 Ranking Values

Rank-order five of the following values in their order of importance to you, with 1 being the most important and 5 being the least.

___ Wisdom	___ Wealth	___ Fame
___ A world at peace	___ Security	___ Health
___ Freedom	___ Fulfillment	___ Love
___ Equality	___ Education	___ Faith

Table 9.3 Attitudinal Scale

Next to each word or phrase, indicate your attitude toward it by writing in the appropriate number: (1) strongly favor, (2) mildly favor, (3) neutral, (4) mildly disfavor, or (5) strongly disfavor.

_____	a. Internet censorship
_____	b. Government bailouts of business
_____	c. Gun control
_____	d. Stricter immigration policies
_____	e. Healthcare reform
_____	f. Lowered drinking age
_____	g. Military spending
_____	h. Medical marijuana

The Internet The Internet offers considerable information about the characteristics of first-year college students, including their attitudes, beliefs, and values, as well as how they spend their time. For example, **www.city-data.com** provides demographic data for the town or city you are researching. Information is provided about the area's levels of income, levels of education, and amount of crime committed. You can also learn about the marital status and sexual orientation of the people in the city or town. Or, you can find out what kinds of automobiles people drive and the lengths of the commute they have. The websites of many universities provide a detailed study of their students, going beyond surface demographics—for example, the ratio of males to females and the number of international students. Each college and university displays this information in different places on its website, but you will not have difficulty locating it. In short, the Internet can be a source of information on your classroom audience.

Tips for Analyzing Your Audience

In addition to the methods of audience analysis described in this section, take some time before you speak to consider some basic questions regarding what you know about the audience. You can use the following questions as a kind of checklist, referring back to it at different points in the speech preparation process.

1. Who invited you to speak? What is the relationship between this person (or these people) and the audience? Is the audience likely to be eager to hear you, or are they required to attend?
2. What can the person who invited you to speak tell you about the audience? Will this person be biased, or can you trust her information?
3. Where will you be speaking? Does the environment offer a warm, hospitable atmosphere? Is the room arranged so audience members will be actively listening to you, or are they likely to be distracted by others, by their phones, or by other noise in the environment?
4. How are the audience members similar to or different from you? Establish your commonalities and consider how you can build on them.
5. What do you know about their backgrounds, hometowns, experiences, and attitudes? Can you link these to your topic and main points?
6. Do their beliefs and values line up with yours? How can you emphasize these areas of agreement? If they do not, how can you show that your differences are not important?

ADAPT TO THE AUDIENCE

Audience analysis yields information about your listeners that enables you to adapt yourself and your message. A speech is not imposed on a collection of listeners; a message is negotiated between a speaker and an audience. Actually, communicators often adapt to their audience's characteristics, even when they are unaware that they are doing so.[3] You cannot be successful at public speaking unless you are willing to learn about your potential audience and adapt to them.

©Hero Images/Getty Images RF

Adapting Yourself

A number of studies have demonstrated the positive effects of adapting to the audience's attitudes: the audience has better recollection of the message, better feelings about the speaker, and attitudes consistent with those of the speaker.[4] A public speaker prepares for an audience by adapting to their expectations. How you look, how you behave, and what you say should be carefully tailored to your audience. You might speak informally and in casual clothes if you are talking to a group of friends. If the audience is a religious group gathered in a church, synagogue, or mosque, you should probably wear more formal clothes and avoid colloquial language.

Adapting Your Language

The language you use in your speech, as well as your gestures, movements, and even facial expressions, should be adapted to your audience. You can use slang with your classmates, but you would not use words like *booty-call* or *all-nighter* within a professional group. Similarly, you would not make humorous faces, wink, or stick your tongue out in a formal setting.

Think about how you might deliver a speech on the topic of healthy eating habits to different audiences: one made up of children, one of older adults, and another of dietitians. How would you adjust your language to most effectively address each group? With children you would probably want to use simple language and visual resources. With the older audience, your visuals may require larger font sizes, or may consist of handouts that can be kept after the speech is through. Finally, with the dietitians, you would likely broach more complex ideas and use more advanced language.

What made Martin Luther King Jr. such an effective orator was his keen ability to adapt his messages for diverse audiences. When speaking to a predominantly African American congregation, his cadence, terminology, and language differed from when he was speaking, for example, to a group of predominantly white lawmakers and legislators.[5] There is power in language and impactful speakers adapt language use to the audience, situation, and purpose of the interaction.

Adapting Your Topic

When we consider topics outside the classroom, it is important to recall the origin of public speaking in ancient Greece. The ancients were well aware of the importance of public debate and oratory. They felt that democracy was possible only through the open discussion of ideas. The founders of the United States similarly valued public speaking, as the First Amendment to the Constitution was devoted to the freedom of speech. Public speaking fosters critical thinking and engagement as citizens.

You should not assume that freedom of speech suggests that you can say anything at any time to any person. Instead, you need to pay special attention to your language choices, your audience analysis and adaptation, and even your delivery choices. For example, it is easy to sound cynical or sarcastic if you do not respect your opponents' points of view. As you speak on controversial topics, you are exercising your constitutional rights. The care you take in your treatment of the topic demonstrates your sensitivity to the rights of others.

Exercise caution in speaking boldly about politics and religion in public speaking situations. Controversial topics, such as gay marriage, banning the ownership of pit bulls, and increased public surveillance may be fine for the classroom, but you should find out from your teacher if he has a list of topics that are off limits. For a number of reasons, some instructors restrict the topics on which students may speak.

Adapting Your Purpose and Thesis Statement

After you have selected your topic, you need to determine your specific purpose in speaking. The **specific purpose** is *the purpose stated precisely as an outcome or behavioral objective and in terms of the audience.* In other words, your specific purpose includes your topic, your audience, and your precise goal in speaking to them. Here are some examples of specific purposes:

©Photo by Marvin Joseph/The Washington Post/Getty Images

> *My audience will be able to explain the difference between the Windows 2016 and Mac OS X platforms.*
>
> *My audience will be able to identify three benefits of cross-racial adoptions.*
>
> *My audience will be able to explain the increase in violence against women in particular countries.*
>
> *My audience will be able to distinguish among military guns, machine guns, handguns, and hunting guns.*

Next, you will determine your **thesis statement**, *a complete statement that reveals the content of your presentation.* The thesis statement is similar to the central idea of a written composition; it forecasts the speech and is often stated early on, generally in the introduction. You can think of your thesis statement as what you would say if you were asked to provide a one-sentence summary of your speech. Here are some examples of thesis statements:

> *The fat-soluble vitamins—A, D, E, and K—are essential to good health and can be found in foods such as eggs, fish, nuts, seeds, cabbage, and cauliflower.*
>
> *You might help a friend or classmate if you know three of the signs of drug abuse, including abrupt changes in school attendance and school work, unusual anger or outbreaks of temper, and deterioration of physical appearance and grooming.*
>
> *The U.S. government needs to balance safety and privacy concerns as a result of terror attacks.*

Just as a speech topic should be adapted to the audience, so should the purpose and thesis statement. For example, would a speech on computer platforms be appropriate in your classroom setting? You might talk about specific essential vitamins and minerals to your speech class, but would that thesis be appropriate for a group of nutritionists? Would you need to adapt to the audience of nutritionists with a more sophisticated treatment of the topic and a slightly different thesis statement? The topic, purpose, and thesis statement are related to each other and should be appropriate for your audience. **Figure 9.3** shows the relationship among the topic, purpose, and thesis statement.

Figure 9.3 From Topic to Thesis Statement

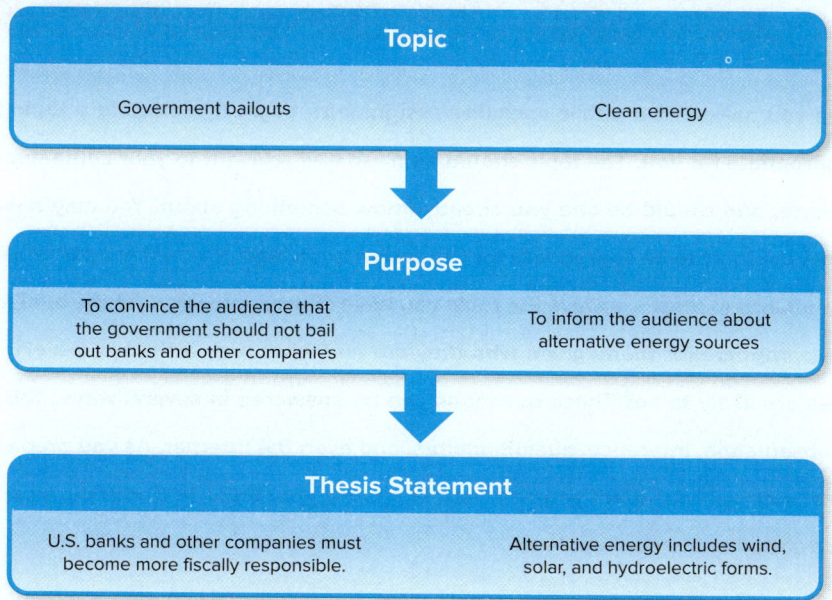

CHALLENGE YOURSELF

How do I know what to talk about when I have to make presentations in school, in the community, and at work? I don't think I know enough about anything to be confident about choosing a topic.

Many speakers are baffled when it comes to choosing an appropriate topic for a speech. At first, the possibilities seem without limit. You are bombarded with information on social media, on television, and in classes. What topic is best for you? Or you might have a very different experience and feel that you have nothing to speak about.

To decide on a topic, try brainstorming and surveying your interests. Keep in mind what is important to the audience and to you. Also, assess your knowledge and commitment to the topic. Ask yourself these questions: How do I spend the bulk of my time each day? What do I feel passionate about? What activities absorb my attention and interest? This kind of self-appraisal may open doors to the discovery of topics important to you. The more invested you are in a topic, the easier it will be to organize and deliver your speech.

Most likely you will need to narrow your topic for the prescribed length of the speech. Do not forget to analyze your audience by observing them, drawing inferences, and even conducting questionnaires and surveys. Consider whether the audience is captive or voluntary; what the demographic features of your audience might be; whether the topic and audience are young or old; and the likely attitudes, beliefs, and values of the audience. All of these considerations will lead you to a topic that is appropriate for you, your audience, and the occasion.

Adapt to the Audience

CHAPTER REVIEW

When you are given a public speaking assignment, begin by selecting a topic that is appropriate for you. The topic should be fresh and relevant to your contemporary audience, and should be one you already know something about. You may need to narrow the topic to be appropriate for the assignment. Next, you will need to consider the audience in more depth: Is the topic you have chosen important to the audience? Is it appropriate for them, given who they are and what their attitudes, beliefs, and values are likely to be? These questions can be answered in several ways. You can use observation, inference, questionnaires, and even the Internet. As you prepare to deliver your speech, adapt yourself, your language, your topic, and your purpose and thesis statement to your audience.

KEY TERMS

brainstorming, 185
commitment, 186
audience analysis, 189
captive audience, 189
voluntary audience, 189
demographic analysis, 189
attitude, 190

belief, 191
value, 191
inference, 193
questionnaire, 194
specific purpose, 198
thesis statement, 198

STUDY QUESTIONS

1. What are some of the methods you can use to select a topic for a speech? Choose one of those methods, and spend 10 minutes selecting a topic for a speech you might give to your classroom audience. Was the method you chose effective? Were the topics you listed reflective of your interests and knowledge?
2. What advice would you give a classmate who is having difficulty narrowing her topic?
3. How can knowing something about your audience's beliefs help you get your message across?
4. What are the four methods you can use to analyze an audience? Can you think of a time, outside the classroom, when you've put one of these methods to use? What were the results?
5. Experienced speakers know how to adapt to their audience. What are some of the ways you can adapt to your audience?

ENDNOTES

1. Mazer, J., & Titsworth, S. (2008). *Testing a common public speaking claim: An examination of students' ego-involvement with speech topics in the basic communication course*. National Communication Association Convention, San Diego, CA.
2. Sklare, G. B., Markman, B. S., & Sklare, A. Values clarification: It's just a matter of timing. *Personnel & Guidance Journal*, 55, 245–248.
3. Clark, H. H., & Murphy, G. L. (1982). Audience design in meaning and reference. In J. F. Le Ny & W. Kintsch (Eds.), *Language and comprehension* (pp. 287–296). New York: Elsevier; Higgins, E. T. (1981). The "communication game": Implications for social cognition and persuasion. In E. T. Higgins, C. P. Herman, & M. P. Zanna (Eds.), *Social cognition: The Ontario symposium* (Vol. 1, pp. 343–392). Hillsdale, NJ: Erlbaum.
4. Cappella, J. N. (2006). Integrating message effects and behavior change theories: Organizing comments and unanswered questions. *Journal of Communication*, 56, S265–S279; Dillard, J., Weber, K. M., & Vail, R. G. (2007). The relationship between perceived and actual effectiveness of persuasive messages: A meta-analysis with implications for formative campaign research. *Journal of Communication*, 25, 613–631; Dillard, J. P., & Ye, S. (2008). The perceived effectiveness of persuasive messages: Questions of structure, referent, and bias. *Journal of Health Communication*, 13, 149–168.
5. Wolfram, W., Myrick, C., Forrest, J., & Fox, M. J. (2016). The significance of linguistic variation in the speeches of Rev. Dr. Martin Luther King Jr. *American Speech*, 91, 269–300.

Blue and Yellow Cube Icon, Connecting Globally Icon, Mountain Icon, Chapter Review Arrows Circle Icon: ©McGraw Hill Education

chapter **10**

Organizing Your Presentation

©Hill Street Studios/Getty Images RF

Your speech will be more likely to accomplish its goals if you can gain and hold your audience's attention, make smooth transitions between major sections, and end with a clear statement of what you want your audience to take away. This chapter will teach you about speech organization by discussing the key elements—the introduction, the body, and the conclusion—as well as how to create an effective outline, an important step in preparing your speech.

LEARNING OBJECTIVES

After reading this chapter, you should be able to:

- Explain the five functions an effective introduction fulfills.
- Describe the six principles for outlining the body of a presentation.
- Explain the four functions an effective conclusion fulfills.
- Demonstrate an understanding of the purpose of a reference list.

THE INTRODUCTION

The **introduction** is *the first part of your presentation*, where you fulfill the five functions listed in **Figure 10.1**. Within the first few minutes of a speech, audience members decide whether they will listen to you. In part, they are deciding whether your topic is important enough to gain their attention. For these reasons you will want to put sufficient time and effort into developing an engaging introduction.

You do not need to fulfill these five functions in the order they are presented in **Figure 10.1**. However, your instructor may prefer this order for all speeches. For other instructors, the functions may occur in any particular order. Gaining audience attention often comes at the beginning, but maintaining attention is an important function throughout the speech. Forecasting the speech's organization often comes toward the end of an introduction, but even that function does not have to be saved for last.

One student, who spoke on the value of eating organic food, began with forecasting the development and organization of the speech. He said, "Because of the expanding global population and rapidly depleting natural resources, processed food is becoming more prominent in our society. I will first present you with some gross facts about processed foods and then I will discuss the nutritious value of organic foods." He followed this forecast with a statement to gain and maintain the attention of his audience, as well as to arouse interest in the topic:

> *Considering the college student lifestyle, ramen noodles sounds like a quick and appetizing dish. The cost-effective and easily fixed meal provides us with*

Figure 10.1 The Five Functions of Introductions

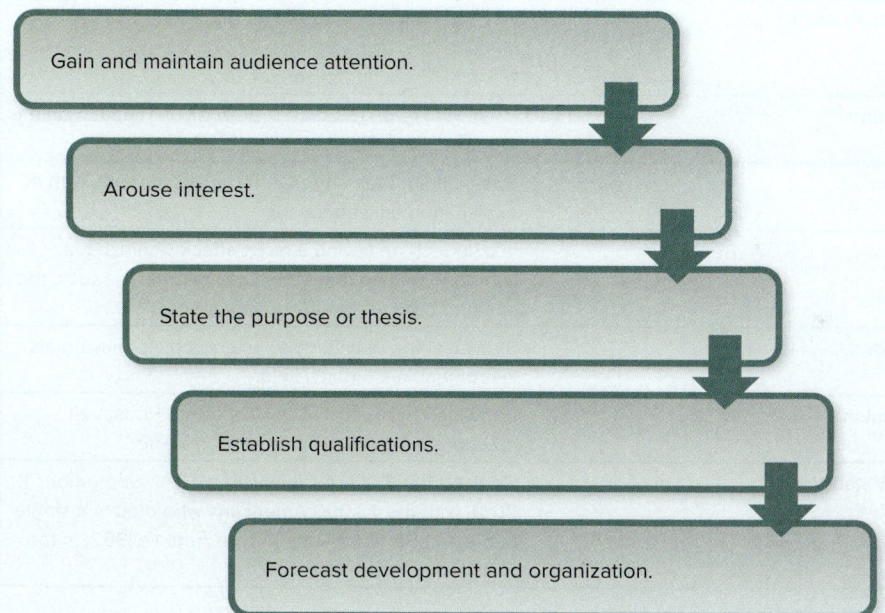

©Katrina Wittkamp/Getty Images RF

temporary satisfaction. However, few of us ever ponder what goes into producing such processed foods and how effectively large corporations monitor the quality of their products.

He then stated his purpose, or thesis, and finished the introduction with his qualification to speak on the topic.

Gaining and Maintaining Audience Attention

Gaining and maintaining attention means involving your audience in your topic in a memorable way. There are many ways that effective speakers draw an audience into a speech topic in a memorable way. Here are some creative suggestions for doing so successfully:

Suggestion	Example
1. Bring to the presentation the object or person about which or whom you are going to speak.	Bring organic food to sample in a speech on organic food.
2. Invite your audience to participate.	Have everyone stand up and perform the exercise you are teaching.
3. Let your clothing relate to your presentation.	A nurse talking about the dangers of not getting a flu shot wears her scrubs.
4. Exercise your audience's imagination.	Have the audience members close their eyes and imagine they are slipping into a cool Minnesota lake when Miami is humid and steamy.
5. Start with sight or sound.	Play "Smoke on the Water" before your speech on the Montreux Jazz Festival.
6. Arouse audience curiosity.	Speak in another language for a few seconds with no explanation until afterward.
7. Role-play.	In a speech on saving a heart attack victim, have someone demonstrate the signs of a heart attack; the speaker then takes appropriate steps.
8. Show a very short video.	Show a video of a German in lederhosen playing an instrument in a Munich field.
9. Present a brief quotation.	Read a short excerpt about Theodore Roosevelt's reaction to the untimely death of his wife.
10. State striking facts or statistics.	Contrast the 3,000 people who died on September 11, 2001, with the 23,000 Americans who died in a single battle, the Battle of Antietam, on April 17, 1862, in the Civil War.

11.	Self-disclose.	Tell audience members something about yourself—related to the topic—that they would not otherwise know: "I lost a job opportunity because of entries on my Facebook page."
12.	Tell a story, a narration.	Tell a story about one of your famous (or infamous) ancestors.

These suggestions for gaining and maintaining audience attention certainly are not the only possibilities; they are suggested to help you think creatively about your own process.

Likewise, there are some attention-getting devices we suggest you avoid. Do not try to gain the audience's attention by doing something unrelated to your topic or something that is overly dramatic. Alternatively, do not begin with mundane statements such as "Today I am going to . . ." or "My speech topic is . . ." Also, do not tell jokes unless you are especially adept at humor. In addition, you might want to try your humor on a subset of your audience or with a group of friends. Refrain from using a rhetorical question as your attention-getter, such as, "How you would feel if you were inappropriately arrested by the police." Instead, relate a compelling story about someone who was inappropriately arrested. Rhetorical questions as attention-catching devices are often overused, are not very creative, and do not usually draw your audience into your speech with impact. Finally, resist bringing a pet, or a very young or very old relative as your attention-getter. You may not be able to control their actions.

Arousing Audience Interest

The second function of an introduction is to arouse audience interest in the subject matter. This is sometimes also called demonstrating listener relevancy for your topic. In a speech on diabetes, you could share how many people have been diagnosed with this disease and the percentage of increase each year. Translate those numbers into the likelihood that members of the audience are likely to develop diabetes, or will have a friend or neighbor who will. By making the topic relevant to those in your audience, you are sure to arouse their interest and show that you have included them in your audience analysis, a topic discussed in **Chapter 9** in detail.

Stating the Purpose or Thesis

The third function of an introduction is to state the purpose or thesis of your speech. Thesis statements include the identification of the speaker's general purpose and specific purpose. The general purpose is either to inform, to persuade, or entertain. The specific purpose identifies a more detailed goal, addressing the question "about what?" People learn more, and are more likely to be persuaded, if they know the speaker's goal. Occasionally, you will want to wait a little longer to share the goal of a persuasive speech, particularly if you think your audience will initially be opposed to your message.

You will recall from **Chapter 9** that a thesis statement is a complete sentence that reveals the content of your presentation. An example of a persuasive thesis statement is, "Today I hope to persuade you that people should be allowed to marry each other whether they are of the opposite sex or of the same sex for at least three reasons." The same topic could also be framed as an informative speech. An example of an informative speech thesis statement on the same topic might be, "Today we will discuss how same-sex couples still face a range of obstacles in legally demonstrating their love to one another." Informative thesis statements refrain from using words like "should/should not," or "must/must not," in the thesis statement itself that imply a speaker may be arguing for a change of policy or behavior. Instead, the thesis statements of informative speeches focus on informational goals.

The following are two additional examples of thesis statements for audiences, which guide the speaker's preparation efforts and informational goals:

Thesis statement for an informative speech: "Identity theft can be avoided, and I will explain five methods you can easily implement."

Thesis statement for a persuasive speech: "After listening to me, you will be eager to join our movement to change the grading system at this college."

Establishing Your Qualifications

The fourth function of an introduction is to describe your qualifications as a speaker on the topic. Establishing your qualifications enhances your credibility. You can talk about your experience, your research, the experts you interviewed, and your own education and training in the subject. Simply stating that you read about the topic or that you studied a topic in high school is insufficient to establish credibility. Be wary about self-praise, but explain why you can speak about the topic with authority.

The following is an example of establishing credibility through self-disclosure: "You probably have noticed that I wear a military uniform on one Friday each month. This is because I fought in the Middle East and now serve in the National Guard—yes, I am a weekend warrior." Another example of establishing your credibility for a topic with less direct individual experience as a speaker might be: "In discussing immigration, I have examined the latest research on the topic and interviewed someone who immigrated to the United States." Having a speaker credibility statement helps the audience understand why they should listen to you on the topic.

Forecasting Development and Organization

The fifth function of an introduction is to forecast the organization and development of the presentation. The forecast previews the main points you plan to cover. Audience members feel more comfortable when they know what to expect.

You might want to forecast the development and organization of your speech just after you have stated the thesis statement, since it is an expansion on the thesis statement. In a speech in favor of same-sex marriages, a speaker might add the following after the thesis statement:

> *Five strong reasons exist for why same-sex people should be allowed to marry: First, it is unconstitutional to discriminate against a specific group of people. Second, homosexuality is not a choice and should not be punished. Third, gay marriage does not hurt anyone, and it does not hurt society. Fourth, gay marriage will increase child adoptions. Finally, gay marriage will bring financial gains for state and local governments.*

Before we move on to a discussion of the body of your presentation, we will look at some tips for strengthening your introduction by avoiding common mistakes:

©Dan Saleinger/Getty Images

1. Do not start talking until you are up in front and settled. Starting your speech on the way up to the lectern is bad form.
2. Do not simply announce your topic; offer an interesting statement to gain the audience's attention.
3. Avoid saying negative things about yourself or your abilities: "I'm not used to public speaking," "I've never done this before," or "I couldn't be more nervous than I am right now." You are supposed to build your credibility in the introduction, not give an audience more doubts about your ability.
4. Do not let your nonverbal unease overcome your message. Crossing your legs, refusing to look at the audience, jingling the change in your pocket, repeatedly pushing your hair off your face—all of these signal to the audience your lack of confidence. Act confident even if you are not.
5. Do not say negative things about your message: "I didn't have much time to prepare this speech," "I couldn't find much information on my topic," or "I really don't know much about this issue." Do the best you can to convey your message, but do not tell the audience to disregard your message.

THE BODY

The **body** is *the largest part of the presentation, in which you place your arguments and ideas, your evidence and examples, your proofs and illustrations, and your stories and testimonials*. When it comes to planning the body of your presentation, you need to decide what information to include and what to exclude. You also need to decide what you will talk about first, last, and in the middle. Your entire message should be included in the body. The introduction paves the way for this message, and the conclusion reinforces or reminds your audience of it. New material should not appear in the conclusion; material introduced in the introduction should be expanded upon in the body.

As mentioned early in this chapter, most speakers begin composing their presentations with the body rather than the introduction, because they need to know the content of the presentation to write an effective introduction. However you decide to draft and organize your speech, you should not underestimate the importance of outlining.

The Principles of Outlining

An **outline** is *a written plan that uses symbols, margins, and content to reveal the order, importance, and substance of your speech*. An outline is used to prepare your speech; it is not to be used in the delivery of the presentation. The outline is a simplified, abstract version of your speech. You will find that learning how to outline can provide you with a useful tool in your classes and at work.

Outlining is easy to learn if you keep six principles of outlining in mind:

Principle 1: Link the outline to the specific purpose and thesis statement. All the items of information in your outline should be directly related to your specific purpose (to inform, entertain, or persuade) and your thesis statement. You will recall that we defined and discussed these terms in **Chapter 9**. Imagine that you are providing an informative speech about a constitutional amendment in your state. Your purpose might be to have the audience describe the scenario if the amendment is defeated and to describe the situation if the amendment passes. Your thesis statement might be, "My audience will understand the proposed ethical standards for public officials, including a revised code of ethics and more effective ways of enforcing this code." You may want to encourage others to stop texting and driving: "Texting and driving results in accidents, deaths, and other long-term consequences." Thus, as you sift through information on your topic, make sure you do not lose sight of this purpose. Use sources of information that address your specific purpose and reinforce your thesis statement well.

Principle 2: Your outline is an abstract of the message you will deliver. As a simplification, the outline should be less than every word you speak but should include all important points and supporting materials.

Principle 3: Each sentence in the outline is a single idea. That is, the outline should consist of single units of information, usually in the form of complete sentences, each of which expresses a single idea.

Principle 4: Your outline symbols signal importance. The **main points**, or *most important points*, are indicated with Roman numerals, such as I, II, III, IV, and V. A 5- to 10-minute message should probably have from one to three main points. **Subpoints** *support the main points,* are of less importance, and are indicated with capital letters, such as A, B, C, D, and E. Ordinarily, two subpoints under a main point are regarded as the minimum. Nothing is magic about the number two; rather, the rule of division states that one item cannot be divided into fewer than two parts.

Principle 5: Your outline margins signal importance. The larger the margin on the left, the less important the item is to your purpose. However, the margins are coordinated with the symbols explained previously; thus, the main points have the same left margin, the subpoints have a slightly larger left margin, the sub-subpoints have a still larger left margin, and so on. The following outline demonstrates how margins illustrate importance.

I. **Many companies are taking a proactive approach related to the issue of workplace diversity.**
    A. One prominent place where companies communicate their value toward diversity is having a diversity statement.
    B. An additional step is to hire a diversity officer, tasked with improving diversity initiatives.
        1. One important initiative for a diversity officer to examine is to analyze the current make-up of their workforce through the lens of diversity.
        2. Another task of an effective diversity officer is to establish standards for workplace diversity complaints.

II. **Some companies take the extra step to create facilities that respect diversity.**
    A. While sometimes controversial, having a unisex bathroom can increase comfort for transgender individuals, clients, and employees.
    B. Providing private spaces for breastfeeding supports working women's desire to maintain a work-life balance.

III. **Diversity goals are best achieved by decreasing the prevalence of hostile work environments through training and awareness.**

Principle 6: Use parallel form. If you are writing a sentence outline, all of your statements should be full sentences. If you are doing a rough draft, all of your statements should be fragments, or phrases. You should not mix sentences, fragments, clauses, single words, and other disjointed thoughts.

The Rough Draft

Before you begin composing your outline, you can save time and energy by (1) selecting a topic that is appropriate for you, your audience, your purpose, and the situation; (2) finding arguments, examples, illustrations, quotations, stories, and other supporting materials from your experience, from written and visual resources, and from other people; and (3) narrowing your topic, so that you can select the best materials from a large supply of available items.

Once you have gathered materials consistent with your purpose, you can begin by developing a **rough draft** of your outline—*a preliminary organization of the outline*. The most efficient way to develop a rough draft is to choose a limited number of main points important for your purpose and your audience.

Next, you should see what materials you have from your experience, from written and visual resources, and from other people to support these main ideas. You need to find out if you have any materials that support your subpoints—facts, statistics, testimony, and examples. In short, you assemble your main points, your subpoints, and your sub-subpoints for your speech, always with your audience and purpose in mind.

The following is an outline exemplifying what a rough draft of a speech looks like.[1]

Citizen Journalism

Introduction

My immediate purpose is to help my audience understand the origins, current uses, and future of citizen journalism.

   I. **What is citizen journalism and what is its importance now and in the future?**
      A. What is citizen journalism?
      B. Why important?
  II. **History**
      A. Origin
         1. When?
         2. Who?
      B. Original uses
 III. **Present**
      A. Reasons for popularity
      B. Complications
  IV. **Future**
      A. Trends
      B. Genres
   V. **Conclusion:** Citizen journalism is growing because of increasing accessibility to new technologies for recording and disseminating news stories.

Your rough draft can have sentences, phrases, or just a word or two to indicate your overall plan for presentation.

Your rough draft should be easy to change; it will evolve as you decide what to keep and what to discard based on your research of your topic.

Your rough draft is an early plan containing cues about what you want to say.

A rough draft of a speech does not necessarily follow parallel form, nor is it as complete as the sentence outline, which often develops out of the rough draft. When you are ready to finalize your outline, you have several options. Key-word and sentence outlines are two possibilities.

The Sentence Outline

A **sentence outline** *consists entirely of complete sentences*. Although it does not contain all the words that will be in the delivered speech, it does provide a complete guide to the content.

The sentence outline that follows is based on a student's speech. The immediate purpose of the presentation was to explain the reasons students should eat breakfast. The action goal of the speech was to persuade classmates to get in the habit of eating breakfast every day. Notice that every entry in the outline is a sentence.[2]

Why All College Students Should Eat Breakfast
Michael Burns

Introduction

I. Many people choose to sleep 30 minutes longer every day rather than take the time to eat breakfast.
   A. How many of you ate breakfast this morning? Your cup of coffee does not count. (*show of hands*)
   B. College students who eat breakfast perform better in classes and are healthier.
   C. Eating breakfast should be a part of all college students' daily schedules.

Body

II. There are many reasons eating breakfast is beneficial.
   A. Breakfast is a great way to jump-start your metabolism and your day.
   B. Students who eat breakfast are healthier than students who don't.
      1. The Centers for Disease Control and Prevention reports that people who eat breakfast are less overweight than people who don't.
      2. The *American Journal of Clinical Nutrition* claims that people who eat a breakfast that includes a glass of orange juice have a stronger immune system.
   C. Students who eat breakfast also perform better in school.
      1. Mayo Clinic doctors have reported that people who eat breakfast regularly have more energy and are able to focus longer on tasks.

2. The American Dietetic Association claims that students who eat breakfast are more likely to have better concentration and problem-solving skills than students who don't eat breakfast.

Conclusion

III. **As college students, we need to eat breakfast daily.**

  A. Eating breakfast every day will make us healthier.

  B. Eating breakfast every day will improve our performance in classes.

  C. Eating breakfast should be just as important to our daily schedules as taking a shower.

©Roy Hsu/Getty Images RF

The Key-Word Outline

A **key-word outline** is *an outline consisting of important words or phrases to remind you of the content of the speech*. This outline shrinks the ideas in a speech considerably more than does a sentence outline. The following key-word outline came from a student's speech. Notice how the key-word format reduces the content to the bare essentials.[3]

The Youth Vote
Amanda Peterson

Introduction

I. **Politicians ignore youth vote**

  A. Most 18- to 24-year-olds don't vote

  B. Statistics on voting

  C. Forecast of the reasons

Body

II. **Youth apathetic to politics**

  A. Sports & beer more interesting

  B. Don't know who represents them

©Blend Images/SuperStock RF

III. **Politics unappealing**
   A. Partisanship
   B. Political scandals

Conclusion

IV. **What solution?**
   A. More focus on youth
   B. More attention on campus

Organizational Patterns

The body of a presentation can be outlined using a number of organizational patterns. Four of them are summarized in **Table 10.1**.

The **time-sequence pattern** is *a method of organization in which the presenter explains a sequence of events in chronological order*. This pattern can be used in both informative and persuasive speeches. The following brief outline is organized in a time-sequence pattern.[4]

©Hill Street Studios/Blend Images /Getty Images RF

Table 10.1 Four Common Organizational Patterns for the Body of a Speech

Organizational Pattern	What It Is	Exemplary Topics
Time-sequence	Chronological order	The future of social media Development of the land grant colleges
Cause/effect	Discusses cause(s) and results	The causes and effects of inflation The causes and effects of binge drinking
Problem/solution	Describes a problem and proposes a solution	Eliminating nuclear waste Helping battered women
Topical-sequence	Identifies 3 to 5 qualities or types of a person, place, or thing	Four reasons to buy a used car Three benefits of trade school

> **How Ford Drove the Auto Industry**
>
> **Jared Fougner**
>
> **Purpose**: I plan to highlight the history of the Ford Motor Company in the United States from its beginnings to today so my audience will be informed about this important foundation of a truly American industry.
>
> I. **Ford started the auto industry.**
>
> II. **In the early years, Ford experimented, developed mass production, and created cars that no other company was creating.**
>
> III. **In the middle years, Ford released the F-series pickup trucks.**
>
> IV. **In modern times, Ford innovated and competed in an ever-tightening market.**

In using a **cause/effect pattern**, *the presenter first explains the causes of an event, a problem, or an issue and then discusses its consequences, results, or effects.* Generally, this pattern is used in persuasive speeches. The presentation may be cause/effect, effect/cause, or even effect/effect. The following outline shows an example of the cause/effect pattern.[5]

> **Confessions of a Smoker**
>
> **Linzey Crockett**
>
> **Purpose**: This speech by a confessed smoker notes the potential effects of smoking on smokers' health, including early death.
>
> I. **Smoking has physiological effects on heart and blood.**
>
> II. **Carbon monoxide increases while oxygen depletes when you smoke.**
>
> III. **As the cigarette burns close to your mouth the dangerous toxins concentrate in the cigarette butt.**
>
> IV. **Smoking cigarettes can and will lead to pulmonary problems like lung cancer and emphysema, diseases that lead to an early death.**

The third pattern of organization, used most often in persuasive presentations, is the **problem/solution pattern**, in which *the presenter describes a problem and proposes a solution.* A message based on this pattern can be divided into two distinct parts, with an optional third part in which the presenter meets any anticipated objections to the proposed solution.

Here you can see what a problem/solution speech in outline form looks like:[6]

Routine Body Shrinking

I. From the time that I was in elementary school, I was overweight.

II. Over the last decade many high-quality studies have proven the benefits of exercise.

III. In five years a well-planned workout regimen helped me lose 130 pounds.

IV. Launching and sustaining a well-structured exercise routine yields benefits uncovered in studies and demonstrated in my own life.

The **topical-sequence pattern**, used in both informative and persuasive presentations, *emphasizes the major reasons the audience should accept a point of view by addressing the advantages, disadvantages, qualities, and types of a person, place, or thing.* The following topical-sequence outline informs the audience about global warming.[7]

Global Warming: What Can You Do?

Purpose: This speech attempts to persuade the audience about implementing steps to avoid even greater global warming and damage to the earth.

I. One smart choice is to buy at a farmers' market to avoid shipping costs and to obtain fresher food.

II. Another smart choice is to buy a fuel-efficient car because such vehicles leave a smaller carbon footprint.

III. Unplug unused electronics because anything turned on means your energy supplier has to burn something that can emit carbon dioxide.

©Blend Images/SuperStock RF

The Body 215

©Caro/Heinrich/Newscom

Transitions and Signposts

Transitions and signposts connect the parts of the speech. A **transition** *typically includes a brief flashback and a brief forecast that tells your audience when you are moving from one main point to another.* Beginning speakers sometimes struggle with delivering transitions. Whereas transitions conveyed in writing are easy for readers to spot and interpret, oral communication requires transitions that are clear and direct so that audiences can stay on track with your message.[8] If a point you are making reminds an audience member of her own experiences with your topic, she may become distracted with her own thoughts for a few seconds. But effective transitions will bring her back to the message of your speech and will signal your moves from one main point to the next. Without effective transitions to guide them, listeners are less likely to remember your main points. Examples of transitions are provided in **Table 10.2**.

Signposts are *ways in which a presenter signals to an audience where the presentation is going.* Whereas transitions are often a sentence or two, signposts can be as brief as a few words. Transitions review, state a relationship, and forecast; signposts merely point. Some examples of signposts are listed in **Table 10.3**.

Tips for Using Note Cards

A key-word outline fits easily on 3-by-5-inch or 4-by-6-inch note cards or on 8½-by-11-inch paper. If you choose note cards, the following suggestions may be useful:

1. Write instructions to yourself on your note cards. For instance, if you are supposed to write the title of your speech and your name on the board before your presentation begins, write that instruction on the top of your first card.
2. Write on one side of the cards only; you may need to use more cards with your key-word outline on one side only, but writing on both front and back is more likely to result in confusion.
3. Number your note cards on the top, so that you are unlikely to confuse their order. If you drop them, you can quickly reassemble them.
4. Write out items that might be difficult to remember. Extended quotations, difficult names, unfamiliar terms, and statistics are items you may want to include on your note cards to reduce the chances of error.
5. Practice delivering your presentation at least two times using your note cards. Effective delivery may be difficult to achieve if you have to fumble with unfamiliar cards. You also need to remember that the note cards can interfere with your gestures.
6. Include delivery cues on your notecards, like "look up here," "gesture at this point," or "convey a serious emotional tone here in the speech."
7. Write clearly and legibly.

Table 10.2 Examples of Transitions

Transition from one main point to another: "Now that we have seen why computers are coming down in cost, let us look next at why software is so expensive."

Transition from a main point to a visual aid: "I have explained that higher education is becoming more and more expensive. This bar graph will show exactly how expensive it has become over the past 5 years."

Transition that includes a review, an internal summary, and a preview: "You have heard that suntanning ages the skin, and I have shown you the pictures of a Buddhist monk and a nighttime bartender who hardly ever exposed themselves to direct sunlight. Now I want to show you a picture of a 35-year-old woman who spent most of her life working in direct sunlight."

Table 10.3 Examples of Signposts

"First, I will illustrate . . ."	"A second idea is . . ."
"Look at this bar graph . . ."	"Another reason for . . ."
"See what you think of this evidence . . ."	"Finally, we will . . ."
"There are three issues with this, first . . ."	"The last argument . . ."

THE CONCLUSION

The **conclusion**, *the end or final part of the speech,* fulfills four functions, which are listed in **Figure 10.2**. These functions need not be fulfilled in the order shown in the figure, but normally they are all fulfilled in the last minutes of a presentation.

Figure 10.2 The Four Functions of a Conclusion

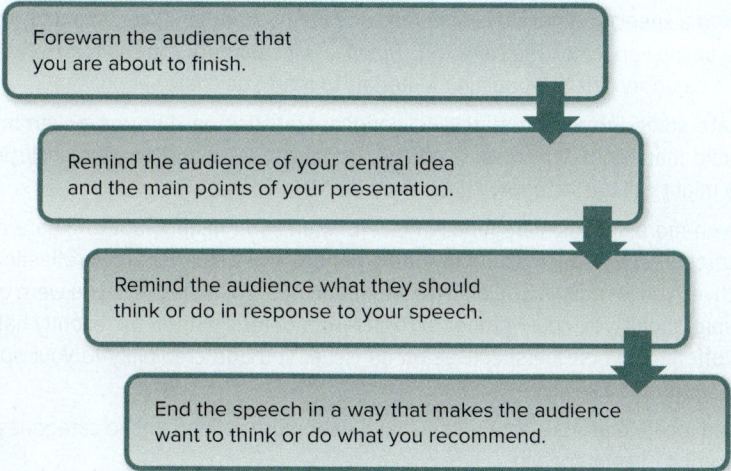

The first function of a conclusion is to warn the audience that the end of the presentation is near. One student signaled the end of her speech by saying, "Five minutes is hardly time to consider all the complications of this issue . . . ." By stating that her time was up, she signaled her conclusion. Another said, "Thus men have the potential for much greater role flexibility than our society encourages . . . ." The word *thus,* like *therefore,* signals the conclusion of a logical argument and indicates that the argument is drawing to a close.

The second function of a conclusion, reminding the audience of your central idea and the main points of your message, can be fulfilled by restating the main points, summarizing them briefly, or selecting the most important point for special treatment. This reminder of the central idea parallels the statement of the purpose and thesis statement in the introduction.

The third function of a conclusion is to specify what you expect audience members to think or do as a result of your presentation. You may want the audience to simply remember a few of your important points, to sign a petition, or to talk to their elected representatives.

The fourth function of a conclusion is to end the presentation in a manner that makes audience members want to think or do as you recommend. This final aspect of your speech is sometimes called the *clincher*. An effective strategy for

CONSIDERING MEDIA

LEARN TO EASILY STORE AND ORGANIZE YOUR WEBSITE LINKS

If you find that you have a hard time locating websites after initial discovery, use online resources to help you stay organized and save time. Live Binders (**www.livebinders.com**) is an online storage and organization resource that lets you easily mark information that you find on the Internet and organize it into subcategories.

- If you are preparing a speech on driving regulations and safety standards, you might find a relevant story in the online version of *The New York Times*. In Live Binders you can mark and store the article under a category like "Introduction Material" to read again later.

- Perhaps you locate some interesting state and national statistics on different governmental websites. You could mark and store these websites for later review and possible inclusion in your speech. You might call this category "Resources for Main Points."

- You might use even more specific categories in Live Binders. You might want to create a category called "Intercultural Perspectives on My Topic" where you gather sources reflecting the range of perspectives you identify as you analyze your audience. For example, if you were giving a speech on "Immigration," you could gather excerpts from op-eds written by recently naturalized citizens. By offering diverse perspectives on an issue, you add credibility to your speech and demonstrate cultural sensitivity.

- As you explore and locate materials, you might also create more refined online categories that reflect each main point of your speech.

crafting a clincher is to return to your attention-grabbing device. For example, if you began with a compelling story, you can end by providing insight to that story using points made in your speech. If you started by providing intriguing statistics, return to that data, or build on it with a fresh statistic that serves to remind your audience of the importance of your topic. You can also close with a quotation: "As John F. Kennedy said, 'Forgive your enemies, but never forget their names.'" Or make use of a literary passage that sums up your concluding message: "We conclude with the words of Ralph Waldo Emerson, who said, 'It is one light which beams out a thousand stars; it is one soul which animates all men.'" Finally, you might decide that your clincher requires some action that demonstrates the point of your presentation—like quickly assembling an electric motor for the class and showing that it works. There are many ways to conclude your speech with energy and excitement, and doing so will ensure your audience remembers your message.

The following is the conclusion of a speech by a first-year student about car phones and teen accidents. The side notes indicate how she fulfilled the functions of a conclusion.

SAMPLE CONCLUSION THAT FULFILLS THE FOUR FUNCTIONS

As you can see, car accidents are the leading cause of death for adolescents 15–20 years of age; therefore, a cell phone in adolescents' hands can be a recipe for disaster. I hope you are now aware of the dangers of teens using cell phones while driving. If you want further evidence, please ask me later.	*Warns that ending is near*
I have covered the basics: 6,000 teens die each year because of car accidents, teenagers' judgments deteriorate greatly with distractions, and 50% of teenagers crash within the first six months of receiving their license.	*Reminds audience of main points: summary*
Cell phone distractions can be easily prevented and can save lives. A law against teen use of cell phones while driving has worked in the first state that adopted such a law. Our state should join them. Next time you hear talk about this proposed law, I hope you will think about the facts I have shared with you and tell others why teenagers should not be allowed to talk on cell phones while driving.	*Specifies what the audience should do*
If you want to keep the roads safer for you and all of your family and friends, you will help get this law in place in our state.	*Ends by recommending an action*

SKILL BUILDER

CRITIQUE YOUR SPEECH INTRODUCTION AND CONCLUSION TOGETHER

Your introduction and conclusion are critical to the success of your speech. They are the first and last things your audience will hear you say, so it's important to make them count.

We suggest you finalize your introduction and conclusion last, after developing the rest of your speech outline. At that point you will have a better sense of how to give your message the impact it needs. When your speech outline is completed, ask yourself the following questions about how your speech should begin and end:

- **Do my attention-grabber and clincher match?** Is there parallelism in how you draw your audience into your speech and how you draw them out of it? If not, revise so they work together. For example, if in the introduction you tell a story to draw your audience in, leave one aspect of that story untold. That untold part of the story becomes your clincher. Or you can start out with an interesting fact and end with another, and then close by connecting the two facts together in a compelling way. When listeners spot the parallelism they will know you are wrapping up your speech.

- **Are the thesis statement and restatement parts of my speech similar enough?** Your thesis statement in your introduction and thesis restatement in your conclusion can be, and probably should be, identical statements. Repetition helps reinforce the central message of your speech.

- **Is the thesis statement concise?** Your thesis is not a preview of your speech. It is a statement that sums up the central message of your speech in one concise statement. Effective thesis statements often take time to think about and develop. Read through your entire speech outline and ask yourself, What is the most important general message that I am hoping to get across? Your answer should help you craft your thesis statement (and restatement). For example, if you are giving a speech on the functions of nursing homes, an effective thesis might be "Nursing homes allow our loved ones to die with dignity."

- **Do my preview and summary statements identify each main point of my speech?** A good preview or summary typically flows from the thesis. Whereas the thesis is a broad one-sentence summary of your speech, the preview and summary are more specific. They unpack the thesis by identifying, in just one or two words, each main point of your speech. For example, for the nursing home speech, the preview and summary statements might be "In discussing nursing homes we will examine [or we examined] staffing considerations, care considerations, and social or engagement considerations." The clincher often follows the summary statement in the conclusion.

- **Does my conclusion contain any information that might negatively impact my credibility?** Beginning speakers sometimes include off-the-cuff remarks in their conclusions that negatively impact their credibility. These should be eliminated from your speech. Don't say things like "I should have prepared more for this speech," "I guess that's all I have to say," or "I'm done." Fulfilling the functions outlined in this chapter will convey to your audience you have wrapped up your speech. Never end your speech with "thank you." If you have fulfilled your speech goal effectively, your audience should be thanking you!

Your instructor may add to this list, depending on the types of speeches you are assigned. **Chapters 13** and **14** address some of the nuances of speech goals further.

THE REFERENCES

When you have completed your outline, you may be asked to provide a list of **references**, or *the sources you used in your presentation.* The main idea behind a reference list is to inform others of what sources you used for your speech and to enable them to check those sources for themselves. Each entry in your references should be written according to a uniform style. Several accepted style manuals can answer your questions about the correct format: *The Publication Manual of the American Psychological Association* (APA), *The MLA Handbook*, and *The Chicago Manual of Style.* Since some teachers prefer MLA and others prefer APA, you should ask your instructor's preference.

CHALLENGE YOURSELF

Once I find out what I'm going to say or write, how do I organize my thoughts in a reasonable manner?

Perhaps you have listened to a speaker who seemed totally disorganized, or who did not have an introduction that gained and maintained your attention or stated the purpose of the talk. Maybe the speaker did not prepare you for the ending. He was speaking energetically and then just stopped without forewarning. Maybe he did not conclude with a memorable statement that helped you recall his message. Or perhaps he did not tell you exactly what he wanted you to take away from his speech.

The way you organize your speech can make a difference in how effectively you get your message across. Always keep in mind the strategies we've covered in this chapter:

- Carefully and creatively consider the functions of your introduction. Gaining and maintaining audience attention, arousing audience interest, stating the purpose or thesis of the speech, establishing your own qualifications to speak on the topic, and forecasting the development and organization of the speech.

- Think about the various ways you can organize the body of the speech. Should you place the most important information first or last? Which organizational plan should you use? How can transitions and signposts help you help the audience follow your train of logic?

- Do not skip the steps of creating a rough draft, followed by a sentence outline, and then a keyword outline that you can actually use to deliver your speech.

- In the conclusion, don't forget to signal that you are almost done speaking, to state exactly what you want the audience to know or do, and to summarize your content in a way that provides a memorable ending.

After you have organized your message as imaginatively and distinctly as you can, ask a friend or instructor to look over your sentence or key-word outline. What advice can he or she offer? Do you tend to have a weak spot in your organization? Most of us do. Consider your weaknesses and pay special attention to them as you polish and prepare your speech. Finally, make sure you don't stumble at the finish line by not practicing the delivery of your structure verbally. Practicing your speech out loud can help identify where you get lost in your structure or whether you need additional notes in your key-word outline.

- You can learn about APA style at **www.apastyle.org/**.
- You can learn about MLA at **https://owl.english.purdue.edu/owl/resource/747/01/**.
- You can learn about the Chicago style at **www.chicagomanualofstyle.org/**.

The reference list is included in your written document; it is not read during the speech. Instead, you will use **oral citations** during the speech at the appropriate time when you are providing specific material you wish to quote or paraphrase. Generally, *you will provide the name of the source, how recent the information is, and the source's qualifications.* Here is an example of an oral citation: "*USA Today* on April 19, 2013, reported that the 'Boston Blast' shone the light on Massachusetts governor Deval Patrick." This source would be listed in the references following correct MLA or APA style. **Chapter 11** provides more depth on how to cite your sources effectively within your outline, within a reference page attached to your speech, and orally during the presentation of your speech.

CHAPTER REVIEW

Now that you are aware of the functions of introductions and conclusions, you can craft effective presentations that will capture your audience's attention and leave them with a memorable point or call to action. But how will you hold your audience's attention between the introduction and conclusion? Use the six principles for outlining the body of the speech, and stay organized by subdividing your main points and subpoints. As you plan your speech, give thought to the organizational pattern that will best serve your purpose, whether it is to persuade or to inform. Remember that an organized speech is much more interesting and easier to follow than a disorganized one.

KEY TERMS

introduction, 203
body, 207
outline, 208
main points, 208
subpoints, 208
rough draft, 210
sentence outline, 211
key-word outline, 212
time-sequence pattern, 213
cause/effect pattern, 214
problem/solution pattern, 214
topical-sequence pattern, 215
transition, 216
signposts, 216
conclusion, 217
references, 221
oral citations, 222

STUDY QUESTIONS

1. What are the five functions of an introduction? Choose one of these functions and describe a time when you were responsible for putting it to use, whether it was in speaking or in writing.
2. How do a rough draft, a sentence outline, and a key-word outline differ from each other?
3. What are the four functions of a conclusion? Which of those functions might you consider most critical in a persuasive presentation, and why?
4. Turn on a radio or television news program or podcast. Listen carefully for oral citations throughout the piece, and keep an informal list of all the sources mentioned. Do any of the sources you listed peak your interest as a listener? How might a list of references help you, as a member of an audience, learn more about this topic?

ENDNOTES

1. Daniel Kalis, a teaching associate, gave this presentation.
2. Michael Burns, Basic Course Director at North Dakota State University, provided this outline for this chapter.
3. Amanda Peterson, an undergraduate at North Dakota State University, composed this outline for a communication course.
4. Jared Fougner, who became a graduate student and was from North Dakota, provided this talk.
5. Linzey Crockett, a student from Chicago, Illinois, wrote and delivered this speech.
6. Greg Heller, an ROTC student majoring in communication, wrote this talk.
7. Emily Holt, a first-year college student, composed this speech.
8. Brownell, J. (2016). *Listening: Attitudes, principles, and skills* (5th ed.). New York: Routledge.

Blue and Yellow Cube Icon, Connecting Globally Icon, Mountain Icon, Chapter Review Arrows Circle Icon: ©McGraw Hill Education

chapter 11

Gathering Information and Supporting Materials

©nd3000/Shutterstock RF

When it comes to preparing your speech, finding and evaluating supporting material is a critical step in the process. The information you present will need to suit your public speaking goal. It should also suit the needs of your listeners, whose thoughts, feelings, beliefs, and actions will be influenced by the information and evidence you put forward.

LEARNING OBJECTIVES

After reading this chapter, you should be able to:

- Explain the challenges of gathering information in the digital age.
- Demonstrate knowledge of the diverse resources available to you through your library.
- Demonstrate effective use of the Internet for finding sources of information.
- Explain the ways you can use practical experience in gathering information.
- Evaluate and properly cite your resources in oral and written formats.

GATHERING INFORMATION IN A DIGITAL WORLD

Let's say you are thinking of buying a car. After speaking to trusted friends and family members about their experiences with vehicles, you decide that a used car is the most practical choice. Next, you might turn to online consumer reports and reviews, recent newspaper articles, recall notices, and independent research studies; you might conduct instant polls among your social networks or an informal interview with a trusted friend who happens to work in the automotive industry.

©Stockbye/Getty Images RF

In each case, your search for relevant information about used vehicles constitutes research. By using a variety of information sources and evaluating them for reliability and relevance, you bring greater insight to your goal of finding the right car, and you are better prepared to make an informed decision.

Data, Information, and Knowledge

Just as you gather information about cars so you can make a high-quality decision about a purchase, you gather information for your speech topic so you can communicate a high-quality message to your audience. To achieve this goal, you need to understand how a researcher creates meaning from data and information, then shares it with others as knowledge. **Figure 11.1** explains what is meant by the terms *data*, *information*, and *knowledge*.

Figure 11.1 The Meaning of *Data*, *Information*, and *Knowledge*

Data are *facts collected from a particular source.*

Example: A runner might wear a special watch that conveys data about her heart rate, pacing, and patterns during a marathon.

Information is *a selective group of facts that you might reference to better understand a set of data.*

Example: A family might organize data about all of their purchases in a financial program, like QuickBooks, in order to see general trends related to their financial management.

Knowledge is *information with meaning attached to it.* Knowledge is a key component of problem solving.

Example: The marathon runner uses information about her running patterns to make decisions about conserving energy for the remainder of the race.

Example: The family tracking their yearly expenditures could use the information they gather to make a budget in order to save for a new purchase.

Data are *facts that have been collected from a particular source*, such as the data a runner collects when wearing a device that measures heart rate. **Information** is *the selective groups of facts that help us understand sets of data*. The runner who keeps a record of her body's physiological patterns when she runs a certain distance might use that information to determine whether to try running a marathon instead of a half-marathon. **Knowledge** is *information with meaning attached to it*.[1] The same runner would use the information she has collected about her physical abilities to focus her training or to pace herself during a long run.

Source: U.S. Coast Guard Photo by Petty Officer 3rd Class Henry G. Dunphy

In other words, when you collect data from a variety of sources, you can then organize it as information of a particular kind; when that information carries meaning that helps you make decisions or think critically about a problem, it takes the form of knowledge. Consider another example:

- A lot of complex *data* exist about alternative energy sources and usage trends.
- If you focus on and collect facts about wind energy, you are forming an *information* base on that topic.
- When you are able to understand this information enough to articulate a position, perhaps reporting some of the benefits and drawbacks of investing in wind-generated energy, you are demonstrating your *knowledge* on that subject.

Once you understand the differences among data, information, and knowledge, you can use the results of your research to present a meaningful message to your audience.

Information Literacy

As a presenter, you can successfully transfer knowledge to your audience by studying and practicing information literacy. **Information literacy** is *the ability to locate, evaluate, and incorporate important information into your own knowledge base*.[2] Given the volume of data and information made available by the Internet, information literacy skills are perhaps more important than ever.

Consider the sheer amount of information on social networking sites like Facebook, YouTube, and Twitter on which users generate loads of new content every minute. Some information science scholars argue that we are merely generating a lot of useless data[3] that do not necessarily contribute to our knowledge.

According to a recent study, 77 percent of participants appreciate having access to a great deal of information on a broad range of topics, as made available on the Internet. However, another 20 percent reported feeling overwhelmed by the prospect of evaluating all the information and sources they encounter.[4] The ability to recognize and filter out irrelevant and inadequate information is an important skill.[5] An information-literate student developing a speech on renewable energy would carefully examine each potential source, keeping in mind the quality of the source in relation to the subtopics she is developing. On the other hand, a student who struggles with information literacy skills would simply select the first sources she comes across, regardless of their quality or relevance to the overall topic.

As an information-literate student, your task is not simply to gather information on a specific topic, but rather to locate information that helps your audience understand that topic better. With an increasing amount of information at your fingertips, you may find it difficult to convert data and information into useful, situated knowledge—that is, knowledge that you and your audience can use when discussing the topic with others.

Information Overload and Information Anxiety

To some extent, having access to plenty of information can help you make good decisions. But having too much information can lead to anxiety, making it difficult to process any new information you encounter.[6] **Information overload** is *the experience of having more data and information than you have the capacity to process in a given time period.*[7] **Information anxiety** is *stress caused by an inability to access, understand, or process information that is necessary to your goal or the task at hand.*[8]

You have likely experienced anxiety and overload before, and chances are you will again. When this happens, make use of the research techniques discussed in this chapter. One of the best strategies for avoiding information overload and anxiety is to start your search for information early. Leave yourself plenty of time to find the best information, as well as to deal with the emotions that might accompany that search.

The Information-Gathering Process

The information-gathering process can be broken down into five critical steps: defining the problem, using diverse strategies, scanning and evaluating, integrating, and organizing. **Table 11.1** outlines these steps and offers examples and tips for applying them to your own information searches.[9]

The first step to any information search should be to define your problem clearly and adequately, which will help you avoid information overload.[10] Next, consider your own knowledge base and determine what useful information you can add to that base. This will immediately limit the scope of your information search: rather than having to sort through every interesting fact you discover in relation to your topic, you will simply evaluate what is relevant to the problem as you have defined it.

Before you begin your information search, construct a concept map, as discussed in **Chapter 9**. A concept map can help you identify areas in which you need to supplement your knowledge with additional facts or with greater depth of coverage or analysis. **Figure 11.2** shows a concept map created to explore the topic of college students and healthcare. A student who creates a concept map like this one might discover she wants to include more coverage of the resources

Table 11.1 The Information-Gathering Process

Define the Problem

Before you begin, define your information problem(s) and consider your goals.
In a speech about healthcare for college students, you might define your problem this way: "I'm curious about the unique healthcare issues college students face."
Tip: As you find more information and learn more about your topic, redefine your problem.

Use Diverse Strategies

Use a range of search techniques and terms:

- "College students and healthcare"
- "College students and health information"
- "College students and health problems"

Tip: Use your library's online catalog and search engines to explore your topic. For instance, pay attention to titles of books and journals that pop up often.

Scan and Evaluate the Information

As one of your main topics, you might choose to discuss where college students go to find health information and how these decisions impact their health. As you scan, you might ask yourself:

- What Internet resources do college students use for information on health?
- How many students follow up by seeing a medical professional?

Discard sources that do not focus specifically on the college student population.
Tip: You don't have to use everything in a source. For example, use only the parts of a research study that relate to your specific topic.

Integrate the Information

This is an opportunity to relate your journal article sources to anecdotes, interviews, and other sources of information.
You might integrate the information you found about college students using the Internet with information you gained from an interview with someone who works at your university health center.
Tip: Create an annotated bibliography in which you summarize your insights from each source.

Organize the Information

Organize and present your information in order to stress particular points.
Consider a way of grouping the information into subtopics—for example, "Costs of Healthcare," "Available Services," and "Care Concerns."
Remember, your method of organization should enhance the audience's current understanding of the topic.
Tip: After completing an annotated bibliography, consider how your insights group together to form your whole topic.

Figure 11.2 A Concept Map Exploring the Topic "College Students and Healthcare"

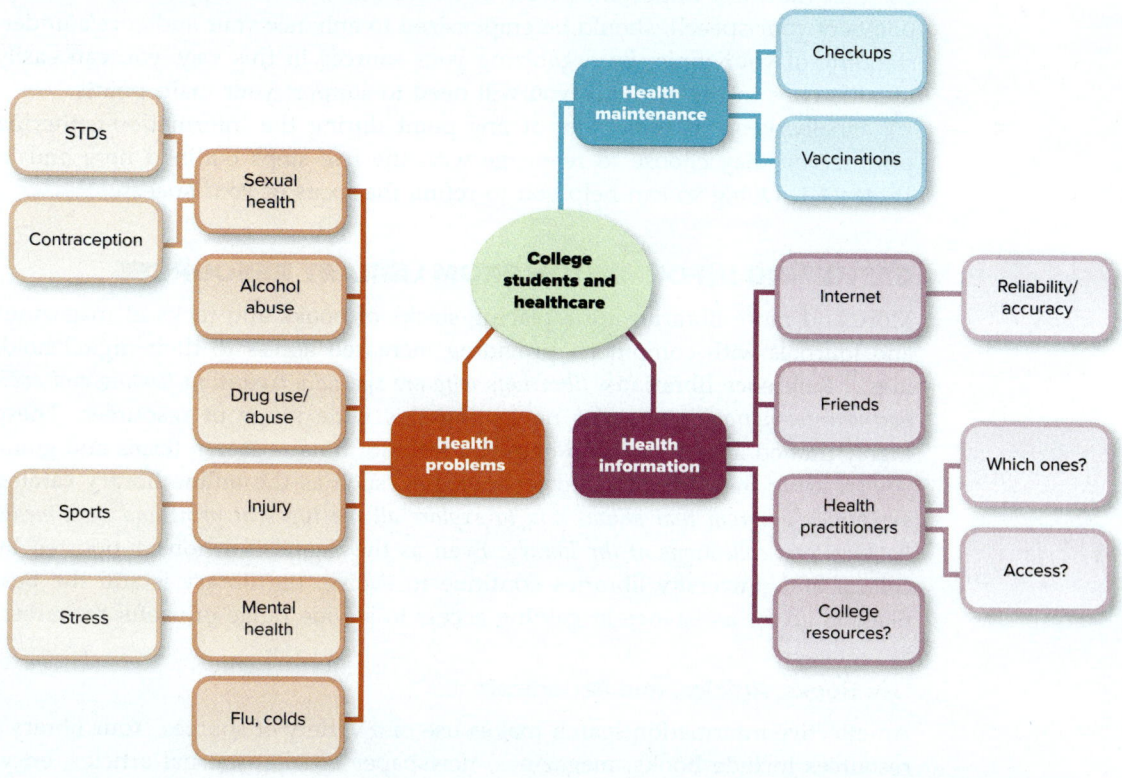

available to students who abuse alcohol. As you continue your research and find new information, you can revise your initial concept map to illustrate more clearly the relationships between aspects of your topic.

Once you define and refine the focus of your topic, the next step in the information gathering process is to use diverse search techniques and terms to explore your topic. When you have located a few high-quality sources, identify key terms that are common to those sources and incorporate those in your search.

Next, as you find new sources, take time to scan and conduct an initial evaluation about how closely it matches the main points and subpoints of your topic as you have defined them. Reviewing the main findings as summarized in the abstract can help you decide if you should scan the entire article or move on to other sources.

As you gather new sources, consider how you might integrate their information with that you have already gathered, including that gained from your own life experiences. Creating an annotated bibliography will help you summarize your thoughts on each new source, including insights into how you might integrate the information into your speech.

Gathering Information in a Digital World **229**

Take the time needed to organize your sources as you gather them. Remember that the most important pieces of information, those supporting the main points of your speech, should be emphasized to enhance your audience's understanding of your topic. By organizing your sources in this way, you can easily identify gaps in the evidence you will need to support your main points.

Finally, keep in mind that at any point during the information-gathering process you may choose to reengage with the five steps outlined here and in **Table 11.1**. Doing so can help you to refine the focus of your speech.

GATHERING INFORMATION FROM LIBRARY RESOURCES

More and more libraries are replacing stacks of books and racks of magazines and journals with computers, providing increased access to their digital holdings.[11] **Reference librarians**, *librarians who are specially trained in finding and evaluating information,* can assist navigating this wide range of resources. These highly trained library staff can help you think of unique search terms and guide you in using the computerized technologies, such as the **online library catalog system**, *a program that allows you to explore all the types of print and multimedia holdings and collections of the library.* Even as the digital functions supported by college and university libraries continue to evolve, the library is still the best place to go for assistance in gaining access to a wide range of useful resources.

Use Books, Articles, and Periodicals

An effective information search makes use of a variety of sources. Your library's resources include books, magazines, newspaper articles, journal articles, encyclopedias, sourcebooks, government documents, almanacs, and multimedia sources, as well as its own special collections. But the most commonly used sources are books, newspapers and magazines, and scholarly journals, described in **Table 11.2**.

As you conduct research for your presentation, focus on the most reliable information you can find. Scholarly articles summarize and build on the research of others and therefore reflect the most current scholarly investigations of your topic. Books and magazines likewise contain information that builds on the work of others. When citing from these sources, keep in mind the difference between primary sources and secondary sources, laid out in **Figure 11.3**.

A **primary source** is *original source material or research.* A **secondary source** is *a source of information that builds on or comments on another's material or research.* Primary sources are firsthand accounts, such as a researcher's publication of the results of an experiment, whereas secondary sources interpret and summarize one or more primary sources. Thus, a newspaper's summary of new study results is an example of a secondary source; the primary source is the originally published study.

The further removed a piece of information is from its primary source, the more open it is to error and bias. If you gather information from a journal article by an author who conducted a survey and conveyed the results, you are citing

Table 11.2 Books, Newspapers and Magazines, and Scholarly Journals

Books
- Contain in-depth information
- Are useful for understanding the general issues, themes, and fundamental principles related to your topic
- Often provide a sense of the history and development of your topic, as well as the interrelationships between your topic and other issues

Newspaper and Magazine Articles (popular press sources)
- Are a great place to start when gauging human interest and understanding current trends, issues, and debates
- Provide diverse perspectives with regard to the core issues related to a topic
- Offer ideas for the introduction or conclusion of a speech, when you might want to include examples of the experiences of others

Scholarly Journal Articles
- Provide an understanding of current and past investigations and research of a topic
- Often have the highest level of peer review before publication

Figure 11.3 Primary Sources vs. Secondary Sources

Primary Sources
- *Original material*
- *For instance, citing the results of a recently conducted survey*

Secondary Sources
- *Material that builds on or comments on another's research*
- *For instance, a newspaper article's summary of a primary source, such as survey results*

a primary source. But if you cite *Newsweek*'s summary of that survey, you are working with a secondary source. The *Newsweek* summary is an interpretation of the survey findings. Secondary sources are fine to use as long as you are aware of how they differ from primary sources, differences that include the potential for error and bias.

Wikipedia is a popular secondary source. Wikipedia listings are written by a community of users rather than, for instance, the scientists who conducted investigations and produced the primary source material. The authors of Wikipedia entries may or may not be relaying credible and reliable information; thus, you should refrain from citing Wikipedia as a source, much as you should never formally cite Facebook, Twitter, or other user-generated content as credible sources in a speech. As much as possible, you want to use primary sources for evidence. Use secondary sources, like newspaper accounts, to build human interest in topics.

©Purestock/Alamy RF

User-generated content (like Facebook and Twitter) can help you begin your search for new or noteworthy information about topics. But you should always ground any social media insights in scholarly evidence and primary sources. For example, if your social media friends constantly talk about television shows, movies, and the Internet, you might decide to develop a speech about media addiction in the age of digital communication. Next, you might supplement your own insights by visiting the library and exploring online databases for relevant and credible information on this topic.

Use primary sources whenever possible. If you find a published summary of research and the summary is from a secondary source, use the information in the summary to locate the actual study (the primary source), and then read and cite directly from that primary source. Newspaper journalists often provide one or two sentences about research studies published in scholarly journals, which is hardly enough to form your own understanding and evaluation of a study. For example, you might read a summary reporting that many elementary school lunches are high in calories and contribute to our national obesity epidemic. You will strengthen your research by locating the study and examining it for yourself. Ask yourself the following questions:

- How many people were part of the study?
- What region of the country was sampled?
- What are some of the most pertinent demographic characteristics of the schools that participated in the study?

Asking these questions will help you gain greater insight, draw more accurate conclusions, and present more reliable information to your audience.

The *way* you present your information is as important as the information itself. Remember that a study's conclusions are almost always preliminary. In a famous instance, researchers studying the impact of working conditions on productivity concluded that environmental factors, like the brightness of the lights in a factory, were responsible for increased levels of productivity. After further analysis, however, they discovered that it was not the lighting that positively affected productivity, but rather the attention paid to the workers by the researchers who were present to conduct the study. This phenomenon, now known as the Hawthorne effect, is an important reminder that research is an ongoing process. Because we cannot study all variables at once, we must draw and state conclusions cautiously.

The best approach, then, is to make "soft" statements about research studies you cite. For example, you might say, "This study suggests," "This study implies," or "This study provides some indication that," instead of "This study proves," or "This study concludes." Remember also to focus your remarks on the new insights generated by a study, which can be found in the "Results" and "Discussion" sections of published articles. If you find anything interesting from the review of literature section of a journal article, then you should look up the primary study yourself rather than rely on the scholar's interpretation of it as a secondary source. Finally, sometimes writers of journal articles use discipline-specific jargon and terminology. Simplify the language and conclusions of journal articles in a way that is appropriate for your audience.

©DreamPictures/Shannon Faulk/Blend Images LLC RF

Use Electronic Databases

Many libraries invest in computer programs that give cardholders full remote access to electronic databases and subscriptions. Whether or not you choose to research remotely, visit the library and ask for help in using these tools. Reference librarians can teach you how to use the unique features each database offers.

Many libraries subscribe to well over a hundred electronic databases that provide abstracts and full-text articles from a range of sources. Some of the most commonly used library databases are listed in **Table 11.3**. If your library does not subscribe to these databases, ask your reference librarian if you have access to similar databases that may include specialized information about your topic.

Use Surveys and Statistics as Evidence

When collecting information from books, popular press sources, and scholarly journal articles, you will encounter surveys and statistics that may be useful in supporting your overall speech topic.

Surveys are *studies that ask a sample of the population a limited number of questions in order to discover public opinions on a particular set of issues*. Surveys, or polls, synthesize the experiences of hundreds or thousands of people. One person's experience with alcohol can have an impact on an audience, but a survey indicating that one-third of all U.S. adults abstain, one-third drink occasionally, and one-third drink regularly provides better support for an argument about the extent of alcohol use in this country. If you're considering citing survey results, first consider these important questions:

> *How trustworthy is the survey source?* An important critical-thinking question to ask is, Who sponsored the survey? A respected newspaper, an objective television or radio network, or a nonpartisan university can produce

Gathering Information from Library Resources **233**

Table 11.3 Commonly Used Periodical Indexes

Academic Search Complete
- Academic Search Complete is updated daily with articles in a wide range of disciplines from over 4,000 scholarly publications.

Communication and Mass Media Complete and Communication Abstracts
- Databases index over 250 journals in communication and media use, updated bimonthly.

LexisNexis and Factiva
- These are often used to access full-text articles from newspapers and magazines, as well as transcripts of news broadcasts and legal cases. Factiva has over 10,000 sources from 159 countries.

Education Full Text
- Education Full Text incorporates publications from over 770 education journals, with more than half of the journals indexed as peer-reviewed publications.

Medline
- Medline is a medical database index from the National Library of Medicine incorporating over 4,000 journals related to healthcare and medicine.

Readers' Guide to Periodical Literature
- This includes over 300 magazine abstracts and 200 full-text magazines published in the United States.

Humanities Abstracts and Social Sciences Index
- These indexes reference both full-text articles and abstracts in art, literature, politics, social psychology, and crime.

trustworthy surveys, but a political party, a company that sells a product related to the survey, or a group with a cause related to the survey topic will likely produce a survey that is biased.

How broad was the sample? Did the survey include the entire nation, the region, the state, the city, the campus, or the class? Larger samples represent a broader viewpoint. In the context of political and other polls, you probably have heard mention of a "margin of error." A survey conducted by sampling a small subset of individuals, and whose results are generalized to a much larger population, contains a significant margin of error. Larger sample sizes reduce the margin of error, which can boost confidence in the accuracy of a poll's results.

Who was included in the survey? Were people selected randomly, or did they volunteer to respond to the questions? From what population were they drawn? If survey responses come from people who called in to a radio talk show, the results will include only the views of people who listen to that show and have an interest in the topic. If people are randomly selected to be in a survey, the results are less likely to be biased by a particular viewpoint. As another example, if you conduct a poll only through Facebook, you are drawing from one kind of population; if you conduct a paper–pencil survey at a shopping mall, you include a different kind of population. Scholarly articles always include information about sampling methods; other publications may be less careful about doing so.

Source: U.S. Census Bureau, Public Information Office (PIO)

GLOBALLY

FINDING RELIABLE AND TRUSTWORTHY STATISTICS

Source credibility should be a top priority for you as a researcher. The following three government websites are credible, nonpartisan resources for data on national statistics.

- **The Bureau of Labor Statistics (www.bls.gov/)** reports on employment and economics.
- **The Congressional Budget Office (www.cbo.gov/)** reports on U.S. spending.
- **The Census Bureau (www.census.gov/)** provides demographic information about U.S. populations, including information on race, ethnicity, income, education, and so on.

But what about finding international statistics? The following websites for statistics can help you provide important global data comparisons in your speech, and in doing so, expand your audience's perspective on your topic:

- **The Central Intelligence Agency World Factbook (www.cia.gov/library/publications/the-world-factbook/)** provides a wealth of data about various topics for 267 different world entities.
- **The European Commission (www.ec.europa.eu/eurostat)** groups and tracks data in nine different macro areas for Europe.
- **The United Nations Institute for Statistics (www.uis.unesco.org)** indexes information about education and literacy; science, technology, and innovation; culture; and communication and information for more than 200 countries.
- **The World Health Organization (www.who.int/gho/en)** tracks more than 1,000 indicators about of health for 194 member partners of the organization.

Although these resources can provide valuable information about life in the "global village," remember that listening to stories shared by people from culturally diverse backgrounds can also yield valuable comparison points for your speech. Try visiting an international student group at your institution. You may find you can connect the international statistics you've gathered to students' own lived experiences.

How representative was the survey sample? For example, *GQ* readers or motorcycle enthusiasts (mostly young males, in both cases) are not typical of the population as a whole, yet many magazines targeted at a specific population survey their readers for opinions, which they then may generalize, introducing a margin of error.

Why was the survey done? Was the survey performed for any self-serving purpose—for example, to attract more readers—or did the government conduct the study to help establish policy or legislation? If the survey sponsor appears to have an agenda, such as selling tobacco products or cell phones, the possibility of bias in the findings or in the sampling is increased.

©BananaStock/PictureQuest RF

Statistics are *numbers used to summarize information or compare quantities*. They can be used as evidence, but they can be difficult to interpret. To make things easier for your audience, instead of saying, "Honda sales increased 47 percent," you could round off the figure to "nearly 50 percent." You could report the number of Honda car sales this year compared with last year. Finally, you could clarify the comparison—for example, by saying, "That is the biggest sales increase experienced by any domestic or imported car dealer in our city this year."

Because numbers are sometimes easier to understand when they appear in print, the public speaker often has to simplify, explain, and translate. For example, instead of saying, "North High had 323,462 high school graduates," say, "North High had over 300,000 graduates." Other ways to simplify a number like 323,462 include writing the number on a board or poster and clarifying by using a comparison, such as, "Three hundred thousand high school graduates are equivalent to the entire population of Lancaster."

You can greatly increase your effectiveness as a speaker if you illustrate your numbers by using visual resources, such as pie charts, line graphs, and bar graphs. When you have such aids, you can both say and show your figures. Also try using visual imagery—for example, "That amount of money is greater than all the money in all our local banks," or "That many discarded tires would cover our city 6 feet deep in a single year."

GATHERING INFORMATION FROM THE INTERNET

Outside of the library, the most frequently used information source is the Internet. In this section, we will review how to conduct effective Internet searches for relevant and accurate information on your topic.

Use Search Engines and Virtual Libraries

The Pew Internet and American Life Project (**www.pewinternet.org**) is a nonprofit organization that researches and studies the ways people incorporate digital technologies into their daily lives. Most recently, Pew reported that 88 percent of American adults use the Internet daily in 2016.[12] Furthermore, 79 percent of Americans using the Internet to research and compare prices of products and engage in e-commerce.[13]

A **search engine** is *a website that is used specifically to search for information.* We use search engines daily for everything from securing directions to exploring online product reviews and examining recent health trends and concerns. As useful as search engines can be, they also have some downsides. For example, they provide a lot of irrelevant information that you, the researcher, need to sift through. Also, they do not always clearly identify the credentials of the authors of the information they turn up. In other words, information found through search engines needs to be carefully evaluated.

Although search engines are the most common means of searching the Internet, another useful tool is a virtual library source. **Virtual libraries** *provide links to websites where some level of review for relevance and usability of the information has been conducted.* A source is not typically listed as part of a virtual library unless it has appeared in an academic journal, at a scholarly convention, or on a reputable website, such as a university or government agency website. **Figure 11.4** presents a list of useful search engines and virtual libraries.

Use Google Scholar

As a beginning researcher, you might struggle to determine which sources are the most critical to your topic. Google Scholar will help you identify what are known as **seminal sources**, *foundational studies or pieces of information that have been heavily cited and have helped advance a line of scholarly inquiry.*

Figure 11.4 Useful Search Engines and Virtual Libraries

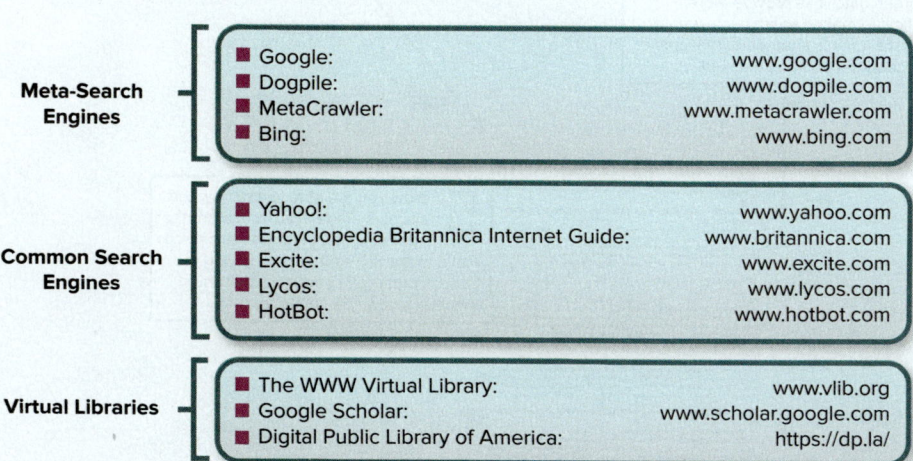

Sometimes the hardest part of putting together a puzzle is seeing how each piece relates to the larger image being constructed. When you use Google Scholar to conduct a search, the results will include the seminal sources related to your topic of investigation. Returning to the puzzle analogy, this site will show you what articles serve as corner and edge pieces of the puzzle that is your overall research topic. For example, **Figure 11.5** explores the results of conducting a search on Google Scholar using the search term "texting while driving."

Figure 11.5 A Google Scholar Search for Articles on Texting While Driving

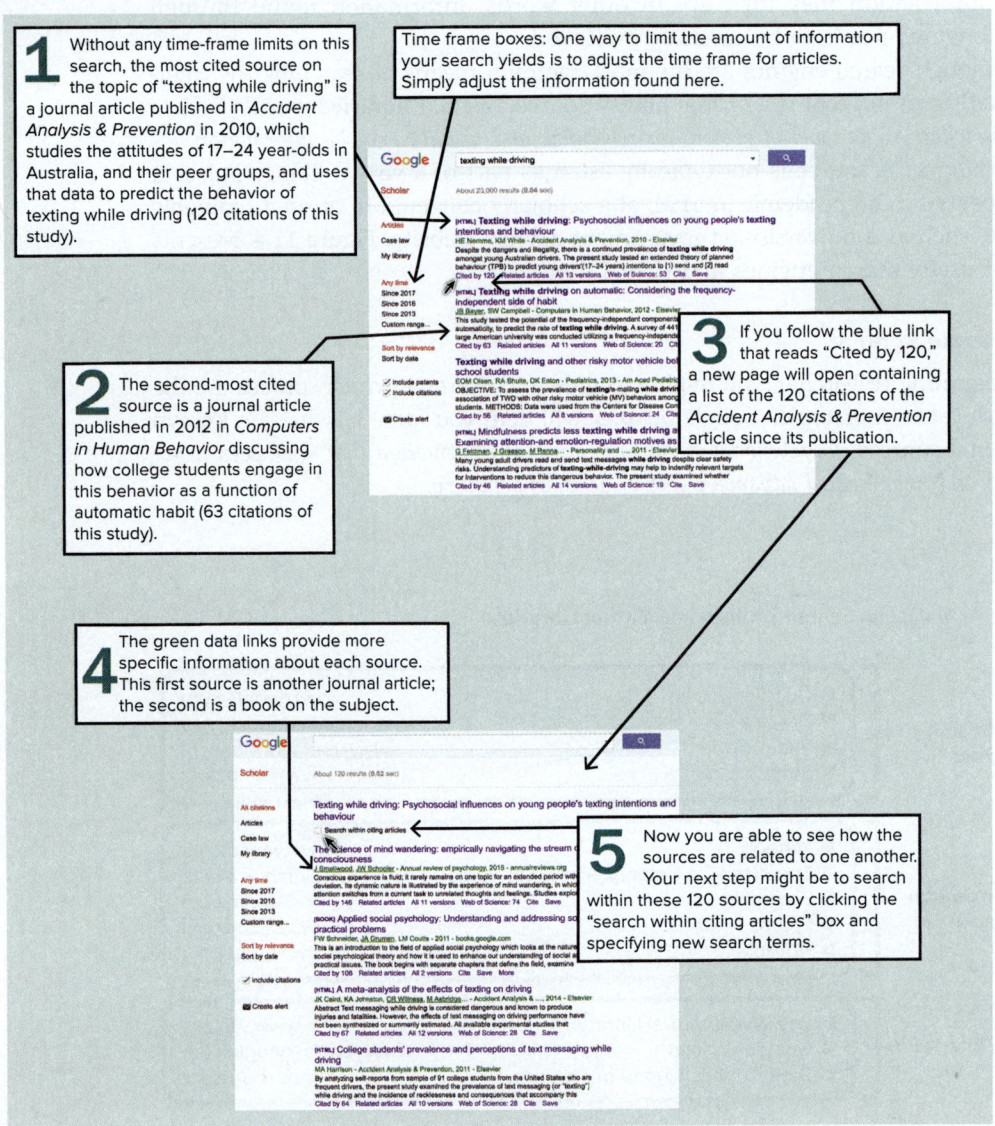

1. Without any time-frame limits on this search, the most cited source on the topic of "texting while driving" is a journal article published in *Accident Analysis & Prevention* in 2010, which studies the attitudes of 17–24 year-olds in Australia, and their peer groups, and uses that data to predict the behavior of texting while driving (120 citations of this study).

2. The second-most cited source is a journal article published in 2012 in *Computers in Human Behavior* discussing how college students engage in this behavior as a function of automatic habit (63 citations of this study).

Time frame boxes: One way to limit the amount of information your search yields is to adjust the time frame for articles. Simply adjust the information found here.

3. If you follow the blue link that reads "Cited by 120," a new page will open containing a list of the 120 citations of the *Accident Analysis & Prevention* article since its publication.

4. The green data links provide more specific information about each source. This first source is another journal article; the second is a book on the subject.

5. Now you are able to see how the sources are related to one another. Your next step might be to search within these 120 sources by clicking the "search within citing articles" box and specifying new search terms.

- The first page of results reflects ten different articles on the topic. The two most cited seminal sources in the list have at least 100 citations since publication. The published work related to either of these two seminal sources could inform the entirety of a speech on texting and driving, since you would not likely need to examine and analyze more than 200 sources.
- One of the benefits of Google Scholar is that it pulls information from a variety of disciplines. For the topic of texting and driving, the top sources are in different fields—criminal justice, communication, and psychology.
- Google Scholar also pulls information from conference proceedings, which do not have as much peer review as other sources. With this in mind, it is your responsibility to evaluate the information in the green line, which provides more details about each source on the list.

Let's say you want to examine only the fourth source in the search shown in **Figure 11.5**. You could copy the source information, take it to your library, and request the article for examination. If you follow the blue link that says "Cited by 46," you will be taken to a new page that shows only the 46 sources that have cited this research study since it was published in 2011.

If you take the information you find about each source to your library, you can get assistance locating each article. In fact, some campuses and universities have integrated their electronic database subscriptions with Google Scholar searches. If this is the case with your library, you will be able to log in to your library account and click on the blue title (a hyperlink). This will take you to a digital copy of the journal article.

A final way that Google Scholar can be helpful is by leading you to sources that are directly related to the scope of your topic. Simply type in the title of a source in quotation marks, and then search through every item that has cited your source since it was published. You might be surprised to learn how much additional relevant information is available.

Applying these strategies to each largely cited source of information helps you find the most precise information in a large body of relevant sources.

Use Internet Search Tools and Resources

A general understanding of search engine logic and functions, such as the strategic use of parentheses, quotation marks, and Boolean operators, will help you limit your searches to the most relevant sources. **Table 11.4** offers tips on how to make the most of your Internet searches.

GATHERING INFORMATION THROUGH PERSONAL EXPERIENCE AND INDEPENDENT RESEARCH

Another way to gain insight into a topic is through personal experience or the experiences of others. When you use **personal experience**, you relate *something that actually happened to you* as evidence for your speech topic.

Table 11.4 Tips for Information Searching on the Internet

Word Stemming	▪ By default, browsers identify any Web page containing the word you entered in the search box. • A search for the speech acronym *INFORM* would return sites with the words *informative*, *information*, *informal*, and *informing*. • To prevent this result, type your search term with a single quote at the end: '*INFORM*'
Phrase Search	▪ If you are looking for a phrase, put the entire phrase in quotation marks. • Typing in *campus safety* will return all sites that contain the two words *campus* and *safety* anywhere on the site. Placing the phrase in quotation marks will return only sites using the phrase in its entirety: "*campus safety.*"
Boolean Operators	▪ Boolean operators allow you to specify *what* you want returned. • Use *AND* in a search box (e.g., *tobacco AND addiction*) to find sources that include both terms. • Use *NOT* in a search box (e.g., *PowerPoint NOT Microsoft*) to find sources with the term before the operator but not after it. • Use *OR* in a search box (e.g., *Gauguin OR van Gogh*) to find sites with one of two possible terms.
Parentheses	▪ Using parentheses allows you to combine Boolean search operators. • Typing the search *(media AND violence) NOT television* will result in websites containing the terms *media* and *violence* but not *television*.

Experience Your Topic

Let's say you are working on a speech about excessive parking fines for student-commuters. You plan to advance the claim that local government should be more accommodating to students who park in residential areas around campus. This is a policy issue. Your personal story as a commuter who can't afford the expensive campus parking lots and who received a $25 fine for parking more than two hours on a city street can be compelling evidence. You have to be careful, however, if your personal experience is unusual. You would have to show that many other students suffered the same treatment, or your "evidence" would sound more like a personal gripe.

One way to gain personal experience is to volunteer for an organization whose goals are related to your general speech topic. Consider the student who joins a political campaign as a volunteer to see how political activism works, or an investigative reporter who takes a job at the restaurant chain whose unfair employment practices she will later reveal in an article. Think of all the material you could gather in just a few hours of working with the campus police, in an animal shelter that takes in abused animals, or in your community, cleaning up a nearby park after a storm.

Your experiences volunteering, including the conversations you have and the activities you observe, can find their way into your speech. For example, if you are asked to develop an informative speech about campus computing, repair, and Internet safety, you could volunteer for a few hours with your campus information technology office. While helping around the office you could ask experts what they look for in detecting potential campus security issues. You could take note of the types of problems the IT experts handle in helping students resolve computing problems in a typical week. Experiencing some aspect of your topic firsthand offers many benefits. You might make contact with people who would make good interview sources. Finally, volunteering demonstrates that you care about your speech topic, boosting your credibility as a speaker.

©Realistic Reflections RF

Conduct Independent Research

Another way to become more directly involved with your topic is to conduct independent research. For example, most classes gather in the minutes before class begins, a brief time when you could ask your classmates their opinion about an issue you plan to discuss. You do not need to construct an entire survey; however, if you decide to, you can refer to **Chapter 9**, where this topic is discussed in detail. Maybe you just want to know how many of your classmates have a particular position on the topic you wish to discuss—for example, what they think of campus parking fines. In your presentation, you can reveal the results.

If you do not have strong, direct experience with your topic, you can engage in independent research by interviewing an expert. Your goal in the interview should be to get the expert talking about his or her experiences and to gather stories you might use as supporting material in your speech. You can do this by constructing open-ended questions—for example, "Can you describe for me some recent initiatives that are targeted toward improving issues of diversity and equality on campus?" or "What do you think the current needs are in relation to diversity, equity, and inclusion on campus?" Either of these questions would generate **expert testimony**, or *information from a source who has enough credibility to speak about a specific topic.* Attorneys often use expert testimony in court—for example, evaluations of psychologists and physicians—to support the innocence or guilt of an individual. Expert testimony can be powerful and persuasive. However, although personal experience and independent research can enhance the overall quality of a speech, they should never be the sole basis for your argument. Make sure you also ground your speech in evidence from scholarly journal articles and books.

CHALLENGE YOURSELF

I am familiar with good habits for finding and evaluating sources, but how do I know if I've chosen the best sources? How do I know when I can stop seeking new information?

Recent research published in the *Journal of Information Science* supports that, by and large, students are familiar with the practices associated with evaluating sources, like those listed in **Table 11.5**. However, the same study suggests that students are more likely to use the sources that are most accessible to them, rather than those that are most pertinent to their research goals.[14]

Your challenge begins with selecting the best and highest-quality sources to suit the needs of your topic and your audience. In this chapter, you've learned some of the steps you can take to improve your information-searching practices. But how will you know when you are done seeking new information? Follow these tips for managing your research process:

1. *Begin the process early.* The processes laid out in this chapter take time. Rushing is likely to lead to increased anxiety and a lower-quality final product.

2. *Don't try to do all the research in one sitting.* Doing anything for too long diminishes your ability to focus on important details. Break up your research into at least three sessions, each focused exclusively on the development of one main point.

3. *Before initiating your second research session, evaluate, synthesize, and integrate the information from your first session.* The information you found in your first session may guide your subsequent research.

4. *Trust yourself.* Your goal is not to find out everything there is to know about your topic. Rather, you should aim to bring out an interesting and unique perspective. Your audience will know if you are genuinely interested in your topic, and your enthusiasm is likely to advance their understanding.

Your credibility is at stake every time you address an audience. You want to use information that will enhance your credibility and show people that you care enough about their time to bring them the very best information you can find on your topic.

EVALUATING, CITING, AND DOCUMENTING YOUR SOURCES

As you gather and evaluate a diversity of sources and incorporate those sources into your knowledge base, remember the importance of source credibility. We have already discussed source credibility in the context of library and Internet research. But in this section we look at another means of evaluating sources and, especially, avoiding plagiarism by citing sources accurately and often.

Evaluate Sources of Information

One way to ensure the credibility of the information presented in your sources is to check them against each other. **Data triangulation** is *the process of verifying and confirming the results or insights from one source of information with other types of* *information on the same topic.* For example, if you are working on a speech about climate change, you might want to incorporate some of what you read in Al Gore's 2006 book *An Inconvenient Truth.* However, because the book came out more than ten years ago, you might decide to verify that the claims advanced in the book are consistent with more current research on climate change. By checking your sources against each other, you ensure the credibility of the information you are presenting, as well as that of yourself as a speaker.

Whatever sources you evaluate, you can apply a consistent set of criteria to test their credibility. Specifically, ask yourself the questions outlined in **Table 11.5**. Throughout your research process, continue to ask these questions about every one of your sources. If you can answer yes to all these questions with certainty, you increase the chances that your sources are valid and trustworthy.

Avoid Plagiarism

Being clear about where you found the evidence you use in your outline and your speech is very important. In doing so, a process called documenting your sources, you rightfully credit the work of other writers and researchers, avoid the very serious consequences of plagiarizing, and demonstrate that you are a credible speaker who has put a lot of good work into gathering and interpreting

Table 11.5 Criteria for Testing Source Credibility

Are there clear markers of credibility for the source?	■ Be cautious of sources without a clear author who has identified credentials. • *Examine the credentials of the author.* Ask yourself, Does the author have a degree or obvious expertise regarding the subject? • *Examine the credentials of the publishing source.* Many journals require double-blind reviews of submissions before publication. Is this true of your source?
Is the source objective?	■ Look for biases in the organization hosting or sponsoring the information or funding the research. • Researching a speech on gun control, you might be especially critical in evaluating information found on the National Rifle Association (NRA) website. • If you are researching Internet addiction, you might be especially wary of any information sponsored by Microsoft.
Does the source draw appropriate conclusions?	■ Credible sources draw conclusions that are appropriate for the study. For example, much survey research is conducted in such a way that the results cannot be applied beyond the study sample. • Examine the Results and Discussion sections of a research study to verify that the conclusions it draws are grounded in the study's results. • Use data triangulation. • Ask yourself, Do the authors draw conclusions that go beyond the data?
Is the information in the source current?	■ Scientific research is self-correcting over time. This means that additional research may detect flaws in earlier thinking and conclusions. Thus, refrain from using sources of information that are out of date. • If you are putting together a speech about smoking and health, do not use antiquated sources that might downplay the dangers of smoking.

information. Therefore, once you identify a source you want to use, cite it properly in three places: the reference list for your speech (or paper), the body of your written work, and the oral delivery of your speech.

An effective **bibliographic reference** is *the complete citation information about a source that you include in the references or works cited at the end of your speech outline.* Your outline should also include **internal references**, *citation information about specific evidence as you present it in the body of your speech.* **Table 11.6** gives examples of the two most common formats for written citations in a "references" or "works

Table 11.6 Proper APA and MLA References

	APA References	MLA References
Newspaper Article—General Style	Last Name, First Initial. (year, month day). Title of article. *Title of Newspaper*, pp. first page, last page.	Author(s). "Title of Article." *Title of Newspaper*, day month year, pp. first page, last page.
Newspaper Article—Example	Manjoo, F. (2012, October 22). Keeping loved ones on the grid. *The New York Times*, pp. D1, D7.	Manjoo, Farhad. "Keeping Loved Ones on the Grid." *The New York Times*, 22 Oct. 2012, pp. D1, D7.
Journal Article—General Style	Last Name, First Initial, Author, B. B., & Author, C. C. (year). Title of article. *Title of Journal*, *volume* (issue), first page–last page. doi: reference number	Author(s). "Title of Article." *Title of Journal*, volume, issue, year, pp. first page–last page.
Journal Article—Example	Kanter, M., Afifi, T., & Robbins, S. (2012). The impact of parents "friending" their young adult child on Facebook on perceptions of parental privacy invasions and parent–child relationship quality. *Journal of Communication*, *62*(5), 900–917. doi: 10.1111/j.1460-2466.2012.01669.x	Kanter, Maggie, Tamara Afifi, and Stephanie Robbins. "The Impact of Parents 'Friending' Their Young Adult Child on Facebook on Perceptions of Parental Privacy Invasions and Parent–Child Relationship Quality." *Journal of Communication*, vol. 62, no. 5, 2012, pp. 900–917.
Website—General Style	Last Name, First Initial. (date of last update). *Site title*. Retrieved from URL	*Name of the Individual Web Page*. Name of the Publisher, date, URL.
Website—Example	Pennsylvania State University. (October 12, 2012). *Penn State takes actions on many Freeh report recommendations*. Retrieved from http://live.psu.edu	*Penn State Takes Action on Many Freeh Report Recommendations*. Penn State University, 2012, news.psu.edu/story/145672/2012/10/12/penn-state-takes-action-many-freeh-report-recommendations.
Interview—General Style	Last Name, First Initial. (year, month day) *Personal Communication*.	Last Name, First Name. Personal Interview, Day month year.
Interview—Example	Hanson, M. (2017, September 10). *Personal Communication*.	Hanson, Mary. Personal Interview, 10 September 2017.

Note: Journal articles that use continuous pagination from issue to issue of the same volume do not need to include the issue number in proper APA style. If an article does not have a doi (digital object identifier) number, you do not have to provide it. Interview references are not typically included in an APA reference list. However, you may want to include some information about interviews you conducted, so that you can count them among your sources.

cited" list—the American Psychological Association (APA) style and the Modern Language Association (MLA) style. Your instructor generally specifies which style you should use. Although the rules may seem picky, using proper citation form is extremely important to good scholarship, as well as to your instructor in assessing your work.

You will also want to make sure you properly cite your sources during your speech. Such **oral citations** *make specific reference, where appropriate, as you present them, to each source you used.* An effective oral citation provides the following three pieces of information:

1. The author(s) of the piece
2. The date of publication (for a Web source, the date it was last updated or was accessed)
3. The name of the publication

You do not need to state the exact title of each source. Simply provide enough information that your audience members can locate your sources if they want to examine your evidence in greater depth. **Figure 11.6** provides an example of

Figure 11.6 Oral Citations for Newspaper Articles, Journal Articles, Websites, and Interviews

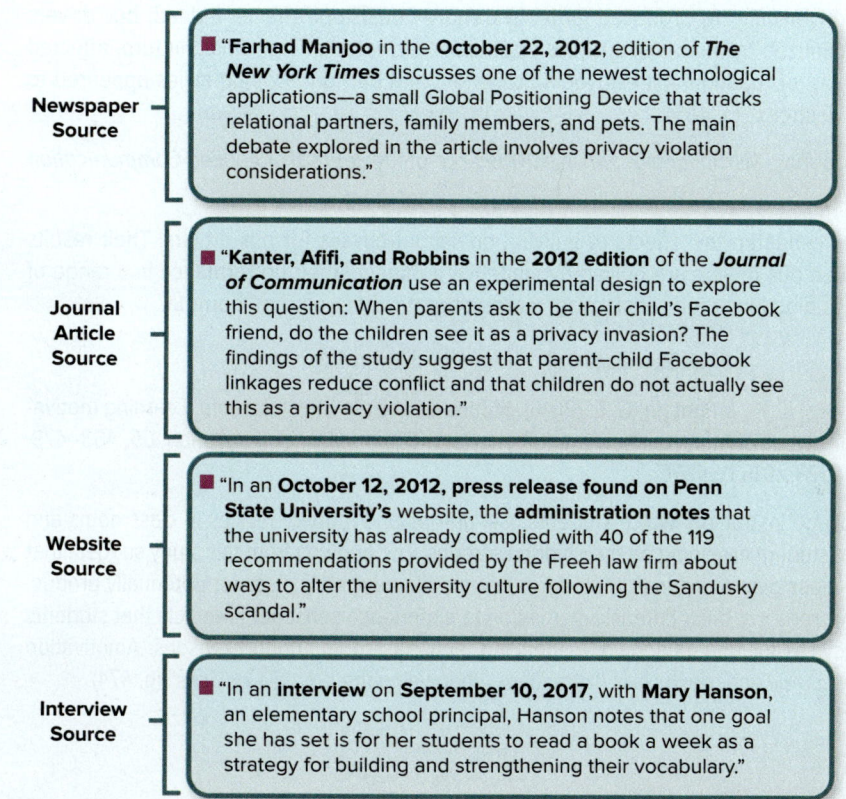

Newspaper Source
- "**Farhad Manjoo** in the **October 22, 2012**, edition of *The New York Times* discusses one of the newest technological applications—a small Global Positioning Device that tracks relational partners, family members, and pets. The main debate explored in the article involves privacy violation considerations."

Journal Article Source
- "**Kanter, Afifi, and Robbins** in the **2012 edition** of the *Journal of Communication* use an experimental design to explore this question: When parents ask to be their child's Facebook friend, do the children see it as a privacy invasion? The findings of the study suggest that parent–child Facebook linkages reduce conflict and that children do not actually see this as a privacy violation."

Website Source
- "In an **October 12, 2012, press release found on Penn State University's** website, the **administration notes** that the university has already complied with 40 of the 119 recommendations provided by the Freeh law firm about ways to alter the university culture following the Sandusky scandal."

Interview Source
- "In an **interview** on **September 10, 2017**, with **Mary Hanson**, an elementary school principal, Hanson notes that one goal she has set is for her students to read a book a week as a strategy for building and strengthening their vocabulary."

Evaluating, Citing, and Documenting Your Sources   **245**

SKILL BUILDER

PRACTICE PROPER ORAL CITATIONS

Effective oral citations show your audience just how hard you have worked to provide them with the most useful information on your topic. Before preparing your first speech, practice delivering effective oral citations by condensing information from your sources into statements that credit the authors of those sources. While it may feel a bit awkward at first, this practice will pay off by building your credibility with your audience.

The following example demonstrates one example of an effective oral citation for a quote on the subject of bullying. Following that are two block quotes and their APA citations. Summarize each of these quotes in your own words preceded by a proper oral citation for the source. Review **Table 11.6** for more examples of effective oral citations. Everything you will need for each oral citation is contained within each APA reference.

Example: Bullying on the School Bus

Reference: Goodboy, A. K., Martin, M. M., & Brown, E. (2016). Bullying on the school bus: Deleterious effects on public school bus drivers. *Journal of Applied Communication Research*, *44*, 434–445. doi: 10.1080/00909882.2016.1225161

Block Quote: "Although observed student-to-student bullying was related to bus drivers' stress at work, student-to-driver bullying produced larger and more consistent effects. Indeed, bus drivers reported being victimized by students, and this victimization created stress, which in turn, affected anxiety while driving, occupational stress, job satisfaction, and burnout. Coping styles appeared to do little to help with stress" (p. 445).

Oral Footnote: Goodboy, Martin, and Brown in a 2016 issue of the *Journal of Applied Communication Research* . . .

Summary: ". . . investigated the effects of bullying on school busses for bus drivers. Their results supported that when bus drivers are bullied by students, it impacts their performance in a range of negative ways, including lower job satisfaction, more occupational stress and burnout."

First Exercise: Cell Phones and Learning

Reference: Stephens, K. K., & Pantoja, G. E. (2016). Mobile devices in the classroom: Learning motivations predict specific types of multicommunicating behaviors. *Communication Education*, *65*, 463–479. doi: 10.1080/03634523.2016.1164876

Block Quote: "College instructors watch students use laptops and mobile devices in classrooms and often wonder what student are doing on their hidden screens. The findings from this study suggest that self-determined actions play a part in how students use mobile devices in class for potentially productive and destructive reasons. IMES [intrinsic motivation to experience sensation] predicts that students will use mobile devices for understanding, influencing, and classroom support reasons. Amotivation predicts that students will engage in class distractions when using their mobile devices" (p. 474).

Oral Footnote:

Summary:

> **Second Exercise: End-of-Life Family Communication**
>
> **Reference:** Keeley, M. P. (2016). Family communication at the end of life. *Journal of Family Communication*, *16*, 187–197. doi: 10.1080/15267431.2016.1181070
>
> **Block Quote:** "After conducting over 150 interviews and collecting hundreds of surveys about FCs [final conversations], I have come to realize that there are numerous EOL [end-of-life] 'backstage' conversations going on in the family. These conversations are occurring among adult children as they observe and/or participate in their parents' death journeys. Family EOL communication can also bring up 'old issues' among the adult siblings such as familial cohesiveness, adaptability, conflict, decision making, and satisfaction, which should be more thoroughly explored as to how they impact the family during their end of life" (p. 194).
>
> **Oral Footnote:**
>
> **Summary:**
>
> Sources: Goodboy, A. K., Martin, M. M., & Brown, E. (2016). Bullying on the school bus: Deleterious effects on public school bus drivers. *Journal of Applied Communication Research*, 44, 434–445. doi: 10.1080/00909882.2016.1225161; Stephens, K. K., & Pantoja, G. E. (2016). Mobile devices in the classroom: Learning motivations predict specific types of multicommunicating behaviors. *Communication Education*, 65, 463–479. doi: 10.1080/03634523.2016.1164876; Keeley, M. P. (2016). Family communication at the end of life. *Journal of Family Communication*, 16, 187–197. doi: 10.1080/15267431.2016.1181070

how you can create an oral citation for a newspaper article, a journal article, a website, and an interview.

In general, during your presentation, do not go too long without referring to a source. Although your instructor will likely tell you the requirements for using sources in your speech, a good rule of thumb is to incorporate one oral reference for each minute of your speech. Using this rule, if you are preparing a five- to six-minute speech, you should orally cite five or six unique sources of information.

CHAPTER REVIEW

This chapter has explored some of the ways you can ground your speeches and written work in the most current, credible, and valuable sources of information. With so much information at hand, you have the very important job of applying these strategies and thus turning data and information into useful knowledge for your audience. By using a diverse range of resources, including your library's holdings, the Internet, and your personal experiences, and methodically triangulating your sources and data, you help ensure that the information you pass on to your audience is both relevant and accurate. Finally, you now know how to evaluate and cite your sources in oral and written formats.

KEY TERMS

data, 226
information, 226
knowledge, 226
information literacy, 226
information overload, 227
information anxiety, 227
reference librarians, 230
online library catalog system, 230
primary source, 230
secondary source, 230
surveys, 233

statistics, 236
search engine, 237
virtual libraries, 237
seminal sources, 237
personal experience, 239
expert testimony, 241
data triangulation, 242
bibliographic reference, 244
internal references, 244
oral citations, 245

STUDY QUESTIONS

1. Name and explain the stages of an effective information-gathering process. How, if at all, does access to digital resources affect these stages?
2. Consider each of the following types of sources, and describe the kind of information you might find in each: books, newspaper articles, and scholarly journal articles.
3. How is Google Scholar different from your typical search engine?
4. Name a topic you could research that would allow you to draw from your personal experience. Name a topic you could research that would be enriched by surveying people in your community. Explain why you chose those topics.
5. What steps would you take to evaluate a source for credibility and document it to avoid being accused of plagiarism?

ENDNOTES

1. Child, J. T., & Shumate, M. (2007). The impact of communal knowledge repositories and people-based knowledge management on perceptions of team effectiveness. *Management Communication Quarterly, 21,* 29–54.
2. Gross, M., & Latham, D. (2007). Attaining information literacy: An investigation of the relationship between skill level, self-estimates of skill, and library anxiety. *Library & Information Science Research, 29,* 332–353.
3. King, B. (2011, January 18). Too much content: A world of exponential information growth. *The Huffington Post.* Retrieved from www.huffingtonpost.com/brett-king/too-much-content-a-world-_b_809677.html
4. Horrigan, J. B. (2016). Information overload. Pew Research Center. Available at http://www.pewinternet.org

5. Eisenberg, M. B. (2008). Information literacy: Essential skills for the information age. *Journal of Library and Information Technology, 28,* 39–47.
6. Eppler & Mengis.
7. Eppler, M. J., & Mengis, J. (2004). The concept of information overload: A review of literature from organizational science, accounting, marketing, MIS, and related disciplines. *The Information Society: An International Journal, 20,* 325–344.
8. Bawden, D., & Robinson, L. (2009). The dark side of information: Overload, anxiety and other paradoxes and pathologies. *Journal of Information Science, 35,* 180–191.
9. Brand-Gruwel, S., Wopereis, I., & Walraven, A. (2009). A descriptive model of information problem solving while using the internet. *Computers & Education, 53,* 1207–1217.
10. Savolainen, R. (2007). Filtering and withdrawing: Strategics for coping with information overload in everyday contexts. *Journal of Information Science, 33,* 611–621.
11. Child, J. T., Pearson, J. C., & Amundson, N. G. (2007). Technology talk: Public speaking textbooks' coverage of information retrieval technology systems. *Communication Quarterly, 55,* 267–281.
12. Pew Internet and American Life (2017, January 12). Evolution of technology: Internet/broadband fact sheet. Retrieved from http://www.pewinternet.org
13. Smith, A., & Anderson, M. (2016, December 19). Online shopping and e-commerce. *Pew Internet and American Life Project.* Retrieved from http://www.pewinternet.org.
14. Kim, K., & Sin, S. J. (2011). Selecting quality sources: Bridging the gap between the perception and use of information sources. *Journal of Information Science, 37,* 178–188.

Blue and Yellow Cube Icon, Connecting Globally Icon, Mountain Icon, Chapter Review Arrows Circle Icon: ©McGraw Hill Education

chapter 12

Communication Apprehension and Delivery

©Steve Hix/Somos Images/Corbis RF

In this chapter we will take a close look at the causes and symptoms of the fear of public speaking, also known as communication apprehension, and share some tips for managing it. But remember, even as you learn to manage the fear of public speaking, practicing is key to effective delivery.

LEARNING OBJECTIVES
After reading this chapter, you should be able to:

- Explain the relationship between delivery and communication anxiety.
- Describe the causes and symptoms of communication apprehension, as well as ways to manage them.
- Describe the four modes of delivery and explain the advantages and disadvantages of each.
- Understand how to apply the vocal aspects of delivery when giving a speech.
- Demonstrate the proper use of your body when delivering a speech.
- List some delivery tips for non-native speakers of English.

WHY CARE ABOUT DELIVERY SKILLS?

Some people believe that it's not what you say, but how you say it, that really counts. According to others, the reverse is true. Actually, both what you say *and* how you say it are important. To better understand this, let's first discuss what *delivery* means.

What Is Delivery?

Delivery is *how your use of voice and body affect the meaning of your presentation.* Effective speakers use their words, voice, and body to communicate a message in a compelling manner. Consider the points in **Figure 12.1** about the importance of delivery skills.[1]

©Brand X Pictures/PunchStock RF

How you look and sound while delivering a presentation affects whether audiences will decide to listen to you. If you look confident and poised, if you speak smoothly and without unintended hesitation, and if your voice sounds strong and authoritative, your audience will perceive you as someone they should listen to.[2]

Perhaps the most striking fact about delivery is how quickly its impact is felt: audiences decide in seconds or, at the most, minutes whether they find you credible as a speaker. Observe fellow students, and watch your instructors, supervisors, managers, and executives at work. Do you judge their competence by how they look and sound? You will likely find that many judgments about speakers' credibility come from their poised appearance and confident voice.

Figure 12.1 Unpacking Delivery

- Effective delivery contributes to the credibility of the speaker.
- Student audiences characterize the poorest speakers by the vocal and physical aspects of their delivery.
- Speakers who are fidgety and nervous, whose voices are monotonous, who maintain little eye contact, and who show little animation or facial expression are perceived as having poor delivery skills.

©Image Source/Getty Images RF

A common cause of poor delivery is public speaking anxiety. A fidgety speaker who makes little eye contact is displaying symptoms of nervousness, which negatively affect her delivery.[3] A presenter who speaks too quickly or softly will lose the attention of the audience. In the next section we aim to demystify public speaking anxiety by examining, first, the reasons speakers get nervous and, second, some strategies for managing those feelings, before and during the speech.

What Is Communication Apprehension?

Given the role of mediated forms of communication in our lives—and the diminishing role of face-to-face interactions—it's no wonder that many of us struggle with nervousness when asked to speak in front of others.

Communication apprehension (CA) is *the fear of communicating with other people, whether that interaction is real or anticipated.*[4] CA can be triggered not only by the act of speaking in front of others but also simply by the thought or anticipation of that interaction. You may not experience any anxiety about your speech until the moment you enter the classroom the day of your presentation. In fact, seeing others give presentations before you present can be just as nerve-racking as presenting yourself.

Nervousness often leads us to make mistakes or to present ourselves in a way that does not look or feel natural. You might even be wondering what you can gain from discussing these fears. Talking about your fears can help, as can reminding yourself that you are not alone. In a recent study, college students were asked to list their biggest fears, and speaking to a group of people was the most commonly identified fear.[5] Over 800 college students listed speaking in front of a group more frequently than any other fear, including the fear of experiencing financial problems, death, or loneliness, as illustrated in **Figure 12.2**.

Experiencing Communication Apprehension

Before examining modes of delivery and the vocal and bodily aspects of presenting, you first need to understand the reasons for communication apprehension and what you can do to overcome it.

CA happens across a range of contexts. Some people experience anxiety only when thinking about speaking in front of groups, whereas others get nervous about interacting one-on-one; some of us experience anxiety in both cases.[6] Generally speaking, **trait apprehension** is *communication anxiety in a variety of settings and under diverse circumstances.*[7] For example, people who exhibit trait-based apprehension are more likely to experience negative self-talk when anticipating an interaction.[8] Leaders with lower levels of trait-based CA are more likely to include a wide range of people in organizational decision-making; leaders with higher levels of trait-based CA tend to handle decision-making on their own.[9]

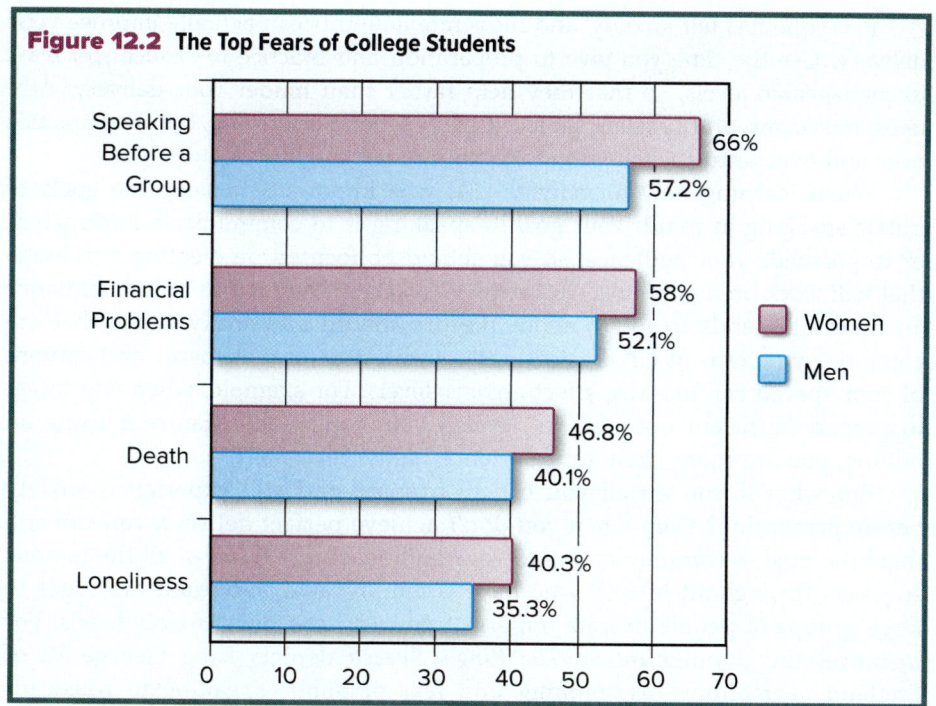

Figure 12.2 The Top Fears of College Students

Source: Dwyer, K. K., & Davidson, M. M. (2012). Is public speaking really more feared than death? *Communication Research Report, 29*, 99–107.

State apprehension, on the other hand, is *communication anxiety in a limited number of settings or circumstances*, such as when speaking to large groups, or when being evaluated. Most people experience some degree of state apprehension, commonly referred to as stage fright or public speaking anxiety. When people experience state-based CA within just the public speaking setting, completing a public speaking course has a tremendous impact in reducing that anxiety.[10] Because trait-based CA can apply to contexts other than public speaking, those who experience it must work to reduce anxiety levels overall in order to improve their interactions.

We often are our own worst critics and incorrectly believe that our audience is judging our presentation skills as harshly as we do. Most often the reverse is true. Because your peers will also be expected to get up and speak, they are more likely to sympathize with your anxiety than to disapprove of it.

The goal of this chapter is not to help you get rid of your anxiety altogether. Experiencing too little or too much anxiety can reduce the overall effectiveness of your communication with your audience. For example, if your anxiety levels are too low, you might overestimate your abilities, underprepare, or establish too casual and relaxed a tone. When your anxiety levels are too high, your delivery can suffer, as when your speech speeds up, your breathing changes, or your body temperature rises and causes your face to turn red.

Why Care About Delivery Skills?

Everyone has felt anxiety, and moderate amounts can actually improve your delivery. Use the time you give to preparation and practice to reduce any fears to manageable levels, so that they help rather than hinder your delivery. Athletes, musicians, and speakers all feel anxiety when performing, but they practice over and over until they are comfortable in front of an audience.

When learning how to manage CA, it is important to keep the goals of public speaking in mind. Your goal in speaking is to communicate information or to persuade your audience, so you should be focused on creating a message that will work on a particular audience. A speaker who focuses on the audience and message tends to forget about the dry mouth and shaky knees that are common symptoms of CA. Factors such as the structural elements and content of your speech can likewise affect anxiety levels. For example, when you forget to prepare sufficient notes, or to develop your topic and organize it using an outline, you are more likely to experience higher levels of CA.

But what if you do all you can to prepare and still experience anxiety before presenting? Even when you don't achieve perfect delivery, you can still meet the goal of communicating to your audience. Just think of all the famous speakers throughout history who have communicated important messages to large groups of people despite imperfect delivery and high anxiety levels. For instance, the popular movie *The King's Speech* depicts King George VI of England overcoming his stammer and fear of public speaking to rouse his people during World War II. Abraham Lincoln reportedly suffered extreme shyness, despite having delivered his memorable and stirring Gettysburg Address.

REDUCE YOUR FEAR OF PUBLIC SPEAKING

In the same way that athletes train and practice to improve their skills, getting over speech anxiety requires commitment and practice. Three techniques that can help you reduce and manage your anxiety levels are systematic desensitization, cognitive restructuring, and skills training. One or more of these techniques may be right for you.

Systematic Desensitization

The first technique we will discuss, **systematic desensitization**, *focuses on progressive relaxation, visualization, and active engagement exercises to help you overcome public speaking anxiety*. To practice systematic desensitization, you will perform a relaxation exercise in your mind. You will then continue to perform the same exercise in progressively more uncomfortable or anxiety-producing scenarios.

You might begin by visualizing yourself successfully accomplishing a small-stakes public speaking exercise, like rehearsing your introduction for a roommate, in a relaxed and comfortable environment, like your living room. When you get home in the evening, actually practice it with your roommate before going to bed. Once you are able to visualize and conquer the smaller task in a relaxed state, you increase the task to something that produces a little more anxiety, like maybe giving the entire speech to your roommate or to a few friends. Eventually, you can work up to using the same technique to practice giving your entire speech to a group whose demographics closely reflect those of your class.

The key to the success of this technique is in returning to a relaxed state before each step toward performing a more high-stakes activity. Make sure you conquer the anxiety involved in the previous small-stakes step before you move on to one that is likely to cause higher levels of anxiety. Another important factor in using this technique is time. It takes time to make even small improvements in managing anxiety, so allow yourself the time you need.

The following steps describe one way to use the systematic desensitization technique when preparing for a speech:

1. Turn off the lights; lie down and think of a situation in which you are totally relaxed and free of stress.
2. Take a deep breath, hold it for a few seconds, and then exhale, repeating with each new breath.
3. Feel the tension leave your body as you exhale each breath.
4. When you reach a relaxed state, visualize yourself doing a small speaking task successfully, such as telling a personal story you know well.
5. Next, practice doing the small activity you visualized in the previous stage. For example, if you are using that personal story to introduce your speech, practice a larger portion of your introduction out loud and by yourself.
6. Finally, start over again with relaxation. This time visualize doing something slightly more difficult than you did before, such as delivering the first main point in the body of your speech. Follow the same sequence of steps.

©amana productions inc./Getty Images RF

Once you have practiced these elements successfully in your mind, you must practice them out loud in order to experience the full effects of this anxiety-reduction technique. For example, you might first begin by practicing delivering a smaller portion of your speech to a wall, then in front of a mirror, and finally to progressively larger groups of people whom you trust.

Research shows that many speakers find that systematic desensitization is highly effective in reducing public speaking anxiety.[12] One reason is that you begin by imagining successes, such as visualizing telling a story you know well, and then build on those positive experiences in the safety of your own imagination.

Cognitive Restructuring

The second method for reducing anxiety in a communication situation is to use the power of positive thinking, also known as **cognitive restructuring**. This method works by *analyzing negative perceptions and developing coping statements*

CHALLENGE YOURSELF

I am really afraid to give a presentation to a large group. I have not done much speaking, and I am worried about how I will appear. Can I do anything to relax and enjoy speaking?

Many times we avoid thinking about or working on a speech until the last possible minute.[8] This is a bit like ripping off a Band-Aid—trying to do everything in one quick motion. This approach actually increases public speaking anxiety.

Research supports that devoting more time to practice before giving your speech will actually lower your anxiety and improve your delivery.[11] Following some simple preparation steps will help you reduce your anxiety and increase your enjoyment of public speaking.

- Practice your speech the first few times using your formal outline, which will have much of your speech content written out.
- Practice your speech out loud. You can pronounce anything more effectively in your head than when you say it out loud. Identify words that are hard for you to say, as well as places where you get tripped up; then correct your delivery before the day of the presentation.
- As you practice, mark up your outline, noting the places where you seem to know the content pretty well, as well as the places where you struggle to recall what to say next. You might decide to add transitions or signposts in the places where your memory fails you.
- Since you won't be reading directly from your outline when you present, create note cards to take with you to the podium. Do not read them word-for-word, however; instead, they should be designed to assist you where you need it most.
- Finally, rehearse using the note cards, so that you are familiar with their contents on the day of the speech. Again, note the places where you continue to have difficulty thinking about what comes next. Either underline or highlight these places to provide yourself with delivery cues.

You do not need to rehearse your speech with a real audience until you are comfortable on your own. If you are feeling particularly nervous, try combining these steps with the systematic desensitization technique described in this chapter.

---

for dealing with a variety of situations. For example, one common negative thought is, "If I forget a part of my speech, I will not do well." But the truth is, one small mistake will not make or break the speech. No one expects a perfect performance.

Our thoughts have a powerful impact on how we experience events, in both positive and negative ways. Sometimes we analyze situations too quickly and attach negative perceptions to them without being mindful of our assumptions. Taking a step back from our assumptions, analyzing our thought processes, and developing coping statements can help break down negative thinking.[13] A coping statement that focuses on what to do if such a thing occurs helps rebuild negative thoughts into positive ones—for example, "I will practice with my note cards, so that I know where I might have issues with memory, and if I forget a part of my speech, I will look at my cards and go to the next piece of information."

To use cognitive restructuring more broadly, you can take the following steps:

1. Create a list of all the irrational and negative self-talk dialogue you experience when thinking about public speaking.
2. Analyze each negative statement and identify a few of the unrealistic or overly negative assumptions you are making in the statement.
3. Develop a coping statement for each negative thought on your list. Be specific and spend as much time thinking about how to overcome those negative thoughts as you did considering them in the first place.
4. Practice the coping statements often until they automatically come to mind when you find yourself contemplating the negative dialogues.

Cognitive restructuring can also help you perceive the public speaking situation differently.[14] Instead of seeing your classroom speech as just another assignment in a required course, you can reframe the situation more positively. For example, speaking to your class is your personal opportunity to sway the thinking of 20 to 30 people who ordinarily would not have come together to listen to your ideas. In other words, you can cope with your negative feelings by redefining the situation as a valuable opportunity to demonstrate what you know, make some friends, and help others in the process.

Skills Training

The third technique for getting over public speaking fears is practice. **Skills training** is *the systematic work you do, through instruction and practice, to develop your public speaking skills.* Rehearsal may sound like common sense, but research supports that consistent practice is one of the most successfully applied techniques for improving public speaking and reducing anxiety.[15]

The first step in using this technique is to recognize that public speaking is a skill that requires work. A student who really wants to become an effective communicator should

- Read and listen for basic instruction.
- Plan a presentation following the instructor's assignment.
- Analyze the audience.
- Practice and deliver the speech.

Furthermore, coaching from the instructor and classmates can help you develop better skills. You are already undertaking this recommendation by reading this book and taking a class in which you will develop greater competence in public speaking.

One example of the skills approach in action is the practiced use of eye contact. Many beginning speakers spend way too much

©Stock Connection/SuperStock

SKILL BUILDER

CONQUER YOUR ANXIETY THROUGH SKILL DEVELOPMENT

If you experience anxiety at the thought of giving a speech, do not worry—you are not alone. Most speakers have some fear of public speaking. One way to conquer your anxiety is to develop your public speaking skills. The more confident you feel, the less anxiety you will experience. Try these steps for preparing your next speech:

1. Practice reading your speech outline alone, out loud, allowing yourself to hold a comfortable position. Vocalize the words and think about your pronunciation, enunciation, and volume projection. Are there places where you trail off, where you could inject more emotion, or where you could be louder? Keep practicing your delivery focusing only on the sound of your voice.

2. Next, stand up and face the wall. Get comfortable on your feet and maintain eye contact with one point on the wall. Are there places in your speech where the content interferes with your ability to make eye contact? The point of public speaking is to communicate complex ideas as simply as you can while still achieving depth and breadth. Simplify the language to improve your delivery.

3. Move to a mirror so you can focus on your facial expressions. Your expressions should appear natural and enhance your verbal message. For example, if your speech is on the topic of domestic violence, your expression should be serious and show concern; if you are speaking on the benefits of regular exercise, you should express a positive energy that conveys health. Are there places where your expressions could better match your message?

4. Next, focus on your posture and gestures. In front of the mirror present as much of your speech as you can remember. Watch what you do with your hands and your body. The first step in eliminating nervous movements is to become more aware of them. Do you grip your hands? Do you play with your glasses or push strands of your hair back behind your ears while you speak? After you know what your nervous movements are, ask a friend to watch you give your speech and to lightly clap every time you exhibit one of these movements. This practiced awareness can help you eliminate these movements while speaking.

5. Finally, after you have practiced by yourself, in front of a mirror, and in front of a friend, use your smart phone to record yourself delivering your speech from start to finish. Watch the whole video with a friend. Evaluate your overall delivery (vocalization, eye contact, facial expressions, and gestures). Identify one thing you do well in each area and one thing you can work on to improve before you give your speech.

Rehearsing your speech is one of the most important things you can do to reduce your public speaking anxiety. Each aspect of delivery described here may seem small and inconsequential, but practicing them separately and then all together can make a huge difference in the effectiveness of your speech. If you have limited time to rehearse, practice the above steps with your introduction and conclusion. Then move to the body of your speech. A strong beginning and ending to your speech will ensure your speech has impact.

time looking at their notes or PowerPoint slides and too little time maintaining eye contact with their audience. Beginning speakers should use a key-word outline for note cards instead of a script, in order to deliver an extemporaneous speech instead of a memorized one. The extemporaneous mode of delivery will encourage eye contact. Over a series of speech-giving opportunities, you will learn to rely much less on your notes and much more on your message and audience. The next section highlights more distinctions between the four modes of delivery for a speech.

Choosing the Right Anxiety-Reducing Technique for You

Now that you are aware of three useful approaches for overcoming CA, you might be wondering which technique you should use. Actually, you can benefit from all these strategies, because each targets different aspects of public speaking anxiety.[16] You might also confer with your instructor to develop a plan that considers your particular anxieties and skills and emphasizes the strategies that will be most helpful to you.[17]

As you can see, working on your delivery skills and managing public speaking anxiety go hand in hand. An important message delivered poorly will fail to engage listeners; however, the same message delivered with confidence and skill can succeed in influencing and informing your audience.

THE FOUR MODES OF DELIVERY

The four modes of delivery are extemporaneous, impromptu, manuscript, and memorized. In your public speaking class, you may be asked to try the impromptu mode for certain assignments. However, most classroom presentations require the extemporaneous mode.

The four modes of delivery vary in the amount of preparation they require. Although all are possible choices for your presentation, speakers are least likely to use the manuscript and memorized modes. The manuscript and memorized modes encourage accuracy but discourage eye contact, audience adaptation, and conversational style. Also, the memorized mode requires much more preparation time than a class with a number of assigned speeches can afford. That is why most public speaking classrooms encourage students to use the extemporaneous mode.

The Extemporaneous Mode

A presentation delivered in the **extemporaneous mode** is *carefully prepared and practiced, but the presenter delivers the message conversationally without heavy dependence on notes.* This mode is message- and audience-centered, with the presenter focused not on the notes but on the ideas being expressed. This mode is characterized by considerable eye contact, freedom of movement and gesture, the language and voice of conversation, and the use of an outline or key words to keep the presenter from reading or paying undue attention to a written script.

Although this mode lends a speech the appearance of spontaneity, don't be fooled; extemporaneous delivery only appears to be spontaneous. Like a talented musician who makes a complicated composition look easy after hours of practice, you need to work hard to make your presentation seem smooth and easy. Extemporaneous delivery allows you to be very flexible and adaptable, to focus on conveying your message to that particular audience. You do not need to use the same words you used when practicing the speech, and you can repeat or explain if you see that the audience is puzzled.

You have seen this mode of delivery in the classroom, in some professors' lectures, sometimes in the pulpit, often in political and legal addresses, and usually in presentations by experienced speakers. This is the mode you will find most useful outside the classroom.

As a student in the communication classroom, you need to avoid overrehearsing your presentation to the point that you memorize it. Most communication instructors and audiences respond negatively to presentations that sound memorized. Any presentation that sounds memorized—and most memorized presentations do—never lets the audience get beyond the impression that the speaker's words are not really his or her own, even if they are.

The Impromptu Mode

©moorboard/Corbis RF

With the **impromptu mode**, *you deliver a presentation without notes, plans, or formal preparation and with spontaneity and conversational language.* You use the impromptu mode when you answer a question in class, when you say who you are, and when you give people directions on the street. You cannot say much in these situations unless you know the answers. Ordinarily, this mode of delivery requires no practice and no careful choice of language, but it does require that you know something about the topic.

The impromptu mode encourages you to "think on your feet" without research, preparation, or practice, so the advantage of the impromptu mode is that you learn how to handle questions about your speech, inquiries about you in a job interview, or questions in class or on the job. The disadvantage of the impromptu mode is that you really do have to know something to provide an adequate response.

The Manuscript Mode

As its name implies, in the **manuscript mode** you *deliver a presentation from a script of the entire speech.* The advantage of this mode is that the presenter knows exactly what to say and reads the words to the audience while giving as much attention to the audience as possible. The disadvantages are that the written message invites a speaker to pay more attention to the script than to the audience and it discourages eye contact and audience feedback.

Politicians, especially those who are likely to be quoted, as well as clergy and professors sometimes use this mode of delivery. Students are rarely asked to use this mode, except when reading a quotation from part of a presentation to the class.

The Memorized Mode

A presentation delivered in the **memorized mode** is *committed to memory*. This mode requires considerable practice and allows plenty of eye contact, movement, and gestures. However, this mode discourages the speaker from responding to feedback, from adapting to the audience during the speech, and from choosing words that might be appropriate at the moment. In other words, memorization removes spontaneity and increases the danger of forgetting.

Politicians, athletes, and businesspeople—those who speak to the same kinds of audiences about the same subjects—often memorize their speeches. Even professors, when they teach a class for the third time in a week, may memorize the lesson for the day.

Choosing the Right Mode of Delivery for Your Presentation

The mode you choose should be appropriate for the message, audience, and occasion. Students use the extemporaneous mode most often in learning public speaking, because that mode teaches good preparation, adaptation to the audience, and a focus on the message. Nonetheless, your mode of delivery does not determine your effectiveness.

Comparing extemporaneous and memorized modes, two researchers concluded that the mode is not what makes a speaker effective. Instead, the speaker's ability is more important. Some speakers are more effective with extemporaneous speeches than with manuscripts, but others use both modes with equal effectiveness.[18]

Frequently, the situation, or context, invites a particular mode of delivery. In a spontaneous toast of a bride and groom, the audience expects a brief, impromptu expression of congratulations; at a political rally, a politician gives some variation of a speech she has delivered many times and in many places (extemporaneous mode); an attorney reads a will to the expectant family (manuscript mode); and an experienced public speaker includes some passage that he has memorized. In the classroom context, the instructor determines the expected mode of delivery.

THE VOCAL ASPECTS OF PRESENTATION

Studying the vocal aspects of presentation is like studying music. The words of a presentation are like musical notes. As people speak, they create a melody. Think of a song that has been covered by two different musicians. Just as musicians can make the same notes sound quite different, affecting their audiences according to the rhythm and mood, for instance, presenters can alter the way they say words in order to get the audience to respond in various ways.

©Kiko Jimenez/Westend61 GmbH/Alamy RF

Some of these vocal aspects were covered in **Chapter 4**, where you learned briefly about nonword sounds. The nine **vocal aspects** of presentation are *projection and volume*, *rate*, *pauses*, *fluency*, *pitch*, *pronunciation*, *articulation*, *enunciation*, and *vocal variety*.

Projection and Volume

Projection is *speaking loudly enough for all to hear*, whereas **volume** is *the relative loudness of your voice*. Audiences (and instructors) get distracted or annoyed when they cannot hear the presenter. You need to be conversational but with a slightly higher volume than you are used to using.

Volume is more than just loudness. Variations in volume can convey emotion, importance, suspense, and changes in meaning. You can use a stage whisper in front of an audience, just as you would whisper a secret to a friend. You can speak loudly and strongly on important points, letting your voice carry your conviction.

Volume can change with the situation. For example, a political rally may be filled with loud, shouted cheers bursting with enthusiasm, whereas a eulogy may be delivered at a lower, respectful volume. An orchestra never plays so quietly that patrons cannot hear, but the musicians vary their volume. Similarly, a presenter who considers the voice an instrument learns how to project softly, loudly, and somewhere in between to convey meaning.

Rate

Rate is *the speed of delivery, or how fast you say your words*. The normal rate for Americans is between 125 and 190 words per minute, but this rate varies widely. You need to remember that your rate of delivery depends on you—how fast you normally speak—and on the situation, audience, and subject matter. People tend to speak more slowly and quietly at a funeral, children listening to a story understand better at slower rates, and complex materials may require more patient timing and more repetition.

Most speech instructors like a presentation to sound conversational yet more formal and careful than street talk. The best advice is to adopt the rate of speaking you use when you talk with others in a conversation. Of course, in front of an audience, you speak as you would in conversation but with a louder voice (increased volume). Try to have a comfortable rate that is slower than a bullet train but not as slow as to induce sleep in your audience. One of the most common areas of improvement for beginning speakers is achieving a rate of presentation that is slow enough for their audience. To improve your rate, consider the needs of your audience: it is difficult to take in information that races past.

Pauses

The third vocal characteristic of speech delivery is the **pause**, *an absence of vocal sound used for dramatic effect, transition, or emphasis*. Presentations are often a steady stream of words without silences, yet pauses can be used for dramatic effect and to get an audience to consider content. The speaker may begin a speech with rhetorical questions:

> Have you had a cigarette today? Have you had 2 or 3? 10 or 11? Do you know what your habit is costing you in a year? A decade? A lifetime?

After each rhetorical question, a pause allows audience members to answer the question mentally. These are pauses correctly used for effect.

On the other hand, **vocalized pauses** are *breaks in fluency that negatively affect an audience's perception of the speaker's competence and dynamism*. These "ahhhs" and "mmhhs" are disturbing and distracting. Unfortunately, even some experienced speakers have the habit of filling silences with vocalized pauses. For example, it is common for speakers to use the word "and" to connect every point in a speech, as if it were all one sentence. Used in this way, "and" is an example of a vocalized pause.

Ask someone you trust to listen to your speech to identify any filler words you tend to use. Each time they hear a vocalized pause, they should drop a marble into a can. The result is a series of irritating interruptions that can help you break your habit. The next step is working to eliminate filler words and to be more comfortable with silent pauses. Many audiences would prefer a little silence to a series of vocalized pauses.

Fluency

The fourth vocal characteristic of delivery is **fluency**, *the smoothness of the delivery, the flow of the words, and the absence of vocalized pauses*. Fluency is not even very noticeable, but lack of fluency is obvious. Someone who struggles with fluency often has awkward pauses in the middle of sentences and must look down at notecards to remember their next point. Under-rehearsed speeches often suffer from disfluencies, whereas speeches practiced too much suffer from too much fluency. You want your speech to sound conversational, but free of awkward pauses. Listeners are more likely to notice errors than the seemingly effortless flow of words in a well-delivered speech. On the other hand, a speaker who seems too slick or smooth-talking is sometimes perceived as dishonest. One study shows that audiences tended to perceive the speaker's fluency and smoothness of presentation as a main determinant of his or her effectiveness.[19]

To achieve fluency, presenters must be confident about the content of their speeches. By knowing what they are going to say and practicing the words over and over, speakers can reduce their use of disruptive repetition and vocalized pauses. If presenters focus on the overall rhythm of the speech, their fluency improves. Speakers must pace, build, and time the various parts of the speech to unite them into a coherent whole.

Pitch

The fifth vocal characteristic of delivery is **pitch**, *the highness or lowness of a speaker's voice—the voice's upward and downward movement and the melody produced by the voice*. Pitch is what makes the difference between the "ohhh" you utter when you

Figure 12.3 **The Control of Pitch**

Controlling pitch does more than make a presentation sound pleasing.

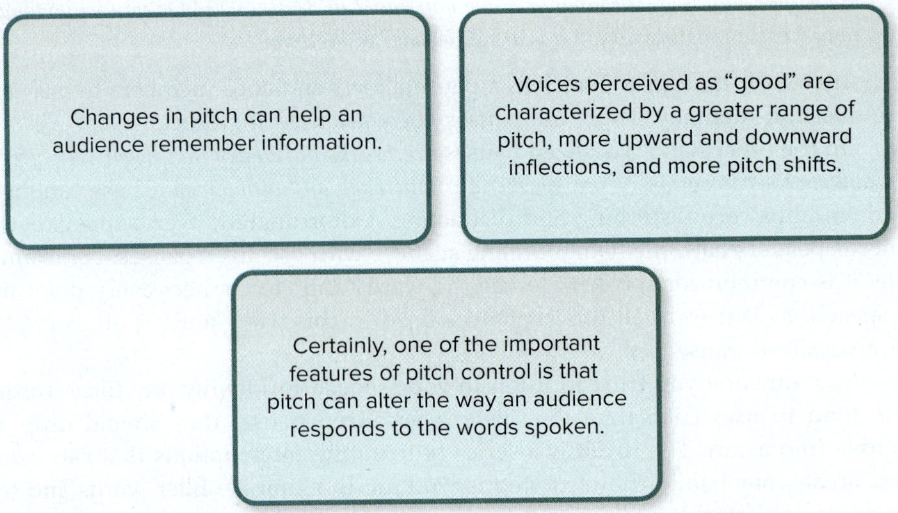

- Changes in pitch can help an audience remember information.
- Voices perceived as "good" are characterized by a greater range of pitch, more upward and downward inflections, and more pitch shifts.
- Certainly, one of the important features of pitch control is that pitch can alter the way an audience responds to the words spoken.

earn a poor grade in a class and the "ohhh" you make when you see someone really attractive. The "ohhh" looks the same in print, but when the notes turn to music, the difference between the two expressions is vast.

The pitch of your voice can make you sound either lively or listless. As a speaker you learn to avoid the two extremes: the lack of change in pitch that results in a monotone and the repeated changes in pitch that result in a singsong delivery. The best public speakers use the full range of their normal pitch (**Figure 12.3**).[20]

Presenters make many subtle changes in meaning by producing changes in pitch. The speaker's pitch tells an audience whether the words are a statement or a question, whether the words mean what they say, and whether the presenter is expressing doubt, determination, irony, or surprise.

Presenters learn pitch control only through regular practice. An actor who is learning to deliver a line has to practice that line many times and in many ways before being sure that most people in the audience will understand the words as intended. An effective presenter rehearses a presentation before friends to discover whether this will be the case. You may sound angry when you do not intend to, doubtful when you mean to sound certain, or frightened when you are only surprised. You may not be the best judge of how you sound to others, so practice with someone who can tell you honestly how you sound.

Pronunciation

The sixth delivery characteristic is **pronunciation**, *the act of correctly articulating words.* The best way to avoid pronunciation errors is to go to an Internet source like Dictionary.com, which provides an audio symbol "🔊" that reveals how to pronounce words. Following is an example of what Dictionary.com says about the word *Urdu*, which names an Asian language. Notice the symbol of a speaker; click on the symbol and the website will provide an audio pronunciation of the word.

Of course, any standard hardcover or online dictionary provides a pronunciation table to help you with new and unusual words. Listening to broadcasters, teachers, and even presenters in your class can increase your vocabulary. One simple way to enhance your pronunciation is to practice your speech out loud. Most people can pronounce anything accurately in their own minds. However, when we involve our vocal system, sometimes there are disconnects between what words we intend to say and what we actually say. You never know what words you might stutter over or have difficulty pronouncing if you never practice beforehand.

> **From Dictionary.com:**
>
> - **Urdu** 🔊 [*oor*-doo, **ur**-; *oor*-**doo**, ur-] one of the official languages of Pakistan, a language derived from Hindustani, used by Muslims, and written with Persian-Arabic letters.

Articulation

The seventh delivery characteristic is **articulation**, *the production of sounds*, which is another important part of enunciation. An example of articulation problems are when you order "dry toast" (without butter) and get "rye toast" or when you asked for a "missing statement" and get a "mission statement." Other times articulation is a problem because you are unfamiliar with a word. For example, a student giving a speech on euthanasia (assisted suicide) had a fine topic, but he called his topic "ee-then-as-ee-ah" instead of articulating it the correct way, which sounds like "youth-in-Asia."

Among the common articulation problems are the dropping of final consonants and "-ing" sounds ("goin'," "comin'," and "leavin'"), the substitution of "fer" for "for," and the substitution of "ta" for "to." An important objective in public presentations, as in all communication, is to articulate accurately.

Enunciation (Pronunciation Plus Articulation)

Enunciation, the eighth vocal aspect of speech delivery, is *the pronunciation and articulation of sounds and words*. Lack of enunciation often occurs because we don't say whole words or we slur over them. A person who says, "I'm gunna be leavin' in the mornin' if I'm feelin' bedder," is trying to say, "I am going to be leaving in the morning if I am feeling better." Another example of enunciation is someone who says "sumpinz up" when she means "something is up."

Rehearsing in front of friends, roommates, or family is a relatively safe way to try out your vocabulary and pronunciation on an audience. Your objective should be to practice unfamiliar words until you are comfortable with them. Also, be alert to the names of people you quote, introduce, or cite in your speech; audiences are impressed when a student speaker correctly pronounces such names as Goethe, Monet, and de Chardin. And your instructor will be impressed if you ask during speech preparation how to pronounce a certain word. That approach is better than just mispronouncing it in a presentation in front of class or at work.

Vocal Variety

The ninth vocal aspect of speech delivery—one that summarizes many of the others—is **vocal variety**. This term refers to *voice quality, intonation patterns, inflections of pitch, and the duration of syllables*. Studies show that vocal variety improves the effectiveness of public presentations:

- A very early study of reading out loud found that audiences retain more information with large variations in rate, force, pitch, and voice quality.[21]
- More recently, researchers studied an audience's comprehension of prose and poetry and found that comprehension decreased 10 percent when the presenter delivered material in a monotone voice.[22]
- Audience members understand more when listening to skilled speakers than when listening to unskilled speakers.[23] They also recall more information both immediately after the speech and at a later date.
- Skilled speakers are more effective, whether the material is organized or disorganized, easy or difficult.[24]
- Good vocalization was found to include fewer but longer pauses, greater ranges of pitch, and more upward and downward inflections.[25]

If you learn how to manage the vocal aspects of delivery, you will be well on your way to impressing listeners with how you look and sound as a speaker. You will also find yourself more comfortable and confident in your role as a public speaker.

THE BODILY ASPECTS OF PRESENTATION

The importance of delivery has been recognized for thousands of years. In the *Rhetorica ad Herennium*, Cicero observed that "delivery is the graceful regulation of voice, countenance, and gesture." This section focuses on the **bodily aspects** of delivery, or *how to use your body to convey meaning*.

Gestures

Gestures are *movements of the head, arms, and hands used to illustrate, emphasize, or signal ideas in a speech*. People rarely worry about gestures in conversation, but when they give a speech in front of an audience, arms and hands seem to be bothersome. Perhaps people feel unnatural because public speaking is an unfamiliar situation.

Do you remember the first time you drove a car, the first time you tried to swim, or the first time you kissed? The first time you give a speech, you might not feel any more natural than you did then. Nonetheless, physically or artistically skilled people make their actions look easy. A skilled golfer, a talented painter, and a graceful dancer all perform with seeming ease. Beginners make a performance look difficult. Apparently, we have to work diligently to make physical or artistic feats look easy.

©Doyle Harrell/Getty Images RF

What can you do to help yourself gesture naturally when you deliver your presentation? The answer lies in connecting your feelings to your behavior. When speakers really care about a topic, you can see their passion in the way they deliver their message: they are more animated, their face shows a range of emotion, their voice is strong, and their eyes connect with yours. Students speaking on a variety of topics from environmental awareness to business ethics have demonstrated that passion and conviction translate into effective delivery.

In addition to focusing on finding a topic you are passionate about, you should also concentrate on your message. Being self-conscious about your delivery or trying to focus too much on a "perfect" delivery can backfire and cause your delivery to seem unnatural. Some students trained in competitive debate exhibit unnatural delivery behaviors that actually cause audience members to become focused so much on delivery that they lose the message of the speech. You should concentrate on your message and do your best to present natural delivery behaviors in your speech.

Another way of learning to make appropriate gestures is to practice a speech in front of friends who are willing to make helpful suggestions. In time, and after many practice sessions, public speakers learn which arm, head, and hand movements seem to help and which seem to hinder their message. For instance, actors spend hours rehearsing lines and gestures, so that they will look spontaneous and unrehearsed on stage. Through practice you, too, can learn to gesture naturally, in a way that reinforces rather than detracts from your message.

Facial Expressions

Your face is the most expressive part of your body. **Facial expressions** consist of *the nonverbal cues expressed by a speaker's face.* Eyebrows rise and fall; eyes twinkle, glare, and cry; lips pout or smile; cheeks can dimple or harden; and a chin can jut out in anger or recede in yielding. Some people's faces are a barometer of their feelings; others' faces seem to maintain the same appearance whether they are happy, sad, or pained.

Because you do not ordinarily see your own face while speaking, you may not be fully aware of how you appear to an audience. In general, speakers are trying to maintain a warm, positive relationship with the audience, and they

CONNECTING GLOBALLY

USING EYE CONTACT OVER MEDIATED CHANNELS

Most Americans believe that direct eye contact signals respect and attention to the listener. But some cultures inside and outside the United States believe that direct eye contact signals disrespect or defiance of authority. Some Native American[26] and Latino cultures, for example, regard it as disrespectful to look others in the eye, and some African cultures perceive it as a threat.

So how should you use eye contact when you are speaking to people with varying backgrounds? Let's say you are on a videoconference call with colleagues who are located in different parts of the world. Consider what eye contact might signal in this context. If strong eye contact is expected, use your recording environment to your advantage. You might place a sticky note on the wall above your camera with a reminder to "Look Here." If you struggle to maintain eye contact, it will probably be easier to look just above the webcam rather than directly into it. You might also place some keyword notes on the wall behind your camera to help you remember important information, like the names of the individuals on the conference call or the main points you want to communicate during the call.

If you worry you won't be able to maintain eye contact, know that there are other ways that you can convey involvement, attention, and respect. You might enhance your other verbal and nonverbal communication signals, like nodding your head while others are speaking. Or you might use verbal messages, like occasionally adding your agreement or saying, "That's a great point. I appreciate your perspective." Small gestures can make a big difference in showing that you are engaged in the conversation.

---

signal that intent by smiling as they would in conversation with someone they like. However, the topic, the speaker's intent, the situation, and the audience all help determine the appropriate facial expressions in a public speech. You can discover the appropriateness of your facial expressions by having friends, relatives, or classmates tell you how you look when practicing your speech. You can also observe how your instructors use facial expressions to communicate.

Eye Contact

Another physical aspect of delivery important to a public speaker is **eye contact**, or *the extent to which a speaker looks directly at the audience*. In conversation we use eye contact to signal turn taking: we can look away while conversing but resume eye contact to signal the other person's turn to speak. Eye contact can also evoke other meanings in presentations:

- Too much eye contact—"staring down the audience"—is too much of a good thing, but too much gazing at notes—lack of eye contact—is poor delivery.
- Audiences prefer the maintenance of good eye contact,[27] and good eye contact improves source credibility.[28]

- Eye contact in a presentation signals your relationship with the audience. If you look at your audience in a friendly way, you signal a warm relationship with them.
- The belief that a person who cannot look you in the eye during conversation may not be telling the truth can be applied to public speaking situations; a speaker's averted eyes may invite the audience to think that he is not telling the truth, even if he is.
- A public speaker who rarely or never looks at audience members may appear disinterested in them, and the audience may resent being ignored.
- A public speaker who looks over the heads of audience members or scans them so quickly that eye contact is not established may appear to be afraid of the audience.

The proper relationship between audience and speaker is one of purposeful communication. You signal that sense of purpose by treating audience members as individuals with whom you wish to communicate, by looking at them for responses to your message.

How can you learn to maintain eye contact with your audience? One way is to know your speech so well that you have to glance only occasionally at your notes. A speaker who does not know the speech well is manuscript-bound. Delivering an extemporaneous speech from key words or an outline is a way of encouraging yourself to keep an eye on the audience. One of the purposes of extemporaneous delivery is to enable you to adapt to your audience, which is not possible unless you are continually observing their behavior to see if they appear to understand your message.

Another way of learning to use eye contact is to scan your entire audience and address various sections as you progress through your speech. Concentrating on the head nodders may also improve your eye contact: in almost every audience, some individuals overtly indicate whether your message is coming across; these individuals usually nod yes or no with their heads. Some speakers find that friendly faces and positive head nodders improve their delivery.

©Image Source/Getty Images RF

Movement

The fourth physical aspect of delivery is **bodily movement**, *what a speaker does with his or her entire body during a presentation.* Sometimes the situation limits a speaker's movement, as might the presence of a fixed microphone, a lectern, a pulpit, or any other physical feature of the environment. The length of the speech can also make a difference; a short speech without movement is less difficult for both speaker and audience than is a very long speech without movement.

Good movement is appropriate and purposeful. A "caged lion" who paces back and forth to work off anxiety is moving inappropriately and purposelessly in relation to the content of the presentation. You should move for a reason, such as walking a few steps when delivering a transition, thereby literally helping your audience "follow you" to the next idea. Some speakers move forward on the points they regard as most important.

Because of the importance of eye contact, speakers should always strive to face the audience, even when moving. Some other suggestions on movement relate to the use of visual aids. Speakers who write on the board during a speech have to turn their backs on the audience. Avoid turning your back by using PowerPoint or Prezi, writing information on the board between classes, preparing a poster ahead of time, or projecting your images on a screen.

You can learn through practice and observation. Watch your professors, teaching assistants, and fellow students when they deliver their speeches to determine what works for them. They may provide positive or negative examples. Refrain from doing distracting things with your body, like repeatedly pushing up your glasses, putting a strand of hair behind your ear, or playing with a ring or other accessory while speaking. When people start noticing these kinds of repeated movements, they can lose focus on the content of your speech.

Using a form like that found in **Figure 12.4** to evaluate your nonverbal delivery while practicing can help you put more thought and purpose behind your speaking practices.

Figure 12.4 An Evaluation Form for Nonverbal Aspects of Delivery

To summarize the material on vocal and bodily aspects of delivery, you should examine the sample evaluation form below. Use this scale to evaluate yourself and others on each of the following items: 1 = excellent, 2 = good, 3 = average, 4 = fair, 5 = weak.

Vocal Aspects of Delivery

_____ Pitch: upward and downward inflections
_____ Rate: speed of delivery
_____ Pause: appropriate use of silence
_____ Volume: loudness of the voice
_____ Enunciation: articulation and pronunciation
_____ Fluency: smoothness of delivery
_____ Vocal variety: overall effect of all of the above

Bodily Aspects of Delivery

_____ Gestures: use of the arms and hands
_____ Facial expression: use of the face
_____ Eye contact: use of the eyes
_____ Movement: use of the legs and feet

DELIVERY TIPS FOR NON-NATIVE SPEAKERS

If you are a student who speaks English as a second language, you may be particularly concerned about your delivery. After all, you must try to remember what you want to say, select the appropriate words, and pronounce them correctly. These concerns differ greatly from one person to another, depending on how comfortable you are with your topic and spoken English. Here are some suggestions for how to work on delivery issues that may be of unique concern to you:

1. *Recognize that you are not alone.* For most speakers, the actual delivery of the speech is what causes the most anxiety. Even native speakers worry that they will forget what they intend to say or that they will say something incorrectly. If you have anxiety about delivery, your classmates will certainly empathize with you.

2. *Give yourself time.* Most of the other suggestions on this list require that you have some extra time to devote to improving your delivery. Perhaps you may need to begin working on your speeches much earlier in comparison with many of your classmates.

3. *Check pronunciation.* With several online pronunciation dictionaries, you can look up words and hear them pronounced. For new and unfamiliar words or words with many syllables, such resources can help you practice correct pronunciation.

4. *Talk with your instructor about reasonable goals.* If you are still working on several pronunciation or grammar issues, you can use your public speaking class as an opportunity to improve. With your instructor's help, identify a short list of items that you can work on over the course of the term. Your practice efforts will be more focused, and your instructor will have a clearer idea of what to concentrate on when giving feedback. If you do not set such objectives beforehand, both you and your instructor may have difficulty concentrating on specific and attainable areas for improvement.

5. *Understand that eye contact is important.* Especially if you come from a culture that does not emphasize eye contact, you should recognize that American audiences value this nonverbal delivery characteristic. To improve your eye contact, you should first get more comfortable maintaining eye contact during conversation. As your eye contact improves during one-on-one interactions, you can work on improving eye contact during speeches.

6. *Practice using audio or video recordings.* By listening to or watching yourself, you will be better able to isolate specific ways to improve your delivery. While observing a recording, make a list of two to four things you could do to improve your delivery; then practice the speech, focusing on those items.

CHAPTER REVIEW

In this chapter, we examined several factors related to improving your delivery. Perhaps the most important argument for improving delivery is the likelihood that you will experience nervousness, or CA, before or during a speech. CA can interfere with your ability to present a strong message. By working on your delivery skills, you can overcome CA and get your message across effectively. You now know several strategies for managing and reducing CA, the four modes of delivery and their appropriate applications, and the delivery skills that are critical to creating a lasting impression on an audience.

KEY TERMS

delivery, 251
communication apprehension (CA), 252
trait apprehension, 252
state apprehension, 253
systematic desensitization, 254
cognitive restructuring, 255
skills training, 257
extemporaneous mode, 259
impromptu mode, 260
manuscript mode, 260
memorized mode, 261
vocal aspects, 262
projection, 262
volume, 262
rate, 262
pause, 262
vocalized pauses, 263
fluency, 263
pitch, 263
pronunciation, 264
articulation, 265
enunciation, 265
vocal variety, 266
bodily aspects, 266
gestures, 266
facial expressions, 267
eye contact, 268
bodily movement, 269

STUDY QUESTIONS

1. How might someone who suffers from state apprehension differ from a person who suffers from trait apprehension?
2. What are the steps of cognitive restructuring, and what are the goals of practicing this technique?
3. When might a manuscript mode of delivery be more appropriate for delivering a speech than an extemporaneous mode?
4. Explain three of the seven vocal aspects of a presentation, and create a goal that you might focus on each area you identify for your next speech.

5. What are the four bodily aspects of presentation? As a listener, which do you find most effective, and why?
6. What advice would you give to non-native speakers to help them feel more comfortable in preparing to deliver a speech?

ENDNOTES

1. Bettinghaus, E. (1961). The operation of congruity in an oral communication situation. *Speech Monographs, 28,* 131–142.
2. Henrikson, E. H. (1944). An analysis of the characteristics of some "good" and "poor" speakers. *Speech Monographs, 11,* 120–124.

   Wyeth, S. (2014, June 5). 14 must haves to be a great public speaker. *INC.* Retrieved from http://www.inc.com
3. Gilkinson, H., & Knower, F. H. (1941). Individual differences among students of speech as revealed by psychological test—I. *Journal of Educational Psychology, 32,* 161–175.

   Smith, J. (2014, June 9). 10 public speaking habits to avoid at all costs. *Business Insider.* Retrieved from http://www.businessinsider.com
4. McCrosky, J. C. (1977). Oral communication apprehension: A summary of recent theory and research. *Human Communication Research, 4,* 78–96.
5. Dwyer, K. K., & Davidson, M. M. (2012). Is public speaking really more feared than death? *Communication Research Report, 29,* 99–107.
6. McCrosky.
7. Allen, M., & Bourhis, J. (1996). The relationship of communication apprehension to communication behavior: A meta-analysis. *Communication Quarterly, 44,* 214–226.
8. Shi, X., Brinthaupt, T. M., & McCree, M. (2015). The relationship of self-talk frequency to communication apprehension and public speaking anxiety. *Personality and Individual Differences, 75,* 125–29.
9. Russ, T. L. (2013). The influence of communication apprehension on superiors' propensity for and practice of participatory decision making. *Communication Quarterly, 61,* 335-348.
10. Hunter, K. M., Westwick, J. N., & Haleta, L. L. (2014). Assessing success: The impact of a fundamentals of speech course on decreasing public speaking anxiety. *Communication Education, 63,* 124–135.
11. Pearson, J. C., & Child, J. T. (2008). The gentle art of persuasion: The influence of biological sex, previous experience, and preparation time on classroom public speaking grades. *Basic Communication Course Annual, 20,* 101–137.
12. Ayres, J., & Hopf, T. S. (1985). Visualization: A means of reducing speech anxiety. *Communication Education, 34,* 318–323.
13. Ayres, J. (1988). Coping with speech anxiety: The power of positive thinking. *Communication Education, 37,* 289–296.
14. Bodie, G. D. (2010). A racing heart, rattling knees, and ruminative thoughts: Defining, explaining, and treating public speaking anxiety. *Communication Education, 59,* 70–105.
15. Pearson, Child, & Kahl.
16. Allen, M., Hunter, J. E., & Donohue, W. A. (1989). Meta-analysis of self-report data on the effectiveness of public speaking anxiety treatment techniques. *Communication Education, 38,* 54–76.

17. Dwyer, K. K. (2000). The multidimensional model: Teaching students to self-manage high communication apprehension by self-selecting treatments. *Communication Education, 49,* 72–81.
18. Hildebrandt, H. W., & Stephens, W. (1963). Manuscript and extemporaneous delivery in communicating information. *Speech Monographs, 30,* 369–372.
19. Hayworth, D. (1942). A search for facts on the teaching of public speaking. *Quarterly Journal of Speech, 28,* 247–254.
20. Black, J. W. (1942). A study of voice merit. *Quarterly Journal of Speech, 28,* 67–74; Woolbert, C. (1920). The effects of various modes of public reading. *Journal of Applied Psychology, 4,* 162–185.
21. Woolbert.
22. Glasgow, G. M. (1952). A semantic index of vocal pitch. *Speech Monographs, 19,* 64–68.
23. Black.
24. Beighley, K. C. (1952). An experimental study of the effect of four speech variables on listener comprehension. *Speech Monographs, 19,* 249–258.
25. Ibid.
26. Martin, J., & Nakayama, T. (2011). *Experiencing Intercultural Communication.* New York: McGraw-Hill, 178–179.
27. Blackman, L. (2017, January 18). New, maybe, finally: Ten powerful speaking tips to ease anxiety. *Naples Daily News.* Retrieved from http://www.naplesnews.com

    Cobin, M. (1962). Response to eye contact. *Quarterly Journal of Speech, 48,* 415–418.
28. Beebe, S. A. (1974). Eye contact: A nonverbal determinant of speaker credibility. *Speech Teacher, 23,* 21–25; Neal, T., & Brodsky, S. L. (2008). Expert witness credibility as a function of eye contact behavior and gender. *Criminal Justice and Behavior, 52,* 1515–1526.

Blue and Yellow Cube Icon, Connecting Globally Icon, Mountain Icon, Chapter Review Arrows Circle Icon: ©McGraw Hill Education

part **4**

Speaking to Inform and Persuade

In this section, you will refine your skills as an informative and persuasive speaker. You will also see how these skills can be applied to a range of speaking contexts, including those you will encounter outside of the classroom. For example, as you enter the workforce, your résumé, cover letter, and interview style will reflect your ability to inform a potential employer of your skills, as well as to persuade that employer to consider you seriously as a candidate.

©Blend Images/ SuperStock RF

CHAPTER 13

Public Presentations to Inform

Prepare an Informative Presentation
Effectively Present Information to an Audience
Skills for an Informative Presentation
Use Visual Resources to Inform
A Sample Informative Speech Outline and Note Cards
Chapter Review

Source: Library of Congress Prints and Photographs Division, Department of the Interior, National Park Service [3b48901u]

CHAPTER 14

Public Presentations to Persuade

Prepare a Persuasive Presentation
Introduce Your Persuasive Presentation
Understand Persuasion
Three Forms of Proof
Organize Your Persuasive Message
Skills for Persuasive Speaking
A Sample Persuasive Speech Outline and Note Cards
Chapter Review

©Eric Audras/Getty Images RF

CHAPTER 15

Using Communication Skills As You Enter the Workplace

Contemporary Jobs in Communication
Producing a Winning Résumé
Writing a Convincing Cover Letter
Mastering the Job Interview
More Tips for the Interview
Building Connections
Chapter Review

chapter 13

Public Presentations to Inform

©Blend Images/SuperStock RF

The goal of informative speaking is to enhance your audience's knowledge and understanding of a topic. In this chapter, you will learn how to determine a goal and purpose for informative speaking. You will also become familiar with skills and techniques for presenting information effectively, including preparing outlines and note cards.

LEARNING OBJECTIVES
After reading this chapter, you should be able to:

- Understand the various goals and purposes of informative presentations.
- Effectively present information to an audience.
- Apply the following basic informative skills to your presentations: defining, describing, explaining, illustrating, using analogies, narrating, and demonstrating.
- Effectively use visual resources to inform.
- Explain the appropriate use of note cards when delivering an informative speech.

PREPARE AN INFORMATIVE PRESENTATION

When you set out to prepare an informative presentation, you must first consider your goals in speaking. To begin, answer the following questions:

1. Why are you delivering the speech? What are your intent, purpose, and goal for informing your audience?
2. What topics lend themselves to informative speaking?
3. What immediate and long-term actions do you expect from your audience as a result of your informative presentation?

Long-range goals were discussed in **Chapter 9**, on topic selection and audience analysis. You may want to review that information as it applies to informative speeches.

What Is Your Goal?

Before you can attempt to speak informatively on a topic, you need to identify your specific goal, or the information you wish to convey. You may want to increase what the audience knows about a topic, teach them something useful, clear up complicated matters, demonstrate something they would find helpful, show how objects or items are related to each other, or share information they might initially think of as boring but that you enliven with your speech. **Table 13.1** lists these general goals and provides specific examples for each.

Table 13.1 Common Goals of Informative Presentations and Examples of Topics

Goals of Informative Presentations	Topic Examples
To increase what your listeners know about a topic	- The newest trends in green design for houses - New clothing designers emerging with spring fashions - What is nanotechnology?
To help your audience learn useful information	- Early steps for avoiding the flu - Chinese customs for greeting and leaving - Travel tips for visitors to Mexico
To clarify complex issues	- How does identity theft work? - How might the United States address its economic problems? - Who was Ponzi?
To demonstrate something useful	- How to save a life with the Heimlich maneuver - The correct way to lift weights - Do-it-yourself wiring
To show how things relate in space	- How to make a man's sport coat - Using electronics in a green residence - Where the major islands of the Caribbean are

What Is Your Purpose?

The **immediate behavioral purposes** of your presentation—*the actions you expect from an audience during and immediately after a presentation*—can be fairly straightforward for an informative presentation. The immediate behavioral purpose isn't usually stated in your speech, but it helps you as a speaker in creating your thesis statement and deciding what content you want to present. Here are some sample purpose statements with immediate behavioral purposes that could be the focus of a speech:

1. *Define words, objects, or concepts.*

    "After hearing my presentation, I want my audience members to be able to provide a meaningful definition for the concept of *eminent domain*."

    Sample statement of purpose for a presentation to define:

    "My purpose is to have my listeners be able to explain to me what powers the government has because of the laws surrounding eminent domain and what the impact can be on private citizens."

2. *Describe objects, people, or issues.*

    "After hearing my presentation, my listeners can describe in a way we can all understand the controversy caused by plans to build a new athletic stadium."

    Sample statement of purpose for a presentation to describe:

    "My purpose is to have my listeners correctly explain back to me the main parts of the controversy surrounding the new athletic stadium."

3. *Distinguish between things.*

    "After hearing my presentation, the audience should be able to distinguish between socialist and democratic positions on state ownership."

    Sample statement of purpose for a presentation to distinguish between things:

    "My purpose is to have my audience show me that they can tell the difference between a socialist position and a democratic position on state ownership."

4. *Compare and/or contrast items.*

    "After hearing my speech, my audience should be able to contrast a real diamond with a cubic zirconia."

    Sample statement of purpose for a presentation to compare and/or contrast:

    "Upon completion of my presentation, members of the audience will be able to accurately identify a cubic zirconia in a collection of authentic diamonds."

EFFECTIVELY PRESENT INFORMATION TO AN AUDIENCE

Audience analysis can help you determine how much the audience members already know and how much you will have to tell them. For example, imagine that you want to talk about the erratic nature of the stock market. If audience members regularly invest in the stock market, they probably know a great deal about market fluctuation and strategies to maximize their investments. However, if your audience is a typical group of undergraduate students, they may need to learn about basic terminology, some history of the stock market, and some examples of good and poor times to invest.

Audience analysis can also help you take advantage of the following tips for presenting information:

- Create information hunger.
- Demonstrate information relevance.
- Use extrinsic motivation.
- Select and design your content.
- Avoid information overload.
- Organize your content.

©Caroline Purser/Photographer's Choice/Getty Images

Each of these tips is discussed in detail in this section. If you have already read **Chapter 10**, you know a great deal about audience analysis. If you have not yet read that chapter, you may want to read it now to fully understand the material here.

Create Information Hunger

An informative presentation is more effective if the presenter can create **information hunger**, *a need for information in the audience*. This is because when you arouse the audience's interest they are likely to learn more.

One method for creating information hunger is to follow a tactic used by journalists. Effective news stories often grab readers' attention by opening with a personal anecdote, then following up with an eye-catching statistic. This strategy piques both the listener's specific and general interest in the topic. For example, you might open a speech on the topic of traffic violations like this:

- **Specific case**: When Justin walked into traffic court this morning, he was facing his third license suspension. The most recent of which included failure to furnish automobile insurance at a traffic stop.
- **General interest:** He joins the 960 thousand Ohioans, whose licences are revoked each year. His offense, among others, pushes the total number of license suspensions a year to almost 3 million, including those with multiple revocations.[1]

Another method is to tap into the audience's curiosity. For example, you might state, "I have discovered a way to add 10 years to my life," or "The adoption of the

Effectively Present Information to an Audience **279**

following plan will ensure lower taxes." In addition, a brief quiz on your topic early in the speech arouses your audience's interest in finding the answers. Unusual clothing related to the topic of your speech (e.g., an EMT uniform) is likely to arouse interest in why you are so attired, and an object you have created (e.g., a homemade windmill that is as tall as you) will probably inspire the audience to wonder how you made it. Following news reporting style and audience curiosity are just two of the many ways to create information hunger.

Demonstrate Information Relevance

Another factor that connects an audience with an informative presentation is **information relevance**, *the importance, novelty, and usefulness of the information to the audience.* Thus, when selecting a topic for an informative presentation, you should carefully consider how relevant it will be to that particular audience. Skin cancer might be a better topic in the summer, when students are sunbathing, than in the winter, when they are studying for finals. A presentation on taxes could be awfully dull; a speech on how present tax laws cost audience members more than they cost the rich might be more relevant, and a speech on three ways to reduce personal taxes might be even more so. However, if your audience happens to be composed of young people who have never paid taxes, none of the three topics might be relevant. Similarly, a speech on raising racehorses, writing a textbook, or living on a pension might be informative but not relevant because of the financial status, occupation, or age of the listeners. Thus, you should exercise some care in selecting a topic that interests the audience, as covered in **Chapter 9**.

Reveal Extrinsic Motivation

The third factor in relating an informative presentation to an audience is **extrinsic motivation**, *the reasons outside the presentation that audience members will benefit from listening to the presentation.* An audience is more likely to listen to and comprehend a presentation if they have good reasons for doing so, especially if they see some potential benefit or reward for themselves.[3] A teacher who tells students to listen carefully because they will be tested at the end of the hour is using extrinsic motivation. A speaker uses extrinsic motivation by telling audience members that, in this speech, they will learn ways to increase their own energy and creativity.

Extrinsic motivation is related to the concept of information relevance. An audience member who would ordinarily lack interest in the economy might find that topic relevant when it is linked to learning about employment trends for college graduates. The audience member's interest in being employable is an extrinsic motivation for listening carefully to the presentation.

Extrinsic motivations need to be mentioned early in a presentation. For example, a statement like, "You will need this background material for the report due at the end of this week," provides extrinsic motivation for managers who

CONNECTING GLOBALLY

IDENTIFYING FAKE NEWS

The dissemination of fake news can distort our perceptions of information and current events and lead to bad decision-making. We are all susceptible to believing fake news stories, especially when they are circulated in our social media networks. So what can we do to avoid falling victim to misinformation and contributing to its spread? Journalist Wynne Davis of National Public Radio offers these six tips:[2]

1. *Pay attention to the website's URL and domain name.* Before you share a story verify that it is connected with a reputable news organization. Even small differences in website domains are important.

2. *Research the author.* Most reputable websites will have plenty of information for you to look at in their "about" section. You should be able to verify information about an author with one or more secondary sources. If the credentials listed on the site seem false or inflated, chances are they are producing fake news.

3. *Look for quotations in the story.* When reputable news agencies produce stories, they seek a range of experts to comment on the issues at hand. If the story has no quotations from experts with credentials, think twice about sharing it.

4. *Research any actual quotations.* Make sure that quotations used in news stories are given proper context. For example, if someone attributes a quotation to the president, that information can easily be verified and read in the proper context. When you see quotations from people you do not know, look for their professional credentials. If they are not provided, read with caution. If they are, a quick Google search can verify those credentials.

5. *Look at the online comments for the story.* Most news organizations allow readers to comment at the end of the story. If these comments indicate that the story is false or inaccurate, you probably should not consider this a valid and reliable source.

6. *Do reverse image searching.* Right click on the images in a story and search them in Google. People who write fake news stories do not usually go to the trouble to include original photos. If you see the same image in a story pop up in multiple places, do the same check with those other sources.

The increased circulation of fake news on web browsers and social media underscores the importance of evaluating the information you gather before presenting it in a speech or sharing it through your own social media networks (see the Chapter 4 Connecting Globally feature on listening to social media).

hear this message from their employer. Similarly, in an informative presentation, you may be able to command more attention, comprehension, and action from audience members if you provide them with some good reasons outside the presentation for attending to your message.

©Don Hammond/Design Pics RF

Design Informative Content

The fourth factor that can help your audience relate to an informative presentation is your selection of **informative content**, *the main points and subpoints, illustrations, and examples used to clarify and inform*. The following principles can help you select your speech content:

- *Audiences tend to remember and comprehend generalizations and main ideas better than details and specific facts.* You should limit your presentations to two to five main points.
- *Relatively simple words and concrete ideas are significantly easier to retain than are more complex materials.* Aim to communicate complex ideas as simply as possible. Long or unusual words may dazzle an audience, but they may also reduce their understanding. Keep the ideas and words at an appropriate level.
- *Humor can make a dull presentation more interesting, but humor does not seem to increase information retention.* Humor also improves the audience's perception of the speaker's character and can increase her authoritativeness when a presentation is dull.
- *Early remarks about how the presentation will meet the audience's needs can create anticipation and increase the chances that the audience will listen and understand.* Whatever topic you select, you should tell audience members early in your presentation how the topic is related to them. This will increase the chances that they will listen.
- *Calling for overt audience response or behavior increases comprehension more than does repetition.* Having an audience do something—such as raise their hands or stand up if they've had a particular kind of experience—provides feedback to the speaker and can be rewarding and reinforcing for both the presenter and the listeners.

Avoid Information Overload

The dangers of information overload while gathering and evaluating sources are discussed in **Chapter 11**. However, as an informative speaker, you must also be wary of the amount of information you present to others. Recall that information overload occurs when you provide more information than the audience can absorb, whether in quantity, complexity, or both. The danger of information overload is that the audience may quit listening to your talk, dismiss your topic, or view you as having less credibility. Information overload is illustrated in **Figure 13.1**.

Figure 13.1 Information Overload in Quantity and Complexity

Information Overload of Quantity
- The speaker tells more than audience members ever wanted to know about a subject, even when they are interested.
- The speaker tries to cram as much information as possible into the time allowed. Unfortunately, this cramming of information decreases understanding.

Information Overload of Complexity
- The speaker uses language or ideas that are beyond the capacity of the audience to understand.
- An engineer who unloads detailed formulas on the audience, or a philosopher who soars into the ethereal heights of abstract ideas, may leave the audience feeling frustrated and more confused than before the speech.

The solution to information overload is to focus on a limited number of main points, include only the best supporting materials, and keep the message at a level the audience can understand. For example, one man wanted to discuss stem cell research. Although this topic is complex and the scientific knowledge about it can be overwhelming, he made the speech highly understandable. He talked about what stem cells are; then he described adult stem cells, embryonic stem cells, umbilical cord stem cells, and pluripotent stem cells. Because he explained the simpler stem cells first, the class could easily grasp the more complex pluripotent stem cells.

Organize Content

In an informative presentation, you can help the audience learn the content by following these organizational recommendations:

1. Tell audience members what you are going to tell them (in the introduction), tell them (in the body), and then tell them what you told them (in the conclusion).
2. Use transitions and signposts to increase their understanding.
3. Tell your audience which points are most important.
4. Repeat important points for better understanding.

SKILL BUILDER

LEARN TO INVOLVE YOUR AUDIENCE

You have probably attended a presentation in which the speaker asks for audience participation. In fact, in any class that isn't a lecture, you are part of an audience whose participation isn't merely requested but is required. As an informative speaker you might involve an audience in the following ways:

- Ask audience members to perform the task being demonstrated—for example, two people dance after you explain the technique of a waltz.
- Have them stand, raise hands, or move chairs to indicate their understanding of the speaker's statements: "Raise your hand if you are familiar with local building codes."
- Have them write answers that will indicate understanding (e.g., "List three ways to lower your blood pressure.").

Involving your audience is a great way to hold their attention and help them remember your message. To decide how you might do so in your next speech, review your completed outline and consider the following questions:

- Do you provide interesting statistics in your speech? You might incorporate that statistic into a question aimed at your audience. For example, if you are giving a speech on maintaining a happy marriage, you might ask your audience to raise your hands if they believe that close to half of all marriages end in divorce. After they've responded, confirm that statistic and cite your source. Then follow up with a compelling point about how the divorce rate might be curbed.
- Where in your speech might you conduct an instant poll? If you are speaking on civic engagement, you might address your audience by saying, "Raise your hand if you have volunteered somewhere in the community this semester." Look at the audience and adapt your response to show that you are listening to them. If few people raise their hands, say, "I hope my speech today can help you see how easy it is to get involved." If many hands go up, say instead, "It's great that so many of you are getting out into the community. Today I'll share some of my experiences doing the same thing."
- Where in your speech could you tell a particularly vivid and compelling story? You might ask your audience to close their eyes and imagine a scenario as you describe something in depth to them.

Involving your audience does not need to be extensive or time consuming. Doing so will show that your speech topic is relevant to their lives.

Audiences can more easily grasp information when they are invited to anticipate and to review the organization and content of your speech. That is why the body of your presentation is bracketed by a preview of what you are going to say and a summary or review of what you've said.

SKILLS FOR AN INFORMATIVE PRESENTATION

When giving an informative presentation, you can rely on certain skills to help you convey your information most effectively. In particular, informative presentations call for the skills of defining, describing, explaining, illustrating, using analogies, narrating, and demonstrating.

Defining

Many people think that definitions are merely explanations found in a dictionary. However, they are much more than that, and there are multiple ways of defining things:

- A **comparison** *shows the similarity between something well known and something less known.* A student explained that tying a bow tie (unfamiliar to most) is the same as tying a shoelace (familiar to all), but since we are unaccustomed to tying a shoelace around our neck, a bow tie is challenging.

- A **contrast** *clarifies by showing differences*—for example, "He was taller than you, he was more heavyset than you, and his hair was darker."

- A **synonym** *defines by using a word or words that are close or similar in meaning to the one you are trying to define*: "A depressed person feels demoralized, purposeless, isolated, and distanced from others."

Source: Photographs in the Carol M. Highsmith Archive, LOC, Prints and Photographs Division

- An **antonym** *defines an idea by opposition*: "A good used car is not full of dents, does not have high mileage, is not worn on the seats, does not leak lots of oil, and has not been involved in a serious accident."

- An **operational definition** *defines by explaining a process.* An operational definition of a cake is the sequence of actions depicted in a recipe.

Definitions are anything but dull; in fact, they are often the cause of great controversy. Consider the following questions pertaining to definitions: When does a collection of cells become a *fetus*? When does a fetus become a *premature child*? Is a *soul* produced with the meeting of sperm and egg? Can *marriage* be between same-sex partners?

Describing

Describing requires presenters to be concrete rather than abstract, specific instead of general, and accurate instead of ambiguous. It also includes using **imagery**, *figures of speech that hit at the senses and stimulate listeners' synapses to see, hear, and feel what the words are saying.*

Look at the following description of Reggie Watts, who started his career as a singer with bands but became a stand-up comedian and performance artist.

> He arrives on stage with enormous amber rings dripping like tree sap from his fingers, his Afro a Miracle-Gro spider plant. Sometimes he's painted a pinkie nail pink. He might be wearing a ridiculous sweater.[4]

Skills for an Informative Presentation

©Douglas Mason/Getty Images

The writer's use of imagery is highlighted. In only two sentences, the words bring this person to life. What this writer demonstrates is that words can paint pictures in the mind that appeal to the senses.

Strong, descriptive imagery is also in the following portrayal of Watts's voice. The highlighted words are especially effective in describing his voice as if it were an entire band.

> Then he lays down a track. He starts with the sound of a kick drum, from deep in his throat, recorded into a loop sampler—a small machine often used by guitarists to layer melodies. He adds a snare with a few controlled exhales. A couple of high notes with his tongue against his teeth. And then he starts to sing, in French or gibberish German. Morphing imperceptibly into a cockney slang, he seems to be talking about something from a human-resources manual or a dating disaster.[5]

Do these words help you picture what Reggie Watts looks and sounds like? You can perform similar magic with your own words if you recognize the potential of speaking with imagery.

Explaining

An **explanation** is *a means of developing an idea that simplifies or clarifies it while arousing audience interest*. An important step in explaining is analyzing, deconstructing, or dissecting something to help the audience understand it. Unless you become skilled at dissecting a concept, your explanation may leave audience members more confused than they were before your presentation. You have to determine what you can do to make a difficult concept more palatable for and accessible to the audience. For example, a biology professor in an article about global warming[6] expressed the problem by explaining how animals and plants are migrating north or climbing higher, if they can, to survive:

> Wild species don't care who is in the White House. It is very obvious they are desperately trying to move to respond to the changing climate. Some are succeeding. But for the ones that are already at the mountaintop or the poles, there is no place for them to go. They are the ones that are going extinct.[7]

In this instance the biology professor knew that global warming is a fairly vague concept. He chose one sign of global warming to reference the idea. Everyone can understand the migration of animals and plants in need of water, food, and tolerable temperatures.

Illustrating

An **illustration** *clarifies by showing what something is.* For instance, if you are talking about lung cancer, you might show photos of affected and unaffected lungs. In discussing the difference between all-wheel and 4-wheel drive, you could show an illustration of the two systems with a diagram. Illustrations can consist of photos, drawings, the objects themselves, or "word pictures."

©Roberto Westbrook/Getty Images

Stories, or narratives, can also provide illustrations. For example, Aesop tells the fable of the lion and the mouse. The mouse awakens the lion by jumping on his head. The lion awakens and is angry. He is about to eat the mouse when he observes that the mouse has made him laugh, and he spares his life. Not too much later, the lion is ensnared and the mouse comes to his rescue. This children's story illustrates that even the small and the weak can sometimes be of help to the large and the strong. Poetry, too, can touch the senses and illustrate ideas that are otherwise difficult to explain.

Using Analogies

An **analogy** is *a comparison of things that are otherwise dissimilar.* "Analogies prove nothing that is true," wrote Sigmund Freud, "but they can make one feel more at home." In other words, linking the known with the unknown can help someone grasp an idea.

The introduction of the iPad, iPod touch, and iPhone was confusing to many potential consumers. Which one or ones should they buy? One advertisement used an analogy; it said that the iPad was like a commuter, the iPhone was like a social networker, and the iPod touch was like a budget-conscious partner in this trio. The analogy worked well in explaining their differences and in suggesting who might want to purchase each one.

Here is another example of an analogy: the U.S. Congress's decision making is like a tug-of-war between two fairly equal teams, neither of which will yield to the other. As a result, nobody wins or loses, but neither does much movement occur. If you are trying to inform an audience on a new or unfamiliar idea, consider linking it to something the audience already knows, and use that to form an analogy.

Narrating

Narration is *the oral presentation and interpretation of a story, a description, or an event.* Narration occurs throughout a range of presentation styles and scenarios, such as the following:

- The dramatic reading of lines from a play, a poem, or another piece of literature
- The voice-over on a series of slides or a silent film to illustrate a point in a speech

- The reading of a letter, a quotation, or a selection from a newspaper or magazine
- The telling of a story or an anecdote from one's life

A person who does the play-by-play account of a ball game is narrating, and so is a presenter who explains what a weaver is doing in an informative presentation on home crafts.

To use narration is to move a little closer to oral interpretation of literature, or even acting, because the narration can be more dramatic than the rest of the presentation. The sections of your presentation that require this kind of special reading also require special practice. If you want to include a few lines of poetry in your presentation, you need to rehearse them so that they have the desired impact.

Demonstrating

Demonstrating is *showing the audience what you are explaining*. Some topics are communicated best through words, others through demonstration. You can talk about CPR, the Heimlich maneuver, fashion trends, and weight lifting, and you can read about these subjects. But nothing aids in the understanding of these topics better than seeing and doing CPR, practicing the Heimlich maneuver, seeing the latest fashion trends, and lifting some weights while learning about them.

Demonstrations are commonly used in everyday life. For example, chefs prepare food on television. Physicians demonstrate a variety of procedures and techniques for medical students. People who want to buy new cars and computers familiarize themselves with products via demonstrations. Clearly, demonstrating is a useful skill in informing others and one you might try in your informative presentation.

USE VISUAL RESOURCES TO INFORM

Visual aids reinforce your verbal message, as well as help you gain and maintain audience attention. **Table 13.2** provides some examples of topics and the visual resources you could use to supplement them.

©Andersen Ross/Blend Images LLC RF

Once you decide which visual resources you will use in your presentation, and how you will use them, you should prepare for any scenario in which the resource might fail, such as the following:

- A speaker has prepared a PowerPoint presentation but encounters compatibility issues when using it with another computer system.
- A presenter plans on singing a particularly poignant aria but has laryngitis on the day of the presentation.
- Someone brings photos to be projected on the screen, but the photos are so tiny that no one can see them.
- A friend agrees to role-play during a speech but has a conflict and must cancel at the last minute.

Table 13.2 Examples of Topics and Visual Resources

Topic	Visual Resource
How to change your own oil	- Use PowerPoint or Prezi photos.
How to succeed in marathons	- Come in running clothes; show the audience how to prepare for, start, and continue the race.
How to make a simple dessert	- Bring and mix the ingredients for a pie, and have the audience salivating as they anticipate dessert.
How to play croquet	- Use croquet mallets and balls.
How to tie knots for rock climbing	- Tie the knots as you describe them.

CHALLENGE YOURSELF

How can I effectively use visual resources in my informative presentation?

As you have already learned, visual resources are not always effective. All of us have watched the hapless speaker who could not exhibit her Prezi because of differences in computer systems, could not show her photos because they were too small, or could not get her dog to perform the tricks it had been taught.

Here is some advice for using visual resources effectively:

- *Be audience-centered.* Do not use foul-smelling, offensive, or disturbing resources.
- *Be ethical.* Do not use dangerous or inappropriate items.
- *Keep the content clear and relevant.* Do not overwhelm the audience with too many facts or figures.
- *Explain the visual resource.* Do not assume that the audience understands its relevance.
- *Understand that using resources takes time.* Explaining a visual resource will take at least two minutes. Therefore, practice and time your speech in advance so you can cut back if necessary.
- *Do not be too simple or too complex.* Consider the audience's level of knowledge on the topic.
- *Strive for professionalism.* Sloppy drawings, print that is too small to be read, and audio that is too soft to be heard will undermine your presentation.
- *Hide the resource when it is not in use.* They are distracting before and after they are used.

In addition to following this advice, consider a few additional tips that your audience is likely to appreciate:

- Make sure everyone in the room can see your visuals. Check the visibility of your visual resources before your speech, during practice; if the classroom is 25 feet deep, have a friend or family member determine if the visual can be read from 25 feet away. If you are planning to hand out a pamphlet or something to your audience, do it at the end of the speech.
- If you do it during your speech, audience members will focus on the handout and will be distracted from your message.
- Finally, do not stand in front of the visual you wish the audience to see; step aside and speak to your audience, not your visual.

Being prepared with a backup plan is essential. Regardless of the types of visual resources you use, you need to practice extensively with them so that they will enhance your presentation rather than distract from it.

A SAMPLE INFORMATIVE SPEECH OUTLINE AND NOTE CARDS

The following is an informative speech outline that was written by Christa Galbraith, a first-year student. The outline is not perfect, but it provides a good example of an informative speech. You will note that this is a complete-sentence outline. Following the outline are the student's note cards, which she used to deliver the speech.

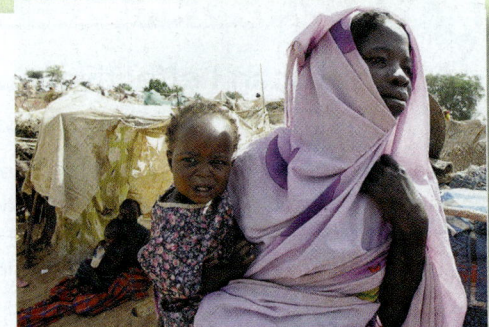
©Cris Bouroncle/Getty Images

Informative Speech Outline
Christa Galbraith

I. Introduction

    A. **Attention Getter:** For the past twelve years, Darfur, Sudan, has been a war-torn region where hundreds of thousands of innocent people have died. The death toll has caused this war to be classified as a Sudanese genocide.

    B. **Listener Relevance:** We all must be educated about the injustices happening around the world, as it is our responsibility to speak up and help those in need.

    C. **Speaker Credibility:** I first heard about the genocide in Darfur in my eighth-grade English class. My teacher was very concerned with human rights and wanted us to be passionate about helping those who were struggling. We spent the semester writing letters to U.S. Congress, starting petitions, and making educational videos for the morning news in the hopes of creating awareness and intervention.

    D. **Thesis Statement:** The genocide in Darfur is a complex regional conflict that has affected the lives of millions of people.

    E. **Preview:** Today, I want to discuss four main points relating to the genocide in Darfur: the basic composition of Sudan and Darfur, the conflict itself, peace agreements, and the current climate.

II. **Body**

   A. **Main Point #1:** Darfur is a region in western Sudan (show picture) that is composed of two main ethnic groups—those who identify as Arabs, and those who identify as Africans. The Arabs tend to live in Northern Darfur, while the Africans reside in Southern Darfur.

   1. **Supporting Point #1:** The Sudanese government, which is mainly composed of Arabs, is believed to favor the country's Arab citizens, who alienated the Africans living in the region.

   2. **Supporting Point #2:** According to Debra A. Miller, the editor of *Current Controversies,* there is also a pronounced difference in the location of Darfur's natural resources. The north has control of the majority of the farmland, while the south is rich in oil. Naturally, this caused tension, as each group wanted some of the other's resources, while keeping their own for themselves (*Current Controversies,* p. 19).

   Transition: The clear division and competition of ethnic groups in Darfur caused unrest and civil war. As the conflict escalated, the government failed to adequately step in. Many Africans felt they weren't being protected.

   B. **Main Point #2:** In April of 2003, two African rebel groups—the Sudan Liberation Army and the Justice of Equality Movement—attacked a military airfield at al-Fashir, killing 75, capturing 23, and destroying seven bombers and helicopter gunships (Miller, *Current Controversies,* p. 19). This humiliated the government and proved that their soldiers were not trained well enough to stop the rebel forces.

   1. **Supporting Point #1:** As an act of punishment, the Sudanese government supplied a volunteer group of Arab militants—called the Janjaweed—with weapons and communication equipment. The Janjaweed then destroyed an entire Darfurian village, murdering and displacing its residents. Robert O. Collins, the author of *A History of Modern Sudan*, explains that they killed and mutilated the men, raped the women, and abducted or killed the children before burning down their homes, stealing their livestock, torching their fields, and destroying all their public buildings (*A History. . .*, p. 289). About 300,000 people have been killed.

©Globe Turner, LLC/Getty Images RF

2. **Supporting Point #2:** Those who survive the attacks are forced to congregate in refugee camps, either near the border of Chad, or in Chad itself. Here they are exposed to disease, malnutrition, and separation from their families. Approximately 3 million people have been displaced.

Transition: As violence escalated, the Sudan Liberation Movement saw the need for peace talks with the Sudanese government.

C. **Main Point #3:** Peace talks have been largely unsuccessful.

   1. **Supporting Point #1:** According to the U.S. Department of State Archives, the first peace agreement was signed in 2006 and required the government to disarm the Janjaweed, provide $30 million for displaced victims, and $300 million, plus $200 million each year after to rebuild the region (U.S. Department of State Archives).

   2. **Supporting Point #2:** However, the violence continued and the need for a second peace agreement arose. The second peace agreement was signed in 2011 and required a compensation fund for victims.

   Transition: Again, this peace agreement has failed to produce results, and the violence in Darfur continues to worsen.

D. **Main Point #4:** According to U.S. Ambassador Smith, in a Darfurian radio interview, "the security situation has deteriorated" since 2011 (Radio Dabanga Interview).

   1. **Supporting Point #1:** The interviewer, Kamal Elsadig, pressured the Ambassador to address issues such as the bombing and murder in civilian areas, as well as the rape that continues in much of Darfur. There is also a lack of water, food, and medical supplies (Interview).

   2. **Supporting Point #2:** Many have noted an increase in violence, not a decrease, since the peace agreement was signed.

   Transition: Though the genocide in Darfur started several years ago, it continues today, and the violence has only escalated.

V. **Conclusion**

A. **Thesis Restatement:** Millions of people have been affected by this nine-year-long genocide over natural resources, ethnic differences, and government revenge.

B. **Main Point Summary:** Hundreds of thousands of Africans are being murdered by the Janjaweed military as an act of revenge. Their villages are terrorized, destroyed, and scattered, causing families to be split up and citizens to take refuge in camps. Peace agreements have been ineffective, and the violence continues today.

C. **Clincher:** We must not turn a blind eye to the injustice and tragedy happening in Sudan. When the safety and rights of others are being undermined, all of our rights are at risk.

References

Collins, Robert. *A History of Modern Sudan.* Cambridge UP, 2008, p. 289.

Miller, Debra. *Current Controversies: Darfur.* Greenhaven Press, 2009, pp. 18–19.

"Q&A: Sudan's Darfur Conflict." *BBC News,* 23 Feb 2010, news.bbc.co.uk/2/hi/africa/3496731.stm.

Smith, Ambassador, dir. "Sudan: Ambassador Smith." Dir. Kamal Elsadig. Radio Dabanga, 19 Sep 2012, allafrica.com/stories/201209200049.html.

United States Department of State. *Darfur Peace Agreement.* 2006. U.S. Department of State Archive. 2001-2009, state.gov/r/pa/prs/ps/2006/65972.htm.

Source: Christa Galbraith

Card #1

Past 12 years–Darfur, Sudan–war-torn–Sudanese genocide.

Educated about the injustices . . . speak up and help those in need.

Learned of genocide in Darfur–eighth grade.

Complex regional conflict–affected millions of people.

Four points: composition of Sudan and Darfur, conflict, peace agreements, and current climate.

Card #2

Darfur-western Sudan (show picture)-two main ethnic groups: Arabs in North and Africans in South.

Sudanese government favors Arabs and alienated the Africans.

Debra A. Miller-Current Controversies, a pronounced difference in location of natural resources. The north-farmland; the south-oil.

Card #3

Miller-April of 2003, two African rebel groups-the Sudan Liberation Army and the Justice of Equality Movement-attacked a military airfield at al-Fashir, killing 75, capturing 23, and destroying 7 bombers and helicopter gunships.

Humiliated government; showed soldiers were not trained well enough to stop rebel forces.

As punishment, government supplied Arab militants-Janjaweed-with weapons & communication equipment.

Destroyed villages, murdering and displacing its residents.

Card #4

Robert O. Collins–A History of Modern Sudan–kill and mutilate the men, rape the women, and abduct or kill the children before burning down their homes, stealing their livestock, torching their fields, and destroying their public buildings.
About 300,000 people killed.
Those who survive–forced to congregate in refugee camps–exposed to disease, malnutrition, and separation from families.
Approximately 3 million people have been displaced.
Violence escalated, Sudan Liberation Movement sought peace talks with the government.

Card #5

Peace talks–unsuccessful.
U.S. Department of State Archives–first peace agreement, 2006, required the government to disarm the Janjaweed, provide $30 million for displaced victims, and $300 million, plus $200 million each year after to rebuild the region.
Violence continued; need for a second peace agreement arose.
Second peace agreement–2011, required compensation fund.
This peace agreement, too, has failed.

A complete-sentence outline and note cards are helpful in the planning and preparation of your speech. However, you would never read either one word-for-word during your delivery. The best practice is to put away the outline and take only your note cards with you to the podium.

Card #6

U.S. Ambassador Smith, in radio interview, "the security situation has deteriorated" since 2011.

Interviewer, Kamal Elsadig, pressured ambassador to address bombing, murder in civilian areas, as well as rape.

Lack of water, food, and medical supplies.

Millions affected—9-year genocide: natural resources, ethnic differences, and government revenge.

Thousands of Africans are being murdered by the Janjaweed military.

When the safety and rights of others are being undermined, all our rights are at risk.

CHAPTER REVIEW

When you are setting out to convey information to an audience, identifying your goal and purpose should be the first step. What immediate and long-term actions would you like your audience to take as a result of your speech? Asking this question can help you identify your goal and purpose, as well as test whether the speech was a success. Just as important is using the skills you have learned for presenting information effectively. Make use of definition, description, explanation, illustration, analogies, narration, and demonstration, and you will keep your audience interested and engaged. Finally, be prepared. The sample sentence outline and note cards in this chapter can help you prepare and deliver your next informative speech.

KEY TERMS

immediate behavioral purpose, 278
information hunger, 279
information relevance, 280
extrinsic motivation, 280
informative content, 282
comparison, 285
contrast, 285
synonym, 285
antonym, 285
operational definition, 285
imagery, 285
explanation, 286
illustration, 287
analogy, 287
narration, 287
demonstrating, 288

STUDY QUESTIONS

1. What is informative speaking? Describe a time when you delivered an informative presentation, in or outside the classroom.
2. What is the difference between the overall goal and the specific purpose of an informative presentation?
3. What are the seven important skills of an informative speaker, and how does each contribute to a presentation?
4. Give an example of a particularly effective or ineffective use of visual resources in a presentation you've attended. Explain why the visuals worked well or did not.
5. What is the purpose of an outline and note cards when it comes to giving your presentation?

ENDNOTES

1. Baird, G. (2011, October 24). New Ohio law lessens penalty for driving under suspension and driving without a license. *The Cleveland Plain Dealer*. Accessed from http://www.cleveland.com
2. Davis, W. (2016, December 5). Fake or real? How to self-check the news and get the facts. *National Public Radio*. Retrieved from http://www.mprnews.org
3. Petrie, C. R., Jr., & Carrel, S. D. (1976). The relationship of motivation, listening, capability, initial information, and verbal organizational ability to lecture comprehension and retention. *Speech Monographs, 43*, 187–194.
4. Tourtelot, N. (2008, December). Lunatic. *Esquire*, 167.
5. Ibid.
6. Harden, B., & Eilperin, J. (2006, December 4–10). Wild species and ski resorts are on the move. *The Washington Post Weekly Edition*, 19.
7. Ibid.

Blue and Yellow Cube Icon, Connecting Globally Icon, Mountain Icon, Chapter Review Arrows Circle Icon: ©McGraw Hill Education

chapter 14

Public Presentations to Persuade

Source: Library of Congress Prints and Photographs Division, Department of the Interior, National Park Service [3b48901u]

In persuasive speaking, your focus is on your immediate purposes as well as on your long-range goals—after all, your aim is to persuade your audience to take some action. When you finish this chapter, you will be able to use evidence to support and argue for your position, describe and provide examples of the three logical forms of proof, and demonstrate the skills used for persuading.

LEARNING OBJECTIVES
After reading this chapter, you should be able to:

- Understand the various goals and purposes of persuasive presentations.
- Know how to effectively introduce your purpose and argument.
- Demonstrate effective use of arguments and evidence.
- Describe and provide examples of the three logical forms of proof.
- Organize a persuasive message effectively.
- Demonstrate effective use of the skills for persuading: providing examples, using comparison and contrast, and using testimonials.

PREPARE A PERSUASIVE PRESENTATION

A **persuasive presentation** is *a message strategically designed to induce change in the audience in some way consistent with your purpose.* The following are some examples of persuasive topics:

New rules are needed for drug use among athletes.
Teachers need to unionize.
Construction and building practices must become greener.
Our country must do its part in helping refugees.
Our legislature must pass laws to control college tuition.

©Jeff Malet Photography/Newscom

Most people misunderstand how persuasion works. Some people think it is all about getting people to do something they would not otherwise do. Actually, *forcing people to unwillingly think or behave as you wish* is not persuasion but **coercion**. Likewise, *tricking people or using fraudulent means to gain compliance* is not persuasion but **manipulation**. Both coercion and manipulation override a person's ability to choose, that is, to make a decision based on sound information and ideas, and are therefore not used by ethical speakers. Persuasion is strategic, but it is neither coercive nor manipulative.

What Is Your Immediate Purpose?

Your presentation should have an **immediate purpose**, *a statement of what you intend to accomplish*. You may want to review that concept as presented in **Chapter 13**, on informative speeches. Given that a single presentation to a captive audience is unlikely to produce dramatic results, you need to be realistic. Thus, a realistic purpose might be something like this: "My immediate purpose is to have my listeners write down the e-mail addresses of legislators so they can communicate with them about lowering our tuition," or "My immediate purpose is to have participants contact their state representatives and express concern about the newly appointed secretary of education." Effective speakers consider their immediate purpose and craft a call to action statement in the conclusion based off of it. For example, in a conclusion you might give out the names and phone numbers of local representatives, ask participants to write them down, and follow up with a call expressing a need for change. Such a statement clearly tells audience members how you expect them to do something different based off of the speech.

What Is Your Long-Range Goal?

In the context of a persuasive speech, you also want to consider your **long-range goal**, *a statement of purposes that could be achieved with continuing efforts to persuade.* You know, for instance, that you are not going to produce a lot of action from a one-shot effort to persuade listeners that more regulation is needed regarding steroid and designer-drug use among athletes. But you also know that, the more your audience hears about this issue from many sources, the more likely something will be done about it. With these thoughts in mind, you could state your long-range goal like this: "My long-range goal is to encourage my listeners to learn more about this issue over time so eventually they may join the effort to push for rules against the use of performance-enhancing drugs in sports."

INTRODUCE YOUR PERSUASIVE PRESENTATION

The introduction for your persuasive presentation has characteristics similar to those of other types of introductions: it seeks to gain and maintain attention, relates the topic to the speaker, and forecasts the organization and development of the presentation. However, a persuasive introduction differs from other kinds of introductions in the way it reveals the purpose of the presentation.

Revealing the Purpose of the Presentation

In an informative presentation, you state clearly at the outset what you want to accomplish and tell the audience what you want them to learn. In a persuasive presentation, however, your listeners may reject your intention to change their thinking or behavior unless you prepare them to listen to you. To do so, you need to analyze the audience to determine when and how you should reveal your immediate purpose.

Have you heard of the "foot-in-the-door" technique? This technique is based on the idea that door-to-door salespeople try to put their foot in the door so home dwellers cannot shut the door without at least listening to the whole sales pitch. Similarly, when you warm your audience to your idea rather than blurting it out at the beginning, you are practicing a kind of foot-in-the-door strategy.

How much are you asking of your audience? **Figure 14.1** explains two possible scenarios. If you aren't asking for much of a change from your audience, you should reveal your purpose and action steps in your introduction. If you think your audience will resist your call for action, reveal your purpose at the outset; then explain the actions you wish them to take at the end, after you have made a strong case.

If you ask your listeners for too much change, you are likely to get a **boomerang effect**—that is, *the audience will like you and your message less after the presentation than they did before.* To avoid the boomerang effect, analyze your audience and decide when you should reveal your purpose.

Figure 14.1 Asking for a Change

How much are you asking of your audience?

Not asking for much of a change?
Reveal your purpose in the introduction of the speech—or your introducer may even reveal the purpose for you.

Need to convince your audience to accept your immediate purpose?
Provide your reasons first and reveal your action step toward the end of the presentation.

(top): ©Stockbyte/Getty Images RF; (bottom): ©Hill Street Studios/Getty RF

What Purposes Are Persuasive?

Most persuasive presentations in the classroom have one of two immediate purposes, adoption or discontinuance, explained and illustrated in **Figure 14.2**. **Adoption** means that *listeners start a new behavior as a result of the persuasive presentation*—for example, they start exercising after you present the risks and prevalence of diabetes. The persuader has some proof of effectiveness if people in the audience state on a post-presentation questionnaire that they are going to take up some new behavior.

Discontinuance is *a persuasive purpose rooted in convincing listeners to stop some current behavior*—for example, to stop taking so much sick leave or to cut down on caffeine intake. Discontinuance and adoption are challenging persuasive purposes well worth your efforts in a presentation. They can change your listeners' lives in very positive ways.

Why Should You Try to Persuade?

Despite decades of messages discouraging overeating, encouraging exercise, and discouraging smoking, U.S. adults are the fattest people on earth, exercise way too little, and continue to die in large numbers from obesity and smoking-related diseases. Given that a multitude of campaigns have failed to change these behaviors, you might start to wonder how anyone would expect you to succeed in a classroom presentation. But you should feel encouraged to know that, in the

Figure 14.2 Examples of Adoption and Discontinuance

The purpose of this poster is *adoption*, meaning that it aims to persuade viewers to do something new—to walk, bike, or take public transportation instead of driving.

This poster persuades viewers to *discontinue* a behavior—in this case, texting while driving.

(left): Source: Courtesy Car Free Day, Metro,DC/carfreemetrodc.org; (right): Source: U.S. Department of Transportation/NHTSA/Distraction.gov

classroom, you will benefit from the opportunity to address your audience directly, face-to-face.

Face-to-face efforts are more persuasive than public service campaigns for at least three reasons. One is that face-to-face communication is among the most effective modes we have. Consider the difference between a public service announcement on television discouraging bulimia and a classroom presentation on the same subject by a classmate who confesses to bulimia and reveals the awful, life-threatening effects of the disease. Which mode—a TV spot or the person herself—would have the most influence on you? As you consider this question, remember that, although we can see almost any entertainer on video, thousands of us show up for concerts because we want to see an entertainer in the flesh.

Face-to-face communication is also compelling because it offers the possibility of spontaneous behavior. For example, Bruce Springsteen has used the stage to speak out against greed in the banking industry—combining entertainment with persuasion in an extremely effective way. Although you might not have the star power of a Springsteen, you may find that people in your classroom audience respond well to your in-person message, delivered in real time, because of its potential to present them with something new, spontaneous, and relevant to them.

The third reason your face-to-face presentation can be especially effective is that your classmates are a captive audience. Thus, you have an opportunity in the classroom to speak about something that really matters to you and to persuade people who might never otherwise have gone to hear a speech about this topic. As members of the classroom audience, they learn about a topic from you, and your persuasive speech has the potential to change their thinking or behavior.

SKILL BUILDER

PERSUADE BY LISTENING AND SEEKING COMMON GROUND

Active listening and seeking common ground are often overlooked as techniques of persuasion. Find someone you trust and respect, and engage them in a conversation on a topic about which you disagree. As you discuss, practice these four skills associated with persuasion:

Seek to understand their unique perspectives. Before you can craft a message that will resonate and persuade, you have to listen to others' perspectives on the issue. Why do they feel the way they do? What aspects of the issue are most important to them? How did they come to form their opinions on the issue? The Skill Builder box in Chapter 2 explains how to engage in active listening and perception checking, which can help you develop greater sensitivity as a listener.

Find common ground and discuss points of agreement. Once you better understand the other person's perspective, respond by focusing on points of agreement. Let's say you are discussing healthcare reform. You might agree that the cost of medicine is too high for the uninsured. So spend some time discussing this point and validating one another's points of view. Doing this builds mutual respect and decreases defensiveness. When people are less defensive, they are more open to the ideas of others.

Be patient, persuasion takes time. We all have had the experience of holding a position on an important issue. Often we are least flexible on issues that correspond with our core beliefs. Rather than trying to change someone's perspective on a deeply held belief, see if you can persuade them to think differently about some aspect that is related, but not central, to the issue. When it comes to the hot-button issues, people change their perspectives slowly, over time. If you are patient, you might find you can persuade others to change their minds.

Learn when to back off. Heated arguments and disagreements rarely move people from their positions. Arguments can instead create defensiveness, making people more resolute and less willing to consider new perspectives. When this happens, back off. Sometimes less communication is better.

UNDERSTAND PERSUASION

To persuade others—whether in school, at home, or at work—you must choose strategies that will work best on your listeners. In other words, audience analysis is key to making the most of the strategies described in this section.

Using Argument to Persuade: Fact, Policy, and Value

Many listeners respond positively to speakers who know how to present a logical argument. Lawyers and debaters are well versed in logical **argument**, *a form of discourse that attempts to persuade*. Arguments consist of propositions, which are the points to be discussed or considered in the argument, and they concern questions of fact, policy, or value.

An example of a **proposition of fact**—*an assertion that can be proved or disproved*—is "College student debt is the highest in history."[1] To demonstrate the accuracy of this fact, you might look at recent statistics about students loans, which demonstrate that the average student in 2016 graduated with over $37,000 in student loan debt, which is 6 percent higher than the amount of student loan debt among 2015 graduates.[2] Or, you could cite a recent *Washington Post* article that notes that the amount of student loan debt shouldered by parents and grandparents, Americans 60 and older, has quadrupled in the past ten years to over $66.7 billion.[3] These facts represent evidence reinforcing the argument that student loan debt is a serious problem for many Americans.

An example of a **proposition of policy**—*a proposal of a new rule*—is the executive order on immigration signed by President Trump in January of 2017, which banned travel to the United States for immigrants from seven predominately Muslim countries. The order also impacted current green card holders and travelers with visas, who were initially unable to get back into the country. When state judges declared the order unconstitutional, President Trump revised the order by removing Iraq from the list of countries and softening the rules as applied to current green card and visa holders. Though concerns about the order's constitutionality still exist, the purpose of this proposition of policy is to increase national security and reduce terrorism threats.[4]

An example of a **proposition of value**—*a statement of what we should embrace as good or bad, right or wrong*—is "We must put security above First Amendment freedoms." To demonstrate the merit of this proposition, you would provide evidence that airline searches, wiretapping, and profiling are more important than our right to protection against unreasonable searches, our expectation of privacy, and our right not to be singled out for negative treatment because of race or ethnicity. Why? Because those violations of rights keep us safe, and we want security more than we want freedoms.

What Is the Difference Between Evidence and Proof?

The term **evidence** refers to *anything, physical or verbal, that helps in forming a conclusion or judgment*, such as DNA results or witness testimony. **Proof**, on the other hand, is *any evidence that the receiver believes*. You might present statistics as *evidence* to support your argument that this country needs a policy solution to the student-debt crisis. If, however, an audience member questioned the source of the statistics or the way the numbers were collected and analyzed, your evidence would not constitute *proof* for that listener. If a lawyer for the prosecution introduces DNA as *evidence* in a criminal trial, but the lawyer for the defense questions the way the DNA was collected or stored, the evidence may not be convincing *proof* for the judge or jury. The relationship between evidence and proof is illustrated in **Figure 14.3**.

Figure 14.3 The Relationship Between Evidence and Proof

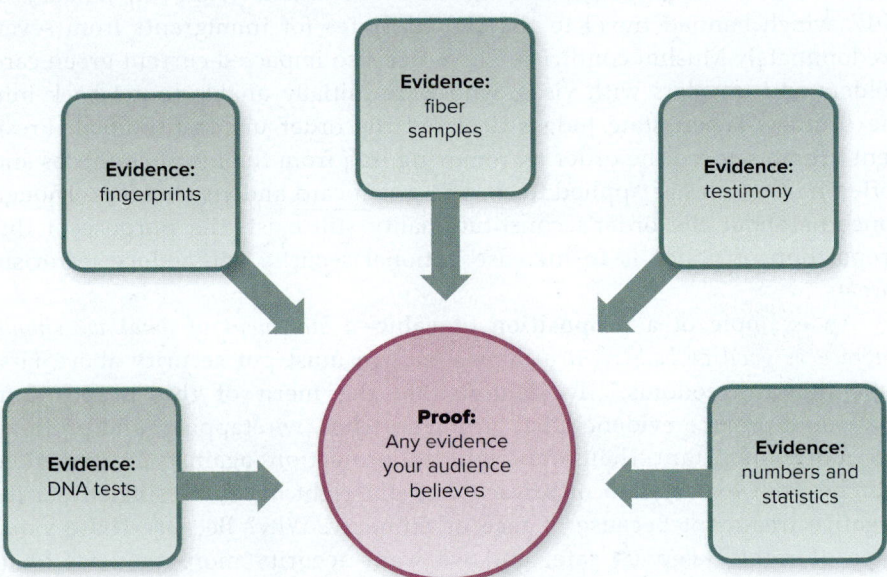

306 Chapter 14 Public Presentations to Persuade

How Can You Test Evidence?

To make your argument as strong as possible, ensure that the evidence you present meets the **tests of evidence**, *standards for demonstrating validity*. To determine if your evidence is strong, ask these questions:

1. Is the evidence consistent with other known facts?
2. Would another observer draw the same conclusions you have, based on this evidence?
3. Does the evidence come from unbiased sources?
4. Is the person who is the source of the evidence qualified by education and/or experience to make a statement about the issue?
5. Is the person who is the source of the evidence credible based on background and reputation?
6. If the evidence is based on personal experience, how typical is that personal experience?
7. If statistics are used as evidence, are they from a reliable source; comparable with other known information; and current, applicable, and interpreted so the audience can understand them?
8. If studies and surveys are used as evidence, are they authoritative, valid, reliable, objective, and generalizable?
9. Are your inferences appropriate to the evidence you are presenting?
10. Have you overlooked any important counterevidence?

An example may help you understand these questions and how to use them. A study was recently conducted at the University of Copenhagen, Denmark. Men between the ages of 20 and 30 who were obese and had a sedentary lifestyle were placed in three groups. The first group did not exercise; the second group exercised about 30 minutes per day or until they burned 300 calories; and the third group exercised about 60 minutes per day or until they burned 600 calories. Although we might guess that the third group lost the most weight, the group that exercised 30 minutes a day actually lost more.[5]

If you were one of the researchers in this study, and you stopped there, concluding that you now had evidence against exercise as a tool for weight loss, you would have failed to fully test your evidence. You would especially have failed to consider questions 1, 2, and 10. Why? The researchers did not stop with that evidence. In looking at the participants' food journals, they discovered that as participants in the third group increased their exercise, they also increased the amount of food they ate. In short, there was a more complex reason the members of the third group lost less weight than those in the second group. The researchers concluded, therefore, that shorter amounts of exercise may be more helpful for those trying to lose weight.[6] For statistics to be considered *authoritative, valid, reliable, objective, and generalizable*, they must be viewed in context. And those who present and interpret them in an argument must not overlook any important counterevidence.

CONNECTING GLOBALLY

CAN PROFILE PICS PERSUADE?

Social media profiles are an expression of identity, from the pictures we post, to the events we highlight and the causes we support. Many people also use social media as a platform for raising awareness about causes they care about and for coordinating meaningful action with those in their network.

An article from *The Washington Post*[7] highlights some examples of groups that have expressed solidarity with social causes using a symbol of their identity—their social media profile pictures.

- In 2009, Iranian protesters showed concern about election irregularities by applying a green filter to their profile pictures.
- In 2014, people in Hong Kong changed their profile pictures to yellow ribbons to show their dissatisfaction with the state of democracy.
- In 2015, people around the world overlaid their photos with a rainbow flag in support for the U.S. Supreme Court decision in favor of marriage equality.
- In 2016, people changed their profile pictures to support the Orlando shooting victims' families and loved ones. The same year, some changed theirs to a black square to demonstrate protest about Donald Trump's victory in the presidential election.

As *The Washington Post* article notes, this new form of activism does not directly influence changes in policy. However, its value lies in raising awareness and building solidarity around important issues. Changes in policy are often inspired by collective actions and expressions of differing opinions. Do you find this type of social media activism persuasive?

THREE FORMS OF PROOF

To persuade an audience you need to know some methods of doing so. Aristotle in his *Rhetoric* wrote about three modes of proof: ethos, pathos, and logos.

Logos refers to *persuasion by using logical argument.*

Ethos refers to *the reputation, authority, and integrity of the speaker.*

Pathos refers to *the use of emotional means of persuasion.*

Over the centuries, these methods have been refined but are still visible everywhere, from advertisements and movie trailers to classroom and office presentations.

Logos, or Logical Proof

One logical structure you can use to formulate your arguments is known as inductive reasoning. An **inductive argument** *provides enough specific instances that the listener can make an inferential leap to a generalization or conclusion.* Consider the example in **Figure 14.4**, which illustrates the structure of an inductive argument for more government programs and support. A series of individual instances, such as unrepaired roads and highways, can lead to an inferential

Figure 14.4 The Structure of an Inductive Argument

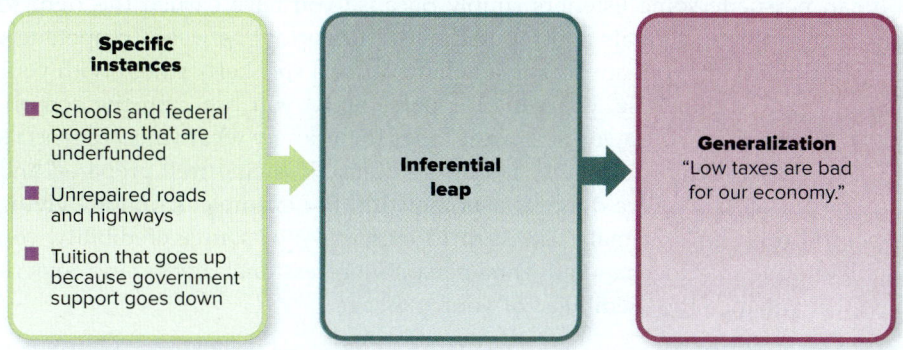

leap, which in turn might lead an audience to conclude that more government support is needed.

Good inductive arguments rely on the particulars of the evidence presented to formulate conclusions. For example, if data shows that online classes fill up faster than face-to-face classes, and that students rate online classes as comparable to face-to-face classes, that evidence might be used to advance the generalization that online classes serve an important function in education today. However, the data described does not provide enough specific evidence to support the conclusion that online classes are better than face-to-face classes. In order to advance this conclusion, additional evidence is needed.

Another logical structure, illustrated in **Figure 14.5**, is deductive reasoning. A **deductive argument** *uses a general proposition applied to a specific instance, or minor premise, to draw a conclusion.* This logical structure is called a **syllogism**, meaning that it *contains a generalization (a major premise) applied to a particular instance (a minor premise) that leads to a conclusion.* For example, consider the generalization that effective leaders involve others in decision-making processes. If your boss does not do so, you might conclude that your boss demonstrates ineffective leadership. Whereas inductive arguments use specific instances to arrive at a conclusion, deductive arguments do the opposite, beginning with a conclusion and applying it to a specific case or instance.

Figure 14.5 The Structure of a Deductive Argument

Ethos, or Source Credibility

You can persuade some listeners simply because you have earned the right to speak, but your credentials and reputation are important as well. Competence, trustworthiness, and dynamism are all elements of a speaker's ethos. With your personal power, expertise, charisma, or personality, you can gain the compliance of your audience, so you will want to let them know what your credentials are. You will also want to establish your credibility by being well prepared and demonstrating that you've done your homework. For example, if you are giving a speech on training animals and want to increase your source credibility, you might interview a dog handler. That person's professional advice and experience will enhance the credibility of your message.

©Purestock/SuperStock RF

Pathos, or Emotional Proof

Emotions play an important role in persuasive speaking. A volunteer speaking about how hospice care can help prolong quality of life might appeal to her audience's emotions by including an uplifting story about how a hospice nurse made a difference. A politician talking about healthcare reform might relate a story about a person who struggles to pay for life-sustaining drugs, appealing to the audience's sense of justice. Emotional appeals can have powerful effects on your audience, so it is important to use them ethically. Sarah McLaughlin's famous commercial for the ASPCA, which combines heart-wrenching music with visual imagery of abused and neglected animals, is so emotionally impactful that it leads many viewers feel guilty or powerless. Toying with people's emotions for the purposes of making a dramatic point is an unethical choice for a public speaker.

The **fear appeal**, *a message designed to frighten or alarm an audience so they will be persuaded to act,* is one of the most common appeals to emotion:

- Political ads focus on impending economic collapse or suggest that only one political party can protect us from an enemy.
- Financial gurus make us feel that we are risking financial ruin if we don't heed their advice.

Fear appeals get us to brush our teeth, use deodorant, and buy certain clothing. As a speaker you can use fear appeals in an ethical manner if you do not exaggerate the threat and if you offer reassurance as well.

In media campaigns regarding teen pregnancy, pathos and fear appeals have been used in a balanced way. Health promoters have found that the most successful campaigns against teen pregnancy include a variety of strategies—for example, they combat positive attitudes toward pregnancy as well as negative attitudes about birth control. They also emphasize negative consequences of sexual intercourse.[8] These messages address emotional issues, but without making exaggerated claims and while providing reassurance.

In contrast, messages that shock people with fear (such as the grim and gripping reenactments of alcohol-related car crashes) often are not effective and may be viewed as unethical. When the appeal to fear is too extreme, the response may be increased anxiety, aggression toward the source of the message, and in some cases unhealthy behaviors to reduce anxiety (e.g., alcohol or drug use).[9] Consequently, an extreme fear appeal is also counterproductive.

ORGANIZE YOUR PERSUASIVE MESSAGE

How do you organize your presentation to achieve your persuasive purpose? Recall the many organizational strategies provided in **Chapter 10**: the time-sequence pattern, cause/effect pattern, problem/solution pattern, and topical-sequence pattern. Another possibility is the Monroe Motivated Sequence, which is especially useful for persuasive presentations, especially when the audience is reluctant to change or to accept a proposed action.

The Monroe Motivated Sequence

Developed by University of Iowa professor Alan Monroe, the **Monroe Motivated Sequence**, *an organizational pattern that includes the following steps: attention, need, satisfaction, visualization, and action,* has been used successfully for four decades and is popular for having five easy-to-follow steps, outlined in **Table 14.1**. Following is an example of a speech using the Monroe Motivated Sequence.

Table 14.1 The Monroe Motivated Sequence

Step 1: Attention

- *Gain and maintain audience attention*, and determine a way to focus it on the content of your presentation.

Step 2: Need

- Once you have the audience's attention, demonstrate how the speech is relevant to them.
- *Arouse a need* for the change you suggest in your persuasive presentation.

Step 3: Satisfaction

- Your speech either presents the information the audience needs or suggests a solution to their needs. You *satisfy the audience* by meeting their needs with your plan.

Step 4: Visualization

- Reinforce your idea in the audience's minds by getting them to see how your information or ideas will help them.

Step 5: Action

- Once the audience has visualized your idea, *plead for action*.
- The audience might remember your main points in an informative presentation and state them to others, or the audience may go out and do what you ask in a persuasive presentation.

SOURCE: This organizational pattern was originally provided by Ehninger, D. & Monroe, A. H., in their multiple editions of Principles and types of speech communication. The most current version of the book is German, K. M., Gronbeck, B. E., Ehninger, D., & Monroe, A. H. (2012). Principles of public speaking (18th ed.). Old Tappan, NJ: Pearson. We Need More Than Antib

We Need More Than Antibiotics to Treat Infections

Purpose: My audience will be able to state the advantages of using multiple drugs to kill dangerous bacteria in our bodies.

Thesis Statement: Serums and phages should be considered, in addition to antibiotics, to kill bacteria.

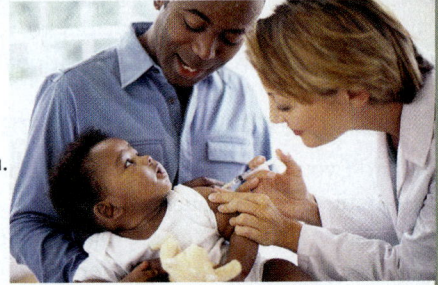
©Ian Hooton/Science Photo Library/Corbis RF

Attention Stage: What is the largest cause of death in the United States? If you have listened to the speeches in this class, you might conclude that it is automobile accidents. Although it is true that automobile accidents kill about 32,000 people a year, a close rival in frequency are infections caught in hospitals. Last year, 30,000 people died from fatal infections they contracted while staying in the hospital. The 30,000 people included newborns, children, middle-aged people, and elderly patients.

Need Stage: Why did all these people die when modern medicine boasts a range of antibiotics with proven effectiveness? Some bacteria are antibiotic-resistant. Last year, in Europe alone, 25,000 people died from bacteria that did not respond to antibiotics. Further, a chief medical officer labeled antibiotic resistance a "ticking time bomb."

Satisfaction Stage: Some pre-antibiotic medications—including serum therapy and bacteriophages (viruses that attack bacteria)—may provide a solution. In the past, medical doctors turned to antibiotics, instead of serums and phages, because antibiotics proved to be a successful treatment for infections. Today, largely because of overuse, we are learning that antibiotics are becoming much less effective. Moreover, serums and phages are more selective in the bacteria they will attack, making them an even more attractive alternative to antibiotics.

Visualization Stage: Imagine a world in which a child in Guatemala who has *Shigella* diarrhea and does not respond to antibiotics is still alive and has a chance to live a fulfilling life. Imagine the middle-aged man who was admitted to the Medical Center at the University of Virginia in 2010—arguably one of the finest medical centers in the world—did not die from an infection treated with antibiotics. Imagine a world where no one needs to worry about dying from an infection treated only with antibiotics.

Action Stage: What can we do to maximize the effectiveness of medicine to rid our bodies of bacteria? We must insist that scientists continue to do research on serums, phages, and other treatments, as well as explore new medical approaches. We also need to insist that our physicians do not take an easy way out by treating all bacteria with antibiotics. Ignoring alternatives to antibiotics may be a matter of life and death for you or someone you love.

Ethical Considerations

Ethics are *a set of principles for right conduct*. Many of our standards for ethical behavior are codified into law. Others are not, but violating them still leads to consequences. The following are some generally accepted ethical standards that govern the preparation and delivery of a persuasive presentation.

1. *Accurately cite sources.* Give credit to the writers, researchers, and thinkers who have provided information you have used.
2. *Respect sources of information.* Demonstrate their credibility as completely as possible.
3. *Respect your audience.* Do not attempt to trick or manipulate them.
4. *Respect those who disagree with you or who offer rebuttals to your argument.* Attack your opponent's evidence, sources, or logic—but not your opponent.

SKILLS FOR PERSUASIVE SPEAKING

Even when your aim is to persuade, you can draw on the skills for informative speaking that were presented in **Chapter 13**. The three skills that lend themselves particularly well to persuasive speaking are providing examples, using comparison and contrast, and using testimonials.

Providing Examples

Examples are specific instances used to clarify your point. They are among the most common clarifying materials. A single, very strong example can help convince an entire audience. For instance, in an argument designed to motivate everyone to vote, you could present a case in which a few more votes would have meant a major change in election results.

Two types of examples are factual and hypothetical. A **factual example** is *based on real circumstances*. Here's one about the expanding role of social media: "Several online memorial sites on Facebook illustrate how social networking sites have started to serve a larger role than simply helping people connect." This is a factual example because it's about a feature of social media (memorial sites on Facebook).

In contrast, a **hypothetical example** is *a fictional but realistic example*. One of your instructors may state on the first day of class, "A good excuse for a student missing class is that he or she has a serious auto accident, ends up in the hospital, and has a signed medical statement from a physician to prove hospitalization for a week. A poor excuse is a student who overslept for a 4 P.M. class and has no explanation for his or her behavior." Either type of example can be brief or extended, but an ethical speaker will reveal whether an example is factual or hypothetical.

CHALLENGE YOURSELF

How can I get others to agree with me, to understand what I know and believe, and to switch to my side on important issues?

You probably already know that persuasion is one of the most difficult of all communication situations. Have you ever tried to persuade a teacher to accept a late paper, to change the grading of an exam, or to give you a higher grade in the class? Perhaps you have attempted to persuade your partner to accompany you on an expensive trip. Maybe you have even endeavored to convince a friend to vote for a different person or to stop using drugs. How successful were you in your endeavors?

In addition to what you've learned in this chapter, consider the advice of Robert Cialdini, a professor at Arizona State University. Professor Cialdini wrote the popular book *Yes—50 Scientifically Proven Ways to Be More Persuasive,* in which he offers the following six principles.

- *Principle of Reciprocity*. People are more likely to say yes to you if you have said yes to them first. If a classmate needs help with a project, show a willingness to step in. You will likely find that he will provide support to you when you ask for it.

- *Principle of Commitment and Consistency*. People have a deep desire to be consistent. Thus, you are more likely to persuade people if you can show them that your position is consistent with their positions on similar matters. For example, you might argue that your friend should support a candidate because environmental issues are a priority for that candidate and your friend has always been concerned with environmental issues.

- *Principle of Authority*. This idea is related to the concept of ethos, mentioned in the chapter. Audiences are persuaded by people in authority and people with expertise. The more you draw on your expertise, whatever it may be, the more likely you are to be persuasive.

- *Principle of Social Validation*. People are more willing to take a recommendation if they see that people similar to them have adopted the proposal. Testimonials from those who agree with you are invaluable as tools of persuasion.

- *Principle of Scarcity*. People find products more attractive to the degree that they are scarce or limited in availability. "Going out of business" sales work because people believe they have a limited time to make a purchase.

- *Principle of Liking*. People are more likely to respond to people they know and like. If you nurture relationships with those in your audience, you are more likely to be persuasive to them.

Think of the last time someone persuaded you to do something. Did any of the factors mentioned above influence you? Now that you know some of the principles of persuasion, and have examples of how you can use them, take opportunities to apply them in your class presentations, as well as your day-to-day life.[10]

Using Comparison and Contrast

As defined in **Chapter 13**, comparison clarifies by linking a familiar instance with an unfamiliar one. If your audience is familiar with one city but not another, you might acquaint them with the unfamiliar city by highlighting what it has in common with the one they know: "New York City and Los Angeles both have immense populations, locations on an ocean, and large international ports." Or you can use contrast, which *emphasizes differences*: "Contrasted with New York City, Los Angeles has far more square miles, a more extensive road system, and a less developed mass transit system." These key similarities and differences help characterize the two cities.

Imagine a friend is attempting to persuade you to buy an electric car, but you have only ever driven gasoline-fueled cars. To make her argument, your friend might point out differences in the impact on the environment and cost to run each type of vehicle (contrast) while explaining similarities in the comfort of the ride and handling (comparison). Comparison and contrast can be used in informative speeches, but they are particularly appropriate for persuasive messages.

Using Testimonials

Testimonial evidence consists of *written or oral statements of others' experience used to substantiate or clarify a point*. We can identify three types of testimonial evidence. **Lay testimony** *consists of statements made by ordinary people that substantiate or support what you say*: a student explains why fellow students should vote for the candidate you have argued is the best. **Celebrity testimony** *consists of statements made by a public figure who is known to the audience*. When former-representative Gabrielle Giffords campaigns for gun-control legislation or Bruce Springsteen endorses Hillary Clinton, they are offering celebrity testimony, and this can be extremely persuasive. Such testimonies are also known as endorsements. Stronger than lay testimony and celebrity testimony is expert testimony. **Expert testimony** *includes statements made by someone who has special knowledge or expertise about an issue or idea*. You might quote a mechanic about problems with an automobile, an interior decorator about quality fabrics, or a political scientist about the possible outcomes of an election.

A SAMPLE PERSUASIVE SPEECH OUTLINE AND NOTE CARDS

The following complete-sentence outline was written by a first-year college student, Calla Price. This outline helped the student plan and organize her talk. She did not use the outline when she delivered her speech; instead, she used the note cards that follow this outline.

Persuasive Speech on Texting and Driving
Calla Price

Introduction

I. **Attention Getter:** Coffee Creamer, named after its color, was my Chevy S-10. That old pickup now sits out in one of our pastures reminiscing on the days before it was totaled. Miserable truck, it just sits there, alone, mangled, and useless after a texting-and-driving accident. The truck might not fear the consequences of texting and driving, but I do.

II. **Listener Relevance:** You have probably written or read a text on your phone while driving, at least once; you may have even had an accident.

III. **Speaker Credibility:** I rolled over my Coffee Creamer because of texting and driving. I could have been killed.

IV. **Thesis Statement:** Texting and driving needs to stop.

V **Preview:** Sometimes accidents end in fatalities. Frequently they bring other consequences that can lead to life-altering physical or emotional impairments. Let's try to find a solution to this problem; let's imagine together what driving could be without a fear of a texting-and-driving accident.

Body

I. **First Main Point:** Texting and driving is dangerous. It is a serious problem in the United States because of the frequency with which it occurs.

  A. The dangers of texting and driving are appalling.

  B. Texting while driving is a serious distraction that increases a driver's chances of getting into an accident.

  C. According to Lisa A. Gardner in a journal article "Wat 2 Do Abt Txt'n & Drv'n," three safety risks are directly related to this behavior.

  1. First, texting takes some of the mental focus away from the task of driving.

  2. Second, texting requires drivers to take one hand off the wheel.

  3. And third, in order to read or write a text, drivers have to look away from the road.

D. The effects of texting-and-driving accidents range from financial burdens to long-term health problems.

1. Fixing car damage costs money, something most college students don't have.
2. Mental health problems can arise after an accident.
   a. Anxiety, depression, and post-traumatic stress disorder (PTSD) are common side effects.
   b. Anne Cameron describes PTSD as having many symptoms, including reliving the event, feeling shame or guilt, being irritable or angry, and experiencing problems with memory.
   c. PTSD symptoms can disappear for years and be triggered again by an unrelated event.

Transition: Clearly, texting while driving is problematic. But the solution is not so clear, because the motivations to text and drive vary from person to person.

II. **Second Main Point:** Texting and driving is a relatively new issue, which means that we are still on the lookout for effective solutions. We do know, however, that in order to solve this problem we need to influence people's decisions directly, and establish laws and regulations against texting and driving.

A. Influencing people to stop texting and driving might be one of the most successful ways of stopping the problem.

1. According to Gardner, peer pressure has been instrumental in changing people's perception—making drunk driving and driving without a seatbelt, for instance, not only illegal, but socially unacceptable. Asking friends not to text and drive while you are in the car may be the most effective way to make them understand you are not comfortable with it. But that is not an easy thing to do. To avoid hard feelings with a friend, Nancy Jackson writes, "Avoid calling or texting your friends if you know they are driving at the time." Ask them not to text you if you are driving as well. These requests should get your message across.
2. Technology also can help influence people. For example, there are now easy-to-install apps that use GPS technology to sense when you are driving, and they send automatic replies to people who text or call when you are on the road. In an article for *USA Today*, Julius Genachowski explains that "new apps block texting or web surfing when the phone is in motion."

B. Laws and regulations against texting and driving also influence people's decisions.
   1. Currently thirty states and the District of Columbia have made texting and driving illegal. Thirty-one states have laws that restrict teens from using their phones while driving. Penalties range from state to state. The national government is regulating states with and without texting and driving laws. According to Jackson, if a state does not have certain laws in place, federal aid for highway maintenance is reduced by 25 percent.
   2. The national government is also making mandatory the development of technology to aid in the prevention of texting and driving, and accidents generally, for cars produced in the United States.

Transition: Can you imagine a world where the solutions worked, and texting and driving wasn't a problem?

III. **Third Main Point:** If texting and driving were considered socially unacceptable, lives would be saved. Moreover, medical bills and mental health problems would be prevented. Think of the benefits of making this problem unacceptable.

   A. The accident rate would decrease.
      1. Accidents would still happen, but the number of accidents that are really serious or hard to get over would decrease.
      2. How many people do you know who have had a texting and driving accident? How many of them drove away with an unwrecked car, an unhurt body, or a healthy mental state?
   B. The fear of accidents that were not your fault would decrease as well.
      1. More drivers would be paying better attention.
      2. Think of how much more attention you have to give others when you know they are texting and driving. Imagine not having to watch other drivers' every move. Imagine not having to worry about your own children texting and driving because our generation put an end to it.

Transition: I cannot stress enough the dangers of texting and driving. I hope I have convinced you to stop putting your life, money, and mental health on the line for the sake of sending a text.

Conclusion

I. **Thesis Statement:** Think of the consequences before you pick up the phone and start texting and driving, or before you let a friend do it.

II. **Main Point Summary:** Put an end to texting and driving.

III. **Clincher:** Texting is not a live-or-die situation. Texting and driving is.

References

Cameron, A. (2007). Exploring posttraumatic stress disorder. *Lesbian News, 33*(3), 24.

Gardner, L. A. (2010). Wat 2 Do Abt Txt'n & Drv'n (aka: What to Do About the Problem of Texting While Driving?). *CPCU Ejournal, 63*(11), 1–13.

Jackson, N. (2011). DN'T TXT N DRV. *Current Health Teens, 37*(7), 6–9.

Julius, G. (2012). Time to put the brakes on texting and driving. *USA Today*. www.usatoday.com/story/opinion/2012/09/24/column-put-the-brakes-on-texting-and-driving/1588157/10

Teens Aware of Texting Dangers, Yet Carry On. (2011). *Professional Safety, 56*(12), 18.

As explained in **Chapter 13**, on informative speaking, a complete-sentence outline and note cards with brief notes can be helpful in the preparation of your speech. However, the idea is not to read from either one while presenting. The complete-sentence outline is a planning tool; the note cards can accompany you to the podium for reference as you speak. The following note cards might be used to deliver the persuasive speech on texting and driving.

Card #1

Coffee Creamer-Chevy S-10.

You have probably written or read a text while driving.

I rolled my truck-I could have been killed.

Texting and driving needs to stop.

Some accidents end in fatalities or other life-altering consequences.

Try to find a solution: Imagine what driving could be without a fear of texting and driving.

Card #2

Texting and driving—dangerous.

Happens frequently in U.S.

Lisa A. Gardner in a journal article "Wat 2 Do Abt Txtn & Drvn,"—three safety risks:
- Takes away some of the mental focus.
- Requires drivers to take one hand off the wheel.
- Requires drivers to look away from the road.

The effects of texting and driving accidents:
- Fixing car damages costs money, which most of us do not have.
- Mental health problems: Anxiety, depression, and post-traumatic stress disorder. Anne Cameron describes PTSD—reliving the event, feeling shame or guilt, being irritable or angry, and experiencing problems with memory.

Card #3

Texting and driving—new issue.

Need to look for effective solutions.

Need to influence people's decisions directly.
- Gardner—peer pressure has been instrumental in changing people's behaviors.
- Nancy Jackson writes, "Avoid calling or texting your friends if you know they are driving at the time."
- Technology—easy-to-install apps that use GPS technology to sense when you are driving and send automatic replies to people who text or call when you are on the road.
- USA Today, Julius Genachowski—"new apps block texting or web surfing when the phone is in motion."

Card #4

Need to establish laws and regulations against texting and driving.
- 30 states + District of Columbia = texting and driving illegal.
- 31 states have laws that restrict teens from using their phones while driving.
- Penalties vary.
- National government-regulating states-Jackson-if a state does not have certain laws in place, federal aid for the highway maintenance is reduced by 25%.
- National government-mandatory to develop technology.

Card #5

Texting and driving-socially unacceptable-lives would be saved.
Benefits of making this problem unacceptable:
- Accident rate would decrease.
- Fear of accidents that were not your fault would decrease.

Think of the consequences before you pick up the phone and start texting and driving, or before you let a friend do it.
Put an end to texting and driving.
Texting is not a live-or-die situation. Texting and driving is.

CHAPTER REVIEW

In this chapter you learned about persuasive speaking and how to prepare and present a persuasive speech. In persuasion, identifying your immediate purpose and long-term goals will help you determine when and how to present your argument, as well as help you use effective evidence. Familiarity with the three logical forms of proof and the skills for persuasion will also help you become a more effective persuasive speaker.

KEY TERMS

persuasive presentation, 300
coercion, 300
manipulation, 300
immediate purpose, 300
long-range goal, 301
boomerang effect, 301
adoption, 302
discontinuance, 302
argument, 305
proposition of fact, 305
proposition of policy, 305
proposition of value, 305
evidence, 306
proof, 306
tests of evidence, 307
logos, 308

ethos, 308
pathos, 308
inductive argument, 308
deductive argument, 309
syllogism, 309
fear appeal, 310
Monroe Motivated Sequence, 311
ethics, 313
examples, 313
factual example, 313
hypothetical example, 313
testimonial evidence, 315
lay testimony, 315
celebrity testimony, 315
expert testimony, 315

STUDY QUESTIONS

1. Draft a list of possible goals of a persuasive speech. How does the nature of the ultimate goal of persuasion differ from that of informative speaking?
2. When should persuasive speakers reveal their purpose? Why does the timing of this revelation matter?
3. How does proof differ from evidence? Describe one scenario from the news, or from your own life, in which evidence was presented that did not qualify as proof.
4. Name and define the three forms of proof. Can you think of a famous public speech that uses two of those three forms? Describe how the speaker used each form of proof to persuade the audience.

5. What are the steps in the Monroe Motivated Sequence? Do you consider the Monroe Motivated Sequence to be an effective means of persuasion? Why or why not?

6. Name the skills that lend themselves to persuasive speaking, and give an example of how you might use each in a persuasive presentation.

ENDNOTES

1. Whitehouse, M. (2011, May 7). Number of the week: Class of 2011 most indebted ever. *Wall Street Journal*.
2. Student Loan Hero (2017, February 8). A look at the shocking student load debt statistics for 2017. *Student Loan Hero*. Retrieved from https://studentloanhero.com
3. Bhattarai, A. (2017, February 11). Student debt now affects a staggering number of elderly Americans. *The Washington Post*. Retrieved from http://www.washingtonpost.com
4. Vitali, A. (2017, March 6). President Trump signs new immigration executive order. *NBC News*. Retrieved from http://www.nbcnews.com
5. Rosenkilde, M., Auerbach, P., Reichkendler, M., Ploug, T., Stallknecht, B., & Sjodin, A. (2012, August). Body fat loss and compensatory mechanisms in response to different doses of aerobic exercise—a randomized controlled trial in overweight sedentary males. *American Journal of Physiology—Regulatory, Integrative and Comparative Physiology*, 303, R571–R579. doi: 10.1152/ajpregu.00141.2012
6. Ibid.
7. Dewey, C. (2015, June 29). More than 26 million people have changed their Facebook picture to a rainbow flag. Here's why that matters. *The Washington Post*. Retrieved from http://www.washingtonpost.com
8. Witte, K. (1997, April). Preventing teen pregnancy through persuasive communications: Realities, myths, and the hard-fact truths. *Community Health*, 22(2), 137–154.
9. Prevention First. (2008). *Ineffectiveness of fear appeals in youth alcohol, tobacco and other drug (ATOD) prevention*. Springfield, IL: Author.
10. Goldstein, N. J., Martin, S. J., & Cialdini, R. B. (2009). *Yes—50 scientifically proven ways to be more persuasive*. New York: Free Press.

Blue and Yellow Cube Icon, Connecting Globally Icon, Mountain Icon, Chapter Review Arrows Circle Icon: ©McGraw Hill Education

chapter **15**

Using Communication Skills as You Enter the Workplace

©Eric Audras/Getty Images RF

Throughout your career, your education will give you a competitive advantage. And strong communication skills, in particular, will be vital every step of the way. This chapter shows how you can communicate your expertise, experience, and education in compelling ways to land one of the estimated 54.8 million job openings during this decade.

LEARNING OBJECTIVES
After reading this chapter, you should be able to:

- Discuss some of the contemporary jobs in the communication field.
- Describe your skills effectively in a résumé.
- Create a compelling cover letter for a job application packet that highlights why a company should hire you.
- Know how to present yourself effectively and appropriately during a job interview.
- Respond to behavioral-based job interview questions to create a lasting impression about you as a candidate.
- Identify at least three ways to network effectively throughout college.

CONTEMPORARY JOBS IN COMMUNICATION

What can you do with a communication degree? The communication field covers many subdisciplines, including public relations, advertising, business communication, journalism, corporate training, and marketing. Some students combine their communication courses with other courses, such as health and wellness, and go on to work in health campaigns against tobacco, excessive alcohol use, or obesity. Others combine communication with political science to serve as a legislative assistant or political analyst. Still others take business courses to prepare themselves to be corporate recruiters, training specialists, or sales representatives. **Table 15.1** lists some of the contemporary jobs recent communication graduates have found.

©Reggie Casagrande/Getty Images

The National Association for Colleges and Employers conducts an annual survey to study trends in national industry demands, hiring, and employment-related practices. Its 2016 Job Outlook survey included representatives from 201 organizations and revealed that hiring new employees with communication skills training is a top priority. In fact, according to employers, a degree in communication is among the top five undergraduate degrees they seek.[1] **Figure 15.1** lists the top five skills that employers look for in a potential employee (on a 1–5 scale ranking), regardless of the candidate's major area of study. Effective verbal communication skills rank at the top of the list.

When it comes to seeking employment, it is likely that the first opportunity you will have to demonstrate your competence as a communicator will be in writing. Most companies will not take the time to interview you unless your résumé and cover letter stand up to the highest level of scrutiny. Thus, you will need to know how to communicate your skills and training effectively to potential employers.

PRODUCING A WINNING RÉSUMÉ

Human resource professionals use a variety of tools—from surveys to background checks—to screen job applicants. But when it comes to your candidacy, the professional résumé remains the most important source of information about you.[2] A good résumé is your starting point in any job search, and it is likely to be critical for securing an interview and an eventual offer of employment. To create a successful résumé, you must consider its style, content, and format.

Style

Style refers to *the way you use language and grammar to construct your written materials*. Although style can range from very formal to very informal, your

Table 15.1 Contemporary Jobs in Communication

Title	Organization
Speech writer	Political campaign
PR professional	Major hospital
Audio editor	Film production firm
Writer/reporter/editor	Newspaper/magazine/television
Social media manager	Retail company
Teacher	High school
Business consultant	Independently employed
Web designer	City government
Administrative assistant	Investment firm
Creative planner	Advertising firm
Motivational speaker	Consulting firm
Tour guide	Travel firm
Manager	Major hotel
Community affairs liaison	Medium-sized city
Fundraiser	Small college
Small-business owner	Privately employed
Teller	Bank
Event planner	Medium-sized city
Flight attendant	Major airline
Government lobbyist	Small midwestern state
Salesperson	Insurance company
Project manager	Publisher

résumé should set a more formal tone, as demonstrated in **Figure 15.2**. Avoid using slang, casual language, or emoji; such attempts to be overly cute or friendly will almost certainly backfire.

Several stylistic conventions are unique to résumés. For example, to describe your skills on your résumé, you should use descriptive clauses that begin with action verbs, rather than using complete sentences beginning with

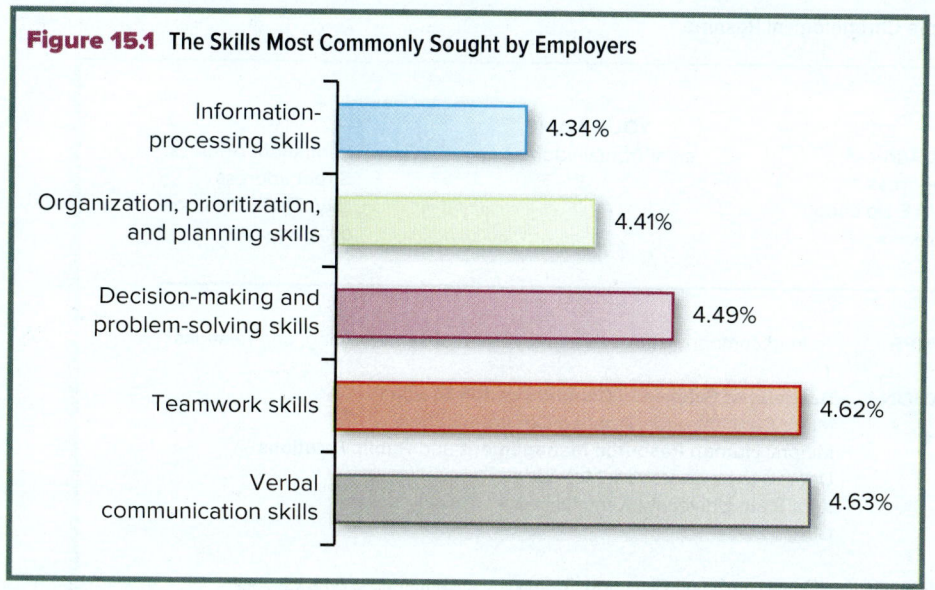

Figure 15.1 The Skills Most Commonly Sought by Employers

the pronoun "I." Many experts recommend action verbs like *planned, supervised,* and *conducted.*³ These words get employers' attention, because they are concrete and indicate what the applicant has done.

Notice in **Figure 15.2** that descriptive clauses related to current employment begin with present-tense action verbs, whereas those related to previous experience begin with past-tense action verbs. Some commonly used action verbs are listed in **Table 15.2**.

Content

Style considerations, of course, mean nothing without the right content. The key content includes your contact information, education, experience, skills, and honors and activities. Without contact information, the rest of your résumé is useless. Every résumé you send out must include complete information about how to reach you, including your e-mail address.

Next, you should pay attention to the information you highlight. Try to think like an employer and keep in mind the prominent functions of the job you are applying for. Then tailor the content to speak to the most crucial aspects of that job. Provide specific information that quantifies your skills and experience; be consistent, concise, and neat.

Quantify information. As much as possible, provide concrete information to illustrate the scope of your accomplishments. For example, "Managed a $30,000 budget for Organization X," is much more precise than, "Managed the yearly operating budget."

Producing a Winning Résumé

Figure 15.2 A Sample Chronological Résumé

YOUR NAME

email@emailaddress.com

Campus Address:		Permanent Address:
Street address		Street address
City, STATE zip code		City, STATE zip code
(xxx) xxx-xxxx		(xxx) xxx-xxxx

OBJECTIVE — To lead company efforts in employee training, mentoring, and relations

EDUCATION
Bachelor of Science in Communication Studies
Major Concentration: **Applied Communication**
Minors: **Human Resource Management** and **Public Relations**
Degree to be conferred: May 2014
Kent State University, Kent, OH
GPA: 3.92

SIGNIFICANT COURSEWORK
- Comm. in Small Grps and Teams
- Organizational Communication
- Public Relations
- Leadership and Communication
- Communication & Conflict
- Org Training and Development
- Human Resource Management
- Layout, Editing, and Design

INTERNSHIP
Personalized System of Instruction   January 2013–May 2013
School of Communication Studies, Kent, OH
- Guided students in their preparation of four speeches for the Introduction to Human Communication course
- Mentored student development of effective study habits for the course
- Assisted the course instructor with lectures, assignments, and in-class developmental exercises
- Evaluated student progress with the instructor in weekly meetings

RELATED EMPLOYMENT
Assistant Manager   June 2011–current
Local Restaurant, Kent, OH
- Train new associates on relevant policies and procedures
- Prepare sales reports and established weekly goals with associates
- Mentor associates in effective customer service strategies
- Conduct associate performance appraisals and quarterly reviews

HONORS & ACTIVITIES
- Lambda Pi Eta National Communication Assoc. Honor Society, President
- School of Communication Studies Senior Scholar, Award Recipient
- Dean's list, 6 semesters in a row

REFERENCES

Name	Name	Name
Professional Title	Professional Title	Professional Title
Company	Company	Company
(xxx) xxx-xxxx	(xxx) xxx-xxxx	(xxx) xxx-xxxx
E-mail address	E-mail address	E-mail address

Table 15.2 Action Verbs for Résumés

Accomplished	Formulated	Ordered	Succeeded
Adapted	Generated	Participated	Supervised
Administered	Handled	Performed	Supplied
Analyzed	Headed	Persuaded	Supported
Balanced	Identified	Prepared	Tabulated
Disbursed	Managed	Revised	Uploaded
Examined	Modified	Searched	Verified
Executed	Notified	Selected	Volunteered
Explained	Obtained	Sponsored	Won
Filed	Offered	Streamlined	Wrote

Be consistent. Whatever stylistic decisions you make about your résumé, adhere to them. If you use bullets to list your job duties, use bullets throughout your résumé. If you put periods at the ends of your bulleted descriptions, do so consistently. If you indent one job title five spaces and underline it, make sure all your job titles are indented five spaces and underlined. Being consistent shows potential employers that you pay attention to detail and are well organized, both of which are qualities that employers value.

Be concise. You do not have to put all your information in a résumé. In fact, view it as an appetizer; you can offer the main course in an interview. Most experts agree that, unless you have more than seven years of work experience, your résumé should not be longer than one page.[4]

Be neat. Given that employers have very limited time to spend reading your résumé, it must make an excellent overall impression. Employers judge you and your capabilities in part on the physical appearance of your résumé. Hiring managers will have a hard time ignoring poor proofreading and sloppiness, and your chances of securing an interview will significantly decrease.

Some résumés, as you can see in **Figure 15.1**, include an **objective statement**, *an articulation of your goal for the résumé*. This statement usually appears first, just below your contact information. Objective statements are important, because they allow you to tailor your credentials and goals to the needs of a particular organization and job description (or the formal duties and scope of a position).[5] The following are examples of objective statements:

- *To apply programming skills in an environment with short deadlines and demanding customers*
- *To achieve consistent improvement in sales profitability of units under my supervision*

Employers also want to see your educational credentials. In summarizing your education, you should include the degrees you have been awarded, your education completion dates (or anticipated completion dates), the schools you've attended, your majors and minors, and your honors or scholarships. The latest U.S. census information surveying people 25 years and older, illustrated in **Figure 15.3**, indicates that completing a bachelor's degree places you among the most highly educated people in the country.[6] Earning a college degree demonstrates to future employers that you are motivated, dedicated, and driven, and completing your degree while earning high grades, working part-time, or involving yourself in extracurricular activities improves your chances of landing a job. If your work history is limited, these educational experiences can help bolster your potential as a job candidate.

Whether you are a freshly minted college graduate or an experienced individual changing jobs or careers, employers will also look at the types of jobs you have held, as well as your job tenures, job duties, and professional accomplishments. When describing your work experience, include a job title, the name of the organization, the dates of your employment, and a description (using action verbs) of your major responsibilities and achievements.

In the list of your previous job duties, list those that are most critical to the job you are applying for first, with the least relevant one last on the list. In adapting your résumé to a particular job, include key words and phrases from

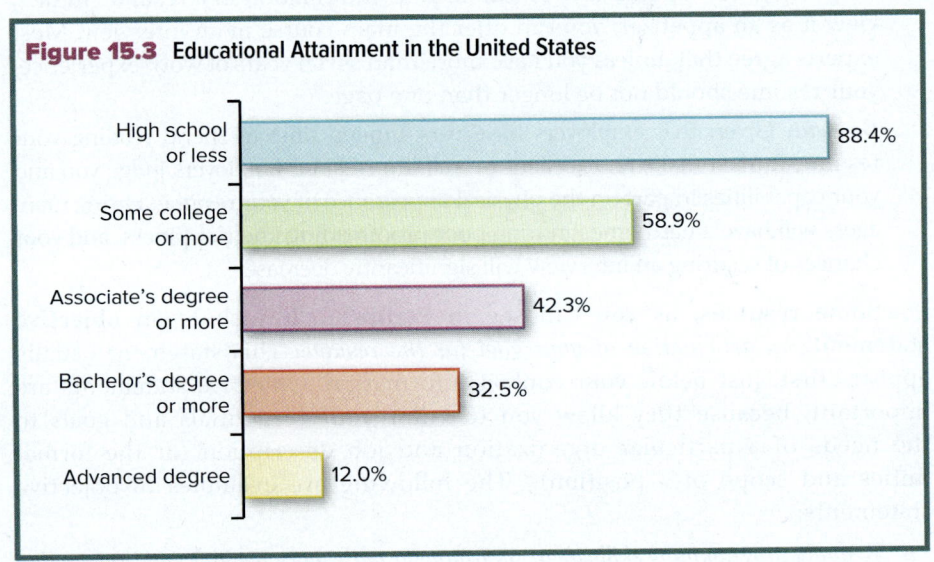

Figure 15.3 Educational Attainment in the United States

- High school or less: 88.4%
- Some college or more: 58.9%
- Associate's degree or more: 42.3%
- Bachelor's degree or more: 32.5%
- Advanced degree: 12.0%

the posted job description. In large organizations, the staff uses electronic databases to search through hundreds of résumés to find perfect matches between jobs and people. If your résumé contains key words from the job advertisement, it is more likely to make the cut.

Some résumés also include a skills section highlighting the candidate's abilities, ranging from the ability to use specialized computer applications to fluency in multiple languages. The skills section of a résumé should be tailored to the job description of the position for which you are applying.

Many college students end their résumés with a list of their campus activities and honors. Involvement in campus and community organizations shows that you are a well-rounded person and are community-minded.

©Oliver Hoslet/EPA/Newscom

Format

There are two main ways to organize your résumé: chronologically, as shown in **Figure 15.2**, and functionally, as in **Figure 15.4**. A **chronological résumé**, which *organizes your credentials over time*, is what most people envision when they think of a résumé. This has long been the standard and, despite technological advances allowing for electronic résumés, it continues to be the most widely accepted format. The purpose of a chronological résumé is to demonstrate your accomplishments over time. You begin with your present or most recent job and continue back to past jobs (see **Figure 15.2**).

A **functional résumé** *organizes your experience by the type of function performed*. If you have had a variety of career paths (such as retail, sales, and advertising), a functional résumé allows you to group these experiences according to the skills you developed and the duties you performed, rather than the places where you developed or performed them. Graduating college students can use a functional résumé to group "professional experience" separately from "other work experience," which may include jobs that do not directly relate to your career goal but nonetheless illustrate your work ethic.

Functional résumés give you an opportunity to focus on the skills and attributes you bring to the work you do. As a college student, perhaps you have held several short-term jobs and worry that your frequent changes in employment will scare off new employers. Your attributes might come from a range of places, such as community-engaged class projects, or groups to which you belong, such as sororities or fraternities. In such cases, a functional résumé will help you

Figure 15.4 A Sample Functional Résumé

YOUR NAME
email@emailaddress.com

Campus Address:
Street address
City, STATE zip code
(xxx) xxx-xxxx

Permanent Address:
Street address
City, STATE zip code
(xxx) xxx-xxxx

OBJECTIVE To lead company efforts in employee training, mentoring, and relations

SKILL SUMMARY Over ten years of experience in customer relations, employee relations, training, project development, and management. Skills across organizations:

- Customer Service & Relations
- Research Skills
- Teamwork/Collaboration
- Teaching & Training
- Microsoft Office Suite
- Staff Supervision
- Organizational Management
- Report Writing
- Professional Presentations

RELEVANT SKILLS

LEADERSHIP AND MENTORING SKILLS
- Instituted an anonymous online employee feedback and response mechanism
- Coordinated diverse service personnel for accurate and timely food delivery
- Trained new employees on the implementation of a shadow mentorship program
- Motivated employees to be more proactive and independent in their areas

PROBLEM-SOLVING AND DECISION-MAKING SKILLS
- Researched and reconciled cash and accounting discrepancies
- Interviewed and hired job candidates
- Responded to unexpected crises and problems from food shortages to missed shifts

CUSTOMER RELATIONS SKILLS
- Listened to and resolved customer concerns and complaints
- Implemented a new procedure for customer complaint responses
- Designed and maintained physical space with customer needs in mind
- Corresponded with the corporate office about staff training and development

EMPLOYMENT HISTORY
Assistant Manager, Target	2012–present
Accounting Office, Walmart	2011–2012
Customer Service Specialist, JCPenney	2010–2011
Assistant Kitchen Manager, Red Robin	2009–2010

EDUCATION
B.S., Communication Studies, Kent State University — Expected: 2014
- Major Concentration: **Applied Communication**
- Minors: **Human Resource Management** and **Public Relations**

HONORS
- Lambda Pi Eta National Communication Assoc. Honor Society, President
- School of Communication Studies Senior Scholar, Award Recipient

REFERENCES

Name
Professional Title
Company
(xxx) xxx-xxxx
E-mail address

Name
Professional Title
Company
(xxx) xxx-xxxx
E-mail address

Name
Professional Title
Company
(xxx) xxx-xxxx
E-mail address

identify the unique experiences you've had, as well as the skills you've gained from them.

If you decide to put together a functional résumé, begin by studying the job for which you are applying. Next, before you begin drafting, make sure you know what attributes the employer is looking for; this is an important step no matter which résumé format you choose. Where can you find that information? Start with the job description, the company's website, and blogs or articles discussing your field. Employers were recently asked to rank a lengthy list of attributes from 0 to 100, based on how important they are to an individual's job candidacy. **Figure 15.5** lists the top ten attributes employers seek when evaluating résumés. The percentage aligned with each attribute reflects the average ranking each attribute received.[7]

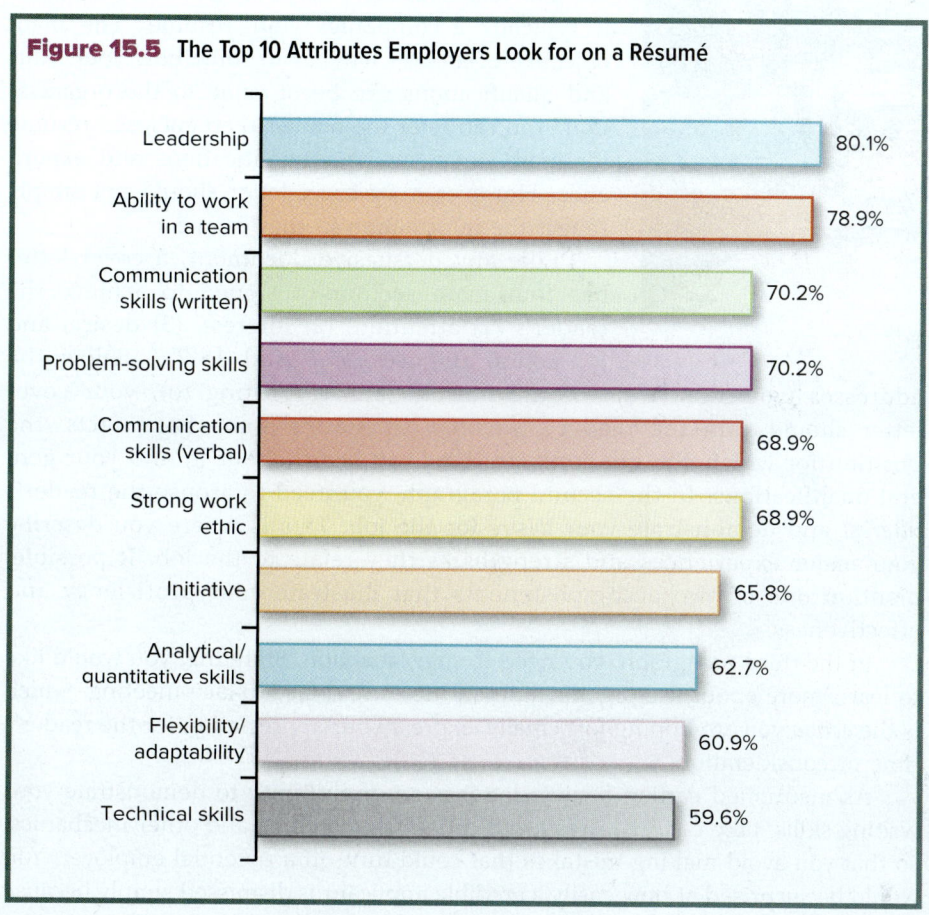

Figure 15.5 The Top 10 Attributes Employers Look for on a Résumé

- Leadership — 80.1%
- Ability to work in a team — 78.9%
- Communication skills (written) — 70.2%
- Problem-solving skills — 70.2%
- Communication skills (verbal) — 68.9%
- Strong work ethic — 68.9%
- Initiative — 65.8%
- Analytical/quantitative skills — 62.7%
- Flexibility/adaptability — 60.9%
- Technical skills — 59.6%

Producing a Winning Résumé **333**

You might consider using some of the attributes listed in **Figure 15.5** as categories in your functional résumé. Some of these, like competent written communication skills, should be demonstrated in the way you present your résumé as well—avoid grammatical errors and use strong action verbs in describing your attributes.

Many colleges and universities have career centers whose staff will critique your résumé and cover letter for free. They also have resources to help you conduct a successful job search and produce a winning résumé. Stop in to your school's career center well before your senior year and become familiar with the services and resources available.

WRITING A CONVINCING COVER LETTER

©Spencer Grant/Photo Edit

A **cover letter** *persuasively illustrates the ways in which you and your credentials match the job description,* and it typically accompanies your résumé. The main objective of a cover letter is to show how your skills and qualifications can be of value to the organization. You can refer the reader to an enclosed résumé for more detail on your qualifications and experience. However, your cover letter should not simply repeat the information in the résumé.

Like any persuasive document, a cover letter has four main sections designed to achieve the reader's (1) attention, (2) interest, (3) desire, and (4) action (**Figures 15.6** and **15.7**).[8] Below the addresses (yours and that of the person you are writing to), your cover letter should gain the reader's *attention* by stating some basic facts: the position for which you are applying, how you heard about it, and your general qualifications. In the second paragraph, you need to arouse the reader's *interest* and demonstrate your *desire* for the job. This is where you describe your major experiences and strengths as they relate to the job. If possible, mention one or two accomplishments that illustrate your proficiency and effectiveness.

In the third paragraph, you need to suggest action. State that you would like to learn more about the organization and to have a face-to-face meeting, which is the *action* you are hoping for. Finally, express your appreciation for the reader's time or consideration.

As mentioned earlier, a cover letter is an opportunity to demonstrate your writing skills; take care with respect to grammar, spelling, and other mechanics, so that you avoid making mistakes that could turn off a potential employer. You would be surprised at how easily a credible applicant is dismissed simply because of correctable errors. If you opt to send e-mail queries to potential employers, remember that they are cover letters, too. Make them formal and persuasive, and include your résumé as an attachment.

Figure 15.6 The Parts of a Cover Letter

HEADING
Your Name
Address
City, STATE, zip code
Phone
e-mail address

INSIDE ADDRESS
Name, Title
Department, Organization
Address
City, STATE, zip code

DATE

SALUTATION: Use title and last name if available (e.g., Dear Dr. Smith or Dear Ms. Jones). Do not use a first name unless you know the person well and are sure this is acceptable. If you do not have a name, use the title (e.g., Dear Employment Manager).

PARAGRAPH I: Gain *attention* and state *purpose:* Indicate the position or type of work for which you are applying. Mention how you heard about the opening or the organization. You may also want to provide a general overview of your qualifications for the position as a preview statement for your letter.

PARAGRAPH II: Arouse *interest* and demonstrate *desire*. Describe your major strengths as they relate to the position you are seeking. If possible, mention one or two recent accomplishments that illustrate your proficiency and effectiveness. Refer the reader to the enclosed résumé for more detail on your qualifications and experience.

PARAGRAPH III: Suggest *action*. Restate your strong interest in the position or organization and your desire for a face-to-face meeting. Include a statement about how the reader may contact you. Finally, express your appreciation for the reader's time and/or consideration.

COMPLIMENTARY CLOSE (Sincerely yours,)

_____
_____

NAME
POSTSCRIPT (Enclosure; Enc.)

Figure 15.7 A Sample Cover Letter

Excited Applicant's Name
Street address
City, STATE zip code
(xxx) xxx-xxxx
email@emailaddress.com

March 20, 2013

Hiring Official's Name
Human Resources, Fab Designs
City, STATE zip code

Dear Hiring Official's Name,

I am writing with interest in a content development position at Fab Designs, a top public relations firm providing high-level professional services to its clients. I hope you will find that my education and experience have prepared me for a position with your firm.

As a content developer at Create, I took on a variety of leadership roles. I led the company's transition to a new design software program and trained all staff in its use, an initiative that helped to increase our sales and make procedures more efficient. I also trained interns in company procedures, as well as managed their day-to-day work flow. I am now interested in putting my content development and leadership skills to use at a larger public relations firm.

For all of these reasons, I am very excited to learn about positions at Fab Designs. I hope to have the opportunity to discuss my qualifications with you in person, and I will look forward to hearing from you soon.

Sincerely,

Excited Applicant
Enclosure

CONNECTING GLOBALLY

USE SOCIAL MEDIA AND FACE-TO-FACE COMMUNICATION IN JOB SEARCHES

If you are an international candidate for a job, mediated communication makes it possible for you to network and interview across great distances. In your job searches, make the most effective use of all forms of mediated communication, including filling out online application materials, keeping your LinkedIn profile up-to-date, contacting possible job leads by e-mail, and making the appropriate follow-up phone calls. These efforts will demonstrate to potential employers your ambition, drive, and desire to put your talents to work for them.

If you are a domestic candidate, you may have the chance to engage in face-to-face communication during your job search. Doing so can make all the difference. When you meet an employer in person, you have the opportunity to show off your personality and skills. Getting to know you personally can help key decision makers differentiate you from all the other candidates.

MASTERING THE JOB INTERVIEW

Before you have the opportunity to meet with a potential employer in a face-to-face interview, you likely will be expected to participate in either a phone or a video-format interview. This is even more likely if the job for which you are interviewing is in another city, state, or country. Advances in interactive communication technology have made these forms of interviewing far less expensive and more reliable than they were even a few years ago.

In a phone interview, you can do several things to use the format to your advantage. If you are being interviewed by a group of people over the phone, keep a notepad handy. When people introduce themselves to you at the beginning, write down each person's name and some type of personal identifier, such as the sound of the person's voice, that will make it easier for you to remember who is speaking. Then, use the interviewers' names as much as possible during the interview to demonstrate that you are friendly and a good listener.

Before you go into any interview, you should know as much as you can about the organization and the functions of the job. Carry out a phone interview in a place where you can spread out all of your notes to use as a reference, if you need them. Choose a location that will be free of distractions, so that you can concentrate as much as possible on the interviewers and the questions being asked.

Another popular format for employment interviews is interactive video. Several Internet-based programs enable video interviews, including Skype, Facetime, ooVoo, and Google Video, each with advantages and drawbacks.[9] Testing any of these technologies beforehand with a friend can help you learn how to use the program, how your image comes across on video, and the optimal lighting and camera angle to achieve the image you desire during your interview.

During video interviews, pay attention to nonverbal communication. Use a set of headphones, if possible, to cut down on distortion and feedback that might be picked up by your or the interviewer's microphone. Also, professional attire is just as important for a video interview as it is with face-to-face interviews; dress professionally.

Carefully consider the environment where you are planning to conduct your video interview. Select a professional location that will positively reinforce your overall credibility with the interviewer—not your home, unless you have a professional office or another location that is free of personal possessions and other potentially distracting objects. Arrange to be interviewed where you can be hardwired to the Internet for your connection (e.g., Ethernet or cable connection); don't take chances by relying on the signal strength and quality of a wireless connection. Do whatever you can to remove any possible distortions or distractions that may occur during a video interview; if someone's voice cuts in and out or your interview has to be disconnected and reconnected, you will lose valuable time that could have been spent interacting with the employer and asking relevant questions.

Do not be surprised if you undergo several rounds of interviews for a position with different people (and in different formats) or experience a group interview, in which multiple people evaluate your responses at the same time. During the interview you must present yourself as a potential asset to the organization, which requires using both verbal and nonverbal communication. Specifically, you want to create a good first impression, speak with clarity, and demonstrate interest.

Create a Good First Impression

First impressions are critical in a job interview. You have about 30 seconds to create a positive first impression. One of the most obvious ways is to dress appropriately. The general rule is to match the style of dress of the interviewer. You can learn about the company's dress code by asking someone who works there, by visiting the organization to observe people, or simply by asking a receptionist at the company. However, if you cannot acquire information about the dress code, you are better off dressing more professionally than casually when you show up for an interview.

©SolStock/Getty Images RF

Taking the time to look professional will demonstrate that you care about the job and your first impressions. For professional positions, conservative dress is typically appropriate—that means dark suits, white shirts or blouses, standard ties for men, dark socks or neutral hose, dark shoes. Be modest in your use of jewelry and cologne. Of course, arrive on time and take cues from the interviewer on how to act while also trying to present yourself in an honest, positive way. For example, use a firm handshake when you meet the interviewer, and if the interviewer stands, you should remain standing.

Speak with Clarity

The way you use grammar can deeply influence the impressions others form about you in professional settings, such as job interviews.[10] Even if you have to pause before responding to questions, organize your answers and avoid slurring your words. Never use potentially offensive language; always use proper grammar. Avoid vocalized pauses ("uh," "um"), verbal fillers ("you know"), and repetitive phrases ("things like that"). If you practice beforehand and you feel confident about your qualifications, you should be able to speak with clarity and precision.

Demonstrate Interest

To be effective in interviews, you must demonstrate interest in the interviewer and the company. One of the most important and meaningful ways to do so is by maintaining strong eye contact with the interviewer.[11] Although you may believe that responding to questions is the central interviewing skill, good listening is also crucial, and it can improve your responses. Use body language to show interest. Smile, nod, and give nonverbal feedback to the interviewer, and thank the interviewer for his or her time and consideration of you as a candidate.

MORE TIPS FOR THE INTERVIEW

Beyond the general interviewing tips discussed in the previous section, there are things you can do to increase your chances of having a successful interview: understand the job and the company and prepare for behavioral-based interview questions.

Understand the Job

A **job description** *defines the content and scope of a position*. Although the format can vary, all job descriptions include at least some of the following information: job duties and responsibilities; the knowledge, skills, and abilities necessary to accomplish the duties; the working conditions; responsibilities in relation to coworkers, supervisors, and external stakeholders; and the extent of the supervision required. You will have studied the job description in order to craft your résumé and cover letter, but it doesn't hurt to return to it before an interview. Doing so will signal to you the types of questions you may be asked and will help you think about your answers and how you will describe your qualifications.

Understand the Company

Job applicants and interviewees lose all credibility when they cannot demonstrate even superficial knowledge of the organization to which they are applying. Taking time to carefully research the company will showcase your initiative, help you be conversant, and prepare you to ask better questions. When appropriate during an interview, signal that you know about the company. For example, if you are asked why you would like to work for the company, say something specific about the company that you admire or have found out from your research.

Besides using obvious sources of information in your research, like the company's website, check your library for specialized resources, such as the Lexis-Nexis Business Insight Solutions or the Bloomberg Businessweek Company Insight Center. These sources can lead you to information about the company's finances, its executive officers, and other pertinent facts. Small businesses may not be indexed in such databases, however; a local library or chamber of commerce may have information about these.

Prepare for Behavioral-Based Interview Questions

Some companies have transitioned to the use of **behavioral-based interview questions**, *which ask the interviewee to describe a situation or an experience that demonstrates skills that are relevant to the position at the company*. Behavioral-based interview questions force the applicant to respond with concrete answers.

The best way to prepare for behavioral-based interview questions is to think about your own work and life history and create what you might refer to as an **experience inventory**, *a story or two from your work history or life that relate to the position you seek and show what kind of person and worker you are*. The prompts in the following nine areas[12] should help you with your inventory:

- *Job skill and overall work experience.* Describe your most significant work accomplishments.
- *Intelligence.* Give an example of a time when you used your fact-finding skills to solve a problem.
- *Maturity and judgment.* Describe an important work decision you have had to make in the recent past. Whom did you consult, and how did you go about making that decision?
- *Responsibility.* Give an example of when you showed initiative and took the lead on a project. Or give an example of a time when you set a goal and achieved it.
- *Relationships.* Describe a project in which others you were working with disagreed with your ideas. What did you do? Or give an example of a time when you motivated others.
- *Resourcefulness.* How do you determine what gets priority in scheduling your time? Or describe a situation when you had several things to do in a limited time, such as study for multiple exams. What led up to the situation? How did you handle it? What was the outcome?
- *Work attitude.* Tell about a time you had to learn something new in a short period of time. Or have you ever had to discipline or counsel an employee or a group member? Explain.

- *Motivation*. Give an example of a time when you motivated others. Tell the most difficult customer service experience you have ever had to handle. What did you do, and what was the outcome?
- *Leadership*. Give an example of a time when you went beyond the call of duty in order to get the job done. Or tell about a time when you were in charge of something and had to let others help you.

When answering behavioral-based interview questions, keep the following guidelines in mind:

- *Be concise.* When preparing, think about the pieces of information that are critical to the point you want to make with a story. Expand or omit according to that central point or theme. Get to the point of your story quickly, so that you can also explain what it means.
- *Select examples that highlight important information about you.* An interviewer asks behavioral-based questions to determine what skills have emerged from your previous experiences. If an interviewer asked you to discuss a time that you used fact-finding skills to solve a problem, you could tell a story that showcased your skill in using the Internet to locate sound research-based sources. For example, you could say, "I know that when I think about problems I like to rely on proven expertise and that I'm good at locating a variety of pieces of evidence on the Internet quickly," and then tell a story that highlights the development of this skill.
- *Explain the moral, conclusion, or lesson learned from your experience.* One way to end a behavioral-based response is to identify explicitly what the story shows about you. If when telling your story you wish to highlight the value of persistence and a sound education, you might say, "When I started looking for sources for a paper, I first consulted my textbook and then I went to the library. Neither of these approaches worked. I then remembered a lesson a professor had taught about using Google Scholar to locate a range of sources on a topic. I applied what I had learned from this professor to the exploration of my paper topic and found exactly the type of information I was looking for. Therefore, not giving up on the task and relying on my education made the difference."

©Suriya Yapin/ Shutterstock RF

- *Connect this lesson to the organization, if possible.* The person asking you behavioral-based questions wants to see how your skills and values merge with the company's work practices. If you can see a way to make that connection for the interviewer, do so. Returning to the example about Internet research, you might say, "I imagine these Internet-based research skills and the need for persistence will also be extremely relevant to the job we're discussing."

SKILL BUILDER

PRACTICE BEHAVIORAL-BASED INTERVIEWING

Ask a classmate or close friend to practice behavioral-based interviewing with you. Choose a real company or organization on which to base your questions. Take turns selecting one of the nine experience inventory areas (job skills and overall work experience, intelligence, maturity and judgment, responsibilities, relationships, resourcefulness, work attitude, motivation, and leadership), and ask each other a behavioral-based question tied to the company you are pretending to interview for.

- Was the experience concisely described?
- Did the example highlight important information about the interviewee?
- Was the moral or lesson learned from the experience clear to the interviewer?
- Did the answer clearly tie back to the organization?

Finish the exercise by offering each other tips on other experiences you might mention with regard to each subject area. What might you do to improve your experience inventory?

BUILDING CONNECTIONS

As you have seen, being able to present yourself effectively in writing and during interviews is crucial to your professional development. Another skill that will play a vital role in opening doors in your profession is building connections, also known as networking.

From your very first college class, you should begin to think about the professional contacts you are making and how you will make the most of those connections. For example, you should think of each of your instructors as a professional resource with connections that may benefit you. Your instructors might eventually write letters of recommendation for you, so going above and beyond what is expected of you in class will help you stand out in their eyes, resulting in stronger letters of recommendation.

Use Social Media to Expand Your Professional Network

One way to strengthen your professional network during college is to make effective use of job-related social media sites, like LinkedIn. They can help you build a strong professional network and learn about what other people in your field are doing with their careers. Don't wait to take steps to strengthen your digital presence—develop your résumé as your studies progress, update it frequently, and post it on a professional social media site.

LinkedIn is the largest professional network on the Internet, operating in over 200 countries with an estimated 187 million members worldwide.[13] Although you should certainly make use of your career center to locate possible job prospects, also post your credentials on LinkedIn, where job opportunities around the globe, and beyond your academic network, could present themselves. Furthermore, you can always use job-related social media to explore ideas with a larger network and get feedback from other professionals. LinkedIn allows professionals to display their credentials and network with people who have similar interests, regardless of where they live.[14]

Using social media can help with professional advancement opportunities as well. But keep in mind that you are not the only one using social media to network and learn about possible job prospects. Many human resource professionals use LinkedIn, Facebook, and other social networking sites to find out about the personal lives of job applicants.[15] Moreover, if you already have a job, but are looking for a better opportunity, protect your privacy and limit who has access to your profile.

One way to prevent possible breakdowns in your private information on social media is to carefully consider the information you make available.[16] Periodically review any posts, photos, comments, and tagged information available through any of your social media networks. Ask yourself if you're comfortable with future employers evaluating you based on that information.[17] If you find information that you or others have posted that could hurt your job search, delete it. Everything connected to you through social media impacts your reputation and networking potential. Use social media cautiously to help ensure that career and networking opportunities remain open to you.[18]

Use Internships as a Networking Opportunity

With so many job openings, you might wonder, "Why should I take the time to complete an internship before applying for a job?" Much like your education, an internship is an investment in yourself and your future. It is true that many degree programs will not require you to complete an internship; however, required or not, an internship could be the best way to start your career.

If you find that putting together a résumé is difficult because you do not have enough work experience in your field, an internship can help you expand your résumé and improve your job prospects.[19] When organizations make hiring decisions, they look for people with strong practical experience. An internship is one way to extend and enrich your education beyond classroom learning.

Internships also give you a short-term, low-risk way to explore various career options.[20] If you are pursuing a degree in the healthcare industry, you might learn through internship experience that you prefer to work with children rather than adults. This knowledge will help you limit the types of positions you apply for and ensure that you will feel satisfied in the career you choose. Or you might like to go into business management but you don't know if you'd prefer to work for a large firm or small company. You could intern with companies of various sizes to learn more about being a leader in both small and large organizational systems. This will also prepare you to speak to prospective employers about your direct experiences in leading a variety of organizational teams.

Finally, internships are a great way to expand your professional network. When you begin your career search at the end of your degree program,

©Steven Debenport/Getty Images RF

weak ties will play a vital role in your job searches. **Weak ties** are *people whom you do not know very well and who do not have a strong relationship with you*, like coworkers, previous internship partners, neighbors, and general acquaintances. On the other hand, **strong ties** are *people with whom you have a well-developed relationship and to whom you turn for advice frequently*. Your strong ties may include close friends, family, and others you know well and trust. All of these connections—but your weak ties, in particular—can help you find job opportunities you may not find on your own.[21]

You should not downplay the value of completing an internship or taking temporary work for a company. In an internship role, you are being assessed as a potential employee in the industry while gaining practical skills that will bolster your résumé. Even though only some internships are paid, even those for which there is no financial compensation offer valuable opportunities to build your skills. In fact, you should think of internships as on-the-job interviews and opportunities to expand your professional network.

Use the Informational Interview to Learn

One final thing that you can do to network, even as you complete your college degree, is to seek out information about the careers that interest you. You can do this by conducting informational interviews with professionals who hold positions to which you aspire. Ask a professional in your field how she got her start in the industry, what it takes to make it, and what advice she might give to someone trying to break into the field in a positive way. Everyone has something to teach you, and an informational interview will only strengthen your prospects. To ensure that you get the most out of informational interviews, there are a few simple steps you can follow before, during, and after the interview.

Before the Interview. Before informational interviews there are a few things you can do to be adequately prepared. First, do your homework. You should be knowledgeable about the company, the person you are interviewing, and any information that is readily available through Internet research. If you are not prepared, the person you are interviewing may feel that you do not value his time.

Second, prepare appropriate questions. The types of questions you ask reveal how much passion and preparation you have put forward. Therefore, you might ask a professional you admire what is unique about his job. Ask questions that can't be answered through information that is readily available.

Next, go into an informational interview with 5–10 questions to guide your time with the interviewee. You want to be prepared, but you do not want to be so rigidly connected to your questions that you miss opportunities to follow up on information that emerges out of the conversation.

Make connections to information you have uncovered in your research, and ask questions that take it further whenever possible. You might ask, "I read in your online profile that early in your career you didn't do much consulting work. How did you make the transition from one type of work to the other?"

CHALLENGE YOURSELF

How in the world am I going to get a job when I graduate? I have limited professional experience and am not all that great at networking. What should I do?

When it comes to networking for your chosen career, informational interviews are an often overlooked method. It can be difficult to make contact with someone who has a wealth of experience in an area in which you hope to work. But keep in mind that people are often happy to talk about the work they do. Asking for professional advice from someone you see as successful is one of the highest forms of flattery. If you do your homework and demonstrate some knowledge of the person and his career, he will more than likely give you advice and perhaps be willing to help you in your job search down the road.

Everyone's professional journey is a little bit different. Don't feel that one person's pathway to success is the only one. After conducting an informational interview with someone you respect, be mindful of what is unique to that person's experience, as well as what you can apply to your own job-search process.

And don't give up. Anything that is worthwhile takes dedication and perseverance. If you learn from others and apply what you learn, you will find that others will seek your advice, too.

Finally, before interviews, ask those you interview if they are comfortable with your using an audio recorder, so that you can focus on their responses and review them later. In addition to asking permission, make sure you have access to the technology. With the advances in smartphone devices and technology, there is a range of tools and applications you can use. If you do not have a way to record an interview, you can borrow a recorder from a friend or check one out from your local library.

During the Interview. When conducting an informational interview, there are several things you should keep in mind that will make the interview more enjoyable. First impressions are critical. Arriving early will help you manage a positive and professional first impression. Throughout the interview act courteously; when it's over, express your appreciation for the person's willingness to talk with you.

Second, be flexible. Your interviewee may answer two or three of your planned questions at once. If this happens, adapt, jump ahead, and go with the flow of the interview. Read the nonverbal cues you learned in **Chapter 3**. If it becomes clear that your subject is talking about something she enjoys, ask an unplanned follow-up question. If she appears to be uncomfortable with the direction of the conversation, move on to another question.

Third, practice active listening techniques during the informational interview. Show that you care about the person's answers. To be sure that you understand the insights your subject is sharing, paraphrase his main points from time to time to demonstrate the care with which you are listening.

Finally, before you end an informational interview, allow the interviewee to ask you questions. Your subject may have questions or additional insights for you, so allow time for them, as well as time to share general reflections.

After the Interview. After an informational interview, take some time to think about and process what you heard during the interview. You may want to jot down some quick reflections or insights you do not want to forget. Make sure the person you interviewed feels appreciated for his time and insights; send a thank-you card in the mail. It's a novelty today to get a card rather than a quick thank-you e-mail. Be specific as you draft your thank-you, and write one thing that you gained from the interview experience.

Finally, if appropriate, ask the people you interview if you can add them to your professional network. Ask if they use LinkedIn, and send a request. They then will be in your network when you finish your education and are looking for a job. You may have additional opportunities to network down the road.

CHAPTER REVIEW

Presenting yourself effectively in writing and orally will open up professional opportunities that would not otherwise be available to you. Begin networking well before you need professional connections; if you wait until the need is critical to your job search, you will find it more difficult to build those relationships. Critically thinking about the information you communicate in these contexts can be the difference between continuing your job search and landing your dream job.

KEY TERMS

style, 325
objective statement, 329
chronological résumé, 331
functional résumé, 331
cover letter, 334
job description, 339

behavioral-based interview
   questions, 340
experience inventory, 340
weak ties, 344
strong ties, 344

STUDY QUESTIONS

1. What are some of the career options related to studying communication? How might communication skills prepare you for a job in your field of choice?
2. Why should you use strong action verbs when creating job function descriptions? Choose three of the action verbs listed in **Table 15.2**, and draft one clause for each that describes your own present or past employment experience.
3. Consider the four main sections that make up a cover letter. How does each of these sections help you persuade a company to hire you?
4. How might you create a strong first impression at a job interview?
5. What are the nine behavioral-based interview question areas? Think of a question for each area that an interviewer might ask you. Next, answer those questions using the advice given in this chapter.
6. What would you do before, during, and after an informational interview to help you build more connections and network more effectively?

ENDNOTES

1. National Association of Colleges and Employers. (2016). *Job outlook 2016*. Retrieved from www.naceweb.org
2. Wright, E. W., Domagalski, T. A., & Collins, R. (2011). Improving employee selection with a revised resume format. *Business Communication Quarterly, 74*, 272–286.
3. Henricks, M. (2000). *Kinko's guide to the winning résumé*. United States of America: Kinko's.
4. Ibid.
5. Bennett, S. (2005). *The elements of resume style: Essential rules and eye-opening advice for writing resumes and cover letters that work*. New York: Amazon Books.
6. United States Census Bureau. (2016). *Educational attainment in the United States: 2015*. Retrieved from https://www.census.gov/topics/education/educational-attainment.html
7. National Association of Colleges and Employers.
8. Krizan, A., Merrier, P., & Jones, C. (2002). *Business communication* (5th ed.). Cincinnati: South-Western.
9. Smith, M. W. (2011, May 21). The best option for video calling. *USA Today*. Retrieved from http://usatoday30.usatoday.com/tech/products/2011-05-21-video-calls_n.htm
10. Lipovsky, C. (2006). Candidates' negotiation of their expertise in job interviews. *Journal of Pragmatics, 38*, 1147–1174.
11. Young, M. J., Behnke, R. R., & Mann, Y. M. (2004). Anxiety patterns in employment interviews. *Communication Reports, 17*, 49–57.
12. U.S. Department of Commerce National Oceanic & Atmospheric Administration. (2013). *Sample interview questions based on nine basic competency areas [report]*. Retrieved from www.esrl.noaa.gov/outreach/student_programs/HelpfulInterviewTips.pdf
13. LinkedIn. (2013, January 7). *About us*. Retrieved from www.press.linkedin.com/about
14. Roberts, S. J., & Roach, T. (2009). Social networking websites and human resource personnel: Suggestions for job searches. *Business Communication Quarterly, 72*, 110–114.
15. Ibid.

16. Child, J. T., Petronio, S., Agyeman-Budu, E. A., & Westermann, D. A. (2011). Blog scrubbing: Exploring triggers that change privacy rules. *Computers in Human Behavior, 27*, 2017–2027.
17. Frampton, B. D., & Child, J. T. (2013). Friend or not to friend: Coworker Facebook friend requests as an application of communication privacy management theory. Computers in Human Behavior, 29, 2257–2264.
18. Child, J. T., Haridakis, P. M., & Petronio, S. (2012). Blogging privacy rule orientations, privacy management, and content deletion practices: The variability of online privacy management activity at different stages of social media use. *Computers in Human Behavior, 28*, 1859–1872.
19. National Association of Colleges and Employers.
20. Branham, L. (2001). *Keeping the people who keep you in business: 24 ways to hang on to your most valuable talent*. New York: American Management Association.
21. Granovetter, M. S. (1973). The strength of weak ties. *American Journal of Sociology, 81*, 1287–1303.

Blue and Yellow Cube Icon, Connecting Globally Icon, Mountain Icon, Chapter Review Arrows Circle Icon: ©McGraw Hill Education

GLOSSARY

A

adoption Listeners start a new behavior as a result of a persuasive presentation.

ageist language Language that denigrates people based on their age, whether young or old.

agenda-setting The process of shaping what topics are considered critical for discussion by society.

aggressiveness Occurs when people stand up for their rights at the expense of others' and care about their own needs but no one else's.

alliteration The repetition of the initial sound of a word.

ambiguous words Words that can be interpreted in multiple ways.

analogy A comparison of things that are otherwise dissimilar.

analytical function The use of critical thinking skills to evaluate and critique an issue or idea.

androgynous Referring to a person who possesses both stereotypically male and stereotypically female traits.

antonym Defines an idea by opposition.

argument A form of discourse that attempts to persuade.

argumentativeness A predisposition to recognize controversial issues, advocate positions, and refute opposing positions.

articulation The production of sounds.

artifacts Ornaments or adornments we display that hold communicative potential.

asynchronous communication Communication that occurs when the people involved experience a delay in interacting with one another and take turns being senders and receivers of information.

attitude A predisposition to respond favorably or unfavorably to a person, an object, an idea, or an event.

attractiveness Includes physical attractiveness, how desirable a person is to work with, and how much "social value" the person has for others.

audience analysis The collection and interpretation of audience characteristics through observation, inferences, questionnaires, and the Internet.

automatic attention We listen in spite of ourselves, without effort.

autonomy and connectedness Having an interest in being close to others, but also needing to maintain a separate identity.

avoidance stage When two partners avoid each other, desiring separation.

B

bargaining The process that occurs when two or more parties attempt to reach an agreement on what each should give and receive in a relationship.

behavioral-based interview questions Interview questions that ask the interviewee to describe a situation or an experience that demonstrates skills that are relevant to the position at the company.

behavioral flexibility The ability to adapt to new situations and relate in new ways when necessary.

belief A conviction, often thought to be more enduring than an attitude and less enduring than a value.

bibliographic reference The complete citation information about a source, which is included in the "references" or "works cited" section at the end of a speech outline.

bodily aspects How to use one's body to convey meaning.

bodily movement What a speaker does with his or her entire body during a presentation.

body The largest part of a presentation, in which the speaker places his or her arguments and ideas, evidence and examples, proofs and illustrations, and stories and testimonials.

bonding stage When a couple communicate their relationship to others.

boomerang effect When an audience likes a speaker and his or her message less after the presentation than they did before.

boundary-crossing media A communication channel whose personal and professional uses span communication contexts.

brainstorming Thinking of as many topics as possible in a limited time to select one that will be appropriate for the audience.

C

captive audience An audience that does not choose to hear a speaker or his or her speech.

cause/effect pattern An organizational pattern in which the presenter first explains the causes of an event, a problem, or an issue and then discusses its consequences, results, or effects.

celebrity testimony Statements made by a public figure who is known to the audience.

channel The means by which a message moves from the source to the receiver of the message.

chronemics The way people organize, relate to, and use time and the messages that result.

chronological résumé A document that organizes a job seeker's credentials over time.

circumscribing stage When the primary focus is on setting limits and boundaries on communication between two people.

cliché An expression that has lost originality and force through overuse.

co-cultural groups Groups that include but are not limited to women, ethnic minorities, gay and lesbian individuals, immigrants and refugees, physically or mentally challenged persons, and even neighborhood gangs and political groups that have formed to promote a cause.

code A systematic arrangement of symbols used to create meanings in the mind of another person or persons.

codependency The tendency to depend on the needs of, or control by, another.

code sensitivity The ability to adapt to the verbal and nonverbal language of the individual with whom we are communicating, regardless of cultural or co-cultural differences.

code switching Shifting from one treatment of language to another based on the audience and place.

coercion When compliance is forced through hostile acts.

cognitive restructuring A technique for reducing public speaking anxiety that focuses on analyzing negative perceptions and developing coping statements for dealing with a variety of situations.

cohesiveness The attachment members feel toward each other and the group.

collectivist cultures Cultures that value the group over the individual.

commitment A measure of how much time and effort people put into a cause.

communication The process of using messages to generate meaning.

communication apprehension (CA) The fear of communicating with other people, whether that interaction is real or anticipated.

communication privacy management (CPM) theory A theory that focuses on the processes people use to decide whether to reveal or conceal private information and how to manage the private information they share with others.

comparison Shows the similarity between something well known and something less known.

complementarity The idea that we sometimes bond with people who provide something we do not have; in turn, we may have qualities or characteristics they lack.

complementing Goes beyond duplication of the message in two channels; the verbal and nonverbal codes add meaning to each other and expand the meaning of either message alone.

compliance-gaining Attempts to persuade another person to do something he or she might not ordinarily do.

compliance-resisting Occurs when targets of influence messages refuse to conform to requests.

computer-mediated communication (CMC) Human-to-human interaction using networked computer environments.

conclusion The end or final part of a speech.

concrete language Words and statements that are specific rather than abstract or vague.

conflict Occurs anytime two or more people have goals they perceive to be incompatible.

conflict management The use of language to resolve issues between or among individuals or groups.

connotative meanings The meanings people come to assign because of personal or individual experience.

content The literal meaning of a message.

context A set of circumstances, including a physical setting, an occasion, or a situation.

contradiction When verbal and nonverbal messages conflict.

contrast Clarifies by showing differences.

co-ownership rules Privacy rules that clarify our expectations for how others will treat our disclosures.

cover letter A document that persuasively illustrates the ways in which a job seeker and his or her credentials match a particular job description.

creative function When imagination meets writing or speaking ability.

criteria The standards by which a group must judge potential solutions to a problem.

cultivation effect The effect of heavy television and media use, which leads people to perceive reality as consistent with media portrayals.

cultural relativism Viewing other cultures as objectively as possible, without judgment.

culture A unique combination of traditions and customs that is transmitted through learning and that shapes the beliefs and behavior of the people who live within them.

D

data Facts that have been collected from a particular source.

data triangulation The process of verifying and confirming the results or insights from one source of information with other types of information on the same topic.

deceptive communication The practice of deliberately making somebody believe things that are untrue.

decoding The process of assigning meaning to an encoded message.

deductive argument Uses a general proposition applied to a specific instance, or minor premise, to draw a conclusion.

defensiveness Occurs when a person feels attacked.

delivery How a person's voice and body affect the meaning of a presentation.

demographic analysis The collection and interpretation of data such as name, age, sex, hometown, year in school, race, major subject, religion, and organizational affiliations.

demonstrating Showing the audience what the speaker is explaining.

denotative meaning The agreed-upon meaning of a word, or the meaning found in a dictionary.

description Giving an account of observed behavior or phenomena.

designated leader Someone who has been appointed or elected to a leadership position.

dialectic theory A theory that suggests that relationships include contrary tendencies or opposing values.

dialogue A conversation, discussion, or negotiation.

differentiating stage When differences are emphasized, as opposed to commonalities.

differentiation and specialization The division of labor in an organization and the degree to which each individual has a unique role and responsibility.

discontinuance A persuasive purpose rooted in convincing listeners to stop some current behavior.

dominant culture The group that has the most power, influence, and rights.

E

emergent leader Someone who exerts influence toward achievement of a group's goal but who does not hold the formal position or role of leader.

empathic listening The attempt to understand another person.

emphasis Using nonverbal cues to strengthen a message.

encoding The process of translating an idea or a thought into words.

enunciation The eighth vocal aspect of speech delivery; the pronunciation and articulation of sounds and words.

ethics A set of principles for right conduct.

ethos The reputation, authority, and integrity of a speaker.

ethnic group Consists of people who share common cultural elements—for example, language or religion—as well as a common history.

ethnocentrism The belief that one's own group or culture is superior to all other groups or cultures.

euphemism A generally harmless word, name, or phrase that replaces an offensive or suggestive one.

evidence Anything, physical or verbal, that helps in forming a conclusion or judgment.

examples Specific instances used to clarify a point.

experience inventory A story or two from an individual's work history or life that relate to the position and show what kind of person and worker he or she is.

experimentation stage The stage in which people make an effort to find some common ground, including background, interests, attitudes, or values.

expert testimony Information from a source who has enough credibility to speak about a specific topic.

explanation A means of developing an idea that simplifies or clarifies it while arousing audience interest.

explicit-rule culture A culture in which policies, procedures, and expectations are more likely to be discussed or negotiated.

extemporaneous mode A carefully prepared and practiced presentation in which the presenter delivers the message conversationally, without heavy dependence on notes.

extrinsic motivation The reasons outside the presentation that audience members will benefit from listening to it.

eye contact The extent to which a speaker looks directly at the audience.

F

facial expressions The nonverbal cues expressed by a speaker's face.

factual example An example based on real circumstances.

fear appeal A message designed to frighten or alarm an audience so they will be persuaded to act.

feedback The receiver's verbal and nonverbal response to the source's message.

figures of speech Expressions that draw relationships that help listeners remember.

fluency The smoothness of the delivery, the flow of the words, and the absence of vocalized pauses.

formal communication Messages that follow prescribed channels of communication throughout an organization.

formal (positional) role An assigned role based on an individual's position or title within a group.

formalization The rules, procedures, and norms that may exist for carrying out work practices.

functional résumé A document that organizes a job applicant's experience by the type of function performed.

G

gatekeeping The process of determining what news, information, or entertainment will reach a mass audience.

gestures Movements of the head, arms, and hands used to illustrate, emphasize, or signal ideas in a speech.

global communication Exchanges between people whose communication practices, patterns, and understandings differ because they come from distinct cultures.

grammatical errors Violations of the formal rules of written and spoken language.

group climate The emotional tone or atmosphere members create within a group.

groupthink A phenomenon that occurs in a group when the desire for cohesion and agreement takes precedence over critical analysis and discussion.

H

hearing The act of receiving sound.

hierarchy The levels of responsibility and relationships within an organization.

hostile work environment harassment It "occurs when unwelcome comments or conduct based on sex, race, or other legally protected characteristics unreasonably interferes with an employee's work performance or creates an intimidating, hostile, or offensive work environment" (FCC).

hurtful messages Messages that create emotional pain or upset; they can encourage the end of a relationship.

hyperbole The use of exaggeration to make a point.

hyperpersonal perspective The understanding that, in certain circumstances, CMC can be beneficial and rewarding, and perhaps even preferable to face-to-face interactions.

hypothetical example A fictional but realistic example.

I

identity management The control (or lack of control) of what we communicate and what it conveys about us.

illustration Clarifies by showing what something is.

imagery Figures of speech that hit at the senses and stimulate listeners' synapses to see, hear, and feel what words are saying.

immediacy When people engage in communication behaviors intended to create perceptions of psychological closeness with others.

immediate behavioral purposes The actions a speaker expects from an audience during and immediately after a presentation.

immediate purpose A statement of what a speaker intends to accomplish in a speech.

implicit-rule culture A culture in which cultural rules are embedded in tradition and followed faithfully.

impromptu mode When a presentation is delivered without notes, plans, or formal preparation, with spontaneity and conversational language.

individualistic cultures Cultures that value individual freedom, choice, uniqueness, and independence.

inductive argument An argument that provides enough specific instances that the listener can make an inferential leap to a generalization or conclusion.

inference A tentative generalization based on some evidence.

influence The power a person has to affect other people's thinking or actions.

informal communication Any interaction that emerges out of social interactions among organization members rather than following the rules of the formal chain of command.

informal (behavioral) role A role that develops naturally or spontaneously within a group.

information The selective groups of facts that help people understand sets of data.

information anxiety The experience of stress due to an inability to access, understand, or process information that is necessary to a goal or task at hand.

information hunger An audience's need for information, as created by the presenter.

information literacy The ability to locate, evaluate, and incorporate important information into our own knowledge base.

information overload The experience of having more data and information than we have the capacity to process in a given time period.

information relevance The importance, novelty, and usefulness of information to an audience.

informative content The main points and subpoints, illustrations, and examples used to clarify and inform.

initiating stage The relational stage that begins with the first impressions someone has of a potential partner.

instrumental function Using language as a directive—a means of getting others to think or do something.

integration stage When two people begin to merge their lives.

intensifying stage When the communication between two people changes and deepens.

intent What a speaker wants to communicate.

intercultural communication Interactions between people from different cultural backgrounds.

interdependence A situation in which people are mutually dependent and have an impact on each other.

internal references Citation information about specific evidence presented in the body of a speech.

interpersonal communication The process of exchanging meaning in interpersonal relationships. Three primary factors distinguish interpersonal relationships: (1) establishing a communicative relationship, (2) generating shared meanings, and (3) accomplishing social goals.

interpersonal relationships Associations between at least two people who are interdependent, who use consistent patterns of interaction, and who have interacted for an extended period of time.

interpretation The assignment of meaning to stimuli.

intimate distance Extends from the body outward to 18 inches; it is the distance used by people who are relationally close.

intrapersonal communication The kind of discussion and decision making that occurs within one's own mind.

introduction The first part of a presentation.

J

jargon The language particular to a specific profession, work group, or culture.

job description Defines the content and scope of a position.

K

key-word outline An outline consisting of important words or phrases to remind a speaker of the content of the speech.

kinesics The way we interpret nonverbal behavior related to movement, such as body language and facial expression.

knowledge Information with meaning attached to it.

L

language The code we use to communicate with each other.

lay testimony Statements made by ordinary people that substantiate or support what a presenter says.

leadership The process of using communication to influence the behaviors and attitudes of others.

linkage rules Privacy rules that clarify someone's need to have others exercise caution about sharing information with certain individuals.

listening The act of interpreting the sounds someone hears, to determine their meaning.

listening for pleasure We listen to relaxing, fun, or emotionally stimulating information.

logos Persuasion by using logical argument.

long-range goal A statement of purposes that could be achieved with continuing efforts to persuade.

long-term memory Memory reserved for facts, figures, and concepts that we know we have to remember.

M

main points The most important points in a speech.

maintenance functions Behaviors that focus on the interpersonal relationships among group members; they are aimed at supporting cooperation and harmony.

management The process of using communication to maintain structure, order, harmony, and the efficiency of procedures and practices.

manipulation Tricking people or using fraudulent means to gain compliance.

manuscript mode Delivering a presentation from a script of an entire speech.

mass communication Involves the use of print and electronic technology by professional communicators to share messages over great distances for large audiences.

mass media The specific means by which we use print and electronic technology to communicate.

meaning Whatever message someone is trying to convey to others, as well as how that message is interpreted.

media convergence The ways in which different technologies have evolved to perform similar outcomes or tasks.

media literacy The ability to think critically about mediated messages and how they influence us.

mediated communication Messages that are transmitted not directly from person to person but through some other communication tool, such as print, electronic, or digital communication devices.

memorized mode When a presentation is committed to memory.

message The verbal and nonverbal expression of the idea, thought, or feeling that one person (the source) wishes to communicate to another person or group of people (the receivers).

metaphor Creatively compares two things that do not at first seem alike.

mindful listening Focusing full attention on the speaker by paraphrasing, smiling, nodding, and providing other nonverbal indicators of conversational engagement.

Monroe Motivated Sequence A problem-solving organizational format (including the steps of attention, need, satisfaction, visualization, and action) that encourages an audience.

M-time A monochromatic time schedule that compartmentalizes time to meet personal needs and to separate tasks from social activities.

multitasking Trying to do two or more tasks at once.

N

narration The oral presentation and interpretation of a story, a description, or an event.

neologisms New words or new meanings for old words that are in the process of entering common use.

noise Any interference in the encoding and decoding processes that reduces the clarity of a message.

nonverbal codes Nonword symbols, gestures, or vocalizations that communicate meaning.

nonverbal communication The process of using wordless messages to generate meaning.

norms The beliefs about how individual members should interact and behave in a particular context.

novelty and predictability The wish to be able to predict events in a relationship; to yearn for the original and new.

O

objectics The study of the human use of clothing and other artifacts as nonverbal codes.

objective statement An articulation of the goal for a résumé.

observations Descriptions of what someone has directly seen, touched, tasted, smelled, or heard.

online library catalog system A program that allows users to explore all types of print and multimedia holdings and collections of the library.

operational definition Defines by explaining a process.

opinion leader A range of people consistently turn to that person for advice and informed perspectives on issues.

oral citations Spoken citations that make specific reference, where appropriate, to each source used in a presentation.

organization Grouping stimuli into meaningful units.

organizational culture The attitudes, values, and beliefs that are common and that characterize the interactions of organization members and the way they work and behave.

outline A written plan that uses symbols, margins, and content to reveal the order, importance, and substance of a speech.

P

paralinguistic features The nonword sounds and nonword characteristics of language, such as pitch, volume, rate, and quality.

paraphrasing Restating another person's message by rephrasing in one's own words.

pathos The use of emotional means of persuasion.

pause An absence of vocal sound used for dramatic effect, transition, or emphasis.

permeability rules Privacy rules that clarify how much private information someone is comfortable with others sharing about specific topics.

perception The process of using the senses to acquire information about the surrounding environment or situation.

perception checking Involves checking in with one's conversational partner to ensure one has a common understanding of an event that has occurred or a common definition of a particular phenomenon.

perceptual constancy Past experiences lead a person to see the world in a way that is difficult to change.

personal bias Letting our own prejudices interfere with our ability to interpret information accurately.

personal distance Ranges from 18 inches to 4 feet, and it is the distance most Americans use for conversation and other nonintimate exchanges.

personal experience Something that actually happened to a speaker.

personal space The distance we maintain between ourselves and others; the amount of space we claim as our own.

persuasive presentation A message strategically designed to induce change in the audience in some way consistent with the speaker's purpose.

phatic communication The most casual and often briefest exchanges that are intended to recognize the existence of another person and demonstrate sociability rather than provide information.

pitch The highness or lowness of a speaker's voice; the voice's upward and downward movement; and the melody produced by the voice.

power The ability to influence others.

prejudice A negative attitude toward a group of people just because they belong to that group.

primary source Original source of material or research.

privacy turbulence When those allowed to access someone's private information have not upheld the stipulated obligations.

problem/solution pattern The organizational pattern in which a presenter describes a problem and proposes a solution.

profanity Language that is vulgar, abusive, or disrespectful of things sacred.

projection Speaking loudly enough for all to hear.

pronunciation The act of correctly articulating words.

proof Any evidence that a receiver believes.

proposition of fact An assertion that can be proved or disproved.

proposition of policy A proposal of a new rule.

proposition of value A statement of what should be embraced as good or bad, right or wrong.

proxemics The study of the human use of space and distance.

proximity The location, distance, or range between persons and things.

pseudolistening Pretending to listen but letting the mind or attention wander to something else.

P-time A polychronic time schedule that views time as "contextually based and relationally oriented."

public distance Exceeds 12 feet and is the distance used most often in public speaking in such settings as lecture halls, churches, mosques, and synagogues.

Q

questionnaire A list of questions developed to obtain demographic and attitudinal information.

R

race A category of people distinguished by inherited features, such as skin color, facial features, or quality of hair.

racist language Language that is insulting because it associates skin color or ethnicity with stereotypical and usually negative characteristics.

rate The speed of delivery, or how fast we say our words.

receiver The intended target of the message.

reference librarians Librarians who are specially trained in finding and evaluating information.

references The sources used in a presentation.

reflexivity Being self-aware and learning from interactions with the intent of improving future interactions.

regionalisms Words and phrases specific to a particular region or part of the country.

regulation The use of nonverbal codes to monitor and control interactions with others.

relational maintenance When a couple begin establishing strategies for keeping the relationship together.

repetition Occurs when the same message is sent verbally and nonverbally, or when someone uses the same word choices over and over again to stress a central point.

responsiveness The idea that we tend to develop relationships with people who demonstrate positive interest in us.

role A part a person plays in a social context.

rough draft A preliminary organization of an outline.

rules of engagement Rules about initiating, conducting, and ending a verbal exchange.

S

scanning and choosing A process of taking in stimuli and choosing what to listen to and how.

search engine A website that is used specifically to search for information.

secondary source A source of information that builds on or comments on another's material or research.

selection The decisions we make to focus on some stimuli—sights, sounds, smells, and other sensations—and neglect others.

selective attention The sustained focus we choose to give to things that are important to us.

self-centered functions Behaviors that serve the needs of the individual at the expense of the group.

self-disclosure The process of making intentional revelations about ourselves that others would be unlikely to know and that generally constitute private, sensitive, or confidential information.

seminal sources Foundational studies or pieces of information that have been heavily cited and have helped advance a line of scholarly inquiry.

sentence outline An outline consisting entirely of complete sentences.

sexist language Language that excludes individuals on the basis of gender.

sexual harassment Unwelcome, unsolicited, repeated behavior of a sexual nature.

short-term memory Where we temporarily store information.

signposts Ways in which a presenter signals to an audience where the presentation is going.

similarity The idea that our relational partners usually like or dislike the same things we do.

simile Creatively compares two unlike things, using the word *like* or *as*.

skills training The systematic work done, through instruction and practice, to develop public speaking skills.

slang Informal, casual language used among equals.

small-group communication The interaction among three to nine people who are working together to achieve an interdependent goal.

social distance Ranges from 4 to 12 feet, and it is the distance used most often to carry out business in the workplace.

social function The use of language to build and maintain relationships.

social media A variety of websites that allow users to connect and interact with acquaintances, friends, family members, organizations, colleagues, and customers all over the world through the exchange of user-generated content.

social undermining An intentional and often planned action meant to socially isolate another person from a larger group.

source Initiates a message.

specific purpose The purpose stated precisely as an outcome or behavioral objective and in terms of the audience.

stagnation stage When relationships are sluggish and do not grow or progress.

state apprehension When someone experiences communication anxiety in a limited number of settings or circumstances.

statistics Numbers used to summarize information or compare quantities.

status Expressed by devoting attention to someone we think is particularly important.

stereotype To treat individuals as if they are the same as others in a given category.

strategic ambiguity Intentional uncertainty and vagueness.

strong ties Relationships that we are highly committed to and that we devote substantial energy to maintaining, regardless of individual circumstances that may occur.

style The way we use language and grammar to construct written materials.

subpoints Points that support the main points of a speech.

substitution Occurs when nonverbal codes are used in place of verbal codes.

supportive communication When communicators listen with empathy, acknowledge the feelings of others, and engage in dialogue to help others maintain a sense of personal control.

surveys Studies that ask a sample of the population a limited number of questions in order to discover public opinions on a particular set of issues.

syllogism A structure that contains a generalization (a major premise) applied to a particular instance (a minor premise) that leads to a conclusion.

symbol Represents an idea, a process, or a physical entity.

synchronous communication Communication that occurs when the people involved interact with one another at the same time as both senders and receivers of information.

synonym Defines by using a word or words that are close or similar in meaning to the one we are trying to define.

systematic desensitization A technique that focuses on progressive relaxation, visualization, and active engagement exercises to help presenters overcome public speaking anxiety.

T

tactile communication (haptics) The use of touch in communication.

task functions Behaviors that directly relate to a group's purpose; they affect the group's productivity.

termination When a relationship stops completely.

territoriality The need to establish and maintain certain spaces as our own.

testimonial evidence Written or oral statements of others' experience used to substantiate or clarify a point.

tests of evidence The standards for demonstrating validity.

thesis statement A complete statement that reveals the content of a presentation.

time-sequence pattern A method of organization in which the presenter explains a sequence of events in chronological order.

topical-sequence pattern An organizational pattern that emphasizes the major reasons the audience should accept a point of view by addressing the advantages, disadvantages, qualities, and types of a person, place, or thing.

trait apprehension When someone experiences communication anxiety in a variety of settings and under diverse circumstances.

transition Typically includes a brief flashback and a brief forecast that tell an audience when a speaker is moving from one main point to another.

trouble talk Exchanges in which people complain about something without expecting a solution.

trust A belief that members of a group can rely on each other.

turning point A transformative event that alters a relationship in some way.

turn taking When one person speaks and the other responds with a certain amount of give and take.

U

uncertainty-accepting cultures Cultures that tend to be tolerant of ambiguity and diversity; they are more often democracies than dictatorships or countries led by powerful royalties.

uncertainty-rejecting cultures Cultures that have difficulty with ambiguity and diversity.

uses and gratifications (U&G) theory A theory that suggests that people use social media to satisfy their own needs and desires.

V

value A deeply rooted belief that governs our attitude about something.

verbal aggressiveness Communication that attacks the self-concepts of other people in order to inflict psychological pain.

verbal communication The use of language to convey meaning.

viral social media campaigns Video messages created with the intentions that people will forward and discuss them through social media and that the messages will be widely seen.

virtual libraries Resources that provide links to websites where some level of review for relevance and usability of the information has been conducted.

vocal aspects The aspects of a presentation that involve the voice: projection and volume, rate, pauses, fluency, pitch, pronunciation, articulation, enunciation, and vocal variety.

vocal cues All of the oral aspects of sound except words themselves.

vocalized pauses Breaks in fluency that negatively affect an audience's perception of the speaker's competence and dynamism.

vocal variety Voice quality, intonation patterns, inflections of pitch, and the duration of syllables.

volume The relative loudness of a speaker's voice.

voluntary audience An audience that chooses to hear someone speak about a particular topic.

W

weak ties Personal relationships to which we are not as committed overall and in which we would not invest as much time and energy to maintain.

word A symbol that has been assigned meaning.

NAME INDEX

A
Aesop, 287
Aristotle, 308

B
Baxter, Leslie, 82
Brown, Chris, 88
Burgoon, Judee K., 49

C
Chai Jing, 122
Cialdini, Robert, 314
Clinton, Hillary, 158, 315
Coban, Aydin, 87
Cooper, Anderson, 104

D
Davis, Wynne, 281
Douglass, Fredrick, 23

E
Edison, Thomas, 158
Emerson, Ralph Waldo, 219

F
Freud, Sigmund, 287

G
Galbraith, Christa, 290
George VI, 254

Gibb, Jack, 85, 87
Giffords, Gabrielle, 315
Goffman, Erving, 146
Gore, Al, 243
Gottman, John, 3

H
Hall, Edward T., 48
Harris, Neil Patrick, 104
Haynes, Colton, 104

J
Janis, Irving, 167

K
Kennedy, John F., 219
King, Martin Luther, Jr., 23, 197
Knapp, Mark, 80, 84–85
Kramarae, Cheris, 104

L
Lincoln, Abraham, 254

M
McLaughlin, Sarah, 310
Mead, George Herbert, 15
Mehrabian, Albert, 46
Middleton, Kate, 84
Monroe, Alan, 311
Montgomery, Barbara, 82

O
Obama, Barack, 101–102

P
Parsons, Jim, 104
Price, Calla, 315

Q
Quintilian, 22

R
Rihanna, 88

S
Sandusky, Jerry, 159
Springsteen, Bruce, 303, 315

T
Todd, Amanda, 87
Trump, Donald, 127, 141, 305

W
Walther, Joseph, 135–136
Watts, Reggie, 285–286
William, Prince, 84
Williams, Richard, 15
Williams, Serena, 15
Williams, Venus, 15

SUBJECT INDEX

A

Abuse
  abusive supervision, 178
  in interpersonal relationships, 87–88, 93
Academic Search Complete, 234
Accommodation, conflict management via, 176
Action
  action model of communication, 9–10
  Action Stage, Monroe Motivated Sequence, 311, 312
  action verbs, 326–327, 329, 334
  audience call to action to, 217, 218–219, 300, 311, 312
  cover letter requesting, 334
Action-oriented listening, 3
Active listening, 64, 68, 304, 345–346
Active perception, 12
Adaptability, employers seeking, 333
Adapting to audience, 196–199
Adaptors, nonverbal communication via, 46
Adoption, of new behavior, 302, 303
Advertising, 23, 122, 193, 287, 310
Advertising Age, 63
Affect displays, 46, 88
Affectionate communication, 88–89
African Americans
  prejudice against, 110
  race of, 101
Ageist language, 33
Agenda-setting, by mass media, 127
Aggressiveness; *see also* Violence
  fear appeals triggering, 311
  in interpersonal relationships, 84, 93
  verbal, 177–178
Alliteration, 23
Alternatives, in problem solving, 168
Amazon Prime, 124
Ambiguous communication
  nonverbal, 54
  verbal, 36
American Psychological Association; *see* APA style documentation
Amish people, 104
Analogies, in informative presentations, 287
Analysis
  analytical function of verbal communication, 24
  of audience, 188–200, 278–279
  of organizational communication, 157–160
  of organizational culture, 153–156
  of problem solving alternatives and outcomes, 168, 169
  skills in, employers seeking, 333
  of social media presence, 146
Androgynous individuals, behavioral flexibility of, 91
Anecdotes, in informative presentations, 279
Annotated bibliographies, 228, 229
Antonyms, 285
Anxiety
  communication apprehension and, 252–259
  fear appeals triggering, 311
  information anxiety, 227
APA style documentation, 221, 222, 244–245, 246–247
Appearance; *see also* Physiological features
  identity management via, 16–17
  nonverbal communication via, 47, 52–54, 251
  physical attractiveness and, 47, 80
  relational development and, 80
Archer, 127
Arguments
  argumentativeness and relational deterioration, 84
  deductive, 309
  inductive, 308–309
  logical *(logos)*, 308–309
  persuasion based on, 305, 308–309
Articles, information gathering from, 230–233
Articulation, 51, 56, 265
Artifacts
  definition of, 52
  nonverbal communication via, 52–54, 56
  organizational culture and, 153, 154, 155
Assigned groups, 161, 162
Asynchronous communication, 129
Attention
  Attention Stage, Monroe Motivated Sequence, 311, 312
  automatic, 66
  cover letter gaining, 334
  introduction garnering audience's, 203, 204–205, 220, 290, 311, 312, 316
  listening and, 66–68
  selective, 66
Attitudes
  audience analysis of, 190, 191, 192, 194–195
  beliefs and, 191, 192 (*see also* Beliefs)
  definition of, 190
  ethnocentrist, 107–109
  intercultural communication and, 101, 116
  interpersonal communication of, 76, 81
  leadership influencing, 170
  media influencing, 128
  organizational culture reflecting, 153
  prejudiced, 105 (*see also* Biases)
  small-group, 168
  social media expressing, 131, 146–147
  values and, 191, 192 (*see also* Values)
  work, job interview discussing, 340
Audience; *see also* Receivers
  adapting to, 196–199
  analysis of, 188–200, 278–279
  captive, 189, 304
  conclusion call to action to, 217, 218–219, 300, 311, 312
  conclusion reminders to, 217, 218
  extrinsic motivation for, 280–281
  information hunger in, 279–280
  information relevance for, 280
  informative content for, 282
  introduction arousing interest of, 203, 206
  introduction garnering attention of, 203, 204–205, 220, 290, 311, 312, 316
  for nonverbal communication, 56
  participation or involvement of, 282, 284
  public speaking to (*see* Public speaking)
  voluntary, 189
Audience analysis, 188–200
  adapting to audience based on, 196–199
  of attitudes, 190, 191, 192, 194–195
  of beliefs, 191, 192, 195

Audience analysis (*continued*)
  of captive *vs.* voluntary audience, 189
  chapter review of, 200
  definition of, 189
  of demographics, 189, 194–195
  inference for, 193–194
  for informative presentations, 278–279
  Internet for, 195–196
  levels of, 189–191
  methods of, 191–196
  observation for, 193
  questionnaires for, 194–195
  tips for, 195
  of values, 191, 192, 194–195
Audio recordings
  of information interviews, 345
  of presentation delivery, 271
Authority, principle of, for persuasion, 314
Autocratic leadership, 172
Automatic attention, 66
Autonomy, in interpersonal relationships, 82, 83, 92
Avoidance
  avoidance stage of relational deterioration, 85
  conflict management via, 176
  of ethnocentrism, 116
  of grammatical errors, 33–34, 39, 334
  of information overload, 227, 282–283
  of plagiarism, 243–247
  of stereotypes, 116
  of word types, in verbal communication, 31–34, 39

B

Bargaining, interpersonal communication for, 90
Behavior
  adoption of new, 302, 303
  behavioral-based interviewing, 340–342
  culture reflecting, 101 (*see also* Culture)
  defensive (*see* Defensiveness)
  discontinuance of, 302, 303
  immediate behavioral purposes of informative presentations, 278
  leadership influencing, 170
  mass media influence on, 124–125
  supportive, 164, 166 (*see also* Supportive communication)

  task functions as, 163–164, 165
  violent (*see* Violence)
Behavioral-based interview questions, 340–342
Behavioral flexibility, 90–92
Behavioral roles, in groups, 163
Beliefs
  attitudes and, 191, 192 (*see also* Attitudes)
  audience analysis of, 191, 192, 195
  conflicts over, managing, 28, 117
  culture reflecting, 101, 108 (*see also* Culture)
  definition of, 191
  ethnocentrist, in superiority, 107–109
  interpersonal communication of, 75
  norms reflecting (*see* Norms)
  organizational culture reflecting, 153
  past experiences coloring, 13
  religious (*see* Religion)
  social media expressing, 131
  values and, 191, 192 (*see also* Values)
Biases
  ethnocentrism as, 107–109, 116
  intercultural communication affected by, 107–110, 116
  personal bias influencing listening, 68, 69
  prejudice as, 105, 109–110
  stereotypes as, 14, 68, 69, 109, 116, 127
Bibliographies, 228, 229, 244
Blogger, 130
Blogs, 130–131
Bloomberg Businessweek Company Insight Center, 340
Bodily movement, 46, 258, 259, 269–270
Body image, media influence on, 122, 125
Body language; *see* Nonverbal communication
Body modifications, 54
Body of presentation
  cause-effect pattern for, 213, 214
  definition of, 207
  in informative presentations, 208, 213, 215, 291–293
  introduction written after, 208
  main points of, 208, 282, 283, 291–293, 316–318
  organizational patterns for, 213–215
  outlining, 208–213, 216, 290–294, 315–319

  in persuasive presentations, 213, 214–215, 316–318
  problem-solution pattern for, 213, 214–215
  signposts in, 216, 217
  subpoints in, 208–209, 291–293
  time-sequence pattern for, 213–214
  topical-sequence pattern for, 213, 215
  transitions in, 216, 217, 317, 318
Boldface, CMC use of, 137
Bonding stage of relational development, 82
Books, information gathering from, 230–233
Boolean operators, 240
Boomerang effect, 301
Boundary-crossing medium, 131–133
Brainstorming, 168, 185–186
Bullying, 87, 178
Bureau of Labor Statistics, U.S., 235
Bystander effect, 105

C

Capitalization, CMC use of, 137–138
Captive audiences, 189, 304
Cause-effect pattern, 213, 214
Celebrity testimony, 315
Cellular technology; *see* Technology
Censorship, 113, 122
Census Bureau, U.S., 4, 101–102, 235
Central Intelligence Agency World Factbook, 235
Certainty
  defensiveness and, 85–86
  uncertainty-accepting *vs.* uncertainty-rejecting cultures, 111–112, 115
Challenge Yourself box
  body language and appearance, 53
  effective listening, 70
  organizational communication analysis, 158
  persuasion, effective use of, 314
  prejudice or hate speech confrontation, 105
  presentation delivery and apprehension reduction, 256
  presentation organization, 221
  sex, honest discussion about, 94
  social media privacy management, 145
  source selection and evaluation, 242
  topic selection, 199

visual resource use, in informative presentations, 289
word use, importance of careful, 39
Channels
  as communication component, 7
  for mediated communication, 124
  models of communication using, 9–11
  opening, for intercultural communication, 116–117
The Chicago Manual of Style, 221, 222
Chicago style documentation, 221, 222
Chronemics, 50
Chronological résumés, 328, 331
Circumscribing stage of relational deterioration, 85
Citations
  accurate, ethics of, 313
  as internal references, 244
  oral, 222, 245–247
City-data.com, 195
Clarification
  comparison and contrast for, 314–315
  definitions for, 37
  examples for, 313
  explanations for, 286
  illustrations for, 287
  small group interaction including, 173
  "what did you mean?" questions for, 37
Clichés, 35
Climate, group, 164, 166–167
Clinchers, 218–219, 220, 294
Closure, organization based on, 11
Clothing
  for job interviews, 338–339
  nonverbal communication via, 52–53, 56
  public speaking choice of, 197
CNN, 127
Co-cultural groups, 103–104, 155
Codependency, in interpersonal relationships, 86–87
Codes
  code sensitivity, 116
  code switching, 30–31
  as communication component, 7–8
  decoding of, 8–11, 25–26, 54
  encoding of, 8–11, 25–26
  language as, 22
  nonverbal, 8, 45–54, 116
  verbal, 8, 116 (*see also* Language; Words)
Coercion, 171, 300

Cognitive restructuring, 255–257
Cohesion, group, 164, 166–167
Collaboration, conflict management via, 176
Collectivist cultures, 110–111, 115
Commitment
  principle of, for persuasion, 314
  to topic, 186–187
Communication
  action model of, 9–10
  channels of, 7, 9–11, 116–117, 124
  chapter review of, 18–19
  components of, 6–9
  deceptive, 84, 93
  definition and description of, 4–6
  face-to-face (*see* Face-to-face communication)
  interaction model of, 10
  intercultural (*see* Intercultural communication)
  interpersonal (*see* Interpersonal communication)
  intrapersonal, 16
  jobs in field of, 325, 326
  listening and (*see* Listening)
  mediated (*see* Mediated communication)
  nonverbal (*see* Nonverbal communication)
  organizational (*see* Organizational communication)
  perception and, 11–18
  phatic, 24
  public presentation of (*see* Public speaking)
  reasons for studying, 3–4
  self-image and, 15–18
  tactile, 50–51, 88
  temporal, 50
  transactional model of, 10–11
  verbal (*see* Verbal communication)
  workplace (*see* Workplace communication)
Communication Abstracts, 234
Communication and Mass Media Complete, 234
Communication apprehension
  cognitive restructuring reducing, 255–257
  definition of, 252
  experiencing, 252–254
  managing and reducing, 254–259
  presentation delivery affected by, 252–259
  skills training reducing, 257–259
  state apprehension as, 253

systematic desensitization reducing, 254–255
  trait apprehension as, 252
Communication privacy management (CPM) theory, 143
  co-ownership rules, 143
  linkage rules, 143
  permeability rules, 143
Comparison and contrast
  in informative presentations, 278, 285
  in persuasive presentations, 314–315
Competition, and conflict management, 176
Complements/complementarity
  nonverbal communication as, 44
  relational development and, 80
Compliance-gaining, 89
Compliance-resisting, 90
Components of communication
  channels as, 7
  codes as, 7–8
  encoding and decoding as, 8–9
  feedback as, 7
  messages as, 6–7
  noise as, 8–9
  people as, 6
Compromise, conflict management via, 176
Computer-mediated communication (CMC), 129–137; *see also* E-mail; Social media
  communication model of, 124
  critical thinking about, 136–137
  definition of, 123
  evaluating interactions, 135–136
  synchronous *vs.* asynchronous, 129
Concept mapping, 188, 227, 229
Conciseness
  in job interviews, 341
  in résumés, 329
Conclusion
  audience call to action in, 217, 218–219, 300, 311, 312
  audience reminders in, 217, 218
  clinchers in, 218–219, 220, 294
  critiquing introduction and, 220
  definition of, 217
  forewarning audience of finish in, 217, 218
  functions of, 217–219
  of informative presentations, 293–294
  main points restated in, 217, 218, 220, 293, 319
  of persuasive presentations, 300, 311, 312, 319
  sample, 219

Concrete language, 38
Confidence, communication study improving, 4
Confidentiality, 175; *see also* Privacy rights
Conflict management and resolution
   accommodation in, 176
   avoidance in, 176
   collaboration in, 176
   communication study improving, 3–4
   competition and, 176
   compromise in, 176
   intercultural communication and, 117
   small-group communication and, 176–177
   tips for effective, 177
   verbal communication for, 25, 28
Congressional Budget Office, 235
Connecting Globally box
   credible statistics sources, 235
   eye contact in intercultural mediated communication, 268
   fake news identification, 281
   focus on yourself-or not-through social media, 29
   job searches via mediated and face-to-face communication, 337
   listening to social media, 67
   mediated communication and workplace privacy, 172
   privacy and security in the global village, 48
   profile pictures for persuasion, 308
   right to be forgotten, 113
   social media around the globe, 122
   take a vacation from social media, 17
   user-generated content reflecting values, 190
   WiFi-connected toys, 78
Connections
   interpersonal relationship connectedness, 82
   memory improved by making, 70
   professional, networking for building, 342–346
Connotative meaning of words, 27
Considering Media box
   website links storage and organization, 218
Consistency
   principle of, for persuasion, 314
   in résumés, 329

Content
   definition of, 64
   deleting, from social media, 144, 145
   informative, 282
   interpersonal communication influenced by, 76–77, 92
   listening to discern, 64
   organization of, in informative presentations, 283–284
   of résumés, 327, 329–331
Context; *see also* Setting
   for communication, 5–6
   for communication apprehension, 252–253
   models of communication using, 10–11
   for nonverbal communication, 55–56
   for social media use, 137–143
Contradiction, nonverbal communication as, 44–45
Contrast; *see* Comparison and contrast
Control, and defensiveness, 85–86
Conversation; *see also* Dialogues
   listening in, 65
   verbal communication rules on, 29–30
Co-ownership rules, 143
Cover letters, 334–336
Creative function of verbal communication, 22–24
Credibility
   conclusion negatively impacting, 220
   of information sources, 230, 232, 233–236, 241, 242–243, 310, 313
   of news stories, 281
   qualifications establishing, 206, 290, 310, 316
   of speaker, delivery affecting, 251
Crisis communication, 138, 140
Criteria
   in problem solving, 167–168, 169
   for testing source credibility, 243
Critical thinking; *see also* Thinking skills
   about mediated communication, 122, 128–129, 136–137, 140–141
   analytical function of verbal communication using, 24
   communication study improving, 3
Cultivation effect of mass media, 127–128
Culture; *see also* Intercultural communication; Race and ethnicity; Religion

   clothing and artifacts reflecting, 52
   cultural characteristics, 110–115
   cultural identity, 108
   cultural norms (*see* Norms)
   cultural relativism, 108
      definition of, 101
   dominant, 103, 155
   global communication and, 67, 138, 142–143
   implicit-rule *vs.* explicit-rule, 112–113, 115
   individualistic *vs.* collectivist, 110–111, 115
   mass media relationship with, 125, 126–128
   M-time *vs.* P-time, 113–114, 115
   nondominant or co-cultural groups, 103–104, 155
   nonverbal communication differences in, 47, 52, 54, 268
   organizational, 153–160
   social media focus influenced by, 29
   uncertainty-accepting *vs.* uncertainty-rejecting, 111–112, 115
Curiosity
   informative presentations peaking, 279–280
   intercultural communication study based on, 107
Cyberbullying, 87

D

Data
   information gathering of, 225–226
   triangulation of, 242–243
Databases, electronic, information gathering from, 233, 234, 239
Deceptive communication, 84, 93
Decision making
   communication study improving, 3
   in groups, 167–169
   groupthink affecting, 167
   skills in, employers seeking, 327
Decoding, 8–11, 25–26, 54
Deductive arguments, 309
Defensiveness
   in groups, 166
   as listening barrier, 69
   persuasion hampered by, 304
   reduction of, 85–86, 87
   relational deterioration and, 84, 85–86
Definitions
   antonyms in, 285
   comparisons in, 285

364   Subject Index

contrasts in, 285
from informative presentations, 278, 285
operational, 285
of problem, in information gathering, 227, 228
synonyms in, 285
verbal communication clarifying, 37
Delivery of presentation; *see* Presentation delivery
Democratic leadership, 171, 172
Demographics
audience analysis of, 189, 194, 195
intercultural communication and shifting, 106–107
Demonstrations, in informative presentations, 277, 288
Denotative meaning of words, 26–27
Description
defensiveness reduction via, 85–86, 87
definition of, 37
imagery in, 285–286
informative presentations leading to, 278, 285–286
job, studying before interview, 339
résumés including, 326–327
verbal communication using, 37, 38
Designated leadership, 170–171
Desire for job, in cover letter, 334
Dialectic theory, 82
Dialogues, 16; *see also* Conversation
Dictionary.com, 264–265
Differentiating stage of relational deterioration, 84–85
Differentiation and specialization, in organizational structure, 157
Disabilities, people with, organizational culture toward, 155
Discontinuance, of current behavior, 302, 303
Discriminatory language, 105; *see also* Biases; Prejudice
Distances
intimate, 49
personal, 49
public, 49
social, 49
Distinctions, in informative presentations, 278
Distractions, as listening barrier, 63, 68–70
Diversity in America, 127
Documentation of sources
APA style, 221, 222, 244–245, 246–247

Chicago style, 221, 222
citations as, 222, 244, 245–247, 313
from information gathering, 221, 222, 228, 229, 243–247, 313
MLA style, 221, 222, 244–245
Dominant culture, 103, 155

E

Economics, intercultural communication study based on, 107
Education
census information on attainment of, 330
credentials from, in résumés, 330
face-to-face *vs.* online, 309
on healthy relationships, 93
informational interviews as source of, 344–346
intercultural communication in, 101
internships enriching, 343
listening in, 64–65, 66
Education Full Text, 234
Egocentrism, as listening barrier, 69
Electronic databases, information gathering from, 233, 234, 239
E-mail
cover letters and résumés via, 334
critical thinking about, 136–137
verbal communication via, 30
Emblems, 46
Emergent groups, 161, 162
Emergent leadership, 170–171
Emoticons, 137
Emotions; *see* Feelings and emotions
Empathy
defensiveness reduction via, 85–86, 87
empathic listening, 65
mindfulness and, 68
Emphasis, nonverbal communication for, 44
Employment-related communication; *see* Workplace communication
Encoding, 8–11, 25–26
Engagement, rules of, for verbal communication, 30–31
English as a second language, 4, 164, 271
Enunciation, 51, 52, 55, 56, 265–266
Equality, defensiveness reduction via, 85–86, 87
Errors
grammatical, 33–34, 39, 334
in perception, 14–15

Ethics; *see also* Values
definition of, 313
dilemmas in small-group communication, 177–179
persuasion consideration of, 300, 313
sexual harassment violating, 178–179
verbal aggressiveness violating, 177–178
work, employers seeking, 333
Ethnocentrism, 107–109, 116
Ethos, 310
Euphemisms, 35–36
European Commission, 235
Evaluation
of CMC and social media interactions, 135–136
defensiveness and, 85–86, 87
of nonverbal aspects of presentation delivery, 270
of problem solving alternatives and outcomes, 168, 169
of sources, in information gathering, 228, 229, 232, 242–243
Evidence
in persuasive presentations, 305–307, 315
proof relationship to, 306
testimonial, 241, 315
tests of, 307
Exaggeration, hyperbole as, 23, 39
Examples
factual, 313
hypothetical, 313
in job interviews, 341
in persuasive presentations, 313
Experiences
connotative meanings reflecting, 27
cover letter describing, 334
experience inventory, 340–341
experiential superiority, as listening barrier, 69
information gathering via, 239–241
job interview questions on, 340–341
perception influenced by past, 13
résumés detailing, 328, 330–334
with topic, 240–241
Experimentation stage of relational development, 81
Expert power, 171
Expert testimony, 241, 315
Explanations, in informative presentations, 286
Explicit-rule cultures, 112–113, 115

Extemporaneous mode of presentation delivery, 259–260
Extrinsic motivation, 280–281
Extroverts, social media use, 133
Eye contact
   in intercultural mediated communication, 268
   nonverbal communication via, 46
   in presentation delivery, 257, 259, 268–269, 271

F

Facebook
   audience analysis using, 190
   gatekeeping by, 126
   global access to, 122
   health communication via, 141–142
   information gathering via, 226, 232, 235
   interpersonal communication and relationships via, 77, 81, 82, 84–85, 137–138
   media literacy and, 129
   organizational communication via, 139
   personality traits and use of, 134
   privacy and, 144–145, 343
   user base, 130
Facetime, 337
Face-to-face communication
   apprehension about, 252
   changing nature of interpersonal, 77
   channels of, 7
   in classrooms, 309
   CMC vs., 135–137
   context of, 5
   conversational partners in, 29–30
   cover letters requesting, 334
   identity management in, 16
   job interviews as, 337–338
   job searches via, 337
   mediated communication or social media affecting, 8, 63, 252
   persuasive presentations, 303–304
   in small groups, 160, 161
   as synchronous communication, 129
Facial expressions; see also Eye contact
   mindful listening and, 70
   nonverbal communication via, 46–47
   in presentation delivery, 258, 267–268
Fact, proposition of, 305
Factiva, 234
Factual distractions, 69
Factual examples, 313

Fake news, 281
Families
   interpersonal relationships in, 79, 91, 92
   leadership and power in, 171
   as relationship-oriented groups, 161, 162
   social media communication in, 137–138
Fear appeals, 310–311
Fear of public speaking; see Communication apprehension
Feedback
   as communication component, 7
   to intercultural communication, 116
   to mediated communication, 124
   models of communication using, 10–11
   to nonverbal communication, 56
Feelings and emotions
   affect displays of, 46, 88
   affectionate communication expressing, 88–89
   apprehension or fear as, 252–259, 310–311 (see also Anxiety)
   conflict management affected by, 177
   fear appeals to, 310–311
   group climate reflecting, 164
   interpersonal communication of, 77, 84, 88–89
   listening stimulating, 65–66
   nonverbal communication conveying, 45–47, 88, 262, 267
   pathos or emotional proof, 310–311
   perception influenced by present, 13
   supportive communication validating, 175
Figures of speech, 23, 39
First Amendment, 197
Flexibility
   behavioral, 90–92
   employers seeking, 333
   in informational interviews, 345
Fluency of presentation delivery, 263
Focus, and listening, 66
Focus groups, 168–169
Foot-in-the-door technique, 301
Forecasting development and organization, 203, 206–207, 290, 316
Formal communication, 157–159
Formalization of organizational structure, 157
Formal roles in groups, 163

404, meaning of, 27
Freedom of speech, 122, 197
Friends with benefits relationships (FWBRs), 78
Functional résumés, 331–334

G

Gatekeeping, 126
Gay, lesbian, bisexual, and transgender individuals
   as co-cultural group, 104
   interpersonal relationships among, 79, 207
   mass media portrayal of, 127
   prejudice against, 109–110
Gender differences
   in cultural influence, 103–104
   gender roles and, 91
   in interpersonal communication, 89, 91
   in listening skills, 3
   in nonverbal communication, 47, 48, 50, 54
   in verbal communication, 32
Gender discrimination, 32, 33
Generalizations, in logical arguments, 308–309
Gestures, 266–267; see also Bodily movement
Glee, 127
Global communication, social media for, 67, 138, 142–143
Google News, 188
Google Scholar, 188, 237–239
Google Video, 337
Government surveillance, 48, 113, 122
Grammatical errors, avoiding, 33–34, 39, 334
Groups
   assigned, 161, 162
   climate and cohesion of, 164, 166–167
   co-cultural, 103–104, 155
   communication competence in, 174–176
   conflict management in, 176–177
   decision making and problem solving in, 167–169
   defensiveness in, 166
   effective interaction in, 173–174, 175–176
   emergent, 161, 162
   ethical dilemmas in, 177–179
   focus groups, 168–169
   function of, 161
   groupthink in, 166–167

leadership in, 169–172
norms and roles in, 52, 162–164, 165
positive relationship cultivation in, 173–179
relationship-oriented, 161, 162
small-group communication, 160–169, 173–180
supportiveness in, 164, 166, 175
task functions in, 163–164, 165
task-oriented, 161, 162
trust in, 164
types of, 161–162

H

Hate speech, 105
Hawthorne effect, 232
Health communication, 138, 141–142
Health Insurance Portability and Accountability Act (HIPAA), 141
Hearing *vs.* listening, 62–63
Hello Barbie, 78
The Hidden Dimension (Hall), 48
Hierarchy, in organizational structure, 156–157
Hispanics
 demographics of, 106
 prejudice against, 110
 race *vs.* ethnicity of, 101–102
 uncertainty-rejecting culture response to, 112
Homosexuals; *see* Gay, lesbian, bisexual, and transgender individuals
Honest communication, 94, 178
Hostile work environment harassment, 32; *see also* Sexual harassment
Hulu, 124
Humanities Abstracts, 234
Humor, in presentations, 205, 282
Hurtful messages, 84, 93
Hyperboles, 23, 39
Hyperpersonal perspective, 135–136
Hypothetical examples, 313

I

Identity
 cultural, 108
 identity management, 16–17
Illustrations, in informative presentations, 287; *see also* Visual imagery
Illustrators, 46
Imagery, in descriptions, 285–286; *see also* Visual imagery
Immediacy, 174–175

Immediate behavioral purposes, of informative presentations, 278
Immediate purposes, of persuasive presentations, 300
Implicit-rule cultures, 112–113, 115
Impromptu mode of presentation delivery, 260
Incivility, 178
An Inconvenient Truth (Gore), 243
Independent research, 241
Individualistic cultures, 110–111, 115
Inductive arguments, 308–309
Inferences
 audience analysis via, 193–194
 definition of, 38, 193
 direct, 193–194
 indirect, 193
 verbal communication making careful, 38
Inflection, 51, 52
Influence
 compliance-gaining as, 89
 compliance-resisting as, 90
 interpersonal communication for, 89–90
 power and, 171
Informal communication, 159–160
Informal roles in groups, 163
Information; *see also* Sources of information
 definition of, 226
 information gathering of, 225–226 (*see also* Information gathering)
 informative presentations providing useful, 277 (*see also* Informative presentations)
 quantifying, in résumés, 327
Informational interviews
 learning from, 344–346
 steps after, 346
 steps before, 344–345
 steps during, 345–346
Information anxiety, 227
Information gathering, 224–249
 from books, articles, and periodicals, 230–233
 chapter review of, 247–248
 on company, prior to interview, 339–340
 concept mapping and, 227, 229
 data in, 225–226
 data triangulation in, 242–243
 digital, 225–230, 231–232, 233, 234, 236–239, 240
 diverse search strategies in, 228, 229

 documentation of sources from, 221, 222, 228, 229, 243–247, 313
 from electronic databases, 233, 234, 239
 evaluating sources in, 228, 229, 232, 242–243
 from independent research, 241
 information anxiety from, 227
 information in, 225–226
 information literacy and, 226–227
 information overload during, 227
 integration of information in, 228, 229
 from Internet resources, 236–239, 240
 knowledge and, 225–226
 from library resources, 230–236, 239, 340
 organization of sources in, 228, 230
 from personal experience, 239–241
 plagiarism avoidance in, 243–247
 primary *vs.* secondary sources for, 230–232
 process of, 227–230
 scanning and evaluating sources in, 228, 229
 seminal sources for, 237
 from statistics, 235, 236
 from surveys, 233–236
Information hunger, 279–280
Information literacy, 226–227
Information overload, 227, 282–283
Information processing skills, 327
Information relevance, 280
Informative content, 282
Informative presentations, 276–298
 analogies in, 287
 audience participation or involvement in, 282, 284
 body of presentation in, 208, 213, 215, 291–293
 chapter review of, 297–298
 comparison and contrast in, 278, 285
 conclusion of, 293–294
 content organization in, 283–284
 creating information hunger with, 279–280
 definitions in, 278, 285
 demonstrations in, 277, 288
 descriptions in, 278, 285–286
 effective presentation of, 278–284
 explanations in, 286
 extrinsic motivation revealed in, 280–281
 goal of, 277

Subject Index **367**

Informative presentations (*continued*)
  illustrations in, 287
  information overload avoidance in, 282–283
  information relevance demonstrated in, 280
  informative content in, 282
  introduction of, 206, 290
  narration in, 287–288
  note cards for, sample, 294–297
  organizational patterns in, 213, 215, 283–284
  outline of, sample, 290–294
  preparation of, 277–278
  purpose or thesis of, 206, 208, 278, 290
  skills for, 284–288
  storytelling in, 284, 287, 288
  topic selection for, 280
  visual aids or resources in, 288–290
Initiating stage in relational development, 80–81
Initiative, employers seeking, 333
Inkblot tests, 11–12
Instagram, 77, 130
Instrumental function of verbal communication, 22
Integration of information, in information gathering, 228, 229
Integration stage of relational development, 82
Intelligence, job interviews discussing, 340
Intensifying stage of relational development, 81–82
Intent
  intentional *vs.* unintentional messages, 6–7
  listening to discern, 64
Interaction
  CMC and social media, evaluation of, 135–136
  interaction model of communication, 10
  patterns of, in interpersonal relationships, 76, 92
  small group member, 173–174, 175–176
Intercultural communication, 100–119
  biases affecting, 107–110, 116
  chapter review of, 117–118
  cultural characteristics influencing, 110–115
  definition and description of, 101–104
  dominant culture in, 103, 155

ethnocentrism affecting, 107–109, 116
eye contact in, 268
improvements to, 116–117
nondominant or co-cultural groups in, 103–104, 155
nonverbal communication and, 47, 52, 54, 268
practicing of, 117
prejudice or hate speech in, 105, 109–110
race and ethnicity considerations in, 101–103, 107–109, 116
stereotyping affecting, 109, 116
study of, 105–107
Interdependence
  definition of, 76
  group and team member, 161
  in interpersonal relationships, 75–76, 83, 92
Interest
  cover letter arousing reader's, 334
  demonstrating, in job interviews, 339
  introduction arousing audience's, 203, 206
  surveys of interests, for topic selection, 185
Internal references, 244; *see also* Citations
Internet; *see also* Mediated communication
  audience analysis via, 195–196
  Google Scholar on, 188, 237–239
  information gathering using, 236–239, 240
  search engines on, 237
  search tools and tips, 239, 240
  virtual libraries on, 237
Internships, 343–344
Interpersonal communication, 74–99
  changing nature of relationships affecting, 77–79
  chapter review of, 94–95
  characteristics of, 76–77
  definition and description of, 75–77
  deterioration of relationships affecting, 83–86
  development of relationships involving, 80–82
  in healthy relationships, 92–93
  improvement of, 88–92
  maintenance of relationships involving, 82–83
  negative relationships affecting, 86–88

online, 67, 77, 78–79, 81, 82, 84–85, 87, 91, 135–136, 137–139
social media for, 67, 77, 81, 82, 84–85, 91, 135–136, 137–139
stages of relationships affecting, 79–86
Interpersonal relationships
  changing nature of, 77–79
  chapter review of, 94–95
  communication in (*see* Interpersonal communication)
  definition and description of, 75–76
  healthy, 92–93
  improvement of, 88–92
  negative, 86–88
  relational deterioration in, 83–86
  relational development in, 80–82
  relational maintenance in, 82–83
  stages of, 79–86
  strong *vs.* weak ties in, 138–139
Interpretation
  of communication, 5
  encoding and decoding words for, 25–26
  of nonverbal communication, 54
  perception based on, 11–12
Interviews
  documentation of, 244, 245
  informational, 344–346
  job, mastering of, 53, 337–342
Intimate distances, 49
Intrapersonal communication, 16
Introduction
  arousing audience interest in, 203, 206
  audience attention garnered via, 203, 204–205, 220, 290, 311, 312, 316
  body of presentation written before, 208
  critiquing conclusion and, 220
  definition of, 203
  forecasting development and organization in, 203, 206–207, 290, 316
  functions of, 203–207
  of informative presentations, 206, 290
  of persuasive presentations, 205–206, 301–304, 311, 312, 316
  purpose or thesis stated in, 203, 204, 205–206, 220, 290, 301–302, 316
  qualifications established in, 203, 204, 206, 290, 316
  tips for strengthening, 207

368 Subject Index

Introverts, social media use, 133
Irreversible interpersonal communication, 76, 77, 93

J

Jargon, 35
Job descriptions, 339
Job interviews
   behavioral-based, 340–342
   company research prior to, 339–340
   demonstrating interest in, 339
   dress code and clothing selection for, 338–339
   experience inventory for, 340–341
   face-to-face, 337, 338
   first impressions in, 338–339
   interactive video, 337–338
   job description studying improving, 339
   mastering, 337–342
   nonverbal communication in, 53, 338–339
   setting for, 337, 338
   telephone, 337
   verbal communication in, 338, 339
Job Outlook survey, 325
Journalism
   fake news *vs.*, 281
   information hunger created in, 279
   social media communication in, 138, 140–141
Judgment, job interviews discussing, 340

K

Key-word outlines, 212–213, 216, 259
Kinesics, 46; *see also* Bodily movement; Facial expressions
The King's Speech, 254
Knowledge
   definition of, 226
   information gathering and, 225–226
   informative presentations to increase, 277
   leadership based on, 170, 171
   of topic, selection based on, 186–187, 199

L

Laissez-faire leadership, 171
Language
   adapting to audience, 197
   ageist, 33
   ambiguous, 36
   clear and simple, 173, 282, 283
   clichés or overused, 35
   concrete, 38
   creative, 22–24
   definition of, 22
   discriminatory, 105
   English as a second language, 4, 164, 271
   ethnic group sharing, 103
   euphemisms in, 35–36
   figures of speech, 23, 39
   informative presentation use of, 282, 283
   instrumental, 22
   intercultural communication and, 101, 103, 107
   "I" *vs.* "you," 177
   jargon, 35
   object, 52–54
   organizational culture and, 153, 154, 155
   profane, 31–32, 39
   public speaking choice of, 197, 282, 283
   racist, 32–33
   regional, 39
   résumé style and choice of, 325–327, 328, 329
   sexist, 32, 33
   slang, 34–35, 39
   verbal communication via (*see* Verbal communication)
   words in (*see* Words)
Lay testimony, 315
Leadership
   autocratic, 172
   communication apprehension influencing, 252
   definition of, 170
   democratic, 171, 172
   designated, 170–171
   emergent, 170–171
   job interviews discussing, 341
   laissez-faire, 171
   management *vs.*, 169–170
   opinion, 141
   organizational, 169–172
   power and, 171–172
   skills in, employers seeking, 333
Learning; *see also* Education
   from informational interviews, 344–346
   lessons learned, job interviews discussing, 341
   listening for, 64–65
   reflexivity and, 117
Legitimate power, 171
Lessons learned, job interviews discussing, 341
LexisNexis, 234
Lexis-Nexis Business Insight Solutions, 340
Library resources
   books, articles, and periodicals as, 230–233
   electronic databases as, 233, 234, 239
   information gathering from, 230–236, 239, 340
   online library catalog system of, 230
   reference librarians assisting with, 230
   statistical data as, 235, 236
   survey results as, 233–236
   virtual libraries, 237
Lies; *see* Deceptive communication
Liking
   bodily movement communicating, 46
   principle of, for persuasion, 314
Linkage rules, 143
LinkedIn
   context for using, 137
   identity management in, 16
   interpersonal relationships via, 77
   organizational communication via, 139
   professional networking via, 342–343, 346
Listening, 60–72
   action-oriented, 3
   active or critical, 64, 68, 304, 345–346
   attention and, 66–68
   barriers to, 63, 68–70
   chapter review of, 70–71
   communication study improving, 3
   conflict management via, 177
   definition of, 63
   empathic, 65
   gender differences in, 3
   hearing *vs.*, 62–63
   importance of, 60, 61–64
   in informational interviews, 345–346
   memory and, 67–68, 70
   mindful, 68, 70
   persuasion by, 304
   practicing effective, 28
   pseudolistening *vs.*, 68, 69
   reasons for, 61–62
   relational, 3

Listening (*continued*)
   supportive communication including, 175
   types of, 64–66
Live Binders, 218
LiveJournal, 130
Logical proof, 308–309
Logos, 308–309
Long-range goals, of persuasive presentations, 301
Long-term memory, 68

M

Main points
   conclusion restating, 217, 218, 220, 293, 319
   limited number of, in informative presentations, 282, 283
   outlining, 208, 291–293, 316–318
Maintenance functions, 164, 165
Management *vs.* leadership, 169–170
Manipulation, 300
Manner, identity management via, 16
Manuscript mode of presentation delivery, 260
Margins of outline, signaling importance, 209
Marriage
   divorce rate, 79, 83–84
   relational deterioration in, 83–86
   relational development to, 82
   relational maintenance in, 82–83
   same-sex, 207
Mass communication, 123–129
   communication model of, 124
   definition of, 123
   media literacy, 128–129
   motivations for consuming, 123–124
Mass media, 123–129
   agenda-setting by, 127
   behavioral influence of, 124–125
   critical thinking about, 128–129
   cultivation effect of, 127–128
   culture relationship with, 125, 126–128
   definition of, 123
   gatekeeping via, 126
   motivations for consuming, 123–124
   time spent consuming, 124
   violence in, 124–125, 127
Maturity, job interviews discussing, 340
Meaning
   basic communication conveyance of, 5
   connotative, 27

decoding as assigning, 8, 25–26
definition of, 22
denotative, 26–27
interpersonal communication generating shared, 75
interpretation of (*see* Interpretation)
of nonverbal communication, 54
verbal communication of, 22, 25, 26–27
words as symbols assigned, 25, 26–27, 75
Media convergence, 123
Media literacy, 128–129
Mediated communication, 120–151; *see also* Internet; Social media; Technology
   chapter review of, 147–148
   computer-mediated communication as, 123, 129–137
   context of, 5, 137–143
   convergence of, 123
   creativity of language in, 23
   critical thinking about, 122, 128–129, 136–137, 140–141
   definition of, 121
   e-mail as, 30, 136–137, 334
   eye contact in, 268
   fake news in, 281
   forms of, 123
   job searches via, 337
   as listening barrier, 63, 65
   mass communication as, 123–129
   mass media for, 123–129
   media literacy, 128–129
   messages via, 7, 121, 124
   motivations for consuming, 123–124
   nonverbal communication and, 136, 137–138, 268
   privacy issues with, 113, 134, 143–146, 172, 343
   reasons for studying, 121–123
   storage and organization of links to, 218
   understanding, 121–123
   user-generated content in, 190, 232
Medline, 234
Memory
   listening and, 67–68, 70
   long-term, 68
   memorized mode of presentation delivery, 261
   right to be forgotten, 113
   short-term, 67–68
Mental distractions, as listening barrier, 69
Merriam-Webster Online, 37

Messages
   body of presentation including, 207
   as communication component, 6–7
   hurtful, in interpersonal relationships, 84, 93
   intentional *vs.* unintentional, 6–7
   interpretation of (*see* Interpretation)
   media conveying, 7, 121, 124 (*see also* Mediated communication)
   models of communication relaying, 9–11
   outlines abstracting, 208
   persuasive, 300, 311–313 (*see also* Persuasive presentations)
   words conveying (*see* Words)
Metaphors, 23, 39
Microblogs, 130–131
Mindful listening, 68, 70
The MLA Handbook, 221
MLA style documentation, 221, 222, 244–245
Mobile technology; *see* Technology
Modern Family, 127
Modern Language Association; *see* MLA style documentation
Monroe Motivated Sequence, 311–312
Motivation
   extrinsic, informative presentations revealing, 280–281
   job interviews discussing, 341
   for mass media consumption, 123–124
   Monroe Motivated Sequence, 311–312
M-time (monochronic time) cultures, 113–114, 115
Multitasking, as listening barrier, 63, 68, 69, 70
Music, listening to, 63, 65–66
MySpace, 130

N

Narration, in informative presentations, 287–288; *see also* Storytelling
National Association for Colleges and Employers, 325
National Domestic Violence Hotline, 88
National security, privacy rights conflicts with, 48
Neatness, in résumés, 329
Need Stage, Monroe Motivated Sequence, 311, 312
Negative statements
   cognitive restructuring of, 255–257

370 Subject Index

introduction avoiding, 207
   in negative self-talk, 252, 255–257
Neologisms, 27
Netflix, 124
Networking
   building professional connections via, 342–346
   informational interviews for, 344–346
   internships for, 343–344
   social media/social networking for, 130–131, 342–343, 346
Neutrality, and defensiveness, 85–86
News reporting
   fake news in, 281
   information hunger created in, 279
   social media communication in, 138, 140–141
The New York Times, 123, 140
Noise
   as communication component, 9
   as listening barrier, 63, 68–70
Nonverbal communication, 43–59
   audience for, 56
   bodily movement as, 46, 258, 259, 269–270
   chapter review of, 56–57
   clothing and other artifacts as, 52–54, 56, 197, 338–339
   as complements, 44
   context awareness for, 55–56
   as contradiction, 44–45
   definition of, 44
   for emphasis, 44
   facial expressions as, 46–47, 70, 258, 267–268 (*see also* Eye contact)
   feedback to, 56
   intercultural communication and, 47, 52, 54, 268
   interpersonal, 88 (*see also* Interpersonal communication)
   interpretation of, 54
   in job interviews, 53, 338–339
   mediated communication and, 136, 137–138, 268
   messages via, 6
   mindful listening and, 70
   nonverbal codes in, 8, 45–54, 116
   physical attractiveness and, 47
   in public speaking, 52, 55, 56, 207, 251, 257, 258, 259, 261–270, 271
   for regulation, 45, 46
   for repetition, 44
   in small-group communication, 174–175
   space as, 48–49, 56

   strategies for improving, 55–56
   as substitution, 45
   time or temporal communication as, 50
   touch or tactile communication as, 50–51, 88
   verbal communication and, 22, 31, 44–45
   vocal cues as, 51–52, 55–56, 251, 261–266, 271
Nonword sounds, 51, 52
Norms
   clothing and artifacts reflecting, 52
   definition of, 163
   group, 52, 162–163, 164, 165
   intercultural communication awareness of, 109, 110, 111
   mediated communication and, 29, 127, 131–133, 145
Note cards
   for informative presentations, 294–297
   for persuasive presentations, 319–321
   presentation delivery using, 216, 259
   tips for using, 216
Note taking, for memory improvement, 70
Novelty, in interpersonal relationships, 82

O

Objectics/object language, 52–54
Objective statements, in résumés, 329, 332
Observations
   audience analysis via, 193
   definition of, 38
   verbal communication making accurate, 38
Occupy movements, 142
Online library catalog system, 230
OoVoo, 337
Operational definitions, 285
Opinion leaders, 141
Oral citations, 222, 245–247
Organization
   cause-effect, 213, 214
   closure as basis of, 11
   of information sources, 228, 230
   of informative presentations, 213, 215, 283–284
   introduction forecasting, 203, 206–207, 290, 316

   Monroe Motivated Sequence for, 311–312
   patterns of, 213–215, 311–312
   perception based on, 11
   of persuasive presentations, 213, 214–215, 311–312
   of presentation, 202–223
   problem-solution, 213, 214–215
   proximity as basis of, 11
   similarity as basis for, 11
   skills in, employers seeking, 327
   time-sequence, 213–214
   topical-sequence, 213, 215
   of verbal communication, 30
   of website links, 218
Organizational communication, 152–182
   analysis of, 157–160
   chapter review of, 179–180
   downward, 159
   formal, 157–159
   global, 142–143
   horizontal, 159
   informal, 159–160
   leadership and, 169–172
   organizational culture and, 153–160
   organizational structure and, 156–159
   positive relationship cultivation and, 173–179
   privacy and, 172
   small-group and team communication in, 160–169, 173–180
   social media for, 138, 139–140, 142–143
   upward, 159
Organizational culture
   communication practices and, 157–160
   definition of, 153
   investigation and analysis of, 153–156
   organizational structure and, 156–159
Organizational structure
   differentiation and specialization in, 157
   formalization of, 157
   hierarchy in, 156–157
   organizational charts depicting, 157–159
   strategic ambiguity in, 157
Outlining
   informative presentations, 290–294

Outlining (*continued*)
    key-word outlines in, 212–213, 216, 259
    links to purpose or thesis in, 208
    main points in, 208, 291–293, 316–318
    margins signaling importance in, 209
    message abstracted in, 208
    parallel form in, 209
    persuasive presentations, 315–319
    principles of, 208–209
    rough drafts of, 209–211
    sentence outlines in, 211–212, 290–294, 315–319
    single idea per sentence in, 208
    subpoints in, 208–209, 291–293
    symbols signaling importance in, 208–209

P

Paralinguistic features, 51–52
Parallelism, 209, 220
Paraphrasing, 37, 70, 177
Parentheses, in Internet searches, 240
Past experiences
    connotative meanings reflecting, 27
    cover letter describing, 334
    experience inventory, 340–341
    information gathering based on, 239–241
    job interview questions on, 340–341
    perception influenced by, 13
    résumés detailing, 328, 330–334
Pathos, 310–311
Pauses, 52, 55, 262–263
Peer reviews, of presentation organization, 221
People, as communication component, 6
People's Climate March, 142
Perception
    active, 12
    chapter review of, 18–19
    communication affected by, 11–18
    definition and description of, 11–12
    differences in, 12–14
    errors in, 14–15
    interpretation in, 11–12
    listening influenced by, 68, 69
    organization in, 11
    past experiences influencing, 13
    perceptual checking, 14–15, 37
    perceptual constancy, 13
    physiological features influencing, 12–13
    present feelings influencing, 13
    process of, 12
    roles influencing, 13
    selection in, 11
    self-image as, 15–18
    subjective, 12
Periodicals
    documentation of, 244, 245
    information gathering from, 230–233
    oral citations of, 245
Permeability rules, 143
Personal bias, listening influenced by, 68, 69; *see also* Biases
Personal distances, 49
Personal experiences; *see* Experiences
Personality traits
    identity reflecting, 17
    social media correlations with, 133–135
Personal space
    intimate distances in, 49
    nonverbal communication via, 48–49, 56
    personal distances in, 49
    public distances in, 49
    social distances in, 49
Perspective
    media/social media influencing, 67, 128
    persuasion of, 304
Persuasive presentations, 299–323
    adoption of new behavior due to, 302, 303
    argument used in, 305, 308–309
    body of presentation in, 213, 214–215, 316–318
    chapter review of, 322–323
    comparison and contrast in, 314–315
    conclusion of, 300, 311, 312, 319
    cover letters as, 334
    definition of, 300
    discontinuance of behavior due to, 302, 303
    ethical considerations with, 300, 313
    ethos or source credibility in, 310
    evidence in, 305–307, 315
    examples in, 313
    face-to-face, 303–304
    introduction of, 205–206, 301–304, 311, 312, 316
    logos or logical proof in, 308–309
    long-range goal of, 301
    Monroe Motivated Sequence for, 311–312
    note cards for, sample, 319–321
    organizational patterns in, 213, 214–215, 311–312
    outline of, sample, 315–319
    pathos or emotional proof, 310–311
    preparation of, 300–301
    principles of persuasion for, 314
    proof in, 306, 308–311
    public service announcements as, 303
    purpose or thesis of, 205–206, 300, 301–302, 312, 316, 319
    reasons to make, 302–304
    skills for, 313–315
    testimonial evidence in, 315
    understanding persuasion, 305–307
Pew Internet and American Life Project, 236–237
Phatic communication, 24
Phrase searches, in Internet searches, 240
Physical distractions, as listening barrier, 69
Physiological features; *see also* Appearance
    perception influenced by, 12–13
    physical attractiveness, 47, 80
    race based on, 101–102
Piercings, 54
Pitch, 51, 52, 56, 263–264
Place; *see* Setting
Plagiarism, avoiding, 243–247
Planners social media users, 134, 135
Planning skills, employers seeking, 327
Pleasure, listening for, 65–66
Policy, proposition of, 305
Political communication, 138, 141, 197, 260, 261
Positional roles in groups, 163
Posture; *see* Bodily movement
Power
    definition of, 171
    expert, 171
    leadership and, 171–172
    legitimate, 171
    punishment, 171
    referent, 171
    reward, 171
Predictability, in interpersonal relationships, 82, 83, 93
Prejudice, in intercultural communication, 105, 109–110
Presentation delivery, 250–274
    articulation in, 265
    bodily movement in, 258, 259, 269–270

chapter review of, 272–273
communication apprehension and, 252–259
definition of, 251
enunciation in, 265–266
evaluation of, 270
extemporaneous, 259–260
eye contact in, 257, 259, 268–269, 271
facial expressions in, 258, 267–268
fluency of, 263
gestures in, 266–267
importance of, 251–254
impromptu, 260
manuscript mode of, 260
memorized, 261
modes of, 259–261
non-native speaker tips for, 271
nonverbal communication in, 52, 55, 56, 207, 251, 257, 258, 259, 261–270, 271
note cards for, 216, 259
oral citations in, 222, 245–247
pauses in, 262–263
pitch in, 263–264
practicing or rehearsing, 221, 255, 256, 257–259, 264, 266, 267, 271
projection and volume in, 262
pronunciation in, 264–265, 271
rate of speech in, 262
vocal aspects of, 52, 55, 56, 251, 261–266, 271
vocal variety in, 266
Presentation of self, on social media, 146–147
Presentation organization, 202–223; *see also specific sections*
body in, 207–217
chapter review of, 222–223
conclusion in, 217–220
introduction in, 203–207, 208, 220
references in, 221–222
Primary sources, 230–232
Prioritization skills, employers seeking, 327
Privacy rights; *see also* Confidentiality
communication privacy management theory on, 143
co-ownership rules and, 143
cultural influences on, 113
health communication and, 141–142
linkage rules and, 143
national security conflicts with, 48
permeability rules and, 143
privacy turbulence and, 144, 145

right to be forgotten and, 113
social media and, 134, 143–146, 172, 343
Problem, defining in information gathering process, 227, 228
Problem orientation, defensiveness reduction via, 85–86, 87
Problem-solution pattern, 213, 214–215
Problem solving
alternatives evaluated in, 168
alternatives identified in, 168
communication study improving, 3
critical criteria in, 167–168, 169
in groups, 167–169
outcome evaluation in, 169
plan implementation in, 168–169
skills in, employers seeking, 327, 333
Profanity, 31–32, 39
Professional success, communication study improving, 4
Projection, in presentation delivery, 262
Pronunciation, 51, 56, 264–265, 271
Proof
emotional, 310–311
evidence relationship to, 306
logical *(logos)*, 308–309
in persuasive presentations, 306, 308–311
Proposition
of fact, 305
of policy, 305
of a value, 305
Protective social media users, 134, 135
Provisionalism, defensiveness reduction via, 85–86, 87
Proxemics, 48–49
Proximity
interpersonal relationships sharing, 77, 80, 93
organization based on, 11
Pseudolistening, 68, 69
P-time (polychronic time) cultures, 113–114, 115
The Publication Manual of the American Psychological Association, 221
Public distances, 49
Public relations
social media communication in, 138, 140
target audience for, 193
Public service announcements, 303
Public speaking
audience analysis for, 188–200, 278–279

fear or apprehension of, 252–259
information gathering and supporting materials for, 224–249
informative presentations in, 206, 208, 213, 215, 276–298
nonverbal communication in, 52, 55, 56, 207, 251, 257, 258, 259, 261–270, 271
persuasive presentations in, 205–206, 213, 214–215, 299–323
presentation delivery in, 52, 55, 56, 207, 216, 221, 222, 245–247, 250–274
presentation organization for, 202–223
topic selection for, 185–188, 197–198, 199, 200, 280
verbal communication in, 23–24, 30
Punishment power, 171
Purpose
adapting to audience, 198–199
of informative presentations, 206, 208, 278, 290
introduction stating, 203, 204, 205–206, 220, 290, 301–302, 316
outline linked to, 208
of persuasive presentations, 205–206, 300, 301–302, 312, 316, 319
thesis statements presenting (*see* Thesis statements)

Q

Qualifications
cover letter stating, 334
ethos from, 310
introduction establishing, 203, 204, 206, 290, 316
résumés detailing, 325–334
source evaluation considering, 243
Quality of speech, 51
Quantifying information, in résumés, 327
Quantitative skills, employers seeking, 333
Questionnaires, audience analysis via, 194–195
Questions
for audience analysis, 194–195, 196
for behavioral-based interviews, 340–342
census, on race and ethnicity, 102
for group norm determination, 162–163
for informational interviews, 344, 345, 346

Questions (continued)
  intercultural communication feedback via, 116
  interpersonal communication via, 94
  listening to responses to, 62
  for organizational culture investigation, 154
  questionnaires of, 194–195
  rhetorical, 205, 263
  source evaluation by asking, 232, 243
  surveys asking, 185, 233–236
  for testing evidence, 307
  for topic selection, 185, 187
  verbal communication using, 37
  "what did you mean?" as, 37
Quotations
  conclusion including, 219
  in fake news, verifying, 281

R

Race and ethnicity
  definitions and descriptions of, 101–103
  ethnocentrism based on, 107–109, 116
  mass media portrayal of, 127
  racist language, 32–33
Rate of speech, 51, 52, 55, 56, 262
Readers' Guide to Periodical Literature, 234
Receivers; *see also* Audience
  channels of communication to, 7, 9–11, 116–117, 124
  as communication component, 6
  feedback from, 7, 10–11, 56, 116, 124
  of mediated communication, 124
  models of communication for, 9–11
Reciprocity, principle of, for persuasion, 314
Reference librarians, 230
References; *see also* Sources of information
  APA style, 221, 222, 244–245, 246–247
  bibliographic, 228, 229, 244
  Chicago style, 221, 222
  definition of, 221
  internal, 244 (*see also* Citations)
  MLA style, 221, 222, 244–245
  oral citations of, 222, 245–247
  organization of, 221–222
Referent power, 171
Reflexivity, intercultural communication improvement via, 117

Regionalisms, 39
Regulation
  nonverbal communication for, 45, 46
  regulators as tool for, 46
Relational listening, 3
Relationship-oriented groups, 161, 162
Relationships
  conflict management and resolution in, 3, 25, 28, 117, 176–177
  cultural influences on, 114–115
  friends with benefits, 78
  hyperpersonal perspective on, 135–136
  interpersonal (*see* Interpersonal relationships)
  job interviews discussing, 340
  listening in, 3, 62, 65
  perceptual checking in, 15
  romantic, 78–79
  same-sex, 79, 207
  small group cultivation of positive, 173–179
  social function of verbal communication for, 24–25
  strong *vs.* weak ties in, 138–139, 344
Religion
  culture, intercultural communication, and, 101, 103, 106, 109, 112
  public speaking on, 197
  stereotypes based on, 109
  uncertainty-rejecting culture response to, 112
Remembering; *see* Memory
Renren, 122
Repetition
  nonverbal communication for, 44
  unrepeatable interpersonal communication, 76, 77, 93
Research
  in books, articles, and periodicals, 230–233
  company, prior to interview, 339–340
  concept mapping and, 227, 229
  data in, 225–226
  data triangulation in, 242–243
  digital, 225–230, 231–232, 233, 234, 236–239, 240
  diverse search strategies in, 228, 229
  documentation of sources from, 221, 222, 228, 229, 243–247, 313
  in electronic databases, 233, 234, 239

evaluating sources in, 228, 229, 232, 242–243
independent, conducting, 241
information anxiety from, 227
information-gathering process in, 227–230
information in, 225–226
information literacy and, 226–227
information overload during, 227
integration of information in, 228, 229
from Internet sources, 236–239, 240
knowledge and, 225–226
from library resources, 230–236, 239, 340
narrowing topic based on, 188
organization of sources in, 228, 230
personal experience informing, 239–241
plagiarism avoidance in, 243–247
primary *vs.* secondary sources for, 230–232
scanning and evaluating sources in, 228, 229
seminal sources for, 237
statistics informing, 235, 236
surveys informing, 233–236
Resourcefulness, job interviews discussing, 340
Responsibility, job interviews discussing, 340
Responsiveness
  bodily movement communicating, 46
  relational development and, 80
Résumés, 325–334
  action verbs in, 326–327, 329, 334
  chronological, 328, 331
  content of, 327, 329–331
  cover letters with, 334–336
  educational credentials in, 330
  experience, job duties, and skills in, 328, 330–334
  format of, 331–334
  functional, 331–334
  objective statements in, 329, 332
  resources for assistance with, 334
  sample, 328, 332
  style of, 325–327, 328, 329
Reward power, 171
Rhetoric (Aristotle), 308
Rhetorical questions, 205, 263
Rituals and routines, organizational culture and, 153, 154, 155
Roles
  definition of, 163

differentiation and specialization of, 157
formal *vs.* informal, 163
gender, 91
group, 163–164, 165
leadership, 170
perception influenced by, 13
social media presentation reflecting, 146–147
task functions for, 163–164, 165
Rough drafts of outlines, 209–211

S

Same-sex relationships, 79, 207; *see also* Gay, lesbian, bisexual, and transgender individuals
Satisfaction Stage, Monroe Motivated Sequence, 311, 312
Scanning
    in information gathering process, 228, 229
    listening involving choosing and, 66–67
Scarcity, principle of, for persuasion, 314
Schools; *see* Education
Searches
    Google Scholar, 188, 237–239
    search engines for, 237
    search strategies, in information gathering process, 228, 229
    tips for successful, 239, 240
Secondary sources, 230–232
The Secret Life of the American Teenager, 127–128
Selection, perception based on, 11
Selective attention, 66
Self
    adapting self to audience, 196–197
    interpersonal communication beginning with, 76, 81, 92
    as listening barrier, 69
    negative self-talk, 252, 255–257
    self-assessment of intercultural communication, 116
    self-centered functions, in groups, 164, 165
    self-centered social media users, 134
    self-disclosure, 81, 206
    self-image, 15–18, 122
    social media focus on, 29
    social media presentation of, 146–147
    social media protection of, 143–146
Semantic distractions, as listening barrier, 69

Seminal sources, 237
Senders; *see* Sources of communication
Sensitivity
    code sensitivity, 116
    diversity sensitivity, 116
    nonverbal sensitivity improvement, 55
    systematic desensitization reducing, 254–255
Sentence outlines, 211–212, 290–294, 315–319
September 11, 2001 terrorist attacks, 106
Setting; *see also* Context
    identity management via, 17
    for job interviews, 337, 338
    for nonverbal communication, 56
    verbal communication rules regarding, 27–29
Sex
    interpersonal communication about, 94
    mass media on, 127–128
Sexist language, 32, 33
Sexual harassment, 178–179
Sharing social media users, 134, 135
Short-term memory, 67–68
Sights, as listening barrier, 69
Signposts, in body of presentation, 216, 217
Silence, 51, 55; *see also* Pauses
Similarity
    organization based on, 11
    relational development and, 80
Similes, 23
Single-parent families, interpersonal relationships in, 79, 91
Skill Builder box
    audience analysis, 192
    audience involvement, 284
    behavioral-based interviewing practice, 342
    cultural identity reflection, 108
    defensiveness reduction, 87
    effective verbal communication and listening skills, 28
    introduction and conclusion critiques, 220
    listening in conversation, 65
    nonverbal sensitivity improvement, 55
    oral citation practice, 246–247
    organizational culture analysis, 156
    perception checks, 15
    persuasion by listening and seeking common ground, 304

    public speaking skill development, 258
    social media presence analysis, 146
Skills
    cover letter describing, 334
    employers seeking specific, 327, 333
    for informative presentations, 284–288
    job interviews discussing, 340
    for persuasive presentations, 313–315
    résumés highlighting, 331, 332
    skills training in presentation delivery, 257–259
    thinking, communication study improving, 3
    in workplace communication, 325, 327
Skype, 337
Slang, 34–35, 39
Small-group communication, 160–169, 173–180
    chapter review of, 179–180
    competence in, 174–176
    conflict management in, 176–177
    decision making and problem solving via, 167–169
    definition of, 160
    effective interaction affecting, 173–174, 175–176
    ethical dilemmas in, 177–179
    group climate and cohesion influencing, 164, 166–167
    group norms and roles influencing, 162–164, 165
    immediacy in, 174–175
    nonverbal, 174–175
    positive relationship cultivation and, 173–179
    supportive, 164, 166, 175
    type of group influencing, 161–162
Social distances, 49
Social goals, interpersonal communication accomplishing, 75
Social media; *see also specific sites (e.g., Facebook)*
    advantages and disadvantages of, 131, 132
    agenda-setting via, 127
    audience analysis using, 190
    as boundary-crossing medium, 131–133
    characteristics of, 132
    contexts for using, 137–143
    co-ownership rules for, 143

Social media (continued)
  creativity of language in, 23
  critical thinking about, 136–137, 140–141
  cultural influences on focus of, 29
  definition of, 129
  deleting content on, 144, 145
  employment affected by, 135, 139–140, 144–145, 172, 342–343
  evaluating interactions, 135–136
  fake news on, 281
  features and uses of, 130–133
  gatekeeping via, 126
  global access to, 122
  global communication via, 67, 138, 142–143
  health communication via, 138, 141–142
  identity management in, 16
  information gathering via, 226, 232, 235
  interpersonal communication and relationships via, 67, 77, 81, 82, 84–85, 91, 135–136, 137–139
  journalism and news reporting via, 138, 140–141
  linkage rules for, 143
  as listening barrier, 63
  media literacy and, 129
  neologisms in, 27
  networking via, 130–131, 342–343, 346
  norms and, 29, 127, 131–133, 145
  organizational communication via, 138, 139–140, 142–143
  permeability rules for, 143
  personality traits and use of, 133–135
  perspective expanded via, 67
  political communication via, 138, 141
  presenting yourself on, 146–147
  privacy and, 134, 143–146, 172, 343
  profile pictures in, for persuasion, 308
  public relations and crisis communication via, 138, 140
  scanning and choosing in, 66–67
  time spent on, 124
  unplugging or vacation from, 17
  user base, 130
  uses and gratifications theory on, 133–135
Social networking sites, 130–131; see also specific sites
Social norms; see Norms

Social Sciences Index, 234
Social undermining, 178
Social validation, principle of, for persuasion, 314
Sounds
  as listening barrier, 69
  nonword, 51, 52
Sources of communication
  channels of communication from, 7, 9–11, 116–117, 124
  as communication component, 6
  feedback to, 7, 10–11, 56, 116, 124
  in mediated communication, 124
  models of communication for, 9–11
Sources of information
  books, articles, and periodicals as, 230–233
  citations of, 222, 244, 245–247, 313
  credibility of, 230, 232, 233–236, 241, 242–243, 310, 313
  data from, 225–226
  data triangulation with, 242–243
  digital, 225–230, 231–232, 233, 234, 236–239, 240
  documentation of, 221, 222, 228, 229, 243–247, 313
  electronic databases as, 233, 234, 239
  evaluation of, 228, 229, 232, 242–243
  independent research results as, 241
  information from, 225–226
  information gathering of, 224–249
  information literacy in use of, 226–227
  integration of, 228, 229
  Internet-based, 236–239, 240
  knowledge from, 225–226
  library resources as, 230–236, 239, 340
  organization of, 228, 230
  overload and anxiety from excessive, 227
  personal experience as, 239–241
  plagiarism of, avoiding, 243–247
  primary vs. secondary, 230–232
  scanning and evaluating, 228, 229
  seminal, 237
  statistics as, 235, 236
  survey results as, 233–236
Space
  informative presentations on spatial relations, 277
  intimate distances in, 49
  nonverbal communication via, 48–49, 56

  personal, 48–49, 56
  personal distances in, 49
  public distances in, 49
  social distances in, 49
  territoriality of, 48
Specific purpose
  adapting to audience, 198–199
  introduction stating, 205–206
Speech Topic Help, 188
Spontaneity, defensiveness reduction via, 85–86, 87
Stagnation stage of relational deterioration, 85
State apprehension, 253
Statistics
  conclusion restating or presenting, 219
  definition of, 236
  information gathering from, 235, 236
  in informative presentations, 279, 284
  in persuasive presentations, 305, 307
Status
  bodily movement communicating, 46
  listening influenced by, 68, 69
Stereotypes
  avoidance of, 116
  as errors in perception, 14
  intercultural communication affected by, 109, 116
  listening influenced by, 68, 69
  mass media and, 127
Storytelling
  in informative presentations, 284, 287, 288
  organizational culture and, 153, 154, 155
Strategic ambiguity, 157
Strategy, defensiveness and, 85–86
Strong ties, 138–139, 344
Style of résumés, 325–327, 328, 329
Subjective perception, 12
Subpoints, outlining, 208–209, 291–293
Substitution, 45
Superiority
  defensiveness and, 85–86
  ethnocentrist belief in, 107–109
  experiential superiority, as listening barrier, 69
Supporting materials; see Information gathering

Supportive communication
	intercultural, 116
	interpersonal, 89
	small-group, 164, 166, 175
Surveys
	definition of, 233
	information gathering via, 233–236
	of interests, for topic selection, 185
Survivor, 161
Syllogism, 309
Symbols
	definition of, 25, 26
	organizational culture and, 153, 154, 155
	outline use of, 208–209
	words as, 25, 26, 75 (*see also* Words)
Synchronous communication, 129
Synonyms, 285
Systematic desensitization, 254–255

T

Tactile communication, 50–51, 88
Taking notes, for memory improvement, 70
Task functions
	definition of, 163
	group roles reflecting, 163–164, 165
	maintenance functions as, 164, 165
	self-centered functions as, 164, 165
Task-oriented groups, 161, 162
Tattoos, 54
Teamwork skills, employers seeking, 327, 333
Technical skills, employers seeking, 333
Technology; *see also* Mediated communication; Social media; Texting
	cyberbullying via, 87
	intercultural communication via, 105–106
	interpersonal communication and relationships using, 77, 78–79, 81, 82, 83, 84–85, 87, 91, 135–136, 137–139
	job interviews using, 337–338
	as listening barrier, 63, 65
Telephone job interviews, 337
Termination stage of relational deterioration, 85
Territoriality, 48
Testimonial evidence
	celebrity testimony as, 315
	expert testimony as, 241, 315
	lay testimony as, 315
Tests of evidence, 307

Texting
	driving and, 63, 68, 238, 303, 316–321
	interpersonal communication and relationships using, 83
	as listening barrier, 63, 65
Thesis statements
	adapting to audience, 198–199
	definition of, 198
	informative, 206, 278, 290
	introduction presenting, 206, 220, 290, 316
	outline linked to, 208
	persuasive, 206, 312, 319
Thinking skills, communication study improving, 3; *see also* Critical thinking
Time
	chronemics or temporal communication, 50
	chronological résumés, 328, 331
	interpersonal relationship duration, 76, 92
	M(onochronic)-time *vs.* P(olychronic)-time cultures, 113–114, 115
	nonverbal communication related to, 50
	social media usage, 124
	synchronous *vs.* asynchronous communication, 129
	time-sequence pattern, 213–214
Topical-sequence pattern, 213, 215
Topic selection
	adapting to audience, 197–198
	age and development of topic and, 187
	brainstorming ideas for, 185–186
	chapter review of, 200
	commitment to topic and, 186–187
	how to select appropriate, 185–187
	for informative presentations, 280
	knowledge of topic and, 186–187, 199
	narrowing topic for, 187–188
	possible topics for, 188
	purpose relationship to, 198, 199
	surveying interests for, 185
	thesis statement relationship to, 198, 199
Touch, 50–51, 88
Trait apprehension, 252
Transactional interpersonal communication, 76, 92
Transactional model of communication, 10–11

Transitions, in body of presentation, 216, 217, 317, 318
Transparent, 127
Trouble talk, 24
Trust, in groups, 164
Turning points, in interpersonal relationships, 82–83
Turn taking, in verbal communication, 30
Twitter
	agenda-setting via, 127
	audience analysis using, 190
	global access to, 122
	information gathering via, 226, 232
	interpersonal relationships via, 77
	journalism and news reporting via, 140
	media literacy and, 129
	political communication via, 141
	scanning and choosing in, 67
	user base, 130

U

U&G (uses and gratifications) theory, 133–135
Uncertainty-accepting cultures, 111–112, 115
Uncertainty-rejecting cultures, 111–112, 115
Under the Dome, 122
United Nations Institute for Statistics, 235
Unrepeatable interpersonal communication, 76, 77, 93
Unworried social media users, 134, 135
U.S. Bureau of Labor Statistics, 235
U.S. Census Bureau, 4, 101–102, 235
U.S. Constitution, 113, 197
User-generated content, 190, 232
Uses and gratifications (U&G) theory, 133–135
Utilitarian social media users, 134, 135

V

Values; *see also* Ethics
	attitudes and, 191, 192 (*see also* Attitudes)
	audience analysis of, 191, 192, 194–195
	beliefs and, 191, 192 (*see also* Beliefs)
	culture reflecting, 108, 109, 110–111, 113, 115, 126 (*see also* Culture)
	definition of, 191
	identity reflecting, 17
	interpersonal communication of, 75, 81

Values (continued)
  opposing, 82
  organizational culture reflecting, 153, 155, 156
  proposition of, 305
  small-group, 168
  social, 80
  social media expressing, 131, 146
  user-generated content reflecting, 190
Verbal aggressiveness, 177–178
Verbal communication, 21–42
  ageist language in, 33
  alliteration in, 23
  ambiguous language in, 36
  analytical function of, 24
  chapter review of, 40–41
  clarification or "what did you mean?" questions in, 37
  clichés or overused expressions in, 35
  code switching in, 30–31
  concrete language in, 38
  conversational partners influencing, 29–30
  creative function of, 22–24
  definition of terms in, 22, 37
  euphemisms in, 35–36
  figures of speech in, 23, 39
  functions of, 22–25
  grammatical errors in, 33–34, 39
  hyperboles in, 23, 39
  inferences made carefully in, 38
  instrumental function of, 22
  interpersonal, 89 (*see also* Interpersonal communication)
  jargon in, 35
  in job interviews, 338, 339
  messages via, 6
  metaphors in, 23, 39
  nonverbal communication and, 22, 31, 44–45
  observations, accurate, in, 38
  paraphrasing in, 37
  practicing effective, 28
  profanity in, 31–32, 39
  racist language in, 32–33
  regionalisms in, 39
  rules of, 27–31
  setting or place influencing, 27–29
  sexist language in, 32, 33
  similes in, 23
  skills in, employers seeking, 327
  slang in, 34–35, 39
  social function of, 24–25
  strategies for improving, 36–39
  turn taking in, 30
  verbal codes in, 8, 116 (*see also* Language; Words)
  visual imagery in, 38
  vocabulary building for, 37–38
  word functionality in, 25–27
  words to avoid in, 31–34, 39
  words to use carefully in, 34–36, 39
Video blogs (vlogs), 130–131
Video-format job interviews, 337–338
Video recordings, of presentation delivery, 271
Vimeo, 129
Violence; *see also* Aggressiveness
  cultural views of, 108
  in interpersonal relationships, 87–88, 93
  mass media, 124–125, 127
Viral social media campaigns, 140
Virtual libraries, 237
Visual aids or resources
  informative presentations including, 288–290
  tips for effective use of, 289
Visual imagery
  in informative presentations, 287
  systematic desensitization using, 254–255
  verbal communication using, 38
Visualization Stage, Monroe Motivated Sequence, 311, 312
Vocabulary, 37–38; *see also* Words
Vocal cues
  articulation as, 51, 56, 265
  enunciation as, 51, 52, 55, 56, 265–266
  fluency of speech as, 263
  inflection as, 51, 52
  nonverbal communication via, 51–52, 55–56, 251, 261–266, 271
  nonword sounds as, 51, 52
  pauses as, 52, 55, 262–263 (*see also* Silence)
  pitch as, 51, 52, 56, 263–264
  presentation delivery and, 52, 55, 56, 251, 261–266, 271
  pronunciation as, 51, 56, 264–265, 271
  quality of speech as, 51
  rate of speech as, 51, 52, 55, 56, 262
  vocal variety with, 266
  volume and projection as, 51, 52, 55, 56, 262
Vocalized pauses, 263
Volume, 51, 52, 55, 56, 262
Voluntary audiences, 189

W

The Washington Post, 308
Weak ties, 138–139, 344
Websites
  documentation of, 244, 245
  oral citations of, 245
  storage and organization of links to, 218
Weibo, 122
Wikipedia, 231–232
Will and Grace, 127
Wolfram Alpha, 146
Women; *see also* Gender differences
  as co-cultural group, 103–104
  gender roles of, 91
  organizational culture toward, 153, 155
  prejudice against, 110
Women's March on Washington, 142, 161
Words
  action verbs as, 326–327, 329, 334
  ageist, 33
  ambiguous, 36
  antonyms of, 285
  to avoid, 31–34, 39
  choice of, 5
  clear and simple, 173, 282, 283
  clichés or overused, 35
  decoding of, 25–26 (*see also* Decoding)
  definition of, 25, 26
  encoding of, 25–26 (*see also* Encoding)
  euphemisms with, 35–36
  functionality of, 25–27
  jargon, 35
  meaning of, 26–27, 75 (*see also* Meaning)
  neologisms as new, 27
  profane, 31–32, 39
  racist, 32–33
  regional, 39
  sexist, 32, 33
  slang, 34–35, 39
  synonyms of, 285
  to use carefully, 34–36, 39
  verbal communication via, 25–27, 31–36
  vocabulary of, 37–38
Word stemming, in Internet searches, 240
Workplace communication, 324–348
  chapter review of, 346–347

conflict management and resolution in, 176–177
cover letters as, 334–336
ethical dilemmas in, 177–179
hostile work environment harassment in, 32
informational interviews as, 344–346
intercultural communication in, 101, 114–115
internships and, 343–344
interpersonal communication in, 91
jargon in, 35
job descriptions, 339
job interviews as, 53, 337–342
leadership and, 169–172, 341
listening in, 61–62, 64, 345–346
management and, 169–170
networking and, 342–346
nonverbal communication in interviews in, 53, 338–339
organizational communication in (*see* Organizational communication)
organizational culture in, 153–160
organizational structure of, 156–159
privacy in, 172
professional success and, communication study improving, 4
résumés as, 325–334
sexual harassment in, 178–179
skill in, importance of, 325, 327, 333

social media affecting employment, 135, 139–140, 144–145, 172, 342–343
verbal aggressiveness in, 177–178
World Health Organization, 235

Y

Yes-50 Scientifically Proven Ways to Be More Persuasive (Cialdini), 314
YouKu, 122
YouTube
   cyberbullying awareness video on, 87
   global access to, 122
   information gathering via, 226
   media literacy and, 129
   personality traits and use of, 134
   user base, 130